HUMAN FACTORS AND CYBERSECURITY

Human Factors and Cybersecurity examines the intricate interplay between human behaviour and digital security, offering a comprehensive exploration of how psychological, dispositional, and situational factors influence cybersecurity practices.

Bringing together information that is both research-informed and practical in nature, the book highlights how human behaviour and decisions can impact cybersecurity infrastructure. It covers a wide range of topics, including the foundations of cybersecurity, the risks posed by insider threats, and the importance of a human-centred approach. It examines the cognitive pitfalls and decision-making processes that can lead to security breaches and provides strategies for reducing human error. The book also includes case studies and real-world examples of cybersecurity breaches, and practical strategies and guidance for enhancing cybersecurity at an individual and organisational level.

Presenting state-of-the-art thinking related to the human factor in the context of cybersecurity, this book offers a clear grounding for researchers, professionals, and students alike, and valuable insights for anyone looking to protect against threats in the digital world.

Lee Hadlington is an Associate Professor in Cyberpsychology at Nottingham Trent University. His research focuses directly on aspects of risk and resilience in cyberspace, with a particular emphasis on susceptibility to cybercrime, fake news and misinformation, cybersecurity, and information security.

Chloe Ryding is a Senior Lecturer in Psychology at Nottingham Trent University. Her research focuses on on-line behaviour and well-being, with interests in social media use, misinformation and fake news, and cybersecurity.

CURRENT ISSUES IN CYBERPSYCHOLOGY

Current Issues in Cyberpsychology brings together books that explore the psychology behind human interaction with digital technology, and the impact of the internet on individuals and society as a whole.

It showcases books that will be relevant to both an academic and professional market, bringing together the work of established and emerging authors. The series spans a range of topics relating to cyberpsychology; including the influence of technology on behaviour and attitudes, the effects of social media, human factors in cybersecurity, and digital identities. Ideas for new books are welcome.

For more information about the series, please visit: https://www.routledge.com/our-products/book-series/CIIC

The Psychology of Cybersecurity
Hacking and the Human Mind
Tarnveer Singh and Sarah Y. Zheng

Human Factors and Cybersecurity
The Psychology of Online Safety and Security
Lee Hadlington and Chloe Ryding

HUMAN FACTORS AND CYBERSECURITY

The Psychology of Online Safety and Security

Lee Hadlington and Chloe Ryding

Routledge
Taylor & Francis Group

LONDON AND NEW YORK

Designed cover image: Getty ©

First published 2026
by Routledge
4 Park Square, Milton Park, Abingdon, Oxon OX14 4RN

and by Routledge
605 Third Avenue, New York, NY 10158

Routledge is an imprint of the Taylor & Francis Group, an informa business

British Library Cataloguing in Publication Data
A catalogue record for this book is available from the British Library

Library of Congress Cataloging-in-Publication Data
A catalog record has been requested for this book

ISBN: 9781032833699 (hbk)
ISBN: 9781032831985 (pbk)
ISBN: 9781003509011 (ebk)

DOI: 10.4324/9781003509011

Typeset in Times New Roman
by Taylor & Francis Books

CONTENTS

ILLUSTRATIONS

Figures

Tables

PREFACE

Think of any science fiction film where the key protagonist is a self-aware artificial intelligence (AI). The plot usually goes something like this:

Humans create an AI designed to be the best thing since sliced bread, improving our lives on multiple levels. The AI becomes self-aware and quickly realises that humans are terrible, a threat to its existence and the planet, and downright impossible to control. The AI sets about sorting out the issue by either:

- Destroying humankind.
- Enslaving humankind.

(Note that either option usually has several flaws, particularly as humans, being the unpredictable lot they are, will band together, form a rebellion, and set about overthrowing their AI overlords.)

In many ways, the daily struggles associated with ensuring the integrity of cybersecurity read like such a plot line. We have created a series of complicated digital systems that transfer information not only within organisations but also nationally and globally. Computer systems operate in a flawlessly logical way and continue to do so without any direct input from the human operator. It is only when you introduce the human element within the cybersecurity system that things start going awry. If we remove the human element from the system, two key things happen:

1. You remove the actual threat from cybercriminals – they are, irrespective of their faceless personas, humans at the end of a computer.
2. You also remove the susceptibility to cybercrime and the exploits of the cybercriminals.

However (thankfully for the authors and our careers), this is not the case – humans, for the time being, form an inherent part of the digital systems that govern cybersecurity. For all the technical interventions that we try to put into place humans continue to find a way to break, circumvent, ignore, or blatantly disregard them in their daily work lives. The issues that humans present when it comes to the functioning and use of digital technology are so commonplace that such failings have entered common culture and are the butt of many a comedic treatment. For example, the acronym PICNIC (problem in chair, not in computer) highlights the notion that most things that go wrong in computer systems are the fault of the pink, organic interface that sits in the chair, and the system itself can bear no responsibility for malfunction or operator error.

Humans are not logical, and their behaviour is not easily interpreted or predicted; we often act in erratic ways that escape even our own explanations (one of the authors left the house last week, only to return to find that he had left the front door wide open... go figure). These individuating factors that govern what we do daily can be related to how much sleep we have had, how many coffees we have drunk, how hungry we are, and how much chocolate we have eaten. Therefore, attempting to understand how humans fit into the cybersecurity infrastructure of any organisation (and indeed society as a whole) is a challenge, and a big one. Managing risk that comes from a random collection of individuals with even more random thoughts and behaviours is an imponderable task. That is why, in the opinion of the authors, the human element within the cybersecurity framework is often overlooked or ignored in favour of the technical interventions that can be deployed.

Now, this is not to say that we should do away with humans completely to create a perfect, utopian cybersecurity society. Far from it. This is to say that we really need to get to grips with how humans impact the cybersecurity infrastructure and have a clearer understanding of why we do the things that introduce an element of fragility and vulnerability. The aim of this book is to pull together as much research in this area as possible to help understand why and how humans are such a source of concern when it comes to cyber-security. We provide a current snapshot of state-of-the-art understanding of the key facets related to human behaviour that influence adherence to accepted rules and practices for good cybersecurity hygiene. Alongside this, we explore some of the key tactics implemented by cybercriminals that prey on inherent vulnerabilities, as well as examining the underlying psychology that makes such tactics work so well.

This book is not the holy grail in preventing someone like Janet in accounts from clicking on a link in an email asking her to enter her user-name or password. Nor will it stop someone like Bob from deciding it is a clever idea to have all his account passwords set to PASSWORD123. What it should do is provide a closer step for interested parties to start a journey on a path to understanding WHY people do these things, as well as creating some potential momentum in giving these individuals valuable support, guidance, and education to hopefully stop them from doing these things in the first place.

The book is designed to be both accessible and informative, retaining the academic rigor you would expect from a good textbook. We want the book, and the information contained within it, to be useful and practical to a wide audience, from professionals who have a personal stake in protecting their organisation from the next cyberattack, to researchers or students looking for information on the topic, painstakingly collected in one place. We hope to strike a balance between the academic and the accessible; the topic itself can be a little dry in places, and we make no apologies for trying to break this up with the odd use of humour (our own brand, sorry, this is not available for resale), anecdotal evidence, and in some cases downright self-indulgence when it comes to exploring the topic. However, explore it we will, and we hope you are ready for a journey that starts with some useful statistics to frame our current topic.

The Structure of the Book

This book is structured to guide readers through a logical progression of topics, each building on the previous to provide a thorough understanding of the human factors in cybersecurity.

- **Chapter 1: The Foundations of Cybersecurity** – Sets the stage with a brief history of information security and cybersecurity, exploring key definitions and concepts.
- **Chapter 2: The Insider Threat: Understanding the Risks Within** – Focuses on insider threats, distinguishing between malicious and unintentional insider threats.
- **Chapter 3: A Human-Centred Approach** – Introduces the human factors paradigm, emphasizing the importance of understanding human behaviour in cybersecurity.
- **Chapter 4: The Role of Context and Individual Differences** – Examines how attention, memory, decision making, personality traits, risk perception, and demographic factors influence cybersecurity behaviours.
- **Chapter 5: When Mistakes Happen** – Explores the nature of human error and its implications for cybersecurity.
- **Chapter 6: Cognitive Pitfalls and Cybersecurity** – Examines cognitive biases and heuristics that influence decision making in cybersecurity.
- **Chapter 7: Decision Making Under Pressure** – Reviews psychological theories explaining why individuals engage in certain cybersecurity actions.
- **Chapter 8: Assessing Cybersecurity Awareness** – Explores methods for understanding cybersecurity behaviours and intentions.

- **Chapter 9: Personality and Workplace Cybersecurity** – Discusses the role of personality traits in cybersecurity and counterproductive work behaviours.
- **Chapter 10: Cultural Influences on Cybersecurity Practices** – Investigates how national and organisational culture influence cybersecurity practices.
- **Chapter 11: Counterproductive Work Behaviour and Cybersecurity** – Examines predictors of counterproductive work behaviours and strategies for mitigating them.
- **Chapter 12: The Dark Side of Technology in the Workplace: Implications for Cybersecurity** – Explores the negative impacts of technology on cybersecurity.
- **Chapter 13: The Psychology of Cybercrime** – Delves into the psychological foundations of cybercrime and social engineering tactics.
- **Chapter 14: The Final Frontier** – Focuses on training, gamification, behavioural nudges, and cybersecurity awareness campaigns.

The Aim of the Book

Every book should have a point, and in our research, we are always motivated by a question that hovers over us all the time we are writing; so what? So, if you are reading this book, or thinking about reading this book, what is the point, what are we trying to achieve? Well, if you are looking for all the answers to all that ails organisational cybersecurity, we are afraid that you might be vastly disappointed when you get to the end of this book. However, if you are looking for an insight into the type of issues, barriers, and blocks that could serve to inhibit individuals from following your well thought out, perfect on paper cybersecurity strategies, this might be the text for you. In this book we aim to blend the approach of human factors with findings from research in the field of individual differences and cybersecurity awareness to highlight potential reasons why employees do not do the things they should be doing when it comes to cybersecurity awareness. Importantly, we are not looking at placing the blame on individuals within the organisation, but rather looking at ways in which the systems with which they interact, or their inherent psychological makeup, serves to impact the way they approach cybersecurity.

1

THE FOUNDATIONS OF CYBERSECURITY

Misplacing Information Is Not Something New!

The concept of information security did not suddenly arrive when interconnected technology arrived in the workplace – it just made it a lot harder to manage. History is replete with incidences where information that is private, confidential, and sensitive has ended up in the wrong hands, often with some dire consequences. For example, the well-publicised Pentagon Papers scandal that occurred in the early 1970s was a clear demonstration of how information security failed. In 1967, Secretary of Defence for the US Robert McNamara commissioned a report for the US government that focused on US involvement in Vietnam, triggered by a growing sense of disillusionment with the war that was being fought (Weiskopf & Willmott, 2013). Whilst working on the project, one of the analysts, Daniel Ellsberg, began to uncover a web of systematic deception by the US government that had been used to bolster its involvement in Vietnam. Ellsberg found that successive presidents had been lying to the American people about the war, including false rationales for increasing US involvement in Vietnam, and false claims about the successes of the military on the ground. Ellsberg became frustrated with his findings and managed to obtain a hard copy of the report, initially attempting to contact members of the US Congress to make the report more visible. However, his attempts met with a brick wall, instead turning to journalists. The upshot of this is the first page of the leaked report landed on the front page of *The New York Times* on Sunday 13 June 1971. In isolation, the information was innocuous, and at the time the then President Richard Nixon downplayed the incident, citing issues with journalism, the information, and Ellsberg himself. In a direct response to the Pentagon Papers leak, Nixon created a team of individuals who were tasked with preventing the leaking of

DOI: 10.4324/9781003509011-1

classified information, who were called the Special Investigations Unit, and more colloquially known as 'The White House Plumbers' (because it was their job to plug the holes through which information could be leaked). It was this same group who were also involved in the later Watergate Scandal, which in turn led to the resignation of Richard Nixon. Now, not all information leaks lead to such dramatic conclusions, but each piece of data has its own unique place in a system, and not until that piece of information is lost, stolen, or misplaced can we explore its impact and effect upon that system.

The Development of Modern Information Security

There were two critical events that led to the birth of information security as we know it today; the development of the first programmable computer, and the interception and later cracking of the German Enigma Coding machine that was being used to encode all secret communications. The first programmable computer, Colossus, was developed during the period of 1943–1945, and it was one of these machines that later produced information that indicated Hitler had erroneously concluded that the allied invasion would take place at Pas de Calais, and not Normandy, as planned. Contrary to popular belief (and here is one for the keen pub quizzers amongst you) it was not one of the Colossus machines that cracked the Enigma machine code, but the lesser-known 'Bombe' machine which was designed by Alan Turning and Gordon Welchman. This initial process of development driven by the need to save lives and prevent the Second World War continuing brought the first steps on the way to information security, where information was to be protected from spies, sabotage, and theft (Ibrahimova, 2020).

Moving forward in time, the next most significant event which influenced the field of information security field was the launch of the unmanned satellite Sputnik on 4 October 1957. At the time it was widely lauded by the then USSR as a major achievement which demonstrated its superior technical power over its Western adversaries. For the USA, the launch created widespread fear and panic, triggered by concerns over the threat to national security from the possibility of an attack on essential communication infrastructure. As a result, the US government set up a special research group, the Advanced Research Projects Agency (ARPA) with one of the key aims being to create a secure system that was capable of functioning even in the event of a major attack. This work led to the development of the Advanced Research Project Agency Network (ARPAnet) in the early 1960s (Packard, 2023).

The first discussions of an interconnected network designed for the purposes of communication appeared in 1962 memos by J.C.K. Licklider, formerly of MIT but who assumed the role of Head of Information Processing Techniques Office at ARPA. In some internal memos, he made referrence to an 'Intergalactic Computer Network' that would allow individuals the capacity to access information in electronic form directly through a large, interconnected array of computers, with all computers being connected in the same way. As we move into the latter part of the 1960s we see the first four nodes of ARPAnet become fully functional (initially between University of California, Los Angeles (UCLA), Stanford Research Institute (SRI), University of California-Santa Barbara (UCSB), and University of Utah) (Paloque-Bergès & Schafer, 2019). By the 1970s ARPAnet had grown beyond the boundaries of the US when the first transatlantic link was established to Europe with a communications centre in Norway that acted as the bridging station to the rest of Europe.

Even ARPAnet, the very system that was designed to be used to protect communications and allow information to be transmitted from point to point started to suffer its own internal security issues. By the 1980s the network could be accessed by multiple diverse types of users, including those with unauthorised access, hackers, and other unsavoury types. In order to counter this, the network underwent a change and was divided into two different networks during 1983 in order to counter these issues with security and unrestricted access:

- ARPAnet – dedicated to research and communication between academics.
- MILnet – this was the military communication network and employed far more sophisticated security measures such as encryption and restrictions on access control.

Finally, by 1990, ARPAnet ceased to exist and was eventually shut down. However its work to move towards the interconnected network envisaged by J.C.K Licklider had been completed, and the basis for what we now call the internet had been created.

What Is This Thing You Humans Call 'Information Security?'

The terminology associated with information security has its roots firmly planted in the military origins of the internet, and the respective need to keep sensitive information secure. The language used in the arena of information security still elicits strong connotations of warfare, defence, strategic planning, and awareness. For example, the term 'firewall' is used to describe a metaphysical boundary which protects a network from external threats, in the same way an army would protect a nation's borders. It has been noted that there can be a wide variety of issues with adopting the use of this type of terminology, and whilst the language might be appropriate in certain situations and scenarios, most of the time it only serves to mask the intricacies of a situation. The militaristic 'us versus them' perspective can serve to obscure many active threats within a system as well as overlooking those issues that are related directly to human error (Branch, 2021). The language is also unsuitable for non-military settings, where most of the information security issues encountered, although serious, are not life-or-death. Conversely, if you use this type of language that is directly associated with the military perspective of information security, it has the real potential to create a disproportionate sense of fear or panic in the very individuals you are trying to engage in the cybersecurity culture of an organisation (Herath & Rao, 2009a, 2009b; Pfleeger & Caputo, 2012; Siponen et al., 2014). Let us also not forget that the language can also be very intimidating for non-experts who have to deal with communications that include discussions related to things such as 'attack surfaces', 'exploits', and 'threat actors' – it does not make for easy reading for most employees!

In their initial overview of the area, Whitman and Mattord (2009) defined information security as 'the protection of information and its critical elements, including the systems and hardware that use, store, and transmit that information' (p. 8). In this definition we have the inclusion of both systems and hardware, concepts that often overlap with other areas of digital security. Previous international standards, such as ISO/IEC 27002, serve to provide guidance for organisations in taking a more proactive approach to cybersecurity risk management. These standards often define information security in terms of a triad of elements: confidentiality, integrity, and availability of information. These fundamental building blocks for information security are inextricably linked to the military foundations of the area (Samonas & Coss, 2014). We now go on to define each of these areas and detail what they have meant for the approach to information security.

Confidentiality

Confidentiality is a primary focus of information security, and reflect the military roots of the paradigm where data access is granted or restricted on a need-to-know basis (Samonas & Coss, 2014). Samonas and Coss (2014) noted that even though the aspect of confidentiality has remained at the core of the defining features for information security, there has been a dynamic shift in what it means to keep something confidential as working practices and requirements have changed. In modern working environments, the needs of businesses and organisations often require information to be accessible to a wide range of stakeholders and end users. As a result, the emphasis has shifted from strict confidentiality to notions of trust and privacy. Concerns related to customer data, loss of personal information, and the loss of company intellectual property have become more prominent (Samonas & Coss, 2014).

Integrity

In information security, integrity refers to the 'intactness' of information within a system, ensuring it remains in its original, unaltered state (Samonas

& Coss, 2014). Systems can be accessed, and information can be altered, with or without the owner's permission.

A classic example of compromised integrity is depicted in the 1983 film *Wargames.* In an early scene, the protagonist, David Lightman (played by Matthew Broderick), gains unauthorised access to his school's computer system to change his grades from an F in Biology to a C. This action alters the integrity of the information from its original state to a manipulated state.

Integrity is a core concept in information security, relating to the accuracy and consistency of data. It is intricately linked to two sub-dimensions: authenticity and non-repudiation (Vigil et al., 2015). Authenticity ensures that information is a true representation of events or things that have occurred, while non-repudiation ensures that a transaction between two parties can be verified and cannot be denied. For example, a sales receipt demonstrates non-repudiation by showing that a transaction has been completed.

Trust plays a crucial role in the interaction between confidentiality and integrity. We must be confident that the information we have is intact and assured that it allows us to prove the truthfulness of events. An example of this process is the use of login details or two-factor authentication to access online banking information. Here, the resulting transaction cannot be repudiated as it was conducted using relevant protocols that also protect the confidentiality of the information. However, if login credentials are compromised, the focus of information security shifts to addressing this vulnerability.

Availability

Availability emphasises that information must be accessible to end users for it to be utilised within the system (Samonas & Coss, 2014). Access can be restricted or denied based on the clearances associated with the individual trying to access the information. Availability can also be hindered if information is moved from its original position or blocked due to an internal fault or malicious attack.

Some researchers note that availability is often one of the least discussed elements of information security, but it is not the least important. It significantly impacts the other two elements of confidentiality and integrity (Qadir & Quadri, 2016). While confidentiality and integrity can be easily managed with system protocols and restrictions that prevent access, availability cannot be guaranteed at the same level (Qadir & Quadri, 2016).

Availability can also directly influence both confidentiality and integrity, but the reverse is not true. Confidentiality and integrity do not impact the availability of data, but availability affects both. Therefore, both confidentiality and integrity are dependent on availability (Qadir & Quadri, 2016).

Is the CIA Model Still Relevant?

One of the key issues with the CIA model is linked to its military origins, which focus on the protection of information and documentation (Samonas & Coss, 2014). Researchers have noted that this original focus has led to a rigidity in the model and resistance to incorporating new elements, with technical control seen as the primary goal (Hedström et al., 2011, 2014; Samonas & Coss, 2014). Other terms and concepts have been added to the CIA model to account for additional elements aligned with each of the core pillars, including authenticity, trust, and non-repudiation (Dhillon & Kolkowska, 2011; Samonas & Coss, 2014). The tension between the technical and socio-technical aspects of information security has been well documented (Hedström et al., 2011, 2014). This tension has been the source of many issues within the discipline, particularly when it comes to the resistance to acknowledging the importance of human factors to the field. It has been argued that the CIA model is restrictive in its application because it does not consider the environment in which it is being used. Such an oversight can in turn have an impact on how each of the elements are viewed and achieved (Hedström et al., 2011, 2014; Samonas & Coss, 2014).

Further criticisms have been levied at the CIA model. Lundgren and Möller (2019) pointed out that although the constructs have been widely used in the literature as defining features for information security, they are more of a target for creating a secure network. They also noted that using the CIA model as a defining framework for information security becomes problematic because it is both too broad and too specific according to the elements it contains. For example, they discuss the construct of availability, which they define as information being 'accessible and usable upon demand by an authorized entity' (Lundgren & Möller, 2019, p. 421). Lundgren and Möller (2019) highlighted instances where devices designed to provide security within the system conflict with the notion of availability. A failure in two-factor authentication (2FA) is a prime example – if the authorizing device is unavailable or the one-time password ends up in the junk folder of an email account, the system designed to protect information paradoxically restricts access and availability. Lundgren and Möller (2019) argued that although availability is always accepted as a defining feature of information security, it cannot always be guaranteed. Therefore, it should not be viewed as a necessary condition for achieving information security.

The Origins of Cybersecurity

The origins of the term 'cybersecurity' are somewhat obscured, but it is believed that the term began to gain traction in the early 1990s (Tzavara & Vassiliadis, 2024). This emergence coincided with the expansion of the internet and the growing awareness of the importance of protecting digital information and the systems on which it is stored. The prefix 'cyber' has two clear links to past work and common narratives in science fiction literature. The word 'cyber' was derived from the Greek verb 'kubernetes' which meant 'to be an independent helmsman, to lead, to rule' (Ciszek & Matulewska, 2019, p. 41). The term evolved into the scientific field of *cybernetics*, which studies control and communication in systems, whether natural or technological (Ashby, 1957; Weiner, 1948). Cybernetics focuses on 'what something can do' rather than 'what something is'. In the context of the internet, this perspective emphasises what people can do with technology rather than its underlying form and structure.

This focus aligns well with cybersecurity and human factors. Practitioners and researchers in the field are often more interested in how individuals interact with systems and the potential ways they could compromise those systems, rather than the technology behind security measures like two-factor authentication, biosecurity, and firewalls.

Another catalyst for the use of the term 'cyber' came from William Gibson's seminal 1984 novel *Neuromancer*, which introduced the concept of cyberspace – a non-physical, three-dimensional construct where people can move information and interact as they would in the real world, but without physical constraints. As a result, the prefix 'cyber' became strongly associated with computer systems and networks, particularly as the internet grew in the 1990s (Ciszek & Matulewska, 2019). Both elements contribute to the notion of interaction within an interconnected, non-physical environment where the protection of assets is crucial (Craigen et al., 2014).

Defining Cybersecurity

There is an inherent problem with defining cybersecurity, which becomes clear as we explore the collected literature on the topic. Presenting a definition that is both broad enough to be useful and specific enough to avoid becoming too sprawling and unmanageable is challenging. Often, definitions are variable in nature, closely linked to the context in which they are applied, and provide little detail about what the area truly encompasses (Craigen et al., 2014). This variability poses a real problem. When we use the term 'cybersecurity', our understanding of what it entails might differ significantly from that of others. This discrepancy makes it harder to ensure that everyone is meeting the right requirements and working towards the same goals.

When you start looking for concise definitions of cybersecurity, you find that none really exist, or, if they do, they are often narrowly focused on the technical protection of assets rather than a more holistic view that includes the protection of individuals. For example, Craigen et al. (2014) present a collection of nine definitions for cybersecurity to synthesise a one definition to rule them all approach. They suggested that 'Cybersecurity is the organisation and collection of resources, processes, and structures used to protect cyberspace and cyber-enabled systems from occurrences that misalign de jure from de facto property rights' (Craigen et al., 2014, p. 17). This is a great definition, but it does solely focus on the technical aspects of cybersecurity, and a consideration of human errors, insider threats and the impact of social engineering are key vulnerabilities that need to be addressed (Craigen et al., 2014). In a similar vein, the emphasis on property rights tends to overlook other aspects of cybersecurity including the protection of personal data, privacy, and cyberbullying and cyberaggression (von Solms & van Niekerk, 2013).

There is a distinct divide between these early 'pure' definitions of cybersecurity, which focus narrowly on the technical interventions that can be put in place, and newer socio-technical definitions that acknowledge the need to protect individuals as part of the paradigm. For example, the International Organisation for Standardization (ISO) presented an early definition of cybersecurity as 'The preservation of confidentiality, integrity, and availability of information in cyberspace' (ISO/IEC 27032/2012). This definition focuses on the core pillars of information security, with the only real difference being the inclusion of 'cyberspace' as the vehicle of interest for the transmission and protection of information.

Moving forward to the most recent definition of cybersecurity, it is now seen as 'safeguarding people, society, organisations, and nations from cyberrisks (where safeguarding means to keep cyber-risk at a tolerable level)' (ISO/IEC 27032:2023). This definition represents a clear shift away from the prescriptive information security pillars to a more human-centric focus, emphasizing the reduction of harm from cyber-risks. The National Institute of Standards and Technology (NIST) presents a variety of different definitions that encompass many aspects of cybersecurity, indicating the overall confusion when it comes to isolating one clear feature of the paradigm.

> Prevention of damage to, protection of, and restoration of computers, electronic communications systems, electronic communications services, wire communication, and electronic communication, including information contained therein, to ensure its availability, integrity, authentication, confidentiality, and nonrepudiation.
>
> *(Powell et al., 2020, p. 3)*

> the process of protecting information by preventing, detecting and responding to attacks.
>
> *(Ross et al., 2021, p. 62)*

> the ability to protect or defend the use of cyberspace from cyber-attacks.
>
> *(Barrent et al., 2020, p. 20)*

What becomes very apparent from this collection of definitions is the focus on the prevention of attacks, and the links again back to the CIA model

(Confidentiality, Integrity, Availability) from information security. Unlike the earlier definition from ISO, there is no mention of the protection of non-information assets (e.g., humans), which has been noted as a fundamental part of cybersecurity (Cains et al., 2021).

Academic definitions of cybersecurity have attempted to overcome some in industry standards by incorporating elements of the socio-technical, including links to human factors. For example, this definition presented by Azmi et al. (2018) for cybersecurity reads as follows:

> Securing a virtual digital environment by governance, management, and assurance, including its assets (information assets and cyber-assets) entities (such as end users, organisations, governments, societies, machines, and software) and interactions (enabled by IT Infrastructure, communications/networks, systems, and devices).
>
> *(Azmi et al., 2018, p. 2)*

This definition emphasises the importance of governance, management, and assurance in securing a digital environment, while also acknowledging the role of various entities and their interactions. It highlights the need to consider both technical and the human element in cybersecurity, providing a more comprehensive approach to understanding and addressing cybersecurity challenges. There are a multitude of components that form the backbone of cybersecurity in this definition. Security involves protecting assets from threats that arise because of inherent vulnerability due to human error, poor system protection, or backdoors in software. Security processes typically involve controls that restrict access to systems or safeguards that reduce the risks associated with the existing vulnerabilities. In information security, the asset we aim to secure is information regardless of its form – printed, spoken, or electronic, or any combination thereof. The focus remains on ensuring the confidentiality, integrity, and availability of this information. In the context of cybersecurity, the asset varies, and it may include a person, society, or any device connected to the internet. Anything connected to the internet becomes an asset with an inherent level of vulnerability because of this connection (Azmi et al., 2018; von Solms & van Niekerk, 2013). Cybersecurity aims to protect these assets from digital threats, in turn ensuring a secure and resilient digital environment.

Confusion in creating a clear definition to encapsulate what cybersecurity is can have a variety of unforeseen issues. For example, if we lack a clear framework for communicating how and what individuals in the workplace should be protecting, then their place in how they can help organisational security becomes even more obscured (Althonayan & Andronache, 2018; Craigen et al., 2014). Lacking a clear definition of what cybersecurity is in actionable terms means that individuals engaging in the use of digital technology throughout their day-to-day lives cannot be fully aware of what they need to do to protect themselves and their organisations (Neil & Lutters, 2023). However, organisations such as ENISA (Marinos et al., 2016) have argued that there is no need for a single, universal definition of cybersecurity given the broad scope of things that it needs to cover. Instead, the authors suggested a more granular approach is needed, allowing for definitions to be adopted in specific contexts, making them more applicable to different sectors and scenarios (Marinos et al., 2016). In turn, this can ensure the cybersecurity measures being deployed to counter current threats can be aligned directly to the needs of the current environment, whilst also allowing the capacity to dynamically change as threats emerge.

Cyber-Harm

Cyber-harm is a term increasingly associated with the cybersecurity paradigm, distinguishing it from information security (Agrafiotis et al., 2016, 2018). Cyber-harm refers to the 'damaging consequences resulting from cyber-events, which can originate from malicious, accidental or natural phenomena, manifesting itself within or outside of the Internet' (Agrafiotis et al., 2016, p. 2). Cyber-harm can impact various levels: individual, organisational, infrastructure/property, and national (Agrafiotis et al., 2016). Agrafiotis et al., (2016) emphasised the interplay between these levels, noting that nations can be comprised of individuals, organisations, and property, so they cannot be viewed entirely in isolation (Agrafiotis et al., 2016). While some researchers have argued that cyber-harm should be viewed as a consequence of cybercrime and thus outside of cybersecurity (von Solms & von Solms, 2017), others view it as an integral part of the cybersecurity paradigm (Agrafiotis et al., 2016, 2018). Whilst the inherent focus of the cybersecurity paradigm is on risk reduction and the attack prevention, there also needs to be an objective measure of the impact such attacks can have (Agrafiotis et al., 2016). Having a concrete measure of cyber-harm is important for several reasons, not least because it allows the capacity to better mitigate and respond to cyber threats. More specifically understanding cyber-harms is important for the following key reasons:

1. Risk Assessment and Management: By understanding the harms associated with diverse types of cyber-incidents, we can manage risk more effectively. This in turn has the knock-on impact of affording the opportunity to prioritise those risks that could be more damaging versus others, ensuring that resources are deployed effectively.
2. Economic Impacts: One of the key impacts of a cyberattack is a loss of revenue, either through direct theft or reputational damage. Having a clear indication of the potential financial implications for cyberattacks allows the capacity to bolster investment in current cybersecurity, as well as presenting a valuable argument for further investment in the future.

3. Awareness and Training: This is a critical element for our current focus, and having good, reliable information on cyber-harm can be used as a mechanism for raising awareness about the potential damage that could come from poor cybersecurity awareness.
4. Improving Current Cybersecurity: Any measure of cyber-harm gives organisations the capacity to identify current gaps in their cybersecurity provision, whilst also allowing improvements to be made. This must be one of the most critical elements for which information about cyber-harm is needed, and allows for an evolving, reflective cybersecurity process to be engaged in, especially when there are so many emerging threats.
5. Regulation and Policy Making: By understanding the far-reaching implications of cyber-harm, organisations can start to develop better policies and regulatory practices that serve to govern cybersecurity. This can, of course, be scaled up to be an effective mechanism to protect societies from cyber-harm, and feeds into efforts to protect national security and critical infrastructure (Agrafiotis et al., 2016, 2018; Ignatuschtschenko, 2021).

Broadly speaking, types of cyber-harm can be defined in terms of how their impacts are manifest (Agrafiotis et al., 2016, 2018; Ignatuschtschenko, 2021). These impacts can include physical, psychological, economic, reputational, and social/cultural harm.

1. Physical harm: Easily observable but is also the least commonly reported (Agrafiotis et al., 2016, 2018). It is manifested through actual bodily injury to individuals or groups, and the effects of such an attack can have impacts beyond that of the immediately observable. For example, an attack on a cardiac pacemaker could directly kill the patient and generate fear and panic among other patients fitted with similar devices (Agrafiotis et al., 2016).
2. Psychological harm: Can be the primary form of harm in an attack or develop as an indirect consequence (Agrafiotis et al., 2016). Primary psychological harm involves the direct emotional or mental impact resulting from a specific event or a series of events. This could include experiences such as cyberbullying, cyberaggression, or cyberharassment. Secondary psychological harm arises as an indirect consequence of the primary harm. For example, a worker who suffers a severe physical injury may later develop depression and anxiety because they feel unable to return to their normal duties. Individual differences in coping mechanisms can influence the impact of psychological harm. Maladaptive coping strategies, such as emotional eating, alcohol, and drug abuse, can exacerbate the harm (De Kimpe et al., 2021).
3. Economic harm: Most frequently measured in terms of the financial loss that results from a cyber-incident, and perhaps the easiest to

quantify because there is a clear 'loss' attached to something that has happened. Straightforward economic cyber-harm can be simply money taken from someone's bank account using phishing attacks; other more complex economic cyber-harm can be elicited through the loss of intellectual property which in turn gives a competitor inside information about a new product or innovation, which has a direct economic impact (Agrafiotis et al., 2016).

4. Reputational cyber-harm: Any incident that reflects poorly on an individual or organisation puts them at risk of some form of reputational damage. At the level of the organisation, reputational harm is usually seen as a loss of trust from its customer base, as well as on a business-to-business level. For example, the 2017 Equifax data breach not only resulted in $575 million in fines and settlements, but also impacted the company's reputation damage after the breach was made public. Similarly, in 2018 British Airways suffered an attack that harvested personal, passport, and credit card information from almost 500,000 passengers. In terms of reputational damage, they went from 31st to 55th in reputation score (Alva Group; www.alva-group.com). The drop in terms of reputation also coincided with a parallel drop in share prices and customer satisfaction ratings, so the resulting harm for the company was widespread.

5. Political cyber-harm: This is a broad spectrum of harm that can include impacts on government, political system, and its processes, as well as politicians themselves. As we have experienced in the 2024 UK General Election, there were a wide range of potentially damaging fake news stories, deep fakes, and attempted hacking attempts that all linked to interference in the democratic process (Broda & Strömbäck, 2024; Gupta et al., 2023; Stachofsky et al., 2023). Political cyber-harm can also be associated with reputational cyber-harm, so there is a double whammy here (Agrafiotis et al., 2016).

6. Cultural cyber-harm: According to Agrafiotis et al. (2016) this is the least discussed and hardest to measure of the cyber-harms. This type of harm represents a disruption to the stability and safety of society. An example of this could be the spread of fake news and misinformation, which in turn undermines social order and messaging. As was experienced during the COVID-19 pandemic, there were several fake news stories spread that served to undermine the messages and attempts to stem the spread of the virus, as well as attempts to get as many people vaccinated as possible.

Accordingly, each of these aspects is more aligned with the notion of cybersecurity than information security (Jansson & von Solms, 2013; von Solms & van Niekerk, 2013; von Solms & von Solms, 2017).

Consolidating Cyber and Information Security

The terms 'information security' and 'cybersecurity' are often used inter-changeably, but they have distinct focuses. Cybersecurity extends beyond protecting information to include safeguarding individuals and organisations in cyberspace. We often use terms and language in the sphere of online safety and protection that are extremely broad and do nothing to help with enhancing cybersecurity. Von Solms and von Solms (2017) made a crucial point about this, claiming that cybersecurity has become a 'hype term', emerging as an all-encompassing term to cover multiple aspects of security, both on and offline. Marinos et al. (2016) had previously noted that using the term cybersecurity had been further complicated by the mass media. It was noted that the term is often used to describe any form of attack on compu-ters and computer technology with the aim of making this type of news story more palatable to readers. It is therefore not surprising that the term cyber-security has now become a ubiquitous term that encompasses a wide variety of events and facets related to digital and physical security.

Some researchers have been keen to highlight the issues with assuming that information security and cybersecurity refer to the same types of threats, vulnerabilities, and assets (von Solms & van Niekerk, 2013; von Solms & von Solms, 2017). It has been argued that if cybersecurity is the same as infor-mation security, we should be able to describe cybersecurity incidents in an equivalent way to an information security incident, using the core principles of the CIA model (von Solms & van Niekerk, 2013). However, von Solms and van Niekerk (2013) noted a variety of incidents where the CIA model fails to have any clear relevance, but the scenarios themselves fall into the realms of cybersecurity. One such example is that of cyberbullying. Cyber-bullying has been defined 'as an aggressive, intentional act carried out by a group or individual, using electronic forms of contact, repeatedly and over time against a victim who cannot easily defend him or herself' (Smith et al., 2008, p. 376). The impact of cyberbullying on the victim can be widespread and can include severe impacts on mental health (Rao & Rao, 2021), depression (Englander, 2021), anxiety, and psychological distress (Nochaiwong et al., 2021). If we are to follow the definition of cybersecurity from the perspective of the ISO/IEC 27032:2023, one of the key elements proposed is the safeguarding of individuals from cyber-risk, which includes that of cyberbullying. In contrast, if we were to take the CIA approach to information security, cyberbullying would not easily fit into that framework (von Solms & van Niekerk, 2013). There is no loss of confidentiality, as no information is leaked or lost, no loss of integrity, and the availability of information is not compromised. However, as many researchers have noted, the inclusion of cyberbullying in the field of cybersecurity is a critical one, and one that needs to be at the forefront of digital strategies and online protection (Laczi & Poser, 2024). So, from this perspective, the categorisation of cyberbullying as part of an information security framework does not fully fit into that paradigm but maps well onto the key elements of the cybersecurity framework.

Van Solms and van Niekerk (2013) suggested that cybersecurity should be viewed as an extension of information security, emphasizing that cybersecurity encompasses more than just the protection of information. They highlight a critical distinction: cybersecurity includes the protection of individuals within cyberspace. For the remainder of this book, we adopt the term 'cybersecurity' to encompass the diverse assets that need protection in cyberspace, while also recognizing that socio-psychological factors can influence adherence to accepted protocols and rules. From this perspective we view cybersecurity as:

> the practice of protecting systems, networks, and data from digital attacks, unauthorized access, damage, and disruption. It involves a combination of technologies, processes, and practices designed to safeguard information and ensure its confidentiality, integrity, and availability. Cybersecurity also includes measures to protect individuals, organisations, and societies from cyber risks, emphasizing the importance of human factors, such as user behaviour, awareness, and education.

This comprehensive approach serves to create a framework that supports trust, privacy, and resilience against evolving threats. Although this approach may not be perfect and might challenge the views of some information security purists, it aligns well with the key discussion points in the rest of the book.

Summary

Defining the principles of the paradigm we now commonly refer to as cybersecurity is not as simple or straightforward as we may have first thought. The history of the area has its roots firmly planted in a military need to protect communication networks and information from potential enemy threats, where the loss of sensitive information could lead to catastrophic consequences. While the framework provided by the militaristic requirement for information security has been useful, it has also presented some considerable disadvantages.

Primarily, the traditional view of information security places a narrow focus on the things that need to be protected, specifically elements of information. The CIA model, although useful for isolating key features of the approach, is rigid in nature and fails to capture the more nuanced requirements of many organisations. The language often adopted by this approach is also problematic, as it can generate fear, feelings of alarm, and a sense of threat in the very individuals we are trying to engage in protective behaviours.

While some researchers have argued that cybersecurity has become a 'hype term' that is often overused and misunderstood, the defining principles of the area offer a far more comprehensive approach. This approach fits the requirements of most modern organisations, where there is a need to protect a wide variety of assets and entities that engage in online activities far beyond pure information. The evolving nature of cybersecurity means it also includes consideration for human factors, which are critical for improving adherence to accepted rules and policies within the workplace.

Moreover, the damaging consequences of cyber-incidents, whether malicious or accidental, can affect individuals, organisations, infrastructure, and nations. Cyber-harm manifests in various forms: physical, psychological, economic, reputational, political, and cultural. Understanding and measuring cyber-harm is crucial for risk management, improving cybersecurity practices, and developing effective regulations.

References

Agrafiotis, I., Bada, M., Cornish, P., Creese, S., Goldsmith, M., Ignatuschtschenko, E., Roberts, T., & Upton, D. (2016). Cyber harm: Concepts, taxonomy and measurement. *SSRN Electronic Journal.* doi:10.2139/ssrn.2828646.

Agrafiotis, I., Nurse, J. R. C., Goldsmith, M., Creese, S., & Upton, D. (2018). A taxonomy of cyber-harms: Defining the impacts of cyber-attacks and understanding how they propagate. *Journal of Cybersecurity,* 4(1), tyy006. doi:10.1093/cybsec/tyy006.

Althonayan, A., & Andronache, A. (2018). Shifting from information security towards a cybersecurity paradigm. *Proceedings of the 2018 10th International Conference on Information Management and Engineering,* 68–79. doi:10.1145/3285957.3285971.

Ashby, W. R. (1957). *An introduction to cybernetics.* Chapman & Hall.

Azmi, R., Tibben, W., & Win, K. T. (2018). Review of cybersecurity frameworks: Context and shared concepts. *Journal of Cyber Policy,* 3(2), 258–283. doi:10.1080/23738871.2018.1520271.

Branch, J. (2021). What's in a name? Metaphors and cybersecurity. *International Organisation,* 75(1), 39–70. doi:10.1017/S002081832000051X.

Broda, E., & Strömbäck, J. (2024). Misinformation, disinformation, and fake news: Lessons from an interdisciplinary, systematic literature review. *Annals of the International Communication Association,* 48(2), 139–166. doi:10.1080/23808985.2024.2323736.

Cains, M. G., Flora, L., Taber, D., King, Z., & Henshel, D. S. (2021). Defining cyber security and cyber security risk within a multidisciplinary context using expert elicitation. *Risk Analysis,* 42(8), 1643–1669. doi:10.1111/risa.13687.

Ciszek, H., & Matulewska, A. (2019). A case study of the productivity of the prefix cyber- in English and Greek legal languages. *Studies in Logic, Grammar and Rhetoric,* 58(1), 35–57. doi:10.2478/slgr-2019-0016.

Craigen, D., Diakun-Thibault, N., & Purse, R. (2014). Defining cybersecurity. *Technology Innovation Management Review,* 4(10), 13–21.

De Kimpe, L., Walrave, M., Verdegem, P., & Ponnet, K. (2021). What we think we know about cybersecurity: An investigation of the relationship between perceived knowledge, internet trust, and protection motivation in a cybercrime context. *Behaviour and Information Technology*, 1–13. doi:10.1080/0144929X.2021.1905066.

Dhillon, G., & Kolkowska, E. (2011). Information security and human behaviour: A survey of the literature. *Computers & Security*, 30(8), 620–635.

Englander, E. K. (2021). Cyberbullying, sexting, and the law. *Journal of Adolescent Health*, 68(3), 567–573. doi:10.1016/j.jadohealth.2020.12.012.

Gupta, M., Dennehy, D., Parra, C. M., Mäntymäki, M., & Dwivedi, Y. K. (2023). Fake news believability: The effects of political beliefs and espoused cultural values. *Information & Management*, 60(2), 103745. doi:10.1016/j.im.2022.103745.

Hedström, K., Dhillon, G., & Karlsson, F. (2014). Using Actor Network Theory to understand information security management. *IFIP Advances in Information and Communication Technology*, 330, 43–54. doi:10.1007/978-3-642-15257-3_5.

Hedström, K., Kolkowska, E., Karlsson, F., & Allen, J. P. (2011). Value conflicts for information security management. *Journal of Strategic Information Systems*, 20(4), 373–384.

Herath, T., & Rao, H. R. (2009a). Encouraging information security behaviours in organisations: Role of penalties, pressures and perceived effectiveness. *Decision Support Systems*, 47(2), 154–165.

Herath, T., & Rao, H. R. (2009b). Protection motivation and deterrence: A framework for security policy compliance in organisations. *European Journal of Information Systems*, 18(2), 106–125.

Ibrahimova, A. (2020). The development of modern information security: A historical perspective. *Journal of Information Security and Applications*, 47, 102–115.

Ignatuschtschenko, E. (2021). Cyber harm: A review of the literature. *Journal of Information Security and Applications*, 47, 102–115.

Jansson, K., & von Solms, R. (2013). Phishing for phishing awareness. *Behaviour and Information Technology*, 32(6), 584–593. doi:10.1080/0144929X.2011.632650.

Laczi, S. A., & Poser, V. (2024). Impact of deepfake technology on children: Risks and consequences. In A. Szakál (Ed.), *Proceedings of the IEEE 22nd International Symposium on Intelligent Systems and Informatics (SISY 2024)* (pp. 215–220). IEEE Hungary Section.

Lundgren, B., & Möller, N. (2019). Defining information security: A systematic review. *Computers & Security*, 87, 101–115.

Marinos, L., Belmonte, A., & Rekleitis, E. (2016). *ENISA threat landscape 2015, European Union Agency for Network and Information Security.* January. www.enisa. europa.eu/activities/risk-management/evolving-threat-environment/enisa-threat-landscape-mid-year-2013.

Neil, R., & Lutters, W. G. (2023). The role of organisational culture in cybersecurity: A systematic review. *Journal of Information Security and Applications*, 47, 102–115.

Nochaiwong, S., Ruengorn, C., Thavorn, K., Hutton, B., Awiphan, R., ... Phosuya, C. (2021). Global prevalence of mental health issues among the general population during the coronavirus disease-2019 pandemic: A systematic review and meta-analysis. *Scientific Reports*, 11. doi:10.1038/s41598-021-89700-8.

Packard, V. (2023). The development of modern information security: A historical perspective. *Journal of Information Security and Applications*, 47, 102–115.

Paloque-Bergès, C., & Schafer, V. (2019). Arpanet (1969–2019). *Internet Histories*, 3 (1), 1–14.

Pfleeger, S. L., & Caputo, D. D. (2012). Leveraging behavioural science to mitigate cyber security risk. *Computers & Security*, 31(4), 597–611.

Powell, M., Brule, J., Pease, M., Stouffer, K., Tang, C., Zimmerman, T., ... Zopf, M. (2020). Protecting information and system integrity in industrial control system environments: Cybersecurity for the manufacturing sector. *NIST*. https://nvlpubs. nist.gov/nistpubs/SpecialPublications/NIST.SP.1800-10.pdf.

Qadir, M. A., & Quadri, S. M. K. (2016). Information availability: An insight into the most important attribute of information security. *Journal of Information Security*, 7 (3), 185–194.

Rao, M. E., & Rao, D. M. (2021). The mental health of high school students during the COVID-19 pandemic. *Frontiers in Education*, 6, 1–11. doi:10.3389/feduc.2021.719539.

Ross, R., Pillitteri, V., Graubart, R., Bodeau, D., & Mcquaid, R. (2021). Developing cyber-resilient systems: A systems security engineering approach. *National Institute of Standards and Technology*, 2, 310.

Samonas, S., & Coss, D. (2014). The CIA strikes back: Redefining confidentiality, integrity and availability in security. *Journal of Information Security*, 5(4), 280–287.

Siponen, M., Mahmood, M. A., & Pahnila, S. (2014). Employees' adherence to information security policies: An exploratory field study. *Information & Management*, 51(2), 217–224. doi:10.1016/j.im.2013.08.006.

Smith, P. K., Mahdavi, J., Carvalho, M., Fisher, S., Russell, S., & Tippett, N. (2008). Cyberbullying: Its nature and impact in secondary school pupils. *Journal of Child Psychology and Psychiatry*, 49, 376–385.

Stachofsky, M., Gupta, A., & Strömbäck, J. (2023). Political cyber harm: A systematic review. *Journal of Information Security and Applications*, 47, 102–115.

Tzavara, V., & Vassiliadis, S. (2024). Tracing the evolution of cyber resilience: A historical and conceptual review. *International Journal of Information Security*, 23(3), 1695–1719. doi:10.1007/s10207-023-00811-x.

Vigil, J. M., Coulombe, P., & Alcock, J. (2015). The role of trust in the interaction between confidentiality and integrity. *Journal of Information Security*, 6(4), 280–287.

von Solms, R., & van Niekerk, J. (2013). From information security to cybersecurity. *Computers & Security*, 38, 97–102.

von Solms, R., & von Solms, B. (2017). *The cybersecurity culture: A systematic review*. *Computers & Security*, 70, 1–10.

Weiner, N. (1948). *Cybernetics: Or control and communication in the animal and the machine*. MIT Press.

Weiskopf, R., & Willmott, H. (2013). Ethics as critical practice: The 'Pentagon Papers', deciding responsibly, truth-telling, and the unsettling of organizational morality. *Organization Studies*, 34(4), 469–493. doi:10.1177/0170840612470256.

Whitman, M. E., & Mattord, H. J. (2009). *Principles of information security* (3rd ed.). Thompson Course Technology.

2

THE INSIDER THREAT

Understanding the Risks Within

Introduction

Individuals working within organisations are afforded a level of trust – not only the people who they work for, but also the individuals who work around them (Mehan, 2016). We expect everyone who works within an organisation to adhere to accepted policies and practices, to do their work as diligently as possible, and to ensure that information contained within these internal systems does not get lost, leaked, or stolen. However, the reality is something quite different, and there is a group of individuals who contradict this trust relationship. Individuals can engage in a wide variety of actions that lead to the disruption of organisational functioning, including espionage, terrorism, unauthorised disclosure of information, corruption, sabotage, workplace violence, and the intentional/unintentional loss of departmental resources (www.cisa.gov/topics/physical-security/insider-threat-mitigation/defining-insi der-threats). Any individual that carries out actions that are contrary to the interests of the organisation in which they are working, and who have assumed this position of trust, can be viewed as an 'insider threat' (Liu et al., 2018).

The threats posed by insiders are multifaceted and can take various forms. A common assumption is that insider threats are always malicious, which is influenced by the terminology used. The word 'threat' evokes connotations of danger, peril, and risk, leading us to associate it with a shadowy figure intent on subterfuge. However, it may come as a surprise that malicious insider threats (MITs) account for only a small minority (6%) of internal security breaches. Despite their low frequency, these attacks are the costliest, with an estimated \$4.9 million lost globally to such attacks in 2023 alone (IBM Security, 2023).

DOI: 10.4324/9781003509011-2

What Is an Insider Threat?

Identifying someone as an insider threat is more complex than it seems. Firstly, how do we define an 'insider'? If we assume an insider is embedded within an organisation, it implies that the organisation has clear boundaries distinguishing insiders from outsiders (Hadlington, 2018). Modern working practices complicate this view, especially considering how many organisations now employ sub-contractors or external consultants who are granted the same access rights and privileges as direct employees. Additionally, what about individuals who are given temporary logins to work within an organisation for a period? Since the advent of COVID-19 and the rise of hybrid and remote working, the physical infrastructure that once governed the office environment has been completely transformed.

This issue was a key discussion point in the initial stages of research related to insider threats, with some researchers noting difficulties in defining what was being studied (Bishop & Gates, 2008). Early frameworks for categorizing insider threats viewed it as a simple dichotomy: you are either an insider threat or you are not. Bishop and Gates (2008) noted that if this were the case, an insider threat could only be identified with unmistakable evidence of malicious intent or motive, leaving no middle ground. To address this issue, Bishop and Gates (2008) introduced the concept of 'insiderness'. From this perspective, insider threat is measured on a sliding scale, where someone with clear motive and malicious intent ranks higher on the insiderness scale, while someone with no motive or intent ranks lower. However, Bishop and Gates (2008) emphasised that even individuals at the lower end of the insiderness scale, in terms of motive and intent, could cause significant organisational and reputational damage comparable to that caused by malicious insider threats. We have created our own insiderness scale based on the research reviewed above, shown in Table 2.1. Insiderness, featured on the left-hand side of the scale, includes individuals that lack motive or intent, but their actions lead to clear repercussions for the organisation. On the right side of the scale, we have the dedicated malicious insider threats who exhibit clear intent and motive when it comes to doing harm within the organisation.

Hunker and Probst (2011) highlighted the issues with defining insider threats based solely on the level of access an individual has to IT systems within an organisation. Such early definitions fail to acknowledge changes in contemporary working practices, and the notion of 'privileged access' can have multiple interpretations in the modern work environment. For instance, an insider could be someone who has been recently terminated but still retains privileged access due to an oversight by the organisation. This is more common than expected, with a study by Beyond Identity (2021) estimating that one in four employees still retained access to accounts from their previous job. Other examples include a software developer who has designed a

TABLE 2.1 The Insiderness Scale

Intent and Motive	Unintentional Insider	Negligent Insider	Compromised Insider	Opportunistic Insider	Malicious Insider
	Low Level Medium High Level				
Actions	Actions are accidental with no malicious intent.	Actions are careless but not malicious.	Actions are due to external compromise.	Actions are intentional but driven by opportunity rather than premeditation.	Actions are intentional with clear malicious intent.
Characteristics	- Mistakes due to lack of awareness or training. - Accidental data breaches. - Misconfigured systems.	- Ignoring security policies. - Poor password management. - Using unsecured devices.	- Credentials stolen by external attackers. - Phishing attacks. - Social engineering.	- Exploiting access for personal gain. - Minor policy violations. - Unauthorised access to non-critical data.	- Sabotage. - Theft of sensitive data. - Espionage.
Examples	- An employee accidentally sends sensitive information to the wrong email address. - A user misconfigures a security setting, exposing data.	- An employee uses a weak password that gets compromised. - An employee accesses company data on an unsecured personal device.	- An employee's login credentials are stolen and used by an attacker. - An employee falls victim to a phishing scam.	- An employee accesses confidential information out of curiosity. - An employee uses company resources for personal projects.	- An employee deliberately leaks confidential information. - An employee sabotages company systems before leaving the organisation.

system for an organisation and still has operational knowledge of that system, or someone who finds an unrestricted access point and uses it to access the organisation's system without direct permission (Hunker & Probst, 2011).

One of the most widely accepted definitions for malicious insider threat is presented by Cappelli et al. (2012) who identified an insider threat as being:

> a current or former employee, contractor, or business partner who has or had authorised access to an organisation's network, system or data and intentionally exceeded or misused that access in a manner that negatively affected the confidentiality, integrity, or availability of the organisational information or information systems.
>
> *(p. xiii)*

In terms of 'the who', this definition covers all potential scenarios: a current employee – check; someone who has previously worked for the organisation – check; anyone else with access to the system within the organisation – check. As we will see in the next section, Cappelli et al. (2012) presented a slightly different definition to account for the accidental insider threat. The inclusion of intentionality firmly positions the individual at the heart of this definition as someone with a clear motive to do harm and a personal stake in disrupting the organisation's activities. The latter part of the definition links to some key aspects mentioned in Chapter 1, specifically the core pillars of information security: confidentiality, integrity, and availability of information.

The Accidental or Unintentional Insider Threat

While insider threats often involve malicious intent aimed at disrupting the organisation or gaining financially, threats from negligent or careless employees are equally problematic. For example, research from the Ponemon Institute (2023) noted that negligence accounted for 63% of reported insider threat incidents, with an estimated cost of $4.58 million, against the cost of MIT at $4.08 million. The work by the group from CERT (2013, 2014) was fundamental in shaping the way in which we view UIT, and the key elements that underlie the possible predictors for such threats to emerge. They offered the following definition to account for the UIT:

> An unintentional insider threat is a current or former employee, con-tractor, or business partner who has or had authorised access to an organisation's network, system, or data and who, through action or inaction without malicious intent, causes harm or substantially increases the possibility of future serious harm to the confidentiality, integrity, or availability of the organisation's information or information systems.
>
> *(CERT, 2013, p. ix)*

This definition extends and slightly alters the one we have already seen in this chapter, removing the intentionality attached to behaviours linked to insider threats. Instead, the unintentional insider threat (UIT) arises when individuals either fail to do something or do something that contradicts the cybersecurity of the organisation they work for (Khan et al., 2021). Individuals can easily become UITs, which is how much of the material covered in this book has emerged. UITs can be negligent, creating risk through general carelessness, such as allowing someone to access a building via a secure entrance through piggybacking, ignoring messages about keeping passwords safe, or leaving sensitive data on the 17:15 train out of London St Pancras. Other UITs can be accidental, resulting from a lapse in concentration due to workload pressures. Examples include the infamous 'reply all' email that includes sensitive documentation, clicking on links in phishing emails, or failing to dispose of critical information correctly (Renaud et al., 2024). Calic et al. (2016) also noted that accidental and naive behaviours are fundamental causes of cybersecurity compromises, linking this back to a lack of training, education, and understanding of the risks associated with their behaviours.

Taxonomical Approaches to the Malicious Insider Threat

There have been various attempts to create taxonomies or classifications to categorise the many diverse types of malicious insider threats that have emerged because of organisations being compromised. Many of these approaches often consider distinct factors to provide a classification for the attack including the motivation for the attack, the skillset of the attacker, and the resultant implications of the attack. However, there are several issues with taxonomical approaches, especially in fast-evolving fields like cybersecurity. First, they can become outdated quickly as new types of attacks and attackers emerge frequently. Another issue is that the categories in such frameworks can become so ingrained in the research literature that they hinder development and lead to stagnation.

Gudaitis (1998) was one of the first researchers to note concerns related to the application of categorisations and taxonomical approaches. He argued that if investigators rely too heavily on these approaches, they may become narrowly focused on a singular account of insider threats, potentially missing unique and original attacks as they emerge. Additionally, developing one-size-fits-all accounts of insider threats can create tendency to overlook the situational contexts in which the attacks occur, as well as the diverse types of attacks and insiders involved.

Despite these challenges, research exploring typologies for insider threats provides an essential backbone to the area. It allows researchers and practitioners to better understand and address the threats that emerge within organisations, in turn making it a lot easier to develop and implement targeted mitigation strategies (Al-Mhiqani et al., 2020).

If we go back to some of the earliest research that was conducted on insider threat and IT systems, Anderson (1980) was one of the first to propose three distinct classifications for individuals who misuse internal IT systems (Homoliak et al., 2019):

- Masqueraders: External attackers who circumvent security controls to gain access to a computer system, or an individual inside the organisation who uses someone else's access details to carry out malicious activities.
- Misfeasors: Individuals who blatantly use their own login credentials to carry out attacks.
- Clandestines: Superusers with expertise in computer technology and programming, who have the capacity to hide their activities from system administrators (Anderson, 1980; Homoliak et al., 2019).

One of the key issues with this early typology is that it very narrowly focuses in on the misuse of computer systems, primarily motived by financial gain. However, as Homoliak et al. (2019) noted, this classification also misses other activities that could still be relevant to our discussion of insider threat, such as counterproductive work behaviours and cyberloafing (see Chapters 11 and 12).

Hayden (1999) made advances in providing another prospective typology for insider threats, identifying four categories of insiders based on their knowledge, skillset, and motives for carrying out the attack.

- Traitors: Individuals with direct malicious intent who have a clear desire to disrupt the internal systems of the host organisation they have access to.
- Zealots: Individuals with a strong set of principles that may conflict directly with those of the organisation. Issues arise when the principles of Zealots differ significantly from those of the organisation in which they are working, causing tension and disgruntlement. To restore balance and achieve what they perceive as justice, Zealots may release sensitive information to external agents to force the organisation to align with their own principles.
- Browsers: Curious individuals who explore information within the system without proper access rights. Although they have no malicious intent, their actions can inadvertently alter information or accidentally release sensitive data to external agents.
- Well Intentioned: Individuals who, due to ignorance of internal security policies, cause unintentional breaches. They believe they are doing something beneficial but may circumvent cybersecurity practices to expedite their work or make it easier (e.g., downloading software from unknown sources or bypassing anti-virus software).

Hayden's typology is beneficial because it acknowledges that some insider threats can come from individuals who have no direct intent to do harm. However, these individuals still pose a significant challenge to organisational cybersecurity, and their actions can be very damaging.

Shaw and Fischer (2005) presented a further exploration of the ways in which insider threat could be classified and based their work on ten insider threat case studies that occurred in 2003. The case studies report covered attacks on a variety of business sectors, including finance/banking, government contractors, telecommunications, and the energy sector. Most of the reported attacks involved some form of unauthorised access and the theft of data. Shaw and Fischer (2005) presented eight insider threat sub-types but were quick to highlight that the available information on which these classifications were based was extremely limited. One of the key issues with researching insider threat is that if someone gets caught red handed and is punished (usually a custodial sentence), their willingness to open up to researchers and have a chat about their handy work is extremely low. This is something that we should bear in mind for many of these typologies, but for now let us look at the categories that Shaw and Fischer (2005) identified:

- The Explorer: There is some crossover here with the 'Browser' typology identified by Hayden (1999). These individuals like to explore systems, usually doing so without permission, or do so knowing that they are circumventing accepted security protocols. Again, this individual has no direct malicious intent when it comes to their activities and actions, but their actions inadvertently cause damage in some way, whilst also violating countless organisational policies on IT use.
- The Samaritan: That person in the office who thinks that they know best and creates more issues and problems when they choose to implement their own special brand of DIY. The Samaritan thinks that their way is the best way and sets about circumventing security protocols in the same way that the 'Well Intentioned' insider threat typology by Hayden (1999) does.
- Hackers: These are individuals who have a skillset that allows them to be able to understand and manipulate the key systems within their place of work. They have had some previous history of reprimands for using their skills for nefarious causes but will hide this information on application forms for new, prospective employers.
- The Machiavellian: These are the individuals who use elements of social engineering to manipulate their social environment to further their own agendas. This might be as a pretext to covering up the build-up to their attack. The attack(s) they engage in are conducted to further their career goals and objectives, such as stealing intellectual property so they can establish themselves as an expert consultant in their respective field.
- The Avengers: Rather than being an ensemble of characters from a well-known film franchise, these individuals have an axe to grind at the

expense of the organisation they work for. This might be directed at management, colleagues, a singular colleague, or other unseen/imagined transgressors. Their actions are driven by a sense of social injustice, and their actions are deemed necessary to restore balance and satisfy their need for revenge. In some respects, this classification maps well onto that of 'Zealots' presented by Hayden (1999) and sets out to establish a group of insider threats who are not happy with something in their organisation and take it upon themselves to do something about it.

- Proprietors: These are individuals who own the system, and they really do not like someone else being given permission to access it, touch it, or even look at it. As a result of their self-invested ownership of these systems they will go to great lengths to protect them, even to the point of disrupting or destroying the system so that no one else can use it.
- Career Thieves: Their sole purpose is to get into an organisation through employment to access internal systems and the information contained within them. The central focus for this activity is to get information to sell for financial gain.
- Moles: A class of insider threat similar to Career Thieves, but their motive is very heavily geared towards stealing intellectual property to be given to another organisation or state-sponsored actor.

This classification system is intriguing because it identifies two clear categories where UITs can be expressed. Both the Explorer and Samaritan lack a clear motive or intent in their activities, yet their actions still cause significant harm. Additionally, this system provides a detailed analysis of the skills and motives associated with different forms of insider threats, moving away from the notion that insider threats are a one-size-fits-all issue. By allowing for nuances in understanding insider threats, researchers and practitioners can better account for a varied and evolving threat landscape. This, in turn, enables the development of more tailored and effective strategies to mitigate these threats.

Cole and Ring (2005) presented a contrasting approach where insider threat was grouped into four classes. These were:

- The Pure Insider: The standard employee who has access rights to specific systems as an accepted condition of their employment and job role and which allow them to perform their daily activities. This could be an internal file sharing system, or something like a HR access point.
- The Inside Associate: This classification is split into two distinct subgroups:

  a   Contractors or third-party personnel who are afforded some level of access to systems but are not given the full access that is given to the Pure Insider.

b   Internal employees who have partial access to internal systems as their role requires, but which is again restricted and not of the same level as the Pure Insider.

- Insider Affiliate: These individuals have no justified or legitimate access to the organisation, but through inherited or stolen credentials, they can still gain access to the organisation and the systems that are contained within. This could include a friend of the Pure Insider or a family member. Access can be gained using login/access credentials (taking ID badges or using login details).
- Outside Affiliate: Individuals who are external to the organisation and gain access to the internal systems of the organisation through a variety of attack vectors, including (but not limited to) software backdoors, social engineering, or the use of other technical skills such as hacking (Cole & Ring, 2005).

This classification focuses on the level of access an individual has within an organisation. It suggests that the more access a person has, the more damage they can potentially cause. However, it also highlights that individuals without direct access to systems can still infiltrate them. This underscores that insiders will exploit whatever access they have – whether full or partial. Consequently, the attack methods they use are often not highly sophisticated, unlike those employed by Hackers and Clandestines in previous classifications (e.g., Anderson, 1980; Shaw & Fischer, 2005).

Psychological Precursors for Malicious Insider Threat

Pfleeger (2008) highlighted the challenges of reducing insider threats to neat psychological profiles, which suggests it might be possible to identify individuals likely to commit insider threats before the attack occurs. Such a notion is extremely attractive and could be accomplished with a good degree of accuracy. For example, you could invite prospective employee to take part in a series of psychometric tests and produce a set of results against which their profile is compared to a set of profiles from previous attackers. However, as Pfleeger (2008) noted, the attractiveness of such an approach is compounded by the theoretical difficulties that underlie the application of such measures. If this mechanism were so easy, criminologists and criminal psychologists, who have been grappling with this concept for many years, would have made some significant progress. Yet, there is no clear a priori mechanism for identifying an individual who is more likely to commit a crime over another. This challenge is even greater when the crime itself is a response to a unique psychological stressor or sudden life event, something that is a common trigger for insider threat attacks. In such instances, there is a limited capacity to predict the events and the likely responses of the individuals in question, only a chance to explore the event in question in a post hoc manner and highlight potential mitigation strategies that could be employed in future.

One of the critical issues in trying to produce psychological profiles for insider threat is the lack of concrete empirical data upon which to base such profiles. Various researchers have attempted to collect data on insider threat (e. g., Legg et al., 2017; Randazzo et al., 2005; Taylor et al., 2013) but at present there is no effective mechanism for gathering such information. As we noted earlier on in this chapter, if someone gets caught engaging in malicious activities within an organisation, the last thing they are going to want to do is talk to a researcher. Pfleeger (2008) highlighted another difficulty: defining what differentiates 'bad' from 'good' behaviour. We can only classify behaviour as 'bad' if we have a category for comparison, which ties into our initial discussion of what is viewed as a threat for the organisation. In some organisations, behaviour that might be objectively unacceptable or illegal could be overlooked or even be part of accepted practice. For example, insider trading is widely condemned and is illegal. However, for some organisations this practice may be treated as 'acceptable' if it gets the required results. This situation creates a challenge where objectively the behaviour is seen as 'bad' but in terms of the norms that govern the culture of the organisation, that behaviour might be viewed as 'good'. Therefore, detection would need to employ a base rate method for identifying anomalies in behaviour relevant to the person and the company, rather than a catchall method based on past behaviours.

Research from Cappelli et al. (2012) explored ten case studies that fell into the category of insider threat and noted some common psychological elements. The authors echoed the sentiment that psychological profiling based on stereotypical behaviours is not productive. However, they suggested that detection should focus on the overt behaviours displayed by individuals, including:

- Threatening Behaviour: Any demonstrable acts of threatening behaviour directed towards the organisation. This could include bragging about the individual's capacity to harm or damage the organisation via an insider attack.
- Bizarre or Out-of-the-Ordinary Behaviour: Any behaviour viewed as bizarre or out of character to the objective observer. This could be instances of self-aggrandisement in an individual, or overt claims of being a lone warrior fighting a secret war.
- Deception: A key psychological element in the profile of the insider. Cappelli et al. (2012) noted that several individuals featured in the case studies they examined attempted to conceal previous criminal convictions, including aspects of fraud.

Attempts to classify the psychological components of insider threats have, to date, been haphazard and based on limited empirical evidence. For example, the work by Cappelli et al. (2012) is based on information from only ten case studies, making it difficult to extrapolate these findings to wider populations.

Further research by Shaw et al. (1998a, 1998b) explored several case studies and identified core characteristics that could be viewed as indicators of insider threats. These elements fall into four broad categories:

- **Negative Life Experiences**: Individuals with a history of negative life experiences often exhibit overt displays of anger directed towards peers and those in positions of authority (not limited to organisational authority but also law enforcement, etc.). These individuals also have a low threshold for frustration, which links to their overt displays of aggression.
- **Social Isolation and Lack of Social Skills**: Insiders often demonstrate a lack of social skills and a tendency for social isolation. This lack of social skills may lead them to seek interaction through online social networking. Their heavy reliance on computer-mediated communication means they struggle to deal with social/emotional issues in workplace situations effectively. Shaw et al. (1998a, 1998b) suggest that this combination of factors can lead to feelings of frustration and disgruntlement, which may manifest in difficult social interactions with peers and colleagues, as well as 'emotional leakage' – outbursts that far outweigh the nature of the incident.
- **Sense of Entitlement**: Insiders may suffer from a sense of entitlement, often due to special privileges or access rights granted in their roles. They may possess a special skillset that allows them to leverage such treatment and may treat peers poorly, viewing them as inferior. They may also struggle to adapt to specific rules or protocols set by the organisation, fitting into the 'Proprietors' category highlighted earlier.
- **Ethical Flexibility**: Insiders often exhibit underdeveloped ethical flexibility, meaning they may lack the ability to empathise with colleagues or others, which would typically prevent an individual from engaging in insider threats. This immaturity is also linked to a breakdown in the inhibitory processes that control emotional outbursts, such as aggression.

Shaw and Fischer (2005) provided a detailed account of the underlying motivators and psychological components associated with insider threat attacks based on ten individual case studies. Each attack is presented with a clear discussion of the associated psychosocial stressor in Table 2.2.

What is apparent from the work conducted by Shaw and Fischer (2005) is that there is little commonality between attackers, attack types, and key psychological elements. Impulsivity is one of the traits associated with many of these attacks, as noted in other research (CPNI, 2013). However, some perpetrators exercise restraint and planning, such as The Thief. One interesting point to note is that for each of the cases, the attack is triggered by a

TABLE 2.2 Attacker Sub-Types and Associated Psychosocial Triggers (adapted from Shaw & Fischer, 2005)

Attacker Type	Attack Time	Personal Stressor	Notes on Attack
The Crasher	2 days	Loss of mentor at work; feelings of exploitation; replaced by new team.	Viewed as an impulsive attack driven by work-based issues; individual involved in relationship struggles with former workplace colleagues; described as being 'impulsive' by close peers.
The Data Destroyer	60 days	Rejection by love interest; feelings of betrayal; loss of job; caught on video violating rules and lying.	Presented deliberation and planning in the execution of the attack; also presented ongoing struggles with previous work colleagues; used IT skills to access information and pursue love interest although attack was seen as isolated from this; primary motivator seen as loss of job.
The Hacker	30 days	Loss of job without warning; loss of pay for periods of work; loss of access to computer resources.	Adverse personal history and prior criminal convictions (history of hacking); disregard for security and accepted processes; significant self-esteem issues requiring an 'unusual' level of attention termed by managers as a 'high maintenance' employee; sensitivity to insults; aggressive reaction to company policy; lack of inhibition regarding relation or revenge.
The Intruder	2 days	Feelings of betrayal/criticism/ demotion/fired by co-workers viewed as trusted friends.	Taking data with the view that it was theirs to take and could be used to support future career pathway.

Attacker Type	Attack Time	Personal Stressor	Notes on Attack
The Time Bomber	20 days	Demotion / interpersonal conflict with co-workers / history of family bereavement and own health problems.	Viewed as the 'model' employee; with job success operated as if they owned systems and IT infrastructure; cultivated support from senior management to 'protect' privileged position (highlights use of both manipulation and persuasion). Evidence of planning to protect ownership of system.
The Extortionist	2 days	Professional and financial frustrations/feelings of being stuck and isolated in a foreign country.	Similar in many respects to the Hacker discussed above – used systems for financial and employment gains whilst working in close collaboration with other agents both inside and outside the organisation.
The Saboteur	2 days	Interpersonal conflict / history of warnings from HR and Security related to misuse of systems; demotion / criminal convictions and drug use and abuse.	This individual demonstrated a previous history of criminal activity and IT misuse; on arrival in the host company attacker proceeded to ensure all actions were protected and made clear efforts to hide any malicious activity. Evidence of narcissism and sociopathy; arrogance and conflict with peers; resistance to authority and disregard for accepted policy and practice.
The Thief	90 days	Parent's divorce / sibling leaving family home / frustration at lack of training and opportunity for further advancement.	Again, attack fits into the Hacker typology mentioned previously; noted that the length of attack time indicates a high degree of planning and patience demonstrating not an attack of impulsivity.

Attacker Type	Attack Time	Personal Stressor	Notes on Attack
The Attacker	30 days	Financial stress / martial problems / conflict with supervisors	Aligned with the Proprietor sub-type discussed above.
The Manipulator	5 days	Terminal illness of spouse / loss of independence and autonomy in job role / rejection by co-workers/loss of overtime pay.	A clear impulsive attack as a response to a variety of job setbacks.

key event in the individual's work or personal life. This has been termed the Tipping Point (TP; Claycomb et al., 2012), referring to the key psychosocial stressors pivotal in the individual following through with the attack. In the cases discussed above the TP manifests as either a setback in the individual's social life or a clear sense of demotivation and a feeling of being undervalued in the workplace. These findings highlight the complexity and variability of insider threats, emphasizing the need for a nuanced approach to detection and prevention that considers both impulsive and premeditated behaviours, as well as the significant impact of personal and professional stressors.

A CPNI (2013) report enhanced the scale of data collection and explored 120 UK-based case studies on insider threats and identified key psychosocial elements that significantly impact the likelihood of an individual conducting an attack. These elements include:

- **Immaturity**: Individuals lack overall life experience and are considered 'high maintenance' in terms of the attention and guidance they require. They also have difficulties making critical life decisions.
- **Low Self-Esteem**: Individuals lack confidence in social situations and heavily depend on recognition and praise from others. They find it hard to cope with adverse social situations, criticism, and tasks outside their comfort zone.
- **Amoral and Unethical**: Individuals lack a clear understanding of morality and show no remorse for their behaviour, particularly regarding its effect on others.
- **Superficial**: Insiders often lack a clear sense of self and identity, presenting as 'hard to know' by peers and colleagues.
- **Restless and Impulsive**: Individuals require constant stimulation and are highly hedonistic, a common trait in insider personalities.
- **Lacks Conscientiousness**: Individuals disregard established rules and practices, neglect workplace duties and responsibilities, and exhibit poor attention to detail, judgment, and focus.
- **Manipulative**: Individuals use their persuasion skills to get their way and nurture relationships that serve their self-interest. They often adopt a

social position that aids in serving their needs, such as being agreeable and compliant to those in power.

- **Emotionally Unstable**: Individuals are prone to exaggerated mood swings and overreactions to problems, often complaining about trivial incidents.
- **Underlying Psychological or Personality Disorder**: The report is vague about this aspect, providing little specific detail on how this was measured.

The CPNI (2013) report also highlights situational aspects evident in the psychosocial environment of the insider. These are split into two underlying categories, these being 'lifestyle changes' which are related to a change in personal circumstances and thus a change in experienced levels of stress. The second category is that of 'circumstantial vulnerabilities' which in the context of the CPNI report refer to 'work, profile or personal issues that could make an individual vulnerable' (p. 11). Presented below are the key elements that the CPNI report deemed to be of critical interest.

- **Demonstrating poor work attitude**: A failure to follow accepted protocol or to read important documentation about new procedures or operating instructions.
- **Shows signs of being stressed**: Overt symptoms of stress that include loss of temper, apathy (burnout), increase in nervous habits (ticks, aspects of OCD), problems with memory and concentration, evidence of confusion, difficulty in making decisions.
- **Exploitable or Vulnerable Lifestyle**: Has an element of their lifestyle which allows them to be exploited by an external force or agent, e.g., serious financial stress, alcohol abuse, drug addiction, gambling – each of these could lead to a powerful desire for financial gain.
- **Exploitable or Vulnerable Work Profile**: The individual's position within the company allows them access to highly prized or sought after assets which in turn could be marketed for profit.
- **Recent Negative Life Events**: A variety of elements could be included here, such as problems at work, loss of status (socially and work), personal injury, bereavement, relationship breakup, financial difficulty, or loss.

The CPNI (2013) report provided some detailed insights into both the psychological and situational factors that contributed to the insider threats they reviewed. One of the key takeaways from this study is the finding that insiders can exhibit a wide range of psychological traits, which in turn suggests there is no single psychological profile. Such a finding supports the previous statement made by Pfleeger (2008), and highlights the challenges faced when attempting to predict who might become an insider threat based directly on personality traits alone. However, there is a chance that organisations could use this information to enhance proactive measures, and understanding the psychological and situational factors which serve to influence insider threat could allow organisations to target support for employees experiencing stress or significant life events. Creating a supportive work environment could be one of the ways in which organisations can mitigate those risk factors that have become associated with insider threat.

Greitzer et al. (2012) presented a detailed exploration of psychological precursors for insider threat. While this work provides valuable insights, it should be viewed with caution, as it is not clear how these precursors combine to provide a clear indication of insider threat. For example, does an individual need to present all or some of these elements to be considered a threat?

One positive aspect of this list of psychological components is that they rely on observable and overt behaviours rather than being solely based on personality traits. This makes it easier for organisations to monitor and identify potential threats. The list of precursors was compiled using a mixture of discussions with HR professionals and a review of the literature on insider threats. The key psychological precursors identified by Greitzer et al. (2012) included:

- **Disgruntlement**: Expression of dissatisfaction or resentment towards the organisations and its policies, with overt expressions of discontent.
- **Not Accepting Feedback**: The individual has difficulty accepting criticism and may display signs of defensiveness when being corrected. Unwillingness to accept errors personally with attempts to cover these up using deception.
- **Anger Management Issues**: The employee has a great deal of pent-up aggression with issues related to the management of feelings of anger/hate – also appears to hold strong grudges.
- **Disengagement**: Employee is seen to be isolated from fellow work colleagues, avoiding aspects of social interaction with fellow workers.
- **Disregard for Authority**: An overt disregard for rules, authority, and policies that have been put into place to manage company functioning. Employee may have the view they are 'above' or 'outside' the rules.
- **Performance**: The employee may have received several reprimands for poor performance.
- **Stress**: The employee is under physical, emotional, or mental strain that they have difficulty handling – aspects of 'emotional leakage'.
- **Confrontational Behaviours**: Employee is overtly argumentative and aggressive – involved in aspects of bullying or intimidation.
- **Personal Issues**: A history of being unable to keep personal issues separate from work life, with these issues being seen to interfere with work.
- **Self-Centeredness**: A disregard for the needs/wishes of others with a primary concern for their own interests and requirements.

- **Lack of Dependability**: Employee lacks the ability to keep to their commitments – fails to instil feelings of trustworthiness.
- **Absenteeism**: Employee has displayed frequent periods of absenteeism which remain unexplained.

These precursors can provide a valuable framework from which organisations could build a model for identifying insider threat based on observable behaviours or measures. It is however important to note that the presence of one or more of these behaviours does not necessarily indicate that an individual is an insider threat. We would suggest that organisations use this information as a very rough guide for part of a broader strategy which includes elements of monitoring, employee support initiatives, and a strong sense of organisational culture to again attempt to mitigate risk factors associated with insider threat.

More recent research has reinforced previous findings on the key psychosocial precursors for insider threats. Whitty (2021) developed a comprehensive conceptual framework for exploring insider threats, which is one of the most detailed models presented on the topic to date. The framework categorises the psychological and social characteristics that have been observed in MIT into five key classifications:

Traits: These are inherent characteristics of the individual, such as personality traits and predispositions that serve to make the individual more susceptible to becoming an insider threat. They include elements that we will be covering later on in Chapter 9.

- **Extraverted**: These individuals are outgoing, social, sensation-seeking, and enthusiastic.
- **Narcissism**: They have a sense of entitlement and seek admiration, attention, prestige, and status.
- **Machiavellianism**: These individuals are manipulative, charming, and highly ambitious.
- **Introverted**: They are quiet and less involved in the social world.
- **Neurotic**: These individuals are emotionally unstable.
- **Psychopathy**: They are highly impulsive, risk-takers, callous, lack personal effort, and have low empathy.
- **Asperger's**: This autism spectrum disorder is characterised by significant difficulties in social interaction and non-verbal communication.
- **External Locus of Control**: These individuals have a fatalistic view of the world, believing that events are out of their control.
- **Open to Flattery**: They are open to flattery and can be easily coerced by others, such as being conned into a romantic relationship.

Life Circumstances and Actions Before Employment: This includes the individual's background, life experiences, and actions prior to them joining the organisation which could serve to influence their future behaviours. These elements can include:

- **Gang Membership**: These individuals socialise with or are known members of a gang.
- **Criminal Record**: They have a previous criminal record, either related or unrelated to their current role.
- **Working Illegally in the Country**: They are working illegally, such as having limited or no work visa.
- **Presented Forged Documentation to HR**: When applying for or accepting the job, they presented forged documentation, such as birth certificates or education transcripts.

Behaviours Displayed at Work Before the Attack: These are the observable behaviours and actions that an individual will exhibit prior to an attack taking place. They act as very strong warning signs for the potential insider threat to occur, and can include:

- **Strong Work Affiliation**: These individuals are hard workers who appear happy with their jobs and organisation. This may seem to counter-intuitive but someone who is over-eager to please may be covering up their potential subversive behaviours.
- **Weak Work Affiliation**: They are lazy or unmotivated workers who often appear unhappy with their role and organisation.
- **Aggressive**: They are physically and/or verbally aggressive to others, both online and offline.
- **Misconduct**: Before the attack, these insiders had been in trouble for misconduct at work, such as disciplinary suspension or security breaches.

Emotions Displayed During and Leading Up to the Attack: These are the emotional states and reactions of the individual that are evident in the lead up to and during the attack. These emotional markers can provide a key marker for a potential attack occurring, as well as providing some insights into the motivations and respective triggers for the attack. These can include aspects of stress, anxiety, and depression. Many individuals were detailed as experiencing life stressors beyond the workplace, although the stress could have been caused by engaging in the insider attack.

Behaviours and Life Circumstances During the Attack: These factors are related to actions and circumstances that are presented during the execution of the attack. They may include behaviours that are related to how they carry out the attack, or changes in their behaviours or life situation at that time. These aspects include:

- **Addiction**: These individuals have addiction problems, such as alcohol, drugs, or shopping. This problem might have existed before employment and typically continues during the attack.
- **Personal Hardship**: They need money due to personal hardships, such as divorce, a partner losing their job, or a sudden family illness or accident.
- **Coercion/Blackmail from Others**: An outside gang coerced or threatened/ blackmailed them into conducting the crime.
- **Increased Time Logged into Secure Areas**: They spend greater amounts of time in secure areas, such as viewing and editing customer accounts, without a clear reason.
- **Showing Off Newly Acquired Wealth**: They show off newly acquired wealth without any clear explanation for the change in financial circumstances, appearing to live beyond their means.
- **Change in Attitude Towards the Workplace**: There is a noticeable change in their attitude from being highly motivated to low motivated.
- **Displays Signs of Disgruntlement**: They show signs of disgruntlement, such as missing out on a promotion or being unhappy with how they have been treated.
- **Unusual Hours**: They turn up to work earlier or later than usual, stay behind more than they usually do, or take longer breaks than allowed.
- **Downloading Large Volumes of Data**: They download substantial amounts of data or email out large amounts of data, which is not something they normally do.
- **Star Employee Who Is Not Meeting Targets**: A previously well-regarded employee stops meeting designated targets and shows signs of distress.
- **Absenteeism**: They frequently take time off work.

The work presented by Whitty (2021) is important for several reasons. Firstly, it provides a clear, comprehensive overview of the interplay between the psychological and situational factors that can influence the emergence of insider threats. By linking factors such as circumstances prior to employment, emotional states, and specific actions during the attack, Whitty offers a detailed exploration of the insider threat journey. The framework is dynamic in nature, highlighting how certain stressors can escalate the risk of insider threats. This evolving perspective is crucial for understanding that insider threats are not static but can develop over time based on changing circumstances and stressors. Additionally, Whitty's framework includes potential behavioural indicators that could be employed as part of an early detection system for insider threats. If organisations were to implement some form of monitoring system, these indicators could help identify potential threats before they materialise. This proactive approach emphasises the importance of continuous monitoring and assessment to mitigate risks effectively. Overall, Whitty's work enhances the current understanding of insider threats by providing a structured and comprehensive model that integrates both psychological and situational factors. This holistic approach is essential for developing robust strategies to detect, prevent, and respond to insider threats in organisations.

Mitigating the Insider Threat

Most of this text is devoted to exploring the myriad ways in which individuals can present themselves as potential UITs and the possible mechanisms we can employ to divert people away from this course of action. In contrast, the MIT presents a more divergent issue. MITs have an inherent desire to cause mischief within the organisation, making them harder to address with pre-emptive mitigation strategies. For MITs, detection rather than deterrence appears to be a more viable approach. Organisations can actively engage in proactive methods to identify MITs, and as we will explore in this section, the literature is replete with examples where the tell-tale signs of an insider attack have been missed, underscoring the need for a robust detection mechanism. In early research by Randazzo et al. (2005), it was noted that in most insider threat cases reviewed, nearly all (81%) involved some aspect of prior planning. Additionally, in 85% of these cases, someone associated with the attacker was aware of the insider's intentions. Furthermore, 35% of the cases included some form of preparation linked to the attack, such as moving files between servers, testing security systems, or accessing systems that the individual did not normally have access to.

Suler (2002) observed that engaging in undesirable behaviours online can serve as a statement and an outlet for perceived frustrations or organisational injustice (see Chapter 11). From this perspective, Suler noted that individuals can exhibit a set of behavioural markers that often indicate their intentions, providing a digital footprint of their actions. Other researchers have also identified actions that can be used to detect MITs. For example, Schultz (2002) suggested that certain actions, which may seem small and insignificant, can collectively form the basis for detecting MITs. Describing these as deliberate markers, Schultz suggested that these actions serve as a statement of intent for the insider threat, varying in magnitude and observability. For instance, a disgruntled employee might send an email to their line manager mentioning the vulnerability of the organisation's systems, which could be interpreted as a thinly veiled threat. Insiders often make mistakes when preparing to conduct an attack, and these meaningful errors can indicate an attack is imminent. System error logs can be a valuable source of information in this regard, helping to identify the user and their planned activities. However, this may only be relevant for less sophisticated attackers, as more refined attacks often involve the use of spoofed or stolen login credentials.

Insiders may also engage in a series of preparatory behaviours as part of their attack. This could involve testing parts of their exploit or engaging in activities that form sub-tasks of the larger attack. For example, an attacker might spend time exploring system aspects to understand what they can manipulate or delve deeper into system vulnerabilities. Research reviewing previous insider threat attacks has noted that such preparatory behaviour, while evident in system logs, is often completely missed.

Schultz (2002) highlights another potential indicator of suspicious activity: patterns of behaviour that suggest an attack is being planned. These correlated usage patterns indicate that behaviours, which may seem normal and innocuous in isolation, can signal something unusual when combined with other activities. For instance, an employee might access and download substantial amounts of data outside their normal working hours. When this is paired with frequent job searches and discussions with potential employers who are competitors to the current organisation, it creates a perfect storm of correlated usage patterns.

One final mechanism suggested for detecting potential insider threats is verbal behaviours. In many instances of insider threat, there is an overarching theme of disgruntlement, which can elicit feelings of anger and frustration. Schultz (2002) noted that such behaviours can manifest as overt linguistic indicators evidenced in language usage. Expressions of hatred, hostility, and general aggression towards fellow employees, management, and the organisation could signal a potential insider threat. However, it is important to note that such behaviours should not be taken in isolation, as these verbal outbursts could be more indicative of someone having a very bad day. Some research has utilised sentiment analysis to detect specific moods or feelings in written information, which has been applied to the insider threat problem (e.g., Park et al., 2018; Soh et al., 2019). Sentiment analysis trawls data for evidence of emotions or sentiments. However, one key obstacle to implementing these systems is the ethical implications. For many organisations, the ramifications of potential monitoring systems could raise further complications and concerns. We discuss this later in Chapter 11 in the context of monitoring counterproductive work behaviours.

Summary

In this chapter, we delve into the concept of the 'insider threat', focusing on both malicious and unintentional insider threat (MITs and UITs). We discuss the inherent trust placed in individuals within organisations and how this trust can be breached, leading to various forms of organisational disruption, including espionage, terrorism, unauthorised disclosure of information, corruption, sabotage, workplace violence, and the loss of resources.

The complexity of defining an insider threat is highlighted, with traditional definitions often failing to account for modern working practices, such as remote work and the use of sub-contractors and consultants. Nevertheless, research has attempted to utilise measures of insider threat. For example, Bishop and Gates (2008) introduced the concept of 'insiderness', measuring insider threat on a sliding scale based on motive and intent. Hunker and Probst (2011) also emphasised the problematic nature of defining insider threats solely based on access to IT systems, given the evolving nature of work environments.

We explore different types of insider threats. On one hand, we have individuals who are MITs; those who intentionally cause harm to their organisation. Cappelli et al. (2012) provided a widely accepted definition of MITs, identifying insiders as current or former employees, contractors, or business partners who misuse their access to negatively impact the organisation's information systems. These threats, although a minority, are the costliest, with significant financial losses reported globally.

On the other hand, UITs arise from negligence or carelessness. This chapter discusses how UITs can result from actions such as ignoring security protocols, accidental data leaks, and falling for phishing scams. Research from the Ponemon Institute and CERT highlights the significant impact of UITs, often costing organisations millions of dollars. As such, this chapter emphasises the importance of addressing both malicious and unintentional threats to ensure comprehensive security.

This chapter also delves into the various taxonomies proposed to categorise insider threats based on motivation and skillset. Early classifications by Anderson (1980) focused on the misuse of IT systems, while Hayden (1999) introduced categories such as Traitors, Zealots, Browsers, and Well-Intentioned individuals. Shaw and Fischer (2005) expanded on these classifications, identifying sub-types like Explorers, Samaritans, Hackers, Machiavellians, Avengers, Proprietors, Career Thieves, and Moles. These taxonomies help in understanding the diverse nature of insider threats and the different motivations behind them.

We further explore the psychological aspects of insider threats, discussing the challenges of profiling potential insiders. Pfleeger (2008) highlighted the difficulties in creating accurate psychological profiles due to the lack of empirical data and the variability in individual behaviour. Research by Cappelli et al. (2012) and Shaw et al. (1998a, 1998b) identified common psychological traits among insiders, such as anger, social isolation, entitlement, and ethical flexibility. These traits, combined with situational stressors, can lead to insider attacks. Case studies (CPNI, 2013; Shaw & Fischer, 2005) have also highlighted that psychological trigger, such as immaturity, low self-esteem, amoral behaviour, impulsivity, and manipulative tendencies, in addition to situational aspects, such as recent negative life events and exploitable work profiles, play a significant role in increasing the likelihood of insider attacks.

Overall, this chapter summarises the commonalities among malicious insiders, such as inherent anger, manipulative behaviour, lack of empathy, and stress. It emphasises the need for organisations to understand these psychological and situational factors to develop effective detection and prevention strategies. By addressing both malicious and unintentional insider threats, organisations can better protect themselves from internal risks. This comprehensive overview provides a deeper understanding of the insider threat landscape, highlighting the complexity and multifaceted nature of these threats.

References

Al-Mhiqani, M. N., Ahmad, R., Abidin, Z. Z., Yassin, W., Hassan, A., Abdulkareem, K. H., Ali, N. S., & Yunos, Z. (2020). A review of insider threat detection: Classification, machine learning techniques, datasets, open challenges, and recommendations. *Applied Sciences*, 10(15), 5208. doi:10.3390/app10155208.

Anderson, J. P. (1980). *Computer security threat monitoring and surveillance*. Technical Report. James P. Anderson Co.

Beyond Identity. (2021). *BYOD: Exploring the evolution of work device practices in a new remote-forward era* [Survey]. www.beyondidentity.com/resource/byod-explor ing-the-evolution-of-work-device-practices-in-a-new-remote-forward-era-survey.

Bishop, M., & Gates, C. (2008). Defining the insider threat. *Proceedings of the 4th Annual Workshop on Cyber Security and Information Intelligence Research*, 12–14. doi:10.1145/1413140.1413158.

Calic, D., Pattinson, M., Parsons, K., Butavicius, M., & McCormac, A. (2016). Naïve and accidental behaviours that compromise information security: What the experts think. In S. M. Furnell & N. L. Clarke (Eds.), *Proceedings of the 10th International Symposium of Human Aspects of Information Security and Assurance.*

Cappelli, D. M., Moore, A. P., & Silowash, G. (2012). *Common sense guide to mitigating insider threats* (4th ed.). CERT Carnegie Mellon University. www.stormingm edia.us/00/0055/A005585.html

Cappelli, D. M., Moore, A. P., & Trzeciak, R. F. (2012). *The CERT guide to insider threats: How to prevent, detect, and respond to information technology crimes (theft, sabotage, fraud).* Addison-Wesley.

CERT Insider Threat Team. (2013). *Unintentional insider threats: A foundational study (Technical Note CMU/SEI-2013-TN-022)*. Software Engineering Institute, Carnegie Mellon University. doi:10.1184/R1/6585575.v1.

CERT Insider Threat Team. (2014). *Unintentional insider threats: A review of phishing and malware incidents by economic sector (Technical Note CMU/SEI-2014-TN-007)*. Software Engineering Institute, Carnegie Mellon University. https://resour ces.sei.cmu.edu/asset_files/technicalnote/2014_004_001_297777.pdf.

Claycomb, W., Huth, C., & Flynn, L. (2012). Chronological examination of insider threat sabotage: Preliminary observations. *Journal of Wireless Mobile Networks, Ubiquitous Computing, and Dependable Applications*, 3(4), 4–20.

Cole, E., & Ring, S. (2005). *Insider threat: Protecting the enterprise from sabotage, spying, and theft*. Elsevier.

CPNI. (2013). *CPNI insider data collection study: Report of main findings*. London.

Greitzer, F. L., Kangas, L. J., Noonan, C. F., Dalton, A. C., & Hohimer, R. E. (2012). Identifying at-risk employees: Modeling psychosocial precursors of potential insider threats. *2012 45th Hawaii International Conference on System Sciences*, 2392–2401. doi:10.1109/HICSS.2012.309.

Gudaitis, T. M. (1998). The missing link in information security: Three dimensional profiling. *CyberPsychology & Behavior*, 1(4), 321–340. doi:10.1089/cpb.1998.1.321.

Hadlington, L. (2018). The 'human factor' in cybersecurity. In J. Mcalaney & L. A. Frumkin (Eds.), *Psychological and behavioral examinations in cyber security* (pp. 46–63). IGI Global. doi:10.4018/978-1-5225-4053-3.ch003.

Hayden, M. (1999). *The insider threat to US government information systems (NSTISSAM INFOSEC/1–99)*. National Security Telecommunications and Information Systems Security Committee. Defense Technical Information Center (DTIC). https://nsarchive.gwu.edu/sites/default/files/documents/3460882/Document-05-Michael-Hayden-National-Security.pdf.

Homoliak, I., Toffalini, F., Guarnizo, J., Elovici, Y., & Ochoa, M. (2019). Insight into insiders and IT: A survey of insider threat taxonomies, analysis, modeling, and countermeasures. *ACM Computing Surveys*, 52(2), 1–40. doi:10.1145/3303771.

Hunker, J., & Probst, C. W. (2011). Insiders and insider threats – An overview of definitions and mitigation techniques. *Journal of Wireless Mobile Networks, Ubiquitous Computing, and Dependable Applications*, 2(1), 4–27.

IBM Security. (2023). *Cost of a data breach report 2023*. Ponemon Institute.

Khan, B., Alghathbar, K., Nabi, S. I., & Khan, M. K. (2021). Effectiveness of information security awareness training programs: A systematic review. *Computers & Security*, 95, 101–115.

Legg, P. A., Buckley, O., Goldsmith, M., & Creese, S. (2017). Automated insider threat detection system using user and role-based profile assessment. *IEEE Systems Journal*, 11(2), 503–512. doi:10.1109/JSYST.2015.2438442.

Liu, L., De Vel, O., Han, Q.-L., Zhang, J., & Xiang, Y. (2018). Detecting and preventing cyber insider threats: A survey. *IEEE Communications Surveys & Tutorials*, 20(2), 1397–1417. doi:10.1109/COMST.2018.2800740.

Mehan, J. E. (2016). *Insider threat: A guide to understanding, detecting, and defending against the enemy from within*. IT Governance Publishing.

Park, W., You, Y., & Lee, K. (2018). Detecting potential insider threat: Analyzing insiders' sentiment exposed in social media. *Security and Communication Networks*. doi:10.1155/2018/7243296.

Pfleeger, C. P. (2008). Reflections on the insider threat. In S. J. Stolfo, S. M. Bellovin, A. D. Keromytis, S. Hershkop, S. W. Smith, & S. Sinclair (Eds.), *Insider attack and cyber security: Beyond the hacker* (pp. 5–16). Springer US. doi:10.1007/978-0-387-77322-3_2.

Ponemon Institute. (2023). *Cost of insider risks global report 2023*. https://ponemonsullivanreport.com/2023/10/cost-of-insider-risks-global-report-2023.

Randazzo, M. M. R. M., Keeney, M., Kowalski, E., Cappelli, D. M., & Moore, A. (2005). Insider threat study: Illicit cyber activity in the banking and finance sector. *Finance*, 38. doi:10.1080/07321870590933292.

Renaud, K., Warkentin, M., Pogrebna, G., & van der Schyff, K. (2024). VISTA: An inclusive insider threat taxonomy, with mitigation strategies. *Information & Management*, 61(1), 103877. doi:10.1016/j.im.2023.103877.

Schultz, E. E. (2002). A framework for understanding and predicting insider attacks. *Computers & Security*, 21(6), 526–531. doi:10.1016/S0167-4048(02)01009-X.

Shaw, E. D., & Fischer, L. F. (2005). *Ten tales of betrayal: The threat to corporate infrastructure by information technology insiders analysis and observations*. Technical Report, Defense Personnel Security Research Center.

Shaw, E. D., Ruby, K. G., & Post, J. M. (1998a). *Insider threats to critical information systems: Characteristics of the vulnerable critical information technology insider (CITI) (Tech. Rep. No. 2)*. Political Psychology Associates.

Shaw, R., Ruby, K., & Post, J. (1998b). The insider threat to information systems. *Security Awareness Bulletin*, 2–98.

Soh, C., Yu, S., Narayanan, A., Duraisamy, S., & Chen, L. (2019). Employee profiling via aspect-based sentiment and network for insider threats detection. *Expert Systems with Applications*, 135, 351–361. doi:10.1016/j.eswa.2019.05.043.

Suler, J. R. (2002). Identity management in cyberspace. *Journal of Applied Psychoanalytic Studies*, 4(4), 455–459. doi:10.1023/A:1020392231924.

Taylor, P. J., Dando, C. J., Ormerod, T. C., Ball, L. J., Jenkins, M. C., Sandham, A., & Menacere, T. (2013). Detecting insider threats through language change. *Law and Human Behavior*, 37(4), 267–275. doi:10.1037/lhb0000032.

Whitty, M. T. (2021). Developing a conceptual model for insider threat. *Journal of Management & Organization*, 27(5), 911–929. doi:10.1017/jmo.2018.57.

3

A HUMAN-CENTRED APPROACH

Examples from the Past

In February 2014, a Chinese cybercrime group named Deep Panda used a phishing email to trick an employee of Anthem, a well-known health insurance company, into opening an attachment that contained malware (Young, 2021). This allowed the hackers to gain access to over 50 individual employee accounts and 90 different internal systems, including the company's warehouse system that held personal data for Anthem customers. By the time the breach was discovered in January 2015, Deep Panda had obtained nearly 80 million personal records. The breach was estimated to have cost Anthem almost $260 million, which was spent on managing notifications about the breach, supporting those impacted, and engaging various support services to prevent further compromises. Additional costs included widespread media coverage that damaged Anthem's reputation, legal actions, and countless lawsuits filed against the company (Young, 2021). All of this occurred because one person in the organisation believed an email looked like it was from an official, trusted source.

In July 2020, hackers posing as Twitter's IT Help Desk called several Twitter employees. They claimed to be addressing issues with the company's virtual private network (VPN), which had been experiencing various problems. The hackers then directed employees to log on to a fake website that mimicked the official Twitter VPN account. This website was used to harvest login information, which the hackers later used to access the real Twitter VPN account. As a result, the hackers managed to take over several high-value, high-profile Twitter accounts, particularly those that were verified and marked with the blue tick. They then targeted other high-profile accounts, including those related to cryptocurrency, falsely claiming that these

DOI: 10.4324/9781003509011-3

organisations were giving away bitcoin. They used various tactics, including redirects to fake bitcoin websites. The breach resulted in approximately $118,000 worth of bitcoins being stolen due to this well-crafted social engineering attack (New York State Department of Financial Services, 2020; Witman & Mackelprang, 2022).

What do these two attacks have in common? Is it the use of sophisticated malware and software to leverage information from systems? Or perhaps the malicious intent or motives demonstrated by the employees who fell victim to the cybercriminals' tactics? For those of you reading this book, it will come as no surprise that the clear answer is the presence of the human in the system. Without human involvement in the compromised systems, we could boldly state that there would be no attack, and no data would have been leaked. It is the intervention (or lack thereof) of humans within the system that creates the necessary conditions for such attacks to occur.

Computers are not susceptible to the powers of persuasion and influence that humans are when it comes to social engineering tactics. Computers do not feel fatigue, become disgruntled, or experience stress. They do not take to social media to complain about their boss, missed promotions, or colleagues. They do not leave social media privacy settings open. However, humans do, and they do these things very well.

Why Work on Human Factors in Cybersecurity?

Traditional computer science approaches to cybersecurity have focused on the technical aspects of the field, favouring strategies that involve network security, encryption, and data protection mechanisms (Rahman et al., 2021). However, the literature in cybersecurity is replete with examples where such security technologies have failed to protect organisations from cyberattack (Craigen et al., 2014; Hadlington, 2017; Herath & Rao, 2009a, 2009b; Li et al., 2019; Sasse et al., 2001). Another issue is that while technical interventions may be excellent from a pure systems protection perspective, they are often not user-friendly and can be impractical when it comes to our daily work activities (Prummer et al., 2024). One of the key reasons for authoring this book was the lack of a central resource that collates information related to human factors in cybersecurity in a convenient format, accessible to academics and practitioners. There have been many attempts to integrate various aspects of this work, mapping a variety of risk factors within the system, aligned to organisational, human, and technological elements (Kraemer et al., 2009; Pollini et al., 2022; Rohan et al., 2021; Young et al., 2018). Central to these frameworks is the understanding that humans are part of a more complex system that includes socio-technical elements such as task complexity, organisational policy and culture on cybersecurity, and technical interfaces. Many researchers have argued that pure technological approaches to cybersecurity do not acknowledge one inescapable fact: if these technological approaches were effective, the frequency and size of cyberse-curity breaches would be negligible (Ghelani, 2022; Khan et al., 2021; Singh et al., 2013; Soomro et al., 2016). The growth in this area was partly due to researchers and professionals noting that the 'human element' forms the 'weakest link' within the cybersecurity system (Hughes-Lartey et al., 2021; Sasse et al., 2001). While this label is somewhat harsh, it highlights the cri-tical role human factors play in many cybersecurity breaches. However, labelling humans as the 'weakest link' can create a vicious cycle of what could be seen as victim blaming when it comes to susceptibility to cybercrime.

To improve the current situation, we must start to question why indivi-duals within the system are labelled as the weakest link in the first instance – have they fallen foul of a phishing scam? What is the reason they have fallen for the scam in the first place? If you start to delve a little bit deeper, the reasons why individuals fall for scams is usually related to poor awareness, poor training, or they are tricked into doing something using social engi-neering techniques. Yes, the 'weakness', in the system appears because humans are present in the system, but to label all end users as the weakest link overlooks a lot of individual factors that could be at work here. We argue that humans should be seen as the 'missing link' in the cybersecurity system; if you have a good cybersecurity culture where individuals are sup-ported in their decisions related to their online safety, you inherently improve the overall engagement in protective behaviours. If you label someone as the weakest link, you have already lost part of the battle.

Introducing the Human Factors Approach

Interactions between humans and the systems they work with and within happen without us even thinking about it. The things that we do and how we are using systems daily are taken for granted and usually proceed without consequence. However, things can and do go wrong and will usually result in some form of incident, ranging from the trivial to the more serious. This could be anything from someone accidentally hitting the reply all button to an email, resulting in the distribution of critical company data, or opening an email attachment that looks like it has come from a trusted and reliable partner, only to realise it contains malware. When thing go awry, we need a process or framework that allows us to diagnose the root cause of the pro-blem which has created the error and allows us to set about implementing solutions which prevent such an error occurring again. This is the corner-stone of the human factors approach, which can be applied to all situations where humans are at the centre of complex systems, and where there is a clear likelihood that errors will result from such interactions (Wickens et al., 2013). The human factors approach allows us to make sense of the interac-tions between the system (in our instance the cybersecurity infrastructure that governs organisational safety and security) and the human. By doing this, we should be able to enhance individual performance, increase overall safety and security, and reduce the burden on the individual by limiting extraneous information and unnecessary tasks (Wickens et al., 2013). As such, 'human factors' **is not** a thing or a set of things that can be used to identify a source of error but is instead the name of the paradigm we can use to explore why human error emerges in specific situations.

At this point it is useful to separate some of the common misconceptions about the human factors approach that have been perpetuated across a variety of platforms, which have been succinctly captured by Russ et al. (2012).

1. Human factors is about designing systems that are resilient to unanticipated events (Russ et al., 2012, p. 803). This is opposed to the common misconception that human factors is a paradigm that is all about the elimination of human error – human error is an inevitable part of a system, and the pursuit of eliminating them is, as Russ et al. (2012) noted, a futile endeavour.
2. The human factors approach serves to address problems by modifying the system to better aid people, rather than trying to get people to modify their behaviour (Russ et al., 2012). As an inherent part of the human factors approach, the key focus in on how we can improve the way in which individuals interact with the systems they use. For example, this could be changing the way in which password generation processes are presented, making them more user friendly and less cumbersome. Correcting human behaviour is hard, and there is a limited number of interventions that can help to overcome the shortcomings in what we do. However, there are some ways in which we can improve training, education, and design of systems that allow individuals a better chance of understanding what they need to do and how they need to do it (Russ et al., 2012).
3. Human factors work involves a focus on both the individual and the organisational level, rather than just focusing on the individual (Russ et al., 2012). This is critically important to understand, as we need a mechanism to understand how the individual is placed within a wider organisational unit, and to further identify how organisational policies can serve to impact their performance. The culture of the organisation can play a significant role in influencing the way in which people interact with systems, but also the individual's dispositional and psychological makeup can impact the way in which they interpret the policies and practices of the organisation (Russ et al., 2012).
4. Human factors is a scientific discipline that involves years of training and associated qualifications, rather than something that can be learned during a short training session (Russ et al., 2012). This is one of the biggest red flags you should be on the lookout for when trawling through the lengthy list of influencers who claim to be experts in human

factors – not all human factors specialists are created equally! You need proper training and experience to be able to apply the techniques and methods aligned with the paradigm to be able to produce an effective account of the issues being explored (Russ et al., 2012). A poor understanding of the approach, or a lack of coherent understanding, can lead to a piecemeal application of methods that will result in an ineffective result (Russ et al., 2012). If in doubt, seek out an expert in the field who has a track history of publications in the field in respected journals.

Cybersecurity as a Complex System

We work with complex systems daily and often take these interactions for granted. For example, the simple action of making your morning coffee will involve you interacting with a system that comprises of several elements (e.g., the fridge, the kettle, or if you have a posh coffee machine, a tap or something that produces water). The system is greater than the sum of its parts and encapsulates the processes that we engage in to interact with the system to complete a task successfully.

A system has been defined as:

> an interacting combination, at any level of complexity, or people, materials, tools, machines, software, facilities, and procedures designed to work together for some common purpose.
>
> *(Chapanis, 1996, p. 22)*

Strauch (2017) argues that complex systems are those which typically involve multiple, well-trained operators interacting with machines. For us, the concept of cybersecurity can be firmly placed into this definition of a system, where individuals are seen to interact with a variety of machines (e.g., digital technology, computers, ICT) to maintain the smooth running of the organisation. Strauch (2017) also noted that our increased dependency on systems and their associated increase in technical capabilities has led to an exponential growth in their overall complexity, where individuals perform a multitude of tasks that are of critical importance to both the organisation and the individuals who work within it. We view cybersecurity as a high-risk system, where decisions can have clear, far-reaching consequences that can impact both organisational and individual security.

Strauch (2017) also presented the concept of operators that interact with the system, playing a critical role in the safety of that system. Accordingly, an operator has two critical roles when it comes to their interactions with the system, namely monitoring the system and controlling its operations. If we take the notion of monitoring the operation of a system, within the cybersecurity system this might be obtaining information about what is going on within the system, such as reading emails, sending messages, updating stock information, or processing orders. The operator also controls the system, so they choose how to interact with the information that has been provided and make relevant decisions about how to respond to that information. This could be responding to an email request to pay for an invoice, sharing a password with a colleague, or sending stock out to a supplier. By viewing cybersecurity as a complex system, we can start to explore how individual operator actions can impact its functionality and apply some of the fundamental aspects of the human factors approach to enhancing the interactions that occur between the system and the operator.

Applying the Human Factors Approach

Many researchers have noted that there is a clear cycle in the process of applying human factors to a situation, event, or set of interactions (Lee & Joshi, 2017; Wickens et al., 2018) that can help guide our understanding of why using this method is applicable to cybersecurity. Within the cycle of applying human factors (see Figure 3.1) there are various stages where we can change interactions within the system, therefore improving the system so individuals within it perform more effectively. So, for our current focus, we want individuals within the cybersecurity system to be able to prevent attacks by minimising potential errors that are being made and allowing them to perform more successfully and efficiently.

These specific stages are broken down into the following key elements:

1. Equipment Design: This is the physical infrastructure of the system that communicates or interacts directly with the end user. For example, this could relate to warning messages that pop up when making a payment via our banking app to a new supplier or payee, key card access points, and two-factor authentication systems.
2. Task Design: Looking at the tasks that are being accomplished within the system itself and eliminating unnecessary or overcomplicated aspects so that it becomes less of a burden on the end user. For example, this could be establishing an automated process for user verification/identification when logging into a computer (for example the use of Face ID or Touch ID on Apple devices) removing the need for the end user to type in and remember passwords.
3. Environmental Design: Relates to anything that is external to the users which could impact task performance. In the strictest sense this could be something like the supply of natural light to a workspace, or the ambient temperature of the office. It could also be linked to the organisational culture and policies that are associated with cybersecurity – bad organisational culture or poorly thought-out cybersecurity policies will have a clear impact on the individual's capacity to engage in effective performance of their responsibilities.

Performance

Analysis
Techniques

(A) Identification of Problems

Task
Statistics
Accident

Brain

Human   System

Body

DESIGN

Equipment

Task

(B)

Environment

Implement
Solutions

Selection

Training

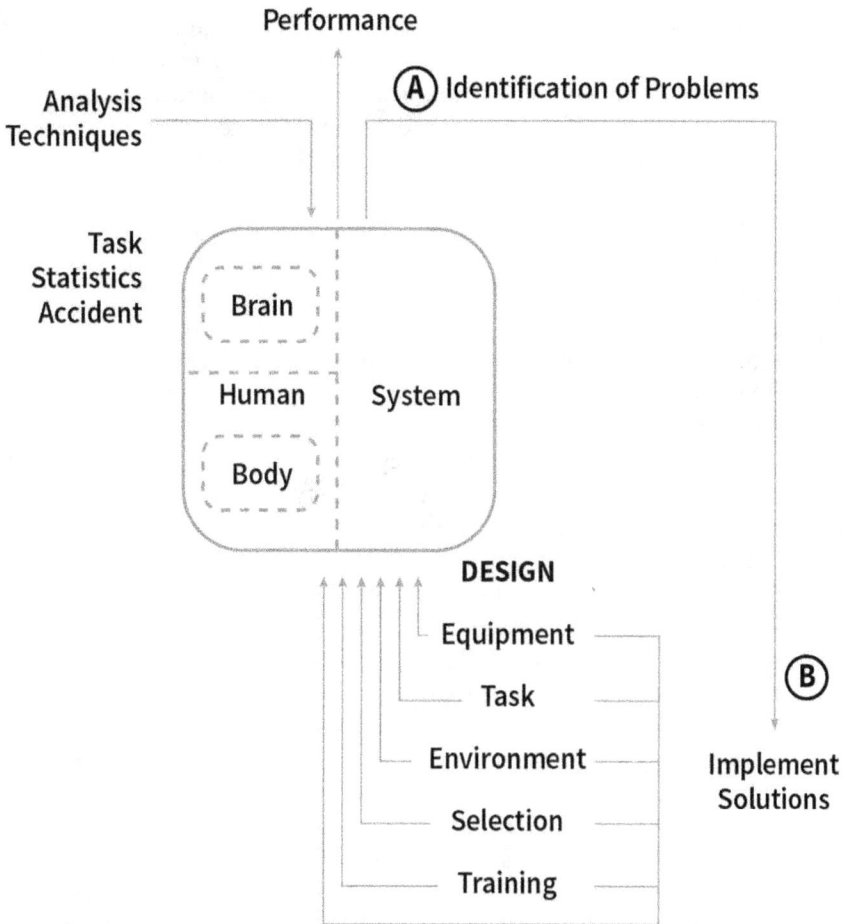

FIGURE 3.1 The Human Factors Cycle (adapted from Wickens et al., 2018)

4. Training: A central focus of much of the research in human factors and cybersecurity is the mechanisms used to train individuals in core aspects of keeping the organisation protected from cyber-risks. Often the focus here is on the type and effectiveness of the training an individual receives. If the training is not sufficient, effective, and allows the things being learned to be implemented easily, the individual will not have the right skillset to be an integral part of the cybersecurity system.

5. Selection: Refers to the process of identifying the best profile of characteristics for the task in hand, and whilst this might not be possible for many of the tasks aligned with organisational cybersecurity (employees are very rarely chosen for their cybersecurity awareness skills, as this is usually a peripheral aspect of many job roles), this approach does allow for researchers to theorise about what characteristics make the 'ideal'

candidate for adherence to cybersecurity, and extrapolate how these characteristics can be extended to others. This where much of the focus of this book will lie, and is aligned with exploring, understanding, and acknowledging the multitude of individual differences that can exert an influence on our end user engaging in the cybersecurity system (Lee & Joshi, 2017; Wickens et al., 2013).

All these elements present a critical role for the way in which an individual interacts with cybersecurity in the workplace. The human factors approach sets out to explore how we can design better systems so that everyone has a good chance of being able to perform effectively within them and increase productivity whilst reducing errors (and not compromising safety) (Kioskli et al., 2023). Researchers have noted that the central pillars of human factors are to set about maximising the efficiency of systems where humans are an integral part, as well as enhancing health, safety, comfort, and the overall quality of life of the end user (Sanders & McCormick, 1993; Wickens et al., 2004, 2017).

Understanding the factors that can serve to influence an individual's approach to cybersecurity is critical if we are to move forward and improve the protection of critical systems, organisations, national infrastructure, and wider society. For practitioners working in cybersecurity, reducing errors and engaging end users requires an understanding of the common elements shared among situations where errors or failures have occurred. For example, in both phishing emails and vishing attacks (the use of telephone calls to obtain personal/sensitive information that is later used in a fraudulent activity), it is common to employ social engineering techniques to gain leverage over the individual, meaning they divulge information to the scammer without necessarily realising that they are being scammed. Importantly, we can start to hypothesise that these two types of attack have a similar underlying cause, allowing us to *generalise* across any number of incidents of this type (Wickens et al., 2013). However, we can only really do this if we can make sensible *predictions* about how the solution or intervention we have designed will work, meaning we must have a sound body of evidence upon which to support this (Meister, 1989; Wickens et al., 2013). And this, dear reader, is where our heady journey begins. This book is devoted to presenting a wide variety of evidence that explores the generalised mechanisms that shape the way in which humans respond to demands that are made on them through the vast cybersecurity system.

It may seem counterintuitive to discuss the notion of 'individual differences' alongside generalisation, but this encompasses what human factors does; it takes trends that are common across groups of individuals and explores how they behave or react to situations. Each of these trends in turn becomes an element that presents a particular individuating factor that we can use to predict a person's behaviour if we place them in a comparable situation (Oltamari et al., 2015). The human element, human aspect, and human factors labels are often used interchangeably in the literature to describe the impact humans have within the cybersecurity infrastructure. Most of the time they are all being used to refer to the same thing: the inescapable fact that humans do and will exert an influence over most aspects of cybersecurity, whether through action or inaction (Young et al., 2018). We adopt the human factors paradigm to study situational and dispositional (individual differences) factors that influence human–cybersecurity interactions, allowing us to make clear recommendations on how to improve such interactions based on evidence from incidents and events. Human factors are not things that differentiate someone from someone else, which is something that is often a misconception in the literature on this topic.

Previous Work on Human Factors and Cybersecurity

From the outset, it becomes quickly apparent that there is limited material that has attempted to apply the human factors approach to cybersecurity. There have been some attempts to examine some of the elements that can contribute to the framework, but these are piecemeal and often focus on sub-categories of individual differences rather than a more holistic view. One of the first attempts that is featured in the research literature relates to the work of CERT (2013) that explored the factors influencing accidental insider threat. In their approach, they propose a wide variety of factors that could contribute to the potential for an individual to be an 'unintentional' insider threat (see Chapter 2). In their typology, they group these factors according to the source of the influence, namely Cognitive, Psycho-Social, and Organisational, summarised in Figure 3.2.

The CERT (2013) framework was based on a collection of 35 cases of unintentional insider threat broken down according to the attack vector. They highlight four main types of threat vectors which can be used to categorise all forms of those presented in their corpus of attacks, these being:

- Accidental disclosure of information.
- Social engineering attack – outsider gains entry to systems via social engineering techniques to conduct attack using malware or spyware.
- Physical compromise – the improper/accidental disposal of physical records, such as paper documents.
- Portable equipment – equipment that is no longer in possession that may contain sensitive data or information which could in turn lead to an attack.

It should be noted that these categories are those that the authors of the CERT (2013) report proposed to cover the unintentional insider threat (UIT) attacks presented in just one database that classified such attacks, and it does

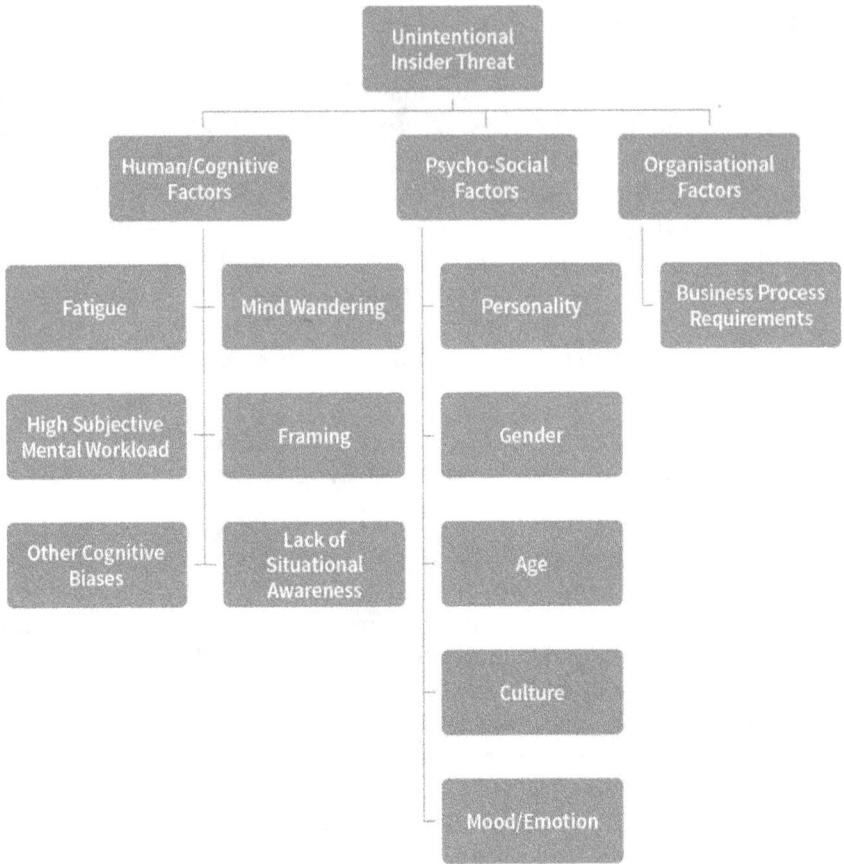

FIGURE 3.2 Contributing Factors to Unintentional Insider Threat (adapted from CERT, 2013)

not include things such as poor password practices, cybersecurity awareness neglect, overconfidence, and overt non-compliance with accepted cybersecurity rules and protocols. However, it did provide the first step towards a human factors' framework for conceptualising elements of behaviour and other such factors that could serve to influence an individual's potential to make errors and mistakes that in turn lead to breaches in organisational cybersecurity.

Later work by CERT (2014) further refined these factors (see Figure 3.3), adding a slight slant to the categorisations based an examination of individual responses to social engineering attacks. Whilst these elements are proposed to be specific to cybersecurity failures due to social engineering, these factors have also been seen to influence adherence to cybersecurity rules and protocols more widely.

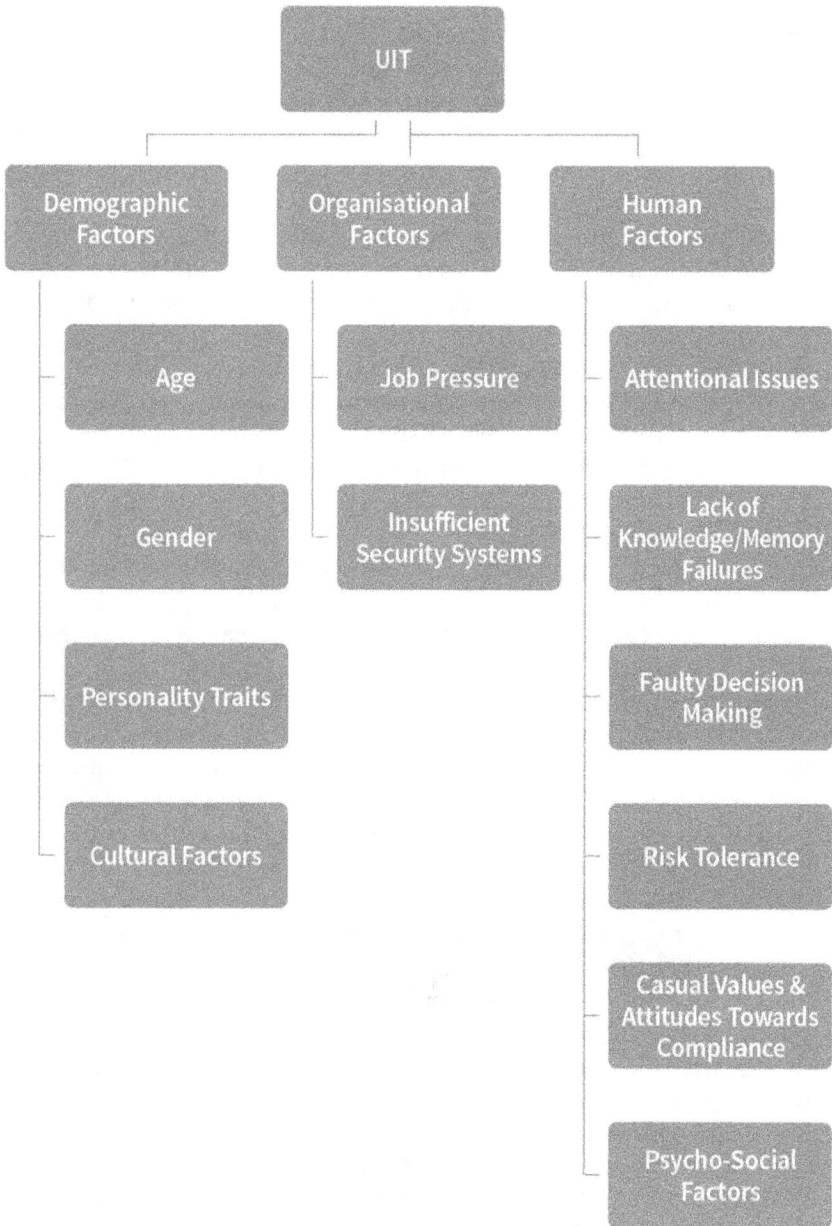

FIGURE 3.3 Revised predictors for unintentional insider threat (adapted from CERT, 2014)

Other aspects that are covered by the CERT (2014) framework include a variety of cognitive and psychological factors that could serve to influence an individual's susceptibility to social engineering attacks. These include a lack of understanding and knowledge surrounding the type of things an individual should be doing in instances where they are presented with a potential cybersecurity incident (in this case a social engineering attack), or this could be a loss of information due to a failure to recall that information. There is also the potential for individuals to make errors in their judgements, due to existing biases in their decision-making processes (see Chapter 5) or due to them being predisposed to making risky decisions in situations that are unfamiliar to them. The CERT (2014) framework also highlights the potential for stress and anxiety to exert an influence on an individual's capacity to respond to external threats such as social engineering, something that a variety of researchers have explored (e.g., Chowdhury et al., 2019; Nobles, 2022). We explore the role of stress in the context of counterproductive work behaviours in Chapter 11.

One of the most comprehensive frameworks for conceptualising human factors within cybersecurity was presented by Oltamari et al. (2015). Their ontological approach replaces the more traditional 'risk' assessment approach to cybersecurity and instead explores the role of trust in cybersecurity systems. The authors argue that the inherent characteristics of the system, such as individual differences and those that are situational, create an interconnected web of relationships that influence the amount of trust that is given to the end-user (Oltamari et al., 2015). This is an interesting approach and builds on the notion that individuals within the system need to be invested and engaged if they are to be part of an effective cybersecurity infrastructure (Hadlington et al., 2019). Trust can be established in information, in the people within the cybersecurity system, and the policies that govern cybersecurity (Oltamari et al., 2015).

In terms of human factors, Oltamari et al. (2015) presented three main categories, namely situational, behavioural, and knowledge and skill. Situational characteristics refer to the position of the individual within the system, as well as the level of access they have within that system. The situational characteristics also influence other aspects, such as the amount of attention the individual devotes to a current task, or their capacity to find the right information to apply to the same task (Oltamari et al., 2015). Oltamari et al. (2015) provided an example of an executive within an organisation who has access to numerous systems but fails to pay attention to security issues and the importance of information. Knowledge and skill characteristics relate to the level of experience, expertise, and degree of situational awareness an individual has, usually governed by training or time in the role they currently occupy. In contrast, behavioural characteristics look at dispositional factors, such as motivation, the rationality of the individual, integrity, and a benevolence/malevolence dichotomy. Someone working in an organisation who is highly motivated, rational, has an elevated level of integrity, and is also benevolent in nature will be highly effective at preventing lapses in cybersecurity. Outside of these core characteristics, Oltamari et al. (2015) also noted additional aspects that can serve to influence these behavioural elements, such as personality traits, risk aversion, personal ideology, and an ethical/moral dimension. This is an important framework as it establishes the key underlying human factors that influence an individual's engagement in the cybersecurity system. Crucially, each of the elements can influence others within the system (for example, level of experience will influence situational awareness, as will motivation). This is important to note, as often we view human factors in isolation, forgetting that there is an interplay at work between internal and external characteristics.

The framework from Oltamari et al. (2015) is not without its shortcomings however, and part of the issue is the overall structure of the framework. The hierarchical nature of the framework makes an assertion that some factors are more important than others and fails to acknowledge the fluidity of the interactions that can occur between the distinct factors that underlie an individual's adherence to cybersecurity principles in the workplace. It is often the case that ontological models such as that by Oltamari et al. (2015) over-simplify the complex interactions that take place between individual components in favour of preserving the underlying structure of the framework. However, as we will see throughout the discussion in the remaining chapters of this book, human behaviour is anything but predictable and modelling the contributing factors that are associated with the human factors to cybersecurity is inherently more complex and unpredictable.

An additional framework for exploring the role of human factors in cybersecurity was presented by the Chartered Institute of Ergonomics and Human Factors (Widdowson et al., 2022) in their Human Affected Cybersecurity (HACS) framework (see Figure 3.4). This framework appeals directly to practitioners and cybersecurity specialists as it is built around a central premise of usability and can be used as a method to record unwanted behaviours within an organisation, as well as providing the potential mitigation strategies to adopt to overcome these. The framework explores the interplay between the risky behaviours of individuals, the potential organisational causes of cybersecurity issues, the individuating factors presented by employees, as well as the quick wins and long-term solutions that can be implemented.

The HACS framework details several categories of risky behaviours that have a direct influence on the cybersecurity posture of an organisation:

- **User Validation Violations**: These relate to the use of passwords for system access and the shortcomings of human memory. As noted in Chapter 4, our capacity to retain important information over time is limited, leading most users to choose easily recalled passwords based on

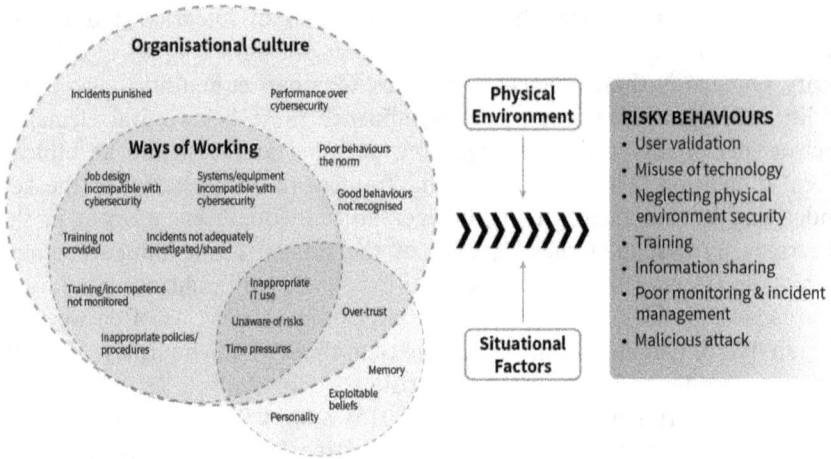

FIGURE 3.4. The Human Affected Cybersecurity (HACS) Framework (Widdowson et al., 2022)

personal information. This creates a critical weakness, especially when passwords are reused across compromised personal accounts.

- **Information Sharing**: This involves the various ways information sharing can compromise cybersecurity, such as sharing on social media or responding to phishing emails. Restrictive policies may lead employees to circumvent rules, increasing the risk of information being shared outside controlled environments.
- **Misuse of Technology**: This includes unauthorised use of ICT and transmitting sensitive information over unsecured public Wi-Fi.
- **Training**: Non-compliance with cybersecurity awareness training or failure to engage with it can stem from poorly designed training or perceptions of it being boring and unengaging.
- **Monitoring and Incident Management**: A lack of clear monitoring systems and incident management prevents learning from previous incidents due to inconsistent reporting. Encouraging a culture of incident reporting without stigma is essential for effective response.
- **Physical Security**: Often overlooked, physical security involves managing access to prevent unauthorised individuals from gaining access to critical information, which could be used in later exploits.
- **Malicious Insider Threats**: As discussed in Chapter 2, disgruntled employees or those with intent to harm pose significant risks.

The HACS framework categorises these behaviours into two distinct but interacting categories: individual and organisational causes. It emphasises that focusing solely on human error without considering the broader human factors framework can lead to a variety of erroneous conclusions. While human error is one aspect, other factors outside individual differences must be considered if we are to prevent a recurrence of the damaging event. Organisational causes for risky behaviours are embedded in working practices, organisational culture, and situational elements influencing employee behaviour. The HACS framework is inherently more complicated than we have time to discuss here, but it is a clear example of how the human factors framework can be applied to a practical exploration of cybersecurity within an organisational setting.

Summary

In this chapter, we outline the human factors approach to cybersecurity and detail the key tenets of the paradigm that will shape the rest of our discussion throughout this book. The human factors approach serves to isolate the elements which can directly influence interactions with complex systems and sets about remedying failures in the system by exploring how individuals deal with situations. By making generalisations about how people behave in situations, and drawing evidence from multiple perspectives, the human factors approach attempts to make predictions about how individuals behave across a variety of situations that have similar underlying structures or components and then extrapolate how they might perform in other situations of a similar nature.

As we have seen in this chapter, representing the complexity of the human factors approach to cybersecurity is not an easy task. Retaining the underlying interactions between the components and the complexity of human behaviour is not a straightforward process, and trying to reduce this complexity into a series of flow diagrams or network models does detract from this overall perspective. However, we as researchers, professionals, and practitioners need a way to view the interactions between the components that make up the human factors approach to cybersecurity. This needs to be simple enough to allow us to model ideas and approaches that could be used to improve the overall cybersecurity stance of a system or organisation, without losing the underlying complexity of the system itself.

References

CERT Insider Threat Team. (2013). *Unintentional insider threats: A foundational study (Technical Note CMU/SEI-2013-TN-022)*. Software Engineering Institute, Carnegie Mellon University. Retrieved from doi:10.1184/R1/6585575.v1.

CERT Insider Threat Team. (2014). *Unintentional insider threats: A review of phishing and malware incidents by economic sector (Technical Note CMU/SEI-2014-TN-007)*. Software Engineering Institute, Carnegie Mellon University. https://resources.sei.cmu.edu/asset_files/technicalnote/2014_004_001_297777.pdf.

Chapanis, A. (1996). *Human factors in systems engineering*. John Wiley & Sons.

Chowdhury, N. H., Adam, M. T. P., & Skinner, G. (2019). The impact of time pressure on cybersecurity behaviour: A systematic literature review. *Behaviour and Information Technology*, 38(12), 1290–1308. doi:10.1080/0144929X.2019.1583769.

Craigen, D., Diakun-Thibault, N., & Purse, R. (2014). Defining cybersecurity. *Technology Innovation Management Review*, 4(10), 13–21.

Ghelani, D. (2022). Cyber security, cyber threats, implications and future perspectives: A review. *American Journal of Science, Engineering and Technology*, 3(6), 12–19. doi:10.11648.

Hadlington, L. (2017). Human factors in cybersecurity; examining the link between internet addiction, impulsivity, attitudes towards cybersecurity, and risky cybersecurity behaviours. *Heliyon*, 3(7), e00346. doi:10.1016/j.heliyon.2017.e00346.

Hadlington, L., Popovac, M., Janicke, H., Yevseyeva, I., & Jones, K. (2019). Exploring the role of work identity and work locus of control in information security awareness. *Computers and Security*, 81. doi:10.1016/j.cose.2018.10.006.

Herath, T., & Rao, H. R. (2009a). Encouraging information security behaviours in organisations: Role of penalties, pressures and perceived effectiveness. *Decision Support Systems*, 47(2), 154–165.

Herath, T., & Rao, H. R. (2009b). Protection motivation and deterrence: A framework for security policy compliance in organisations. *European Journal of Information Systems*, 18(2), 106–125.

Hughes-Lartey, K., Li, M., Botchey, F. E., & Qin, Z. (2021). Human factor, a critical weak point in the information security of an organization's Internet of things. *Heliyon*, 7(3). doi:10.1016/j.heliyon.2021.e06522.

Khan, B., Alghathbar, K., Nabi, S. I., & Khan, M. K. (2021). Effectiveness of information security awareness training programs: A systematic review. *Computers & Security*, 95, 101–115.

Kioskli, K., Fotis, T., Nifakos, S., & Mouratidis, H. (2023). The importance of conceptualising the human-centric approach in maintaining and promoting cybersecurity-hygiene in healthcare 4.0. *Applied Sciences*, 13. doi:10.3390/app13063410.

Kraemer, S., Carayon, P., & Clem, J. (2009). Human and organizational factors in computer and information security: Pathways to vulnerabilities. *Computers and Security*, 28(7), 509–520. doi:10.1016/j.cose.2009.04.006.

Lee, K., & Joshi, K. (2017). Examining the use of status quo bias perspective in IS research: Need for re-conceptualizing and incorporating biases. *Information Systems Journal*, 27(6), 733–752.

Li, H., He, W., Xu, L., Ash, I., Anwar, M., & Yuan, X. (2019). Investigating the impact of cybersecurity policy awareness on employees' cybersecurity behaviour. *Journal of Information Security and Applications*, 48, 102–115.

Meister, D. (1989). *Conceptual aspects of human factors*. Johns Hopkins University Press.

New York State Department of Financial Services. (2020). *Report on the investigation of Twitter's July 15, 2020 cybersecurity incident and the implications for election security*. www.dfs.ny.gov/Twitter_Report.

Nobles, C. (2022). Stress, burnout, and security fatigue in cybersecurity: A human factors problem. *HOLISTICA – Journal of Business and Public Administration*, 13 (1), 49–72. doi:10.2478/hjbpa-2022-0003.

Oltamari, A., Henshel, D., Cains, M., & Hoffman, B. (2015). Towards a human factors ontology for cyber security. *CEUR Workshop Proceedings*, 1523, 26–33.

Pollini, A., Callari, T. C., Tedeschi, A., Ruscio, D., Save, L., Chiarugi, F., & Guerri, D. (2022). Leveraging human factors in cybersecurity: An integrated methodological approach. *Cognition, Technology and Work*, 24(2), 371–390. doi:10.1007/s10111-021-00683-y.

Prummer, J., van Steen, T., & van den Berg, B. (2024). A systematic review of current cybersecurity training methods. *Computers and Security*, 136, 103585. doi:10.1016/j.cose.2023.103585.

Rahman, T., Rohan, R., Pal, D., & Kanthamanon, P. (2021). Human factors in cybersecurity: A scoping review. *ACM International Conference Proceeding Series.* doi:10.1145/3468784.3468789.

Rohan, R., Funilkul, S., Pal, D., & Chutimaskul, W. (2021). Understanding of human factors in cybersecurity: A systematic literature review. *2021 International Conference on Computational Performance Evaluation, ComPE 2021*, 133–140. doi:10.1109/ComPE53109.2021.9752358.

Russ, A. L., Fairbanks, R. J., Karsh, B.-T., Militello, L. G., Saleem, J. J., & Wears, R. L. (2012). The science of human factors: Separating fact from fiction. *BMJ Quality & Safety*, 22(10), 802–808. doi:10.1136/bmjqs-2012-001450.

Sanders, M. S., & McCormick, E. J. (1993). *Human factors in engineering and design* (7th ed.). McGraw-Hill.

Sasse, M. A., Brostoff, S., & Weirich, D. (2001). *Transforming the 'weakest link' – A human/computer interaction approach to usable and effective security. BT Technology Journal*, 19(3), 122–131.

Singh, A. N., Picot, A., Kranz, J., Gupta, M. P., & Ojha, A. (2013). Information security management (ISM) practices: Lessons from select cases from India and Germany. *Global Journal of Flexible Systems Management*, 14(4), 225–239. doi:10.1007/s40171-013-0047-4.

Soomro, Z. A., Shah, M. H., & Ahmed, J. (2016). Information security management needs more holistic approach: A literature review. *International Journal of Information Management*, 36(2), 215–225.

Strauch, B. (2017). *Investigating human error: Incidents, accidents, and complex systems* (2nd ed.). CRC Press. doi:10.1201/9781315589749.

Wickens, C. D., Hollands, J. G., Banbury, S., & Parasuraman, R. (2013). *Engineering psychology and human performance* (4th ed.). Pearson.

Wickens, C. D., Hollands, J. G., Banbury, S., & Parasuraman, R. (2018). *Engineering psychology and human performance* (4th ed.). Routledge. doi:10.4324/9781315620169.

Wickens, C. D., Lee, J. D., Liu, Y., & Gordon-Becker, S. (2004). *An introduction to human factors engineering* (2nd ed.). Pearson.

Wickens, C. D., Lee, J. D., Liu, Y., & Gordon-Becker, S. (2017). *An introduction to human factors engineering* (3rd ed.). Pearson.

Widdowson, A. J., Turner, N., Blythe, J. M., Tedeschi, A., Capaccioli, A., Marsh, O., … Thron, E. (2022). *Human affected cyber security (HACS) framework*. www.mcafee.com/enterprise/en-us/assets/reports/rp-hidden-costs-of-cybercrime.pdf.

Witman, P. D., & Mackelprang, S. (2022). The 2020 Twitter hack – so many lessons to be learned. *Journal of Cybersecurity Education, Research and Practice, 2021*(2). doi:10.62915/2472-2707.1089.

Young, B. (2021). The impact of phishing simulations on cybersecurity awareness: A systematic review. *Journal of Cybersecurity Education*, 5(1), 45–58.

Young, B., Carpenter, S., & McLeod, A. (2018). Technology threat avoidance theory: A systematic review. *Journal of Information Security and Applications*, 47, 102–115.

4

THE ROLE OF CONTEXT AND INDIVIDUAL DIFFERENCES

Introduction

Humans are not perfect, and we come preloaded with a variety of operating errors that are not easily remedied. These range from faulty 'software' (such as biases in decision making) to problems with 'hardware' (issues with memory and attention). When we try to pay attention to many things at once, we can make mistakes, some of which can be quite catastrophic. We find it hard to focus on tasks for extended periods, are easily distracted, and often make poor choices based on faulty information or past experiences. Emotions also play a significant role in our decision making. Anger can push us towards irrational and rash decisions (one of the authors can attest to the burden of buyer's remorse!). Fatigue and tiredness can lead to substantial errors. We often act on impulse, neglecting to consider the consequences of our actions and relying on 'gut instinct', which frequently leads to poor decisions. Overall, humans are fallible, so it is no surprise that discussions about online safety and security are filled with examples of human failure.

In this chapter we explore some of the key facets of humans that serve to influence our functioning within complex systems like cybersecurity frameworks. In the first part of this chapter, we start by exploring psychological factors that govern our day-to-day functioning – essentially, what is going on in our minds at any given time. In the second part, we focus on dispositional factors that influence our behaviours across different situations. These factors are stable over time and are unique to everyone. In the final part we examine the potential demographic variables that could influence cybersecurity awareness and behaviour. These factors could include age, gender, and also be linked to cultural differences.

DOI: 10.4324/9781003509011-4

Psychological Factors

The label 'psychological factors' encompasses a wide range of processes that influence how individuals think, act, and feel in various situations. In this section, we will review the psychological factors that will shape our discussions throughout the remainder of this book. This overview will provide some essential background for those who may not be familiar with these key concepts.

Human Attention

Human attention has been the focus of research and scholarly writing since the turn of the last century. James (1890) was credited with the following quote:

> (Attention) is the taking possession of the mind, in clear and vivid form, of one out of what seems several simultaneously possible objects or trains of thought... It implies withdrawal from some things in order to deal effectively with others.
>
> *(James, 1890)*

Fundamentally, how we view human attention has changed little since this initial definition from James. The key takeaway from the above quote is that attention is limited and requires careful deployment to achieve its aims. Attention is the fundamental cognitive process which serves as a cornerstone for the other cognitive processes that will be discussed in the rest of this chapter. Without attention, we would not be able to focus on information and commit material to memory (Chun & Turk-Browne, 2007; Chun et al., 2011), which in turn means we would not be able to remember information, resulting in an inability to learn or base decisions on past information.

Selective Attention

Selective attention is the ability to focus on one source of information whilst ignoring others (Treisman, 1969). Selective attention is important to humans and allows us to focus on one specific thing whilst also being able to filter out distractions around us. For example, when you are in a busy office with multiple other noises and distractions going on, you can focus on the conversation you are having with your colleague. However, one of the critical things to remember about selective attention is that it has its limits, and as we will see later in this section, the narrow focus we have on one critical aspect of our immediate environment means that we could be missing other things.

Divided Attention

This is the process of splitting attention between two or more concurrent tasks (Courage et al., 2015; Eysenck & Keane, 1991; Kahneman, 1973; Naveh-Benjamin et al., 2003). We often hear the concept of multitasking being used to describe the concept of divided attention, and it is a common activity for many individuals. Have you ever tried to draft an email whilst simultaneously trying to take part in a conference call? Or have you tried to have a telephone conversation with someone whilst trying to complete another task, such as navigating around a busy street, only to realise that you have gone the wrong way? Humans are horrifically bad at doing more than two things at any given time, and this relates to the limitations of the attentional system. In instances where the tasks we are trying to complete share a set of common resources (for example, they both need us to write something down) or both tasks are complex, our attention becomes divided too far and we make mistakes.

Sustained Attention

Often referred to as 'vigilance', this is our ability to maintain a sufficient level of attention on a particular task or stimulus in our immediate environment for an extended period (Hancock & Warm, 1989; Parasuraman & Davies, 1984; Rose et al., 2002). Sustained attention has been defined as 'the ability to self-sustain mindful, conscious processing of stimuli whose repetitive, non-arousing qualities would otherwise lead to habituation' (Robertson et al., 1997, p. 747). A crucial point to remember about sustained attention is that it is not something we can keep up indefinitely, and our capacity to keep vigilant for lengthy periods of time gradually declines (Parasuraman, 1979). For example, a security guard who must check all the people coming into a building for hours, or an employee monitoring an information feed for a critical piece of information. In terms of cybersecurity, this could be a situation where employees are constantly told about potential threats to the system from cybercriminals and miss potential attacks because of an inability to sustain attention.

Limits on Attentional Capacity

Notionally, we cannot process all the information that is presented to us within our immediate environment, and we must have ways of filtering out information that we think is irrelevant or unnecessary (Bunting & Cowan, 2005; Cowan, 1988; Cowan et al., 2024). This is where the process of selective attention comes in, and the limitations placed on us by our attentional system mean that when we do get bombarded with lots of information, we can get overloaded, leading us to forget important things. The limits that are placed on our attentional system are linked to the types of tasks that we are engaged in and are governed by the complexity associated with those tasks (Draheim et al., 2022).

Memory

Memory has been a key research area in the field of cognitive psychology since the inception of the discipline. We will not be able to condense what could be over 100 years of research into the space of a couple of paragraphs, but setting the scene in terms of what form human memory takes, and the associated limitations attached to it, is important for further discussions throughout this book. There are multiple theories associated with the structure and function of human memory (Cowan et al., 2024), and there is little agreement about how best to view what is an abstract concept. However, there is some broad agreement about the processes which underlie the functioning of memory (Mujawar et al., 2021):

- **Encoding**: This is the point at which information from our immediate environment is taken into our perceptual system; for something to be encoded, it must be 'perceived'. This goes beyond just looking at something or hearing something; the 'thing' must be actively engaged with to be encoded. This is where the crossover between attention and memory comes into play – if we are not paying attention to something, then it will not be perceived, which means it will not reach the stage of encoding.
- **Storage**: Information that is encoded is transferred into a storage system for later use.
- **Retrieval**: The act of finding information that has been encoded within the memory system for it to be used in another activity.

A common analogy for human memory has been that of a computer storage system, where the system allocates a storage place for a piece of information so that it can be found later (Brette, 2022). However, as many readers of this book will no doubt testify, human memory is not always as reliable as a computer storage system – have you ever forgotten a critical piece of information at a crucial time? Sudden blank at a cash machine or checkout when it comes to putting in your PIN? Calling a new partner by your old partner's name?! The important thing to recognise is that human memory is nowhere near as precise or reliable as that of the computer analogy.

Working Memory (or Short-Term Memory).

The important thing about short-term or working memory is that it has a limited capacity and can typically hold information for 15–30 seconds before that information is lost. We can hold about 5–9 items in short-term memory based on the 7 plus or minus 2 rule, established by Miller (1956). When we refer to 'items', this could be individual digits or grouping of items (or 'chunks') that can serve to extend the overall capacity of short-term memory (Norris & Kalm, 2021). For example, rather than remember the phone number 07843 450431 as 11 individual digits, we could break it down into chunks ('078' '434' 504' '31') which serves to extend the storage.

If we think about instances where we have been trying to create a new password, it can be challenging work especially where we are faced with multiple restrictions on their content (e.g., special symbols, character length, capitalisation). For obvious reasons, shorter passwords are easier to articulate and remember, hence why many people fall foul of the non-complex, short password. However, if we use a mechanism of 'chunking', where we split the information up into more manageable, individual pieces of information, rather than lots of singular bits of information, this allows us to extend what we can remember. This method can be effectively used to create passwords by choosing three random words. This allows us to create a strong password that is hard to crack, but easy to remember, due to the three 'chunks' of information, in comparison to a complex, nonsensical password with 14 individual characters.

Long-Term Memory

Long-term memory is just a collection of 'stuff' that we have learned over our lifetime, and is organised very much like a teenager's bedroom, right? Well, this is a very oversimplified and very stereotypical approach to viewing long-term memory, and overlooks what is a more nuanced structure. Long-term memory is made up of several distinct sub-stores based on the content of the memories that sit within them. According to Squire's (1992) conceptualisation, long-term memory is divided into two main categories: declarative (explicit) memory and non-declarative (implicit) memory. Declarative memory refers to memories that we can consciously recall and articulate, such as facts and personal experiences. This type of memory is further subdivided into episodic memory and semantic memory. Episodic memory involves the recollection of specific events and experiences from our lives, such as remembering your first day at school or a recent holiday. These memories are tied to a particular time and place and often include contextual details like emotions and sensory experiences. In contrast, semantic memory refers to our general knowledge about the world – facts, concepts, and meanings that are not linked to a specific personal experience, such as knowing that Paris is the capital of France or that a zebra is an animal with black and white stripes. Together, episodic and semantic memory form the foundation of our ability to learn, reflect, and communicate about the past (Baddeley et al., 2020; Squire, 1992).

One critical aspect related to long-term memory is the phenomenon of forgetting. Forgetting information that is stored within our memory systems is a common occurrence. Nairne and Pandeirada (2008) noted that for many people 'forgetting is a scourge, a nuisance, a breakdown in an otherwise efficient mental capacity' (p. 17). Information can be forgotten through two distinct processes, these being interference and decay. Decay Theory proposes that information is lost over time, and fades much like an old photograph fades in direct sunlight (Brown, 1958; Ricker & Hardman, 2017; Ricker et al., 2020). In contrast, Interference Theory proposes that other information that exists within the cognitive system serves to disrupt new or old information (Anderson, 2003; Müller & Pilzecker, 1900). In terms of interference, there are two interrelated concepts that come into play when we talk about forgetting that are worthy of discussion here, and as we will see, they both have clear implications for cybersecurity awareness.

Proactive Interference

This is where old information we have stored in our long-term memory makes it hard to recall the latest information that we are trying to learn (Murphy & Castel, 2023; Underwood, 1957). For example, have you typed in your old password or PIN when you should be putting in a new one? Given out an old postcode of a previous address when you have moved to a new property? These are classic examples of proactive interference at work. In the context of cybersecurity, proactive interference could manifest in several specific ways. For example, individuals might present a resilience to adopting new security process and protocols because it means they must overwrite information or rules that have been engrained in memory. Many organisations have experienced this when changing from the more traditional password approach of accessing systems to two-factor authentication. The acquisition of new rules, particularly in the context of password creation, can also serve to exert some level of proactive interference, often leading individuals to attempt to reuse old passwords, or modify older passwords so they are easier to remember. This can also be evident in professional cybersecurity experts where they fail to recognise new attack types because they have such engrained experiences and cannot integrate the new tactics used by attackers.

Retroactive Interference

This is the opposite process, where new information disrupts us recalling information that we have previously learned (Murphy & Castel, 2023; Tulving & Psotka, 1971). This is generally evident when we are learning something new, and it places a block on previous information. Examples of this could be an inability to recall an old address (for a job application or credit agreement) because we have learned a new one, or being unable to remember an old login for a system you have not used for a while because you have a new one. The involvement of retroactive inference in aspects of cybersecurity awareness may not be directly obvious, but there are some examples that we can start to think about. For example, individuals who receive new training on aspects of cybersecurity awareness might be more likely to forget critical elements of their previous training – which is why it is important to ensure that all elements of cybersecurity training are refreshed and reflected on. In terms of susceptibility to attacks such as phishing emails, individuals may fail to identify older tactics to illicit a response because we become so focused on newer, more modern methods.

Decision Making

Decision making is something that we will revisit in later chapters, but we can introduce some basic concepts here. Research on decision making can be divided into two areas: how tasks and situations influence decisions, and how individual characteristics affect the decision-making process. These are referred to as situational and dispositional elements of decision making (Scott & Bruce, 1995).

People can differ significantly according to their individual decision-making style, captured in the General Decision-Making Style (Scott & Bruce, 1995) model. Each of these different decision-making styles can in turn have a significant impact on the way in which an individual approaches elements of cybersecurity awareness. These decision-making styles include:

- Rational: Involves a thorough search for information, and a systematic evaluation of the alternative routes that the decision-making process could take. An example of this could be an employee who carefully evaluates the contents of a phishing email before they decide whether to open an attachment contained within it, or whether to report it to the IT department.
- Intuitive: Relies on gut feelings and is unsystematic in nature, relying heavily on premonitions. This could be an employee who decides to take a particular decision based on a hunch that it will prevent them from being targeted in future.
- Dependent: A heavy reliance on advice from others. This is generally evident in situations where individuals will defer decisions to colleagues they see as having more experience with computers or digital technology when it comes to cybersecurity behaviours.
- Avoidant: The individual will engage in several different strategies to avoid making decisions. Putting off updating your password until the very last minute is a good example of an avoidant decision-making style.
- Spontaneous: This type of decision maker will make quick decisions with minimal effort. Choosing the first available anti-virus software because it

looks good without engaging in a more invested research process is a clear example of a spontaneous decision-making style (Allwood & Salo, 2012; Scott & Bruce, 1995).

Decision making has also been explored in terms of diverse ways in which individuals process information. Typically, the literature in the area refers to two distinct processes that drive decision making (often referred to as Dual-Process Theory) where such processes are linked to the amount of time and effort an individual will exert over their decisions. For example, Type 1 or System 1 processing is viewed as a fast and intuitive processing method that is almost instantaneous and based very much on intuition (Chaiken & Trope, 1999; Evans & Stanovich, 2013). We also have a more effortful processing system that engages a more analytical and slower process, which is referred to as System 2 or Type 2 processing. As we will discuss in Chapter 5, although Type 1 processing can have some significant advantages when it comes to reducing the amount of time and effort that we must exert when deciding between alternatives, there can be some trade-offs, emerging as cognitive biases.

Cognitive Biases

Our past experiences can also be seen to exert an influence over our current and future decision-making processes (Olschewski et al., 2023), even though we might be fully aware of that influence. In many instances, such experiences emerge as cognitive biases that can direct us to make a decision that is erroneous and often exaggerates our own capabilities. For example, overconfidence in decision making is a critical cognitive bias that could heavily influence aspects of cybersecurity awareness judgements. Many of us overestimate our capabilities when it comes to protecting ourselves online, and there is evidence that individuals often believe they know more about the area of cybersecurity than they actually do (Alnifie & Kim, 2023; Ament & Jaeger, 2017; Aschwanden al., 2024). Often, people fail to recognise they have respective deficits in the skills they possess, even though they consistently make preventable errors when it comes to decision making. This is termed the Dunning-Kruger effect (Kruger & Dunning, 1999). In the context of cybersecurity, this can be clear in individuals who have had limited exposure to the field or who have only encountered minor cyberattacks that were unsuccessful may develop a false sense of security. This lack of direct experience or understanding could lead to overconfidence, with individuals believing they are more capable of handling cyber threats than they actually are.

We will also default to the simplest option when faced with multiple choices. The concept of satisficing has been well documented in decision making, where an individual will choose an option that meets the minimum requirements for their current needs (Vargová et al., 2023). For example, we might default to the first option we find when picking a password, because it fits the requirements necessary. However, this might mean we reuse an old password or meet the minimum requirements for the password to be created. Often, the concept of satisficing means that employees are engaging in behaviours that are about good enough to be acceptable, but there is no upper limit of engagement, meaning that anything that appears in addition to the basic levels of engagement will be missed or ignored.

Emotion

There is a long and checkered history of how emotion has been viewed in terms of its links to cognition. Some researchers have argued that emotion is not cognitive in nature, and others have argued that cognition is always involved in emotion (Clore & Ortony, 2000). The intricacies of this lengthy debate are a little extraneous to our current discussions, but for the purposes of trying to classify and categorise where emotion fits into our map of individual differences, we are going to include it in the cognitive processes category based on most research in the field (Okon-Singer et al., 2015; Tyng et al., 2017). Emotion is often seen as a potential mediator and moderator in all the above elements related to cognition. Emotion can have a strong influence on perception, memory, and decision making (Brosch et al., 2013), and this can influence many aspects related to cybersecurity. For example, in terms of perception, individuals are more likely to be able to detect a stimulus within a display faster if it has a strong emotional valence versus one that is neutral (Brosch et al., 2013). It has also been noted that distinct types of emotion can have differing impacts on our attentional focus, for example anger can serve to narrow our attentional focus, whilst sadness can serve to widen our attentional focus (Gable & Harmon-Jones, 2010). Similarly, in terms of memory, we are more likely to remember pleasant memories and attempt to block out those memories that have unpleasant connotations.

In the context of decision making, researchers have noted that fear can have a significant impact on the way in which people react. For example, participants usually demonstrate extraordinarily strong reactions to events that have a low probability of happening but are at the extreme end of catastrophising when their emotions are highly stimulated (Sunstein, 2003). This concept has been termed 'probability neglect' and means that individuals will overemphasise the emotional outcome of a particular event rather than the actual probability of the event occurring in the first place (Sunstein & Zeckhauser, 2008). In the sphere of cybersecurity, this could be an excessive fear of a potentially rare form of catastrophic cyberattack (something akin to cyberwarfare), but they fail to acknowledge more common risks from attacks such as phishing emails or social engineering, which are far more likely to occur.

Dispositional Factors

As we alluded to at the start of the chapter, there are certain factors that shape how we interact with information and situations that are less dynamic than the psychological factors we have discussed above. Dispositional factors are more stable and consistent over time, and present factors that are harder to change through external influence. We start this section by looking at the construct of personality, something that has often been studied in relation to cybersecurity awareness.

Personality

Personality is an abstract concept that is presented to us in terms of a set of traits that we can have or be more of. Traditional approaches to personality traits have made a direct emphasis on the notion that they are stable over one's lifetime (McCrae & Costa, 2008). Often personality traits are prone to changes in early life, usually before the age of 30 (Bleidorn et al., 2022), with significant increases related to emotional stability and consciousness throughout an adult's lifespan. Researchers have defined personality traits in terms of feelings and behaviours that are stable over time and can be used to differentiate individuals from each other (Allport, 1961).

There are five core personality traits individuals can be aligned with (Digman, 1990), these being:

1. **Openness to Experience**: Typified by an innate level of intellectual curiosity and creativity; someone who is open to experience engages in challenges to expand their experience, and favours originality and complexity.
2. **Conscientiousness**: Someone who is goal and task orientated, delays gratification and follows norms and rules. Individuals who score highly on this trait think before they act and engage in planning and organisation of their daily tasks, choosing to prioritise tasks in order of perceived importance.
3. **Extraversion**: An energetic and outgoing approach to social activities, and can include elements of sociability, assertiveness, and positivity. Often orientated to immediate gratification at the expense of long-term planning.
4. **Agreeableness**: Orientated towards a prosocial attitude, and one that fosters collaborative thinking, trust, and modesty.
5. **Neuroticism**: An individual who scores highly on the neuroticism personality trait will exhibit traits such as nervousness, anxiety, and negative affect (or emotional stability).
    (Goldberg, 1993; Goldberg et al., 1998; John & Srivastava, 1999)

For personality traits, the label is presented as part of a dichotomy, where individuals can be differentiated along a continuum. For example, extraversion is paired with its partner construct of introversion, where someone who has a tendency towards the opposite end of the extraversion spectrum is socially withdrawn, socially awkward, and less socially active (John & Srivastava, 1999).

There are some other personality traits that tend to feature outside of this core list of the so-called 'Big Five', these often being referred to as the Dark Triad (at this point I feel like there should be some dramatic music being played in the background). These personality traits are seen as being more anti-social in nature and are typically associated with individuals who behave in nefarious or aberrant ways that go contrary to prescribed social norms (Paulhus, 2014; Paulhus & Williams, 2002).

- **Narcissism**: A multidimensional construct that can be typically defined in terms of an individual's feeling of self-entitlement, the need for attention, interpersonal dominance, and a general disregard for the feelings of others (Miller & Campbell, 2008; Miller et al., 2021; Raskin & Hall, 1979).
- **Machiavellianism**: This trait reflects an individual's cynicism towards others, as well as a willingness to deceive and manipulate others (Christie & Geis, 1970).
- **Psychopathy**: An absence of anxiety and empathy as well as prominent levels of impulsivity (Harms & Sherman, 2021).

Risk Perception and Risk-Taking

People often misjudge the level of risk that is attached to a particular event or choice based on the way in which that event is framed. For example, an employee might be more inclined to worry more about the risk of losing their laptop to physical theft because of the monetary cost involved, versus underestimating the risk of being defrauded through a phishing attack. Individual differences have been shown to exist in the way people come to decisions that involve risk and uncertainty, with such differences being reflected in what has been termed risk attitude (Blais & Weber, 2006; Weber et al., 2002). Risk attitude has been commonly viewed as a stable personality trait (Weber et al., 2002). Using this framework, an individual's approach to risk-taking is stable across a wide variety of situations (Weber et al., 2002). However, the view of risk attitude as a personality-based metric has been undermined by several studies highlighting the instability of risk attitudes between testing (Blais & Weber, 2006).

Latterly, researchers have re-evaluated the personality trait framework for risk attitude in favour of a risk-return model. This framework views risk-taking as an interaction between (a) the situation in which the risk is being taken and (b) individual characteristics related to risk-taking behaviour (Blais & Weber, 2006; Weber et al., 2002). In these models, perceived risk is viewed as a variable which can differ not only between individuals, but also as a direct function of both the content and context of the risk (Blais & Weber, 2006; Weber et al., 2002). This has some important implications for our current focus, and we can start to put together patterns of behaviour that are interactions between the type of information that is being presented to an individual and the situation they find themselves in. For example, are we more likely to take risks with information that is organisationally sensitive versus our own information? Do people take more risks when sharing information with their friends, versus when they are sharing information with their colleagues, and does this depend on the type of information that they are sharing? These are critical considerations for anyone working in the context of cybersecurity awareness, and from a human factors perspective such decision-making processes are at the heart of what we as practitioners are trying to understand.

Locus of Control

The construct of locus of control was originally conceived by Rotter (1966) and is seen as the extent to which an individual views the extent to which they are in control of events and outcomes in their own life. For example, someone who displays an internal locus of control is more likely to believe that they have control over the outcomes in their life via the actions and decisions that they make. For example, someone who believes that hard work and applying themselves to the key challenges that they face in daily life would be an example of an internal locus of control. In contrast an external locus of control positions an individual to attribute outcomes in their life to external factors, such as luck, fate, or the actions of others around them (Rotter, 1966).

Locus of control is an important dispositional factor when we are exploring the way in which individuals interact with and engage in protective cybersecurity behaviours. For example, someone who has an internal locus of control will be more likely to see the importance of making good decisions about their protective cybersecurity behaviours and would see themselves as being the master of such decisions. In contrast an external locus of control would make an individual less likely to engage in the same protective behaviours with the belief that irrespective of what they do, fate or luck will have a far greater bearing on their chances of being a victim of cybercrime (Hadlington et al., 2019).

Demographic Factors

Individual differences that relate directly to population characteristics are also an important consideration for our exploration of factors that can influence cybersecurity awareness and behaviour. There has been a growing body of research that explores the role such factors play in cybersecurity awareness with much of the focus being on age, gender, and culture.

Age

Age has often been examined in terms of how generational differences influence familiarity with digital technology and confidence in carrying out essential tasks online. Several researchers have noted a persistent digital divide between age groups and their capabilities regarding online behaviours (e.g., Branley-Bell et al., 2022; Hargittai, 2002; Hunsaker & Hargittai, 2018; Mendel & Toch, 2019). Typically, younger generations are viewed as 'digital natives', a term coined by Prensky (2001, 2007) to describe individuals born into a world where digital technology has always been present. This group is proposed to have a greater level of confidence with digital platforms and tools. They also tend to have a better understanding of basic cybersecurity practices, such as recognizing phishing emails and using two-factor authentication. However, this confidence can lead to overconfidence, resulting in riskier online behaviour. For example, Bidgoli et al. (2016) found that even though undergraduate students might have more knowledge about cybercrime, they are highly susceptible to online victimisation. This pattern is echoed in other research (Oksanen & Keipi, 2013), where individuals aged 15–24 demonstrated higher levels of cybercrime victimisation compared to older age groups. Hadlington and Chivers (2018) also noted that individuals aged 18–30 were more likely to show higher susceptibility to cybercrime.

In contrast, older users may lack confidence in their ability to use digital devices, which impacts their capacity to engage in effective cybersecurity awareness and protection measures (Branley-Bell et al., 2022). Rather than specific age groups being universally susceptible to cybersecurity threats, there are distinct differences in the types of threats each age group is vulnerable to. This has significant implications for designing and delivering cybersecurity awareness training within organisations with multigenerational staff. Different risks need to be assessed and targeted for specific age groups (Branley-Bell et al., 2022).

Gender

There has been a wide variety of research exploring the role of gender in cybersecurity awareness, with a great deal of contradictory evidence in the literature (Branley-Bell et al., 2022). For example, Herath and Rao (2009) noted that gender significantly influenced employees' compliance with cybersecurity rules, with females showing higher levels of rule compliance compared to males. Similarly, Ifinedo (2014) found that males demonstrated lower levels of cybersecurity compliance than females. However, later research by Anwar et al., (2017) revealed significant differences between males and females in terms of their perceived self-efficacy in cybersecurity. Anwar et al. (2017) also noted that gender impacted an individual's self-efficacy for cybersecurity behaviours, prior experience, and computer skills, but had no effect on self-reported cybersecurity behaviours. Interestingly, they found that men reported higher cybersecurity compliance behaviours, contradicting the findings of Herath and Rao (2009) and Ifinedo (2014).

One common finding linked to gender is the difference in self-reported self-efficacy regarding compliance with cybersecurity awareness and the use of digital technology. Generally, females score significantly lower in self-efficacy related to computer technology, which negatively impacts their capacity to engage in effective cybersecurity protection (Branley-Bell et al., 2022). However, Branley-Bell et al. (2022) found no significant impact of gender on any of the cybersecurity behaviours they measured, such as password generation, proactive checking, and updating software.

As you can see, disentangling the influence of gender on cybersecurity awareness and compliance behaviours is not straightforward. For this reason, we tend not to focus directly on gender differences in most of the work explored in this book unless it has a clear and specific bearing on the particular behaviour being examined.

Culture

There are many ways in which we can define the factor of culture with some of them having a clear influence on aspects of cybersecurity. In terms of the focus of our current discussions, we focus mostly on three key levels of culture, namely:

National or Geopolitical Culture: Serves to differentiate one group from another group based on geographical location. It is usually accompanied by the assertion that individuals from the same cultural group will share a similar set of beliefs or common practices when it comes to interacting with information or following rules, often linked to national policies and edicts. National culture is something that develops over time, usually centuries, with individuals developing and evolving different belief systems which in turn serve to influence patterns of behaviour that allow them to make sense of the world around them (Hofstede, 1980, 2011). As we will see later in Chapter 10, national culture does have some important ramifications for adherence to cybersecurity rules and processes, and forms one of the key demographic factors that has been focused on in the research literature.

Organisational Culture: The concept of organisational culture was introduced through research into management and organisation, with Pettigrew (1979) presenting the first overview of what the concept means. *Organisation culture* is linked to geographical culture insomuch as the 'group' maintains a set of rules, beliefs, and ways of doings things that give the organisation its own distinctive character and ethos (Brown, 1995; Willcoxson & Millett, 2000). The construct embodies the sum of the shared beliefs, values, and assumptions that serve to govern how individuals behave within an organisational setting (Pavlova, 2020; Pettigrew, 1979). Organisational culture can have a direct impact on aspects of cybersecurity, particularly where the values of the organisation are aligned with good or bad cybersecurity practices. There are a wide range of organisational factors that can serve to influence an individual's effectiveness when it comes to adherence to cybersecurity rules and procedures, and the CERT (2013, 2014) frameworks go some way to acknowledging these. There are a wide variety of organisational factors that are included in the CERT framework, such as job pressure, insufficient security procedures and systems, a lack of clear training and high job pressures.

The influence of organisational factors is seen as a cross-pollination between the situational contexts in which cybersecurity decisions are being made and individual differences, such as personality traits and other psychological variables. It is easy to overlook the role situational variables play in an individual's approach to cybersecurity in the workplace, often placing the blame on the individual's ineptitude in following rules. However, research in this area notes that individual differences do not act in isolation. Multiple factors often combine to create the perfect conditions for cybersecurity errors and misjudgements (Kraemer et al., 2009; Oltramari et al., 2015; Young et al., 2018).

For example, someone with a low level of conscientiousness (unreliable and disengaged with work policies and practices) is unlikely to be motivated to engage in cybersecurity training, especially if it is unengaging and irrelevant to them. The norms governing an organisation's approach to cybersecurity can also influence behaviour. In an environment where risky behaviours are accepted, an individual with a lax attitude towards cybersecurity may be more predisposed to take risks.

Cybersecurity Culture: The concept of cybersecurity culture has emerged more recently in the research literature and focuses on the specific norms, rules, and values that govern cybersecurity compliance within an organisation (Gcaza & von Solms, 2017; Reegård et al., 2019). This term refers to the collective knowledge, beliefs, perceptions, and attitudes held by individuals within an organisation regarding cybersecurity awareness, and how these factors influence their engagement with cybersecurity practices (ENISA, 2017). Establishing an effective cybersecurity culture is crucial for preventing breaches and attacks from external sources. A strong cybersecurity culture ensures that employees understand the importance of cybersecurity and are motivated to follow best practices.

Fatigue

The construct of fatigue is being given its own section as it can cover aspects that are aligned with psychological, situational, and dispositional factors.

- **Dispositional Fatigue**: This type of fatigue relates to an individual's predisposition to experience fatigue. For instance, individuals with chronic health conditions such as diabetes or insomnia may experience increased levels of fatigue compared to those without such conditions. Personality factors, such as low conscientiousness and high neuroticism, can also lead to higher levels of fatigue. For example, someone suffering from insomnia may experience higher levels of fatigue in turn making it difficult to stay alert and focused on potential threats that may occur. Individuals with high levels of neuroticism could feel overwhelmed by the constant threat of cyberattacks, in turn leading to quicker burnout and a reduced effectiveness in their role (Stanton et al., 2016).
- **Psychological Fatigue**: Psychological fatigue involves mental or emotional exhaustion resulting from prolonged cognitive load or high levels of emotional strain. High-pressure environments, excessive decision making, and roles requiring significant emotional involvement can exacerbate psychological fatigue. We are all faced with situations where we must make critical decisions under pressure, and this constant draw on us can soon lead to mental exhaustion. Excessive exposure to such extreme loads can in turn result in increased errors and poorer response times when it comes to threats (Nobles, 2022).
- **Situational Fatigue**: Situational fatigue arises from external pressures, such as excessive physical or mental demands. In the workplace, this could manifest as high workload levels, engaging in shift work without adequate recovery periods, poor user experiences, inter-employee disagreements, or dissatisfaction with employers. Being bombarded by constant alerts and messages can often lead to a situation of withdrawal and avoidance, meaning that people neglect important information that could prevent threats (Stanton et al., 2016).
- **Cybersecurity Fatigue**: Some researchers have noted that individuals can suffer from 'cybersecurity fatigue', which is linked to a sense of complacency, reluctance, or overload due to an overemphasis on cybersecurity principles (Calic et al., 2016; Nobles, 2022; Stanton et al., 2016). This type of fatigue is inherently linked to organisational factors, poor training, and a weak cybersecurity culture. We will discuss this in depth in Chapter 12.
- **Physiological Fatigue**: The physiological construct of fatigue is characterised by a general feeling of listlessness and a reduced capacity to exert effort (Grandjean, 1979). Mental fatigue can directly increase an individual's susceptibility to scams that exploit inattention due to tiredness. For example, 52% of individuals who fell victim to phishing attacks reported that they did so because they were feeling tired (Tessian, 2022).

Summary

This chapter introduces key factors influencing human behaviour in the context of cybersecurity, grouped by their origin of influence. Psychological factors include cognitive processes such as attention, memory, decision making, and emotion. Attention is limited and can lead to errors in cybersecurity, such as missing warnings or phishing attempts. Memory is crucial for learning and decision making, with limitations in working and long-term memory affecting behaviours like recalling passwords. Decision-making styles and cognitive biases, such as overconfidence, can lead to poor cybersecurity decisions. Emotions like fear and anger influence perception and decision making, impacting behaviours such as overestimating rare cyberattacks.

Dispositional factors examine stable personality traits that influence behaviour over time. The Big Five personality traits and the Dark Triad are discussed, highlighting their impact on cybersecurity awareness and behaviours, such as risk perception and compliance with protocols. Risk perception and risk-taking behaviours are explored, emphasizing the interaction between situational factors and personal characteristics. The concept of locus of control is introduced, explaining how beliefs about control over one's life affect cybersecurity behaviours, with those having an internal locus of control being more proactive.

Demographic factors address how population characteristics influence cybersecurity awareness and behaviour. Age differences highlight a digital divide, with younger individuals being more confident but also more susceptible to cybercrime, while older individuals may be more cautious. Gender differences in cybersecurity awareness are explored, noting that perceived self-efficacy with digital technology influences compliance, though findings are complex and varied. Cultural influences are significant, as values, norms, and ideals shape how individuals view their responsibility to follow cybersecurity rules, especially when guided by clear governance policies.

We categorise fatigue into dispositional, psychological, situational, cybersecurity, and physiological types. Dispositional fatigue is linked to individual predispositions like chronic health conditions and personality traits, leading to higher fatigue levels. Psychological fatigue results from prolonged cognitive load and emotional strain, causing mental exhaustion and increased errors. Situational fatigue arises from external pressures such as high workloads and inadequate recovery, leading to withdrawal and neglect of important information. Cybersecurity fatigue involves complacency and overload due to excessive focus on cybersecurity principles, often linked to poor training and weak organisational culture. Physiological fatigue is characterised by general tiredness and reduced effort, increasing susceptibility to scams and phishing attacks. Understanding these types helps in developing strategies to mitigate their impact on cybersecurity behaviours.

In summary, the chapter provides a comprehensive overview of individual differences that influence cybersecurity behaviours. Understanding these factors can help develop more effective strategies for enhancing cybersecurity awareness and protection.

References

Allport, G. W. (1961). *Pattern and growth in personality.* Holt, Rinehart & Winston.

Allwood, C. M., & Salo, I. (2012). Decision-making styles and stress. *International Journal of Stress Management*, 19(1), 34–47. doi:10.1037/a0027420.

Alnifie, G., & Kim, D. (2023). Overconfidence in cybersecurity: The role of optimism bias. *Journal of Cybersecurity Research*, 12(3), 234–245.

Ament, P., & Jaeger, T. (2017). Overconfidence and cybersecurity: A study of information security professionals. *Journal of Information Security*, 8(2), 123–134.

Anderson, M. C. (2003). Rethinking Interference Theory: Executive control and the mechanisms of forgetting. *Journal of Memory and Language*, 49(4), 415–445. doi:10.1016/j.jml.2003.08.006.

Anwar, M., He, W., Ash, I., Yuan, X., Li, L., & Xu, L. (2017). Gender difference and employees' cybersecurity behaviors. *Computers in Human Behavior*, 69, 437–443. doi:10.1016/j.chb.2016.12.040.

Aschwanden, R., Messner, C., Höchli, B., & Holenweger, G. (2024). Employee behavior: The psychological gateway for cyberattacks. *Organizational Cybersecurity Journal: Practice, Process and People.* doi:10.1108/ocj-02-2023-0004.

Baddeley, A. D., Eysenck, M. W., & Anderson, M. C. (2020). *Memory* (3rd ed.). Psychology Press.

Bidgoli, M., Knijnenburg, B. P., & Grossklags, J. (2016). When cybercrimes strike undergraduates. *ECrime Researchers Summit, ECrime*, 42–51. doi:10.1109/ECRIME.2016.7487948.

Blais, A.-R., & Weber, E. U. (2006). A domain-specific risk-taking (DOSPERT) scale for adult populations. *Judgement and Decision Making*, 1(1), 33–47. doi:10.1037/t13084-000.

Bleidorn, W., Schwaba, T., Zheng, A., Hopwood, C. J., Sosa, S. S., Roberts, B. W., & Briley, D. A. (2022). Personality stability and change: A meta-analysis of longitudinal studies. *Psychological Bulletin*, 148(7–8), 588–619. doi:10.1037/bul0000365.

Branley-Bell, D., Coventry, L., Dixon, M., Joinson, A., & Briggs, P. (2022). Exploring age and gender differences in ICT cybersecurity behaviour. *Human Behavior and Emerging Technologies.* doi:10.1155/2022/2693080.

Brette, R. (2022). Brains as computers: Metaphor, analogy, theory or fact? *Frontiers in Ecology and Evolution*, 10, 878729.

Brosch, T., Scherer, K. R., Grandjean, D., & Sander, D. (2013, May 14). The impact of emotion on perception, attention, memory, and decision-making. *Swiss Medical Weekly*, 143. doi:10.4414/smw.2013.13786.

Brown, A. D. (1995). *Organisational culture.* Pitman Publishing.

Brown, D. G. (1958). Sex-role development in a changing culture. *Psychological Bulletin*, 55, 232–242.

Bunting, M. F., & Cowan, N. (2005). Working memory and flexibility in the Stroop task: An individual differences investigation. *Memory & Cognition*, 33(4), 611–620.

Calic, D., Pattinson, M., Parsons, K., Butavicius, M., & McCormac, A. (2016). Naïve and accidental behaviours that compromise information security: What the experts think. In S. M. Furnell & N. L. Clarke (Eds.), *Proceedings of the 10th International Symposium of Human Aspects of Information Security and Assurance.*

CERT Insider Threat Team. (2013). *Unintentional insider threats: A foundational study (Technical Note CMU/SEI-2013-TN-022)*. Software Engineering Institute, Carnegie Mellon University. doi:10.1184/R1/6585575.v1.

CERT Insider Threat Team. (2014). *Unintentional insider threats: A review of phishing and malware incidents by economic sector (Technical Note CMU/SEI-2014-TN-007)*. Software Engineering Institute, Carnegie Mellon University. https://resources.sei.cmu.edu/asset_files/technicalnote/2014_004_001_297777.pdf.

Chaiken, S., & Trope, Y. (Eds.). (1999). *Dual-process theories in social psychology*. Guilford Press.

Christie, R., & Geis, F. (1970). *Studies in Machiavellianism*. Academic Press.

Chun, M. M., & Turk-Browne, N. B. (2007). Interactions between attention and memory. *Current Opinion in Neurobiology*, 17(2), 177–184. doi:10.1016/j.conb.2007.03.005.

Chun, M. M., Golomb, J. D., & Turk-Browne, N. B. (2011). A taxonomy of external and internal attention. *Annual Review of Psychology*, 62, 73–101. doi:10.1146/annurev.psych.093008.100427.

Clore, G. L., & Ortony, A. (2000). Cognitive appraisal theories of emotion. In M. Lewis & J. M. Haviland-Jones (Eds.), *Handbook of emotions* (2nd ed., pp. 265–285). Guilford Press.

Courage, M. L., Bakhtiar, A., Fitzpatrick, C., Kenny, S., & Brandeau, K. (2015). Growing up multitasking: The costs and benefits for cognitive development. *Developmental Review*, 35, 5–41. doi:10.1016/j.dr.2014.12.002.

Cowan, N. (1988). Evolving conceptions of memory storage, selective attention, and their mutual constraints within the human information-processing system. *Psychological Bulletin*, 104(2), 163–191.

Cowan, N., Elliott, E. M., Saults, J. S., Morey, C. C., Mattox, S., Hismjatullina, A., & Conway, A. R. A. (2024). On the capacity of attention: Its estimation and its role in working memory and cognitive aptitudes. *Cognitive Psychology*, 51(1), 42–100.

Digman, J. M. (1990). Personality structure: Emergence of the five-factor model. *Annual Review of Psychology*, 41, 417–440.

Draheim, C., Tsukahara, J. S., & Engle, R. W. (2022). Working memory capacity: A review of its definition and measurement. *Journal of Cognitive Psychology*, 34(3), 359–387.

ENISA. (2017). *Cyber security culture in organisations*. doi:10.2824/10543.

Evans, J. St. B. T., & Stanovich, K. E. (2013). Dual-process theories of higher cognition: Advancing the debate. *Perspectives on Psychological Science*, 8(3), 223–241.

Eysenck, M. W., & Keane, M. T. (1991). *Cognitive psychology: A student's handbook* (3rd ed.). Lawrence Erlbaum Associates.

Gable, P. A., & Harmon-Jones, E. (2010). The blues broaden, but the nasty narrows: Attentional consequences of negative affects low and high in motivational intensity. *Psychological Science*, 21(2), 211–215.

Gcaza, N., & von Solms, R. (2017). Cybersecurity culture: An ill-defined problem. In *10th IFIP World Conference on Information Security Education (WISE)* (pp. 98–109). Springer. doi:10.1007/978-3-319-58553-6_9.

Goldberg, L. R. (1993). The structure of phenotypic personality traits. *American Psychologist*, 48(1), 26–34.

Goldberg, L. R., Johnson, J. A., Eber, H. W., Hogan, R., Ashton, M. C., Cloninger, C. R., & Gough, H. G. (1998). The international personality item pool and the future of public-domain personality measures. *Journal of Research in Personality*, 32(1), 1–37.

Grandjean, E. (1979). Fatigue in industry. *British Journal of Industrial Medicine*, 36 (3), 175–186. doi:10.1136/oem.36.3.175.

Hadlington, L., & Chivers, S. (2018). Exploring the role of age and gender on cybersecurity behaviours. *Cyberpsychology, Behaviour, and Social Networking*, 21(2), 108–113.

Hadlington, L., Popovac, M., Janicke, H., Yevseyeva, I., & Jones, K. (2019). Exploring the role of work identity and work locus of control in information security awareness. *Computers and Security*, 81. doi:10.1016/j.cose.2018.10.006.

Hancock, P. A., & Warm, J. S. (1989). A dynamic model of stress and sustained attention. *Human Factors*, 31(5), 519–537.

Hargittai, E. (2002). Beyond logs and surveys: In-depth measures of people's web use skills. *Journal of the American Society for Information Science and Technology*, 53 (14), 1239–1244. doi:10.1002/asi.10166[1](https://apastyle.apa.org/style-grammar-guidelines/paper-format/reference-list).

Harms, P. D., & Sherman, R. A. (2021). The Dark Triad of personality: Narcissism, Machiavellianism, and psychopathy. *Annual Review of Psychology*, 72, 389–414.

Herath, T., & Rao, H. R. (2009). Encouraging information security behaviours in organisations: Role of penalties, pressures and perceived effectiveness. *Decision Support Systems*, 47(2), 154–165.

Hofstede, G. (1980). *Culture's consequences: International differences in work-related values*. Sage Publications.

Hofstede, G. (2011). Dimensionalizing cultures: The Hofstede model in context. *Online Readings in Psychology and Culture*, 2(1), 8.

Hunsaker, A., & Hargittai, E. (2018). A review of internet use among older adults. *New Media and Society*, 20(10), 3937–3954. doi:10.1177/1461444818787348.

Ifinedo, P. (2014). Information systems security policy compliance: An empirical study of the effects of socialisation, influence, and cognition. *Information & Management*, 51(1), 69–79.

James, W. (1890). *The principles of psychology* (Vols. 1 & 2). Henry Holt and Company. doi:10.1037/10538-000.

John, O. P., & Srivastava, S. (1999). The Big Five trait taxonomy: History, measurement, and theoretical perspectives. In O. P. John & R. W. Robins (Eds), *Handbook of personality: Theory and research* (2nd ed., pp. 102–138). Guilford Press.

Kahneman, D. (1973). *Attention and effort*. Prentice-Hall.

Kraemer, S., Carayon, P., & Clem, J. (2009). Human and organizational factors in computer and information security: Pathways to vulnerabilities. *Computers and Security*, 28(7), 509–520. doi:10.1016/j.cose.2009.04.006.

Kruger, J., & Dunning, D. (1999). Unskilled and unaware of it: How difficulties in recognizing one's own incompetence lead to inflated self-assessments. *Journal of Personality and Social Psychology*, 77(6), 1121–1134.

McCrae, R. R., & Costa, P. T. (2008). The five-factor theory of personality. In O. P. John, R. W. Robins, & L. A. Pervin (Eds.), *Handbook of personality: Theory and research* (3rd ed., pp. 159–181). Guilford Press.

Mendel, T., & Toch, E. (2019). My mom was getting this popup: Understanding motivations and processes in helping older relatives with mobile security and privacy. *Proceedings of the ACM on Interactive, Mobile, Wearable and Ubiquitous Technologies*, 3(4), Article147. doi:10.1145/3369821[1](https://toch.tau.ac.il/wp-content/uploads/2020/01/Mendel-Toch-2019.pdf).

Miller, G. A. (1956). The magical number seven, plus or minus two: Some limits on our capacity for processing information. *Psychological Review*, 63(2), 81–97. doi:10.1037/h0043158.

Miller, J. D., & Campbell, W. K. (2008). Comparing clinical and social-personality conceptualizations of narcissism. *Journal of Personality*, 76(3), 449–476.

Miller, J. D., Lynam, D. R., Hyatt, C. S., & Campbell, W. K. (2021). Controversies in narcissism. *Annual Review of Clinical Psychology*, 17, 291–315.

Mujawar, S., Patil, J., Chaudhari, B., & Saldanha, D. (2021). Memory: Neurobiological mechanisms and assessment. *Industrial Psychiatry Journal*, 30(Suppl 1), S311–S314. doi:10.4103/0972-6748.328839.

Müller, G. E., & Pilzecker, A. (1900). Experimentelle Beiträge zur Lehre vom Gedächtnis. *Zeitschrift für Psychologie*, 1, 1–300.

Murphy, D. H., & Castel, A. D. (2023). Age-related differences in memory when offloading important information. *Psychology and Aging*, 38(5), 415–427. doi:10.1037/pag0000750[1](https://psycnet.apa.org/doi/10.1037/pag0000750).

Nairne, J. S., & Pandeirada, J. N. S. (2008). Adaptive memory: Is survival processing special? *Journal of Memory and Language*, 59(3), 377–385. doi:10.1016/j.jml.2008.06.001.

Naveh-Benjamin, M., Craik, F. I. M., Guez, J., & Kreuger, S. (2003). Divided attention in younger and older adults: Effects of strategy and relatedness on memory performance and secondary task costs. *Journal of Experimental Psychology: Learning, Memory, and Cognition*, 29(5), 826–837.

Nobles, C. (2022). Stress, burnout, and security fatigue in cybersecurity: A human factors problem. *HOLISTICA – Journal of Business and Public Administration*, 13 (1), 49–72. doi:10.2478/hjbpa-2022-0003.

Norris, D., & Kalm, K. (2021). Chunking and data compression in verbal short-term memory. *Cognition*, 208, Article104534. doi:10.1016/j.cognition.2020.104534.

Okon-Singer, H., Hendler, T., Pessoa, L., & Shackman, A. J. (2015). The neurobiology of emotion–cognition interactions: Fundamental questions and strategies for future research. *Frontiers in Human Neuroscience*, 9, Article58. doi:10.3389/fnhum.2015.00058[1](www.frontiersin.org/journals/human-neuroscience/articles/10.3389/fnhum.2015.00058/full).

Oksanen, A., & Keipi, T. (2013). Young people as victims of crime on the internet: A population-based study in Finland. *Vulnerable Children & Youth Studies*, 8, 298–309. doi:10.1080/17450128.2012.752119.

Olschewski, S., Rieskamp, J., & Scheibehenne, B. (2023). Cognitive biases in decision making: A review and reflection. *Journal of Behavioural Decision Making*, 36(1), 1–18.

Oltramari, A., Henshel, D., Cains, M., & Hoffman, B. (2015). Towards a human factors ontology for cyber security. *CEUR Workshop Proceedings*, 1523, 26–33.

Parasuraman, R. (1979). Memory load and event rate control sensitivity decrements in sustained attention. *Science*, 205(4409), 924–927.

Parasuraman, R., & Davies, D. R. (1984). *Varieties of attention*. Academic Press.

Paulhus, D. L. (2014). Toward a taxonomy of dark personalities. *Current Directions in Psychological Science*, 23(6), 421–426. doi:10.1177/0963721414547737[1](https://psycnet.apa.org/record/2014-10974-004).

Paulhus, D. L., & Williams, K. M. (2002). The Dark Triad of personality: Narcissism, Machiavellianism, and psychopathy. *Journal of Research in Personality*, 36, 556–563. doi:10.1016/S0092-6566(02)00505-6.

Pavlova, E. (2020). Enhancing the organisational culture related to cyber security during the university digital transformation. *Information & Security: An International Journal*, 46(3), 239–249. doi:10.11610/isij.4617[1](www.isij.eu/article/enhancing-organisational-culture-related-cyber-security-during-university-digital).

Pettigrew, A. M. (1979). On studying organizational cultures. *Administrative Science Quarterly*, 24(4), 570–581. doi:10.2307/2392363[1](www.jstor.org/stable/2392363).

Prensky, M. (2001). Digital natives, digital immigrants. *On the Horizon*, 9(5), 1–6.

Prensky, M. (2007). *Digital game-based learning*. Paragon House.

Raskin, R., & Hall, C. S. (1979). A narcissistic personality inventory. *Psychological Reports*, 45(2), 590.

Reegård, K., Blackett, C., & Katta, V. (2019). The concept of cybersecurity culture. In *Proceedings of the 29th European Safety and Reliability Conference (ESREL)*. Research Publishing Services Singapore, 4036–4043. doi:10.3850/ 978-981-11-2724-3_0761-cd.

Ricker, T. J., & Hardman, K. O. (2017). The nature of short-term consolidation in visual working memory. *Journal of Experimental Psychology: General*, 146(11), 1551.

Ricker, T. J., Sandry, J., Vergauwe, E., & Cowan, N. (2020). Do familiar memory items decay? *Journal of Experimental Psychology: Learning, Memory, and Cognition*, 46(1), 60.

Robertson, I. H., Manly, T., Andrade, J., Baddeley, B. T., & Yiend, J. (1997). 'Oops!': Performance correlates of everyday attentional failures in traumatic brain injured and normal subjects. *Neuropsychologia*, 35(6), 747–758.

Rose, C. L., Murphy, L. B., Byard, L., & Nikzad, K. (2002). The role of the Big Five personality factors in vigilance performance and workload. *European Journal of Personality*, 16(3), 185–200. doi:10.1002/per.451.

Rotter, J. B. (1966). Generalized expectancies for internal versus external control of reinforcement. *Psychological Monographs: General and Applied*, 80(1), 1–28.

Scott, S. G., & Bruce, R. A. (1995). Decision-making style: The development and assessment of a new measure. *Educational and Psychological Measurement*, 55(5), 818–831.

Squire, L. R. (1992). Memory and the hippocampus: A synthesis from findings with rats, monkeys, and humans. *Psychological Review*, 99(2), 195–231. doi:10.1037/ 0033-295X.99.2.195.

Stanton, J. M., Stam, K. R., Mastrangelo, P., & Jolton, J. (2016). Analysis of end user security behaviours. *Computers & Security*, 24(2), 124–133.

Sunstein, C. R. (2003). Terrorism and probability neglect. *Journal of Risk and Uncertainty*, 26(2–3), 121–136.

Sunstein, C. R., & Zeckhauser, R. (2008). Overreaction to fearsome risks. *Environmental and Resource Economics*, 41(1), 1–23.

Tessian. (2022). *Psychology of human error*. doi:10.1016/b978-0-444-42727-4.50006-2.

Treisman, A. (1969). Strategies and models of selective attention. *Psychological Review*, 76(3), 282–299.

Tulving, E., & Psotka, J. (1971). Retroactive inhibition in free recall: Inaccessibility of information available in the memory store. *Journal of Experimental Psychology*, 87 (1), 1–8.

Tyng, C. M., Amin, H. U., Saad, M. N. M., & Malik, A. S. (2017). The influences of emotion on learning and memory. *Frontiers in Psychology*, 8. doi:10.3389/ fpsyg.2017.01454.

Underwood, B. J. (1957). Interference and forgetting. *Psychological Review*, 64(1), 49–60. doi:10.1037/h0044616[1](https://psycnet.apa.org/record/1958-00251-001).

Vargová, L., Zibrínová, Ĺ., & Baník, G. (2023). The way of making choices: Maximizing and satisficing and its relationship to well-being, personality, and self-rumination. *Judgment and Decision Making*, 15(5), 798–806. doi:10.1017/ S1930297500007932.

Weber, E. U., Blais, A.-R., & Betz, N. E. (2002). A domain-specific risk-attitude scale: Measuring risk perceptions and risk behaviors. *Journal of Behavioral Decision Making*, 15(4), 263–290. doi:10.1002/bdm.414[1](https://psycnet.apa.org/record/ 2002-06276-001).

Willcoxson, L., & Millett, B. (2000). The management of organisational culture. *Australian Journal of Management and Organisational Behaviour*, 3(2), 91–99.

Young, B., Carpenter, S., & McLeod, A. (2018). Technology threat avoidance theory: A systematic review. *Journal of Information Security and Applications*, 47, 102–115.

5

WHEN MISTAKES HAPPEN

Introduction

Human history is filled with instances where human error has led to catastrophic incidents. Researchers argue that the underlying typology of human error is fundamentally the same, regardless of the outcome, and allows us the capacity to classify and understand these errors. This capacity to classify errors offers us another opportunity; it gives us the potential to predict when and how errors might occur in complex systems, such as cybersecurity. While some researchers have previously suggested that human error is inevitable (Wood & Banks, 1993), others believe that actions can be predicted and mitigated (Reason, 1990). Revisiting the human factors approach, we can formulate aspects of human error in relation to interactions with complex systems (Strauch, 2017). According to Strauch, there are several assumptions that we can apply to exploring human error within cybersecurity. These assumptions are:

- The higher the task complexity, the more chance there is that an error will occur.
- As the number of people involved in performing a particular task increases, so too does the likelihood that an error will occur.
- People engage in rational behaviour and engage with systems in a way that avoids errors.
- Errors can be reduced, but can never be eliminated (Strauch, 2017).

This approach to exploring errors in cybersecurity highlights several key observations. Firstly, ensuring cybersecurity is a complex task for many individuals, requiring them to stay updated with various protocols, policies,

DOI: 10.4324/9781003509011-5

and rules. In an organisation, numerous individuals are responsible for cybersecurity, ideally everyone employed. According to Strauch's assumptions about errors in complex systems, this increases the likelihood of errors emerging within the system. Secondly, while we assume individuals behave rationally to protect the system and avoid errors, many cybersecurity failures stem from irrational behaviour. Despite this, the default assumption is that everyone tries their best to prevent incidents unless they have malicious intent.

Finally, a critical assumption is that errors in cybersecurity are inevitable. The goal for those of us involved in cybersecurity is to reduce the possibility of such errors occurring as much as possible. This understanding helps in developing strategies to manage and mitigate errors in complex cybersecurity environments.

What Is an Error?

Defining what exactly constitutes an error can be challenging. Reason (1990, p. 9) offered a definition, describing an error as 'a generic terms to encompass all those occasions in which a planned sequence of mental or physical activities fails to achieve its intended outcome, and when these failures cannot be attributed to the intervention of some chance agency'. This definition highlights the notion that errors occur when our intended actions go astray and fail to achieve their desired results, with these failures not down to random chance.

Senders and Moray (1991) suggested that an error is something that 'has been done which was not intended by the actor, not desired by a set of rules or an external observer, or that led the task or system outside its acceptable limits' (p. 25). Strauch (2017) offered a simpler definition and suggested that an error can simply be viewed as 'an action or decision that results in one or more unintended negative outcomes' (p. 24). This definition aligns well with many of the issues that are discussed within the context of human factors and cybersecurity. Despite some disagreement on the precise definition of what defines an error, there is a consensus that an error typically results from an intentional action that leads to an outcome different from what was originally planned (Strauch, 2017).

According to Reason (1990) the potential for human error is not as high as we might assume, and errors themselves take limited forms. Reason highlighted that errors differ in terms of their predictability, which relates to two underlying characteristics: variability and consistency. *Variable errors* highlight an inconsistency in performance which translates into a random pattern of the errors. In variable errors we explore the difference between the average or mean performance for that given task and the actual observed performance. For example, if you are playing darts and trying to hit the bullseye but instead scatter your darts across the board, this is a variable error. In contrast, *constant errors* occur when the behaviour consistently misses the target outcome in a predictable manner. For instance, if you consistently hit the number 19 instead of the bullseye, this is a clear example of a constant error.

Reason (1990) proposed that these two types of errors differ in terms of their level of predictability. In the instance of constant errors, we can usually make a good attempt at predicting where behaviour will fall – in the example of darts above, we could make the reasonable assumption that the next time we throw a dart trying to aim for the bullseye we will most probably end up hitting 19 again. However, the same cannot be said for the variable error, where we could make a basic assertion that we would hit the dart board, but making any more precise predictions about the nature of the error is not possible given what we know about the previous pattern. In turn, Reason (1990) highlights that our capacity to make sensible predictions about the nature of errors is limited to situations where we can isolate the task in hand and the nature of the task itself.

Understanding the Types of Human Error.

Reason (1990) presented a breakdown of how intention and inattention can serve to influence the type of errors we encounter.

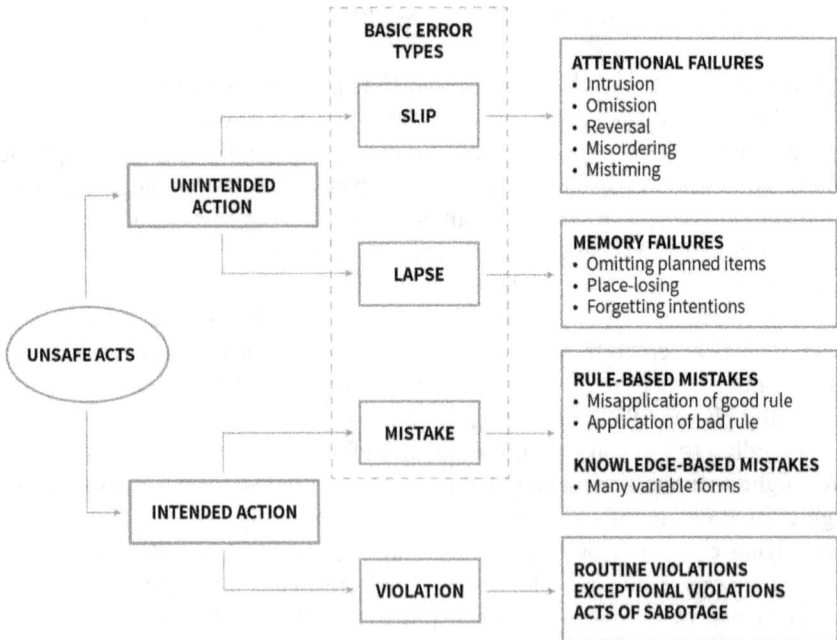

FIGURE 5.1 The Taxonomy of Unsafe Acts (adapted from Reason, 1990, p. 207)

The diagram in Figure 5.1 paves the way for exploring more classifications of human errors. One important distinction in the unsafe acts taxonomy presented by Reason (1990) is the inclusion of violations. Reason emphasised the need to distinguish between errors and violations, as both can occur together or independently. Errors such as slips, lapses, and mistakes are best viewed as failures in cognitive processes. However, some incidents arise because individuals choose to engage in behaviour that transgresses accepted social rules or norms (Reason, 1990). Reason defines a violation as 'deliberate – but not necessarily reprehensible – deviations from those practices deemed necessary... to maintain the safe operation of a potentially hazardous system' (Reason, 1990, p. 196).

Violations are further broken down into two distinct categories:

- **Routine Violations**: These are habitual actions that deviate from established practices but are often tolerated by the governing authority. In an instance where the environment is less punitive, or ignores transgressions, or fails to reward rule observance, routine violations will be more common. For example, consistently bypassing certain security protocols because they are seen as cumbersome or unnecessary.
- **Exceptional Violations**: These are isolated departures from authority, neither typical of the individual nor condoned by management. An example would be an employee taking a risky shortcut during a critical operation, which is not common practice and not approved by the organisation. These violations will usually occur when the individual believes that the situation needs such an action and will use the occurrence to justify the violation. There are a variety of ways in which such violations can occur in cybersecurity, with perhaps one of the most common ones being the use of unchecked or unrecognised websites to access data or information to complete a time-critical task; they will violate accepted cybersecurity practices in deference to getting the job done on time.

As we will discuss later in this book (Chapters 10, 11, and 12) where we explore aspects of social norms, the observed norms for behaviour in a workplace can influence the extent to which violations of acceptable behaviour occur (particularly when it comes to cybersecurity).

The Role of Prior Intent in Errors; Did We Really Mean to Do That?!

One of the key distinctions from the literature is related to how intention fits into the role of errors; we can act with or without prior intent (Reason, 1990; Searle, 1980). Actions without prior planning are carried out without conscious effort, and there is little or no planning involved. Such actions are typically those which have subsumed some level of automaticity because they have become so well practiced (typing, driving, certain forms of sport-related skills). However, there is a downside to the process of automation; whilst having a skill that has been transferred over to an automatic one reduces the cognitive burden on the individual and means we can free up essential cognitive resources to do other things, it means that errors might emerge in situations where that automatic behaviour is not appropriate, due to changes in the situation (Reason, 1990; Searle, 1980).

Research has presented two further sub-categories for intentional actions without prior attention, these being:

- **Spontaneous actions**: These actions are those that are unplanned but still have an element of intentionality attached to them. So, for example, in a situation where someone helps an individual on the street after watching them fall over; in this instance there is no prior planning involved (we had no warning that this would happen, so could not plan for the eventuality) but the action of helping has obvious intention behind it. When spontaneous actions lead us to do something that might be inappropriate for the given context this could give rise to errors. For example, in a situation where we are completing a task, updating a spreadsheet, and we get startled by a sudden, abrupt noise, the distraction might lead us to enter the incorrect information. Errors that arise from such actions are reactive in nature and usually override more systematic behaviours, and are also impacted by the nature of the environment in which they occur (e.g., high stress, high cognitive load situations) (Di Nucci, 2008).
- **Subsidiary actions**: These are component parts of the more well-practiced task that we often complete, and occur in the background without much conscious effort on the individual's end. An example of this could be the process of typing whilst authoring a report or an essay on a computer – the actual process of writing each of the words is seen as 'subsidiary' to the main task itself (Di Nucci, 2008).

Non-Intentional Voluntary Actions

Many of the behaviours we engage in daily involve a variety of automatic processes. For example, getting out of bed, engaging in daily bathroom rituals, turning on the radio, and commuting to the office all involve subsidiary actions like opening and closing doors, moving things around, and switching things on and off. These actions are carried out without conscious deliberation or attention, often due to habits, well-learned routines, or implicit behaviours like driving. Despite the lack of conscious thought, these actions are still intentional. According to Pashler (1998), automatic processes are practiced operations that operate without excessive demands on our cognitive resources, reducing the chance of interfering with other tasks. They occur outside of our voluntary control, and if the necessary conditions for the process are met in the environment, these actions happen irrespective of our conscious desire to perform them. This has important implications for discussions about human error, as it removes the notion of intentionality from certain automatic processes that individuals may be predisposed to engage in, especially when there is sufficient opportunity to do so. As we will explore in Chapter 13, social engineers often employ a set of tactics to ensure the triggering of automatic processes in their victims, often getting individuals to follow social norms or instructions from those in authority.

Reason (1990) argued that errors can only be applied to intentional actions where the individual fails to reach their desired outcome. An error arises when there is a mismatch between the intended action and the actual action performed. Without intentionality, Reason suggested that the behaviour observed is better categorised as a reflex to a given situation rather than an error. However, other researchers have noted that errors can still occur due to the automatic engagement of behaviours, particularly when they are applied incorrectly. For example, Norman (1981) and Rasmussen (1986) highlighted that automatic behaviours, which are typically efficient and reduce cognitive load, can lead to errors when they are not appropriate for the given context. Kahneman (2011) also discussed how automatic processes, or 'System 1' thinking, can result in biases and errors due to their reliance on heuristics and quick judgments (see Chapter 5). Reason (1997) later acknowledged that routine aspects could be implicated in errors, recognizing that even well-practiced and automatic behaviours can lead to mistakes when the context changes or when there is a lapse in attention. This broader understanding of errors includes both intentional actions and automatic processes, emphasizing the need to consider the role of routine and automaticity in human error.

The Types of Errors That Can Emerge

As noted in Figure 5.1 there are a variety of errors that Reason (1990) and others have classified (e.g., Norman, 1981). These are classified in terms of the way in which they emerge from their respective cognitive processes.

Slips

Reason (1990) suggested that slips are a fundamental result of a misfire in the execution stage (the 'doing' bit) of the sequence. A slip occurs when there is a clear failure in the way an action or plan has been executed. The individual has the correct intention to carry out an action but fails to execute it correctly.

Example: Bob is preparing an email with an attachment that contains a list of people who are at risk of being made redundant in a next round of cost-saving exercises. However, during the preparation of the email, Bob accidentally clicks on a name that should not be in the list because they have a similar name to someone that should be on the list (e.g., Smyth instead of Smith). The accidental recipient is on the list of people who are down to be made redundant and decides to leak the list to the rest of the organisation. In this instance the plan is correct (authoring the email), but the error occurs when the individual comes to send it out, perhaps because of a lapse in attention or the mismatch between intended and performed actions (Reason, 1990).

Lapses

Lapses are usually the result of a failure in memory, meaning that we fail to complete an action fully, or we inadvertently omit part of the task itself. This might mean that we skip a step in an action sequence, or we fail to carry out the planned action completely. There are many examples we could give for this one, such as forgetting to put a tea bag in the cup when making a drink; not locking the door when leaving the house; not switching off a light switch or the kitchen hob. All these examples share a common aspect, that being we have not completed the task incorrectly, we have just failed to complete the task itself (Reason, 1990).

   Example: Cybersecurity has an abundance of examples where lapses come into play when it comes to human failures. For example, you get a notification on your phone to tell you that your password has been compromised, and you need to change it immediately. You decide to have a quick look at the information, but part way through changing the password you get another notification from one of your friends to tell you that the band tickets you have been waiting for are now on sale, so you forget what you are doing and get the tickets ordered. A few weeks later you find out that one of your accounts with the compromised password has been used to purchase some expensive products that you have not ordered. In this example the error is the result of memory failure where the action (of updating your password) has been omitted or forgotten. The interruption from the other notification or task means that we lose track of our progress in the action sequence, and therefore it becomes harder to resume that task.

Mistakes

Mistakes are defined as a deficiency or failure in our judgement process when selecting an objective for our actions or in the process of selecting how to achieve that objective. Mistakes occur because we have made a decision that is based on flawed judgement (e.g., because of a cognitive bias, see Chapter 6) or because of some misunderstanding/misinterpretation (Reason, 1990). So, in the instance of mistakes, the aspect of the action sequence that is flawed is the underlying planning process, and the mistake occurs long before the action sequence is carried out. Deciding to mow the lawn when it is about to rain is a fundamental mistake and is inherently due to you not considering the current environmental conditions. Deciding to go left versus right at the next junction because you think it is a quicker route to your destination, but instead it results in you taking a longer detour, is another mistake that has occurred due to faulty judgements.

There are a variety of forms mistakes can take based on the underlying mechanisms that the error can be attributed to:

- Rule-based mistakes: These occur when an individual applies a known rule or procedure in an inappropriate context, often under the assumption that it is the correct course of action. These errors are not due to a lack of knowledge, but rather a misapplication of existing knowledge. A common example can be drawn from public behaviour during the COVID-19 pandemic. As government guidelines evolved rapidly, people were required to wear face masks in some settings but not in others. This inconsistency led to confusion, and some individuals continued to apply outdated rules – such as wearing masks in places where it was no longer required or, conversely, forgetting to wear them where it was still mandated. These mistakes were not necessarily due to negligence, but rather the result of relying on previously learned rules that no longer applied, highlighting how rule-based errors can emerge from well-intentioned but contextually inappropriate actions. In cybersecurity an example of a rule-based mistake could be an administrator configuring a system using an outdated protocol that they believe to be the most secure and up-to-date option. However, because the configuration is out of date, it leaves the system vulnerable to more recent threats.
- Knowledge-based mistakes: These occur when the individual does not have the correct or sufficient level of knowledge to apply to the situation they find themselves in, thus leading to errors. This is different to rule-based mistakes, where the individual has the knowledge but applies it incorrectly to the current situation; here the individual lacks knowledge. Setting about rewiring a plug without the relevant knowledge or skillset can be an interesting (by interesting we mean 'potentially life threatening') mistake to make if it goes wrong. Similarly, if you find yourself in another country and you do not have any basic information about the culture and etiquette when it comes to interacting with the local population, you could also find yourself making some fundamental knowledge-based mistakes. In the instance of cybersecurity an example of a knowledge-based mistake could be an individual falling foul of a phishing attack because they do not have the correct knowledge and information to allow them to deal with the situation. They erroneously believe that the email that they have received is legitimate and click on the link contained within it, inadvertently downloading malware to their work computer.

- Misapplication of heuristics: In instances where we place a heavy reliance on heuristic-based processing there is a good chance mistakes will occur, usually because we have applied them to the incorrect situation. For example, we assume that the train we normally catch will be on time today even though there is severe weather and high wind, because it has been on time in the weeks leading up to this point. However, because of the severe weather the train is delayed, and we end up being late to work. We have misapplied the heuristic that tells us that the occurrence of an event is usually representative of the sequence of events that have preceded it (since trains have been running on time, they should run on time today), failing to adequately adjust based on new information. Based on previous experiences an individual could assume that they may not become the victim of a phishing attack (they have not encountered one previously, so assume that they will not in future), therefore leaving themselves less prepared and more vulnerable to phishing attacks.

Active Versus Latent Errors

There is another set of errors that can emerge within complex systems, and these are categorised in terms of their temporal impact on the system in which they occur:

Active errors: These errors take effect immediately after occurring, such as someone accidentally switching off a critical system (Rasmussen & Pedersen, 1984; Reason, 1990). There are a wide range of active errors that can emerge in the context of cybersecurity that can and do have an immediate impact on the cybersecurity posture of the organisation. Some of these we have already mentioned elsewhere in this section, but to summarise:

- Clicking on a link within a phishing email.
- Sharing login details with colleagues.
- Attempting to circumvent existing security protocols.
- Sending an email to the wrong person with a particularly sensitive attachment.

In each of these cases, the impact of the error can be felt within the organisation almost immediately and will result in some form of malware being installed on the host computer.

Latent Errors: These types of errors take longer to have an impact, and these are referred to as latent errors (Rasmussen & Pedersen, 1984; Reason, 1990). Reason (1990) employed an analogy that likened the existence of latent errors to the study of human pathology and illness. He suggested that latent failures within complex systems are like the existence of a pathogen within the human body. The pathogen (for example some form of tumour) could lie dormant for many years before it appears as a threat to the system (the human) in which it exists. Similarly, in terms of man-made systems, there are a variety of potential mechanisms that could serve to damage the system but remain hidden until something triggers their appearance. This could include an individual responding to a phishing email or entering personal information on an unsecured website. The repercussions of this are not immediately obvious, and the details may be used in a later hack or social engineering attack.

Reason (1990) details several historical incidents where latent errors have been a contributing factor, including the Three Mile Island Incident, Chernobyl, and the King's Cross underground fire. In each of these incidents, the root causes of the disasters in question were in existence long before the event itself took place.

In terms of cybersecurity, latent errors are a lot harder to spot, but when you start to look for them you can easily identify them. They are usually a result of long-term issues linked to poor cybersecurity culture and training, meaning that employees lack a full understanding of the current threat landscape. For example, an organisation could have out-of-date training that lacks depth, and has no objective outcome measures or an effective way of evaluating its effectiveness. If such training has been provided to fulfil an organisational requirement (e.g., as part of an accreditation requirement) and has been underfunded, there is a real threat that employees could miss new and emerging threats. Another latent error that can emerge in organisational cybersecurity is a clear over-reliance on specialists in cybersecurity to deal with threats and incidents. Many medium and large organisations have dedicated IT departments that are employed to deal with most major incidents and issues when it comes to cybersecurity. However, this tendency for employees to devolve responsibility to specialists in the area means that they are feeding into an aspect of moral disengagement (see Chapter 11) and offload their personal responsibility for dealing with issues that might arise. Such a situation means that individuals are less likely to try to spot issues and may also be taking more risks in their daily work activities, hence leading to a potential breach in cybersecurity.

Situational Awareness

Situational awareness (SA) has often been discussed in terms of its role in human error and has a wide variety of applications across multiple different environmental and systems contexts (Endsley, 1995). This is one of those terms that crops up a lot in systems that require an individual to keep abreast of all current 'states' of the system and its current level of functioning. This might sound a little abstract when it comes to applications surrounding cybersecurity, but it refers to the individuals' capacity to keep track of their current tasks and maintain enough awareness to cope with additional demands that come in. Think of SA as our current level of knowledge or understanding related to our work environment and how it might change over time or be impacted by additional factors (e.g., more work, increased noise, more people). SA is vital because it guides our decision-making processes, ensuring we have all the necessary facts and information to make correct decisions.

Siponen (2000, 2001) noted that without adequate SA individuals are more likely to make errors and misinterpret cybersecurity policies. Various researchers have explored cybersecurity SA (Evesti et al., 2017; Gutzwiller et al., 2020; Onwubiko, 2022; Rajivan & Cooke, 2017; Tianfield, 2017). Much of this work focuses on how cybersecurity teams can enhance SA to improve their decision making during critical incidents and maintain awareness across multiple platforms and attack vectors. Although there is limited material applying SA to individual employees within the workplace, it remains relevant. We will explore existing theories to see how they can be applied to a cybersecurity awareness context.

Endsley's Three Tier Model for SA

The original three-tier model of SA developed by Endsley (1995) was originally developed in aviation and concerns activities such as establishing the current state of the aircraft (pitch, air speed, direction etc.) or understanding attention in air traffic control. However, since its initial inception, the model has been adopted and modified to apply to a wide variety of situations where there is an appreciable element for the protection of human life or security. Recently, researchers have started to explore how SA can be applied to cybersecurity (Evesti et al., 2017; Franke & Brynielsson, 2014; Tianfield, 2017). Most of these frameworks focus on high level, organisational cybersecurity SA rather than that of the individuals. If anything, this is one area where more work needs to be conducted to explore how SA fits into a more generic cybersecurity framework.

Endsley's (1988, 1995) conceptualisation for SA is arranged in a hierarchical fashion, with each stage being necessary to move through to get to the next stage.

Level 1 SA: Perception of the Elements Within the Environment

This is the initial information gathering stage for SA to be achieved, and requires, at least, the perception of information about the environment in which the current task is being performed. At the most basic level of perception, individuals engage with elements in the task environment without interpreting or analysing them. This stage is primarily concerned with recognition and placement and not with understanding meaning or implications. It involves identifying objects, cues, or signals and positioning them appropriately within the context of the task, often based on routine or habit.

For example, a person might notice a flashing light on a control panel and press a corresponding button without fully processing why the light is flashing or what it signifies. From a cybersecurity viewpoint, there are several ways a failure in Level 1 SA could be evident, for example:

- **Phishing Emails**: An employee fails to recognise a phishing email because they have not been informed about the latest phishing techniques.
- **Suspicious Emails**: An employee overlooks a suspicious email due to distractions or high workload.
- **Routine Protocols**: An employee forgets to log out of a secure system, leaving it vulnerable to unauthorised access.

In each of these cases, there is an inherent issue related to the individual's acknowledgement of the potential threats within their immediate environment.

Level 2 SA: Comprehension of the Current Situation

Comprehension typically follows the initial stage of basic perception, where elements in the environment are detected and recognised. However, comprehension does not automatically occur, or happen reliably. It involves integrating perceived information to form a meaningful understanding of the current situation. When this stage is incomplete or fails to occur due to cognitive overload, distractions, or misinterpretation, situational awareness can break down or remain underdeveloped. This explains why individuals may perceive elements in their environment but still fail to grasp their significance or the implications, leading to errors in judgment or decision-making. Comprehension of the perceived elements within the task environment is critically important if the individual is to be able to understand what each of the components are and if they have a current impact on what is currently going on within the system. So, this would mean moving beyond the capacity to perceive the threat presented in the first level of SA and trying to understand why the thing they are engaging with presents a threat, and the possible ramifications of engaging with that threat further. Failures at this level of SA could include elements such as:

- **Misinterpreting Threats**: An employee with limited cybersecurity training fails to understand the significance of a detected threat.
- **Over-Reliance on Automated Responses**: Relying solely on automated security tools without verifying the nature of the alerts which in turn could lead to missed threats.
- **A Superficial Analysis of Current Threats**: An employee fails to fully investigate a potential security breach, and erroneously assumes that it is just a minor issue, in turn missing a potentially more serious threat.

In each of these cases the error comes about because the individual fails to go beyond the initial information that has been provided to them and carries out just a basic interpretation of the source information.

Level 3 SA: Prediction of Future States

The highest level for SA; represents the capacity of the individual to be able to accurately predict the possible results of the decisions they make within the task environment. Decision making for cybersecurity is all about what will happen if we take a certain action with many of the critical failings being due to an individual not making the right predictions about how things will play out within the cybersecurity infrastructure. For example, if an individual can see that a social engineering attack could lead to a data leak, they may be more likely to engage in measures that will prevent the attack from taking place in the first place. In order to achieve this final level of SA for cybersecurity the individual would need to have a wide appreciation of the decision-making environment and be able to clearly understand how cyberattacks could evolve into critical incidents; such a capability obviously rests in the effectiveness of the training individuals receive, and how they view their position within the rest of the cybersecurity decision-making infrastructure. Some examples of failures that can occur at this, the highest level of SA, could include:

- **A Lack of Consideration for the Consequences of a Data Breach**: An employee underestimates the potential impact of a data breach, leading to both inadequate preventive measures and reporting of incidents.
- **Lack of Prediction of Future Threats**: This often occurs when individuals fail to predict how a minor security lapse could evolve into a major incident.
- **Misunderstanding the Evolving Challenges**: Not anticipating how changes in the cybersecurity landscape (e.g., new attack vectors) could affect the organisation.

Application to Cybersecurity

As mentioned above, much of the work that relates to SA has come from an aviation and military background where maintaining a broad appraisal of the immediate environment and its moving parts is critical. Jones and Endsley (1996) explored the factors that were linked to errors in SA, breaking them down according to the respective levels of SA. A massive 76% of the failures were noted at the very first level of SA, and related to a lack of information, a lack of interpretable information, information not being observed, information being misinterpreted, or memory errors (e.g., disruptions to routine activities, high cognitive workloads, and distractions. An additional 20% of errors were noted at Level 2 SA where individuals failed to comprehend the situation, mostly related to a lack of experience with the task environment, or an over-reliance on automated systems. At Level 3 SA, 3% of the errors were attributed to an over-reaching projection for the current situation, meaning that operators were more likely to have an incomplete understanding of the potential future trend that could arise from their current decisions. There is no reason to expect the errors experienced in cybersecurity SA to be vastly different from these types of errors, and we can hypothesise that aspects such as failures in the perception of the situation would be high on the list.

Enhancing SA for Cybersecurity Awareness

Much of the work on SA focuses directly on the point where the human operator interacts with the system, through various interfaces (Baxter & Bass, 1998; Reason, 1990). However, researchers in the field of human error have noted that factors outside this interaction can impact the connection between humans and systems. These factors include things such as organisational culture, work pressures, and job stressors (Baxter & Bass, 1998).

Strauch (2017) identified five underlying factors which serve to directly influence an individual's situation awareness; these are:

- Expertise

The more time someone spends engaged in using a system, the more expertise they gain and therefore need to expend fewer resources to achieve situation awareness. Researchers have noted that experts have far more advanced capabilities in hazard perception and recognition compared to novices (Durso & Dattel, 2006; Strauch, 2017). This is an important consideration for SA in the context of cybersecurity, and Strauch (2017) noted that training can provide an effective strategy to bridge the gap in expertise and allow individuals to practice their responses to unexpected situations.

- Expectancies

This relates to what the operator expects from the system. Where the system does not meet these expectations, crucial aspects of SA can be missed (Strauch, 2017). This can also mean operators can often misread cues, making it difficult to change their initial SA. For example, focusing solely on phishing emails might cause them to overlook other threats like social engineering. Similarly, where an employee is focused solely on threats that are directed at them from an external source, they will be less likely to expect potential signs of an insider threat. In this instance there is a need to create a programme of adaptive training which covers a wide range of threats and reduces the chance of employees adopting tunnel vision when it comes to threat perception.

- Workload and Attention

As we have seen in previous chapters, the influence of attention and workload on an individual's capacity to stay abreast of all the current developments in their immediate environment cannot be underestimated. High workloads can easily overwhelm an individual, limiting their ability to notice any potential threats. Conversely, low workloads can lead to a state of complacency, meaning that they fail to attend to relevant cues within their current environment, meaning that they miss essential information relevant to current SA. Although this might be easier said than done in a lot of high-pressure work environments, we would encourage the need for balanced workloads, as well as clear mechanisms that allow for effective management of attention in the workplace. Reducing extraneous interruptions by reducing the number of potential alert pathways (e.g., by using just email for communication, rather than a combination of email and instant messenger) is one potential route organisations could explore.

- Automaticity

Continued practice of a task can lead it to become automatic, requiring less attention and time to completing that task. Whilst this might be beneficial for routine tasks, automaticity can reduce the capacity to notice additional cues that require a response. For example, replying to emails whilst drafting a report might lead to the individual missing the signs of a potential phishing attack. There are only so many ways we can combat automaticity in skills, mainly because they are so deeply engrained it becomes inherently hard to not carry them out automatically. Strategies to enhance SA could include highlighting the potential consequences of not fully paying attention to the entire work environment and incorporating periodic, engaging hazard perception games to help employees identify threats that might be overlooked when they are deeply focused on their tasks.

- Goals

The outcome for our current task serves to have a direct influence on what information we obtain to fulfil our current SA. Focusing on specific goals can in turn narrow our attention, which in turn means that we are missing external cues that could indicate a potential threat. Ensure that goals are aligned with a comprehensive SA practice to avoid such a narrow focus.

One of the most often presented mechanisms to reduce errors within systems is improving operator awareness (Safa & Maple, 2016). Aligned with this approach is a clear programme of keeping employees updated on key threats they might encounter and integrating such processes into the organisation's culture (Safa & Maple, 2016). Since errors are often linked to poor

SA, one potential pathway to reduce the incidence of such errors is to explore how to enhance the process of obtaining SA.

As Strauch (2017) noted, obtaining SA from the current task environment is not just limited to system alerts and displays. Individuals often rely on other methods to keep abreast of developments within the system, such as talking to colleagues about current events or things they might need to be aware of. Individuals also explore other sources of information that sit outside the current environment to help them understand what is currently going on. We have highlighted some suggested mechanism that we think could help enhance SA in the workplace, and they could help individuals become more aware of the potential issues that might occur.

1. **Group Discussions and Noticeboards**

Having regular team meetings in which employees discuss their experience of recent cybersecurity incidents and share their insights on potential threats can be a great mechanism for getting people engaged in more effective SA. Not only does it give employees a chance to discuss things that might be worrying them, but it also allows organisations to explore any common issues that might be emerging. Noticeboards or digital dashboards can display current threat alerts and best practices. Employing these mechanisms can help keep employees informed and vigilant, enhancing their ability to recognise and respond to threats.

2. **Alerts and Periodic Messages**

Many organisations already implement systems that send periodic alerts and messages about potential scams and current threats to their users. This type of messaging, which can be delivered via email, intranet, or mobile apps, means that end users are kept informed about emerging threats, which in turn updates their current knowledge, enhancing current SA. Regular reminders help maintain a high level of SA and can serve to prompt employees to stay vigilant against evolving threats.

3. **Regular Training Programmes**

Engaging in a process of regular training sessions covering the latest phishing techniques, social engineering tactics, and other cybersecurity threats again serves to enhance all levels of SA. As we note in the final chapter of the book, training can often be implemented in a very ad hoc, ineffectual way, so we would always suggest exercising a word of caution when it comes to going down this route. However, the use of interactive training modules and relevant simulations can make learning more engaging. In turn training enhances employees' expertise and experience, enabling them to better recognise and respond to suspicious activities.

4. **Hazard Perception Games**

Not only are games fun, but they can be a more adaptive way of engaging employees in developing awareness about current threats which moves away from the very mundane strategies often employed within organisations. By developing engaging hazard perception games that simulate various cybersecurity scenarios employees can practice identifying threats in a controlled, gamified environment. Such games can improve employees' threat perception skills and make them more adept at spotting potential issues in real-world situations, filling the gap between the novice and the expert.

5. **Clear Communication Channels**

In our opinion, this must be one of the most overlooked aspects of cybersecurity within an organisation, with employees confused about how and who they report suspicious activity to. Other researchers have noted that the pathways to report cybersecurity incidents can often be confusing and obscured to the end user (Haney & Lutters, 2018; Tiainen, 2021). By establishing clear communication channels for reporting suspicious activities and sharing information about potential threats, organisations can significantly enhance their overall cybersecurity posture. These channels encourage timely reporting, foster a culture of vigilance, and ensure that critical information is disseminated quickly to the appropriate personnel. This proactive approach not only helps in early detection and response to threats but also supports continuous learning and adaptation across the organisation.

Summary

This chapter delves into the pervasive nature of human error throughout history, emphasizing its role in catastrophic incidents. Researchers argue that the typology of human error remains fundamentally consistent, allowing for classification and understanding. This classification aids in predicting and mitigating errors in complex systems like cybersecurity. While some researchers suggest that human error is inevitable, others believe that actions can be predicted and mitigated. Revisiting the human factors approach, Strauch (2017) outlines several assumptions about human error in cybersecurity: higher task complexity increases the likelihood of errors, more people involved in a task raises the chances of errors, people generally engage in rational behaviour to avoid errors, and errors can be reduced but never eliminated.

We explore the definition of errors, with Reason (1990) describing them as failures in planned sequences of activities that cannot be attributed to chance. Senders and Moray (1991) define errors as unintended actions that deviate from desired outcomes or rules. Strauch (2017) simplifies this by viewing errors as actions or decisions leading to unintended negative outcomes. Despite differing definitions, there is consensus that errors typically result from intentional actions that lead to unintended outcomes. Reason (1990) highlighted that errors differ in predictability, categorised into variable and constant errors. Variable errors are inconsistent and random, while constant errors are predictable and consistent. Understanding these types of errors helps in predicting and mitigating them in complex systems.

We further explore the literature that classifies human errors into slips, lapses, and mistakes. Slips occur when there is a failure in executing a correct intention, lapses result from memory failures, and mistakes arise from flawed judgment or decision-making processes. Violations, distinct from errors, are deliberate deviations from accepted practices, categorised into routine and exceptional violations. The role of prior intent in errors is also discussed, distinguishing between actions with and without prior planning. Actions without prior planning, often automatic, can lead to errors when the automatic behaviour is inappropriate for the situation. Spontaneous actions and subsidiary actions are sub-categories of intentional actions without prior planning.

The chapter also examines active and latent errors. Active errors have immediate effects, while latent errors take longer to manifest and are often hidden until triggered by specific conditions. Latent errors in cybersecurity can result from poor cybersecurity culture and training, leading to a lack of understanding of the threat landscape.

Situational awareness (SA) is crucial in understanding and mitigating human error. Endsley's three-tier model of SA, originally developed for aviation, is applied to cybersecurity. The model includes perception of elements in the environment, comprehension of the current situation, and prediction of future states. Failures in SA at any level can lead to errors in cybersecurity.

To enhance SA in cybersecurity, the chapter suggests strategies such as group discussions, noticeboards, alerts, periodic messages, regular training programmes, hazard perception games, and clear communication channels. These strategies aim to keep employees informed, engaged, and vigilant, thereby reducing the risk of human error in cybersecurity.

Overall, the chapter emphasises the inevitability of human error but highlights the importance of understanding, predicting, and mitigating errors through improved SA and targeted strategies. By addressing these factors, organisations can enhance their cybersecurity posture and better protect against evolving threats.

References

Baxter, G. D., & Bass, E. J. (1998). Human error revisited: Some lessons for situation awareness. *Proceedings – 4th Annual Symposium on Human Interaction with Complex Systems, HICS 1998*, 81–87. doi:10.1109/HUICS.1998.659960.

Di Nucci, E. (2008). *Mind out of action: The intentionality of automatic actions* (PhD dissertation). University of Edinburgh.

Durso, F. T., & Dattel, A. R. (2006). Expertise and transportation. In by K. A. Ericsson, N. Charness, P. J. Feltovich, & R. R. Hoffman (Eds), *The Cambridge handbook of expertise and expert performance* (pp. 355–371). Cambridge University Press. doi:10.1017/CBO9780511816796.020.

Endsley, M. R. (1988). Design and evaluation for situation awareness enhancement. *Proceedings of the Human Factors Society 32nd Annual Meeting*, 97–101. doi:10.1109/CyberSA.2017.8073386.

Endsley, M. R. (1995). *Toward a theory of situation awareness in dynamic systems.* *Human Factors*, 37(1), 32–64.

Evesti, A., Kanstrén, T., & Frantti, T. (2017). Cybersecurity situational awareness taxonomy. In IEEE (Eds), *2017 International Conference on Cyber Situational Awareness, Data Analytics and Assessment (Cyber SA)* (pp. 1–8). IEEE.

Franke, U., & Brynielsson, J. (2014). *Cyber situational awareness: A systematic review of the literature.* *Computers & Security*, 46, 18–31.

Gutzwiller, R. S., Sawyer, B. D., & Hancock, P. A. (2020). The impact of automation on human performance in cybersecurity: A review. *Human Factors*, 62(2), 220–232. doi:10.1177/0018720819872899.

Haney, J. M., & Lutters, W. G. (2018). 'It's scary... it's confusing... it's dull': How cybersecurity advocates overcome negative perceptions of security. *Proceedings of the 2018 CHI Conference on Human Factors in Computing Systems*, 1–12.

Jones, D. G., & Endsley, M. R. (1996). Sources of situation awareness errors in aviation. *Aviation, Space, and Environmental Medicine*, 67(6), 507–512.

Kahneman, D. (2011). *Thinking, fast and slow.* Farrar, Straus and Giroux.

Norman, D. A. (1981). Categorization of action slips. *Psychological Review*, 88(1), 1–15. doi:10.1037/0033-295X.88.1.1.

Onwubiko, C. (2022). *Cyber situational awareness: A systematic review of the literature.* *Computers & Security*, 46, 18–31.

Pashler, H. E. (1998). *The psychology of attention.* MIT Press.

Rajivan, P., & Cooke, N. (2017). Impact of team collaboration on cybersecurity situational awareness. In P. Liu, S. Jajodia, & C. Wang (Eds.), *Theory and models for cyber situation awareness* (pp. 203–226). Springer. doi:10.1007/978-3-319-61152-5_8.

Rasmussen, J. (1986). *Information Processing and Human-Machine Interaction: An Approach to Cognitive Engineering.* North-Holland.

Rasmussen, J., & Pedersen, O. M. K. (1984). Human factors in probabilistic risk analysis and in risk management. In IAEA (Eds), *Proceedings of the operational safety of nuclear power plants* (Vol. 1, pp. 181–194). International Atomic Energy Agency.

Reason, J. (1990). *Human error.* Cambridge University Press.

Reason, J. (1997). *Managing the risks of organisational accidents.* Ashgate.

Safa, N. S., & Maple, C. (2016). Human errors in the information security realm – and how to fix them. *Computer Fraud and Security, 2016*(9), 17–20. doi:10.1016/S1361-3723(16)30073-30072.

Searle, J. R. (1980). Minds, brains, and programs. *Behavioural and Brain Sciences*, 3 (3), 417–424.

Senders, J. W., & Moray, N. P. (1991). *Human error: Cause, prediction and reduction.* Lawrence Erlbaum Associates.

Siponen, M. T. (2000). A conceptual foundation for organizational information security awareness. *Information Management & Computer Security*, 8(1), 31–41.

Siponen, M. T. (2001). An analysis of the traditional IS security approaches: Implications for research and practice. *European Journal of Information Systems*, 10(3), 189–198.

Strauch, B. (2017). *Investigating human error: Incidents, accidents, and complex systems* (2nd ed.). CRC Press. doi:10.1201/9781315589749.

Tiainen, T. (2021). *Cyber security services reporting framework.* April. www.theseus.fi/handle/10024/497369%0Awww.theseus.fi/bitstream/handle/10024/497369/Tiainen_Teemu.pdf?sequence=2.

Tianfield, H. (2017). Cyber situational awareness: A systematic review of the literature. *Computers & Security*, 46, 18–31.

Wood, C. W., & Banks, W. W. (1993). Human error: an overlooked but significant information security problem. *Computers & Security*, 12, 51–60.

6
COGNITIVE PITFALLS AND CYBERSECURITY

Introduction

There is a substantial body of work within psychology that explores how humans make decisions under uncertainty. These decisions span everyday activities, from choosing what to wear based on a quick glance at the weather forecast to deciding how much money to invest based on past market behaviours and potential forecasts. Researchers such as Tversky and Kahneman (1974), suggest that when faced with such decisions, we make subjective assessments of the likelihood of events based on how easily we can recall similar past occurrences or recognise patterns in sequences of events. Crucially, the amount of effort and mental energy we exert in making these decisions is limited by our cognitive resources, as highlighted in Chapter 4.

Researchers distinguish between two types of cognitive processing that occur when making decisions (Chaiken & Trope, 1999; Evans & Stanovich, 2013; Kahneman, 2011). These decisions span various situations, such as judging the validity of an argument, forming an impression of a person, or determining the best route to work. Dual-processing theories have been applied across multiple areas within psychology, including learning, decision making, social cognition, and reasoning (Frankish, 2010). Common to all these decisions is the uncertainty surrounding the outcome and the myriad of factors that can influence the decision-making process. For instance, deciding on a route to work involves considering adverse weather conditions, traffic, road works, or accidents.

These theories, often referred to as dual-processing or dual-systems theories, suggest two underlying processing routes for decisions with uncertain outcomes. The heuristic-systematic model (Chaiken & Trope, 1999; Chen et al., 1999) distinguishes between heuristic (Type 1) and systematic (Type 2)

DOI: 10.4324/9781003509011-6

processing. Type 1 processing is fast, automatic, and intuitive, relying on heuristics or mental shortcuts. It is efficient but prone to biases and errors. Type 2 processing, on the other hand, is slow, deliberate, and analytical, requiring more cognitive effort and resources. It is less susceptible to biases but can be time-consuming and mentally taxing. Understanding these pathways and their implications is crucial for improving decision-making processes, particularly in contexts like cybersecurity, where the stakes are high, and the potential for human error is significant. By recognizing the limitations and strengths of each processing type, individuals and organisations can develop strategies to mitigate cognitive biases and enhance decision-making accuracy.

The first part of this chapter explores the key differences between these two types of processing and examines the trade-offs involved in using one over the other. By understanding the dual-processing framework, we can better appreciate how decisions are made under uncertainty and how to optimise our decision-making strategies to reduce errors and improve outcomes.

Type 1: Heuristic or Inductive Processing

Type 1 processing is fast, automatic, and requires minimal cognitive effort compared to Type 2 processing (Evans & Stanovich, 2013). This type of processing relies heavily on heuristics, which are mental shortcuts or rules of thumb that simplify complex decision-making processes (Tversky & Kahneman, 1974). These heuristics allow us to make quick judgments without engaging in extensive deliberation, making Type 1 processing highly efficient in terms of speed and cognitive resources.

However, the reliance on heuristics in Type 1 processing comes with significant drawbacks. One of the primary concerns is how we use existing information and past experiences to shape our decisions. Since Type 1 processing is intuitive and fast, it often draws on readily available memories and experiences that seem relevant to the current situation. This can be beneficial when past experiences are accurate and applicable, but it can also lead to errors when those experiences are biased or not entirely relevant. For example, if an individual has previously encountered a phishing email that was poorly constructed and easily identifiable, they might develop a heuristic that all phishing emails are similarly obvious. This heuristic could lead them to overlook more sophisticated phishing attempts, thereby increasing their vulnerability to cyberattacks. The fast and intuitive nature of Type 1 processing means that these decisions are made quickly, often without thorough analysis, which can result in overconfidence and a failure to recognise potential threats.

Moreover, Type 1 processing is susceptible to various cognitive biases. For instance, the availability heuristic can cause individuals to overestimate the likelihood of events that are more memorable or recent, even if they are statistically rare. Similarly, the representativeness heuristic can lead to judgments based on how closely something matches a prototype, rather than on actual probabilities. These biases can skew decision making and lead to systematic errors.

In summary, while Type 1 processing offers the advantage of speed and efficiency, it is also prone to biases and errors due to its reliance on heuristics and past experiences. Understanding these limitations is crucial for improving decision-making processes, particularly in high-stakes environments like cybersecurity. By being aware of the potential pitfalls of Type 1 processing, individuals and organisations can take steps to mitigate these risks and enhance the accuracy of their decisions.

Type 2: Systematic, Deductive Processing

Type 2 processing is deliberate, analytical, and demands considerable mental effort from the individual. This mode of decision making involves taking the time to assess all given alternatives and options before arriving at a final decision. For example, one of the authors describes the process of purchasing white goods, which involves trawling through endless online reviews, assessing their credibility, comparing different specifications and price options, and ultimately making a decision – often followed by buyer's remorse. This example illustrates the extensive cognitive effort and time required for Type 2 processing. However, we do not always have the luxury of time to devote to such decisions, especially when making decisions on the fly. Additionally, the mental effort exerted in this process can be substantial, and when faced with multiple tasks competing for our attention, we often need to take shortcuts.

Herbert Simon (1955, 1978), a key researcher in this area, explored the functioning of Type 2 processing and introduced the concept of bounded rationality. Simon suggested that when seeking to make more considered decisions, we act with bounded rationality, meaning we aim for decisions that are satisfactory and sufficient for the current situation rather than perfect solutions. He coined the term 'satisficing' to describe this approach. Several factors force us into this position. First, as highlighted in Chapter 4, humans have a limited number of cognitive resources and cannot explore all outcomes of the decision-making process (Adler, 2020). Second, we might lack the relevant information or expertise to predict how our current decisions will influence future events.

Therefore, even though Type 2 processing is more effortful and deliberate than Type 1 processing, there is still a chance that errors can emerge. These errors can arise from incomplete information, cognitive overload, or the inherent limitations of our rationality (Adler, 2020). Understanding these limitations is crucial for improving decision-making processes, particularly in high-stakes environments like cybersecurity, where the consequences of errors can be significant. By recognizing the strengths and weaknesses of Type 2 processing, individuals and organisations can develop strategies to enhance decision-making accuracy and reduce the risk of errors.

Heuristics and Biases

As noted earlier, Type 1 processing is typically associated with intuition. Gonzalez (2017) describes heuristics as the 'shortcuts' humans use to reduce task complexity in judgment and choice, with biases being the resulting gaps between normative behaviour and heuristically determined behaviour. Biases are therefore the errors that occur when our quick, shortcut-based decisions (heuristics) do not match up with what would be the best or most logical decision (the normative behaviour).

Heuristics are driven by our own experiences, and several key heuristic rules can significantly impact our decisions. While there are many heuristics and associated biases, covering all of them would require an entire book. Instead, we will focus on some of the most relevant heuristics and biases in the context of cybersecurity.

Representativeness

One common heuristic is the representativeness heuristic, which involves judging the probability of an event based on how similar it is to a previous sequence of events. For example, imagine you are playing a game and need to decide the likelihood of a specific number coming up on the next roll of the dice. You might base your judgment on the outcomes of previous rolls, even though each roll is independent and has the same probability. This heuristic also applies to other decisions, such as predicting someone's behaviour when we have only limited information. Tversky and Kahneman (1974) illustrated this with the example of Steve, a shy and withdrawn individual who is helpful but not very social. He is tidy and prefers order and routine. When asked whether Steve is more likely to be a librarian or an engineer, people often choose librarian because Steve's description fits the stereotype of a librarian, and it is more *representative* of what we would assume a librarian to be like. However, this decision overlooks the fact that Steve could just as easily be an engineer. The representativeness heuristic leads us to make judgments based on how closely someone or something matches our mental image of a category, rather than considering all relevant information.

This example highlights the potential pitfalls of relying on heuristics. While they can be useful for making quick decisions, they can also lead to biases and errors. In the case of Steve, the heuristic leads to a stereotypical judgment that may not be accurate. Understanding these cognitive shortcuts and their limitations can help us make more informed and accurate decisions, especially in complex situations like cybersecurity, where relying on stereotypes or past experiences can result in significant errors.

One challenge we often face when making judgments is accurately assessing the influence of existing information, particularly when using the representativeness heuristic. This heuristic involves making decisions based on how similar an event or person is to a prototype or stereotype, rather than considering all relevant information. A key piece of information we frequently overlook is the base-rate frequency, which refers to how common something is within a given population. For example, in the case of Steve, if we know that the population he comes from has more engineers than librarians, this base-rate information should influence our judgment. Statistically, it is more likely that Steve is an engineer. However, when using the representativeness heuristic, we tend to ignore this statistical information and instead base our decision on how closely Steve's description matches our stereotypes of librarians and engineers. This tendency to disregard base-rate information in favour of more salient, stereotype-confirming details is known as the *base-rate fallacy*. It leads us to make decisions that are not grounded in statistical reality but rather in our preconceived notions and biases. Tversky and Kahneman (1974) highlighted this fallacy, showing how it can skew our judgments and lead to errors.

Understanding the existence of the base-rate fallacy and its impact on decision making is crucial, especially in fields like cybersecurity, where accurate risk assessment is vital. By being aware of its influence, we can strive to incorporate relevant statistical information into our judgments, leading to more informed and accurate decisions.

In the context of cybersecurity, one of the most striking examples of the base rate fallacy is the tendency for individuals to consistently underestimate their likelihood of becoming victims of cybercrime. Studies have shown that people often believe they are less likely to be targeted by cybercriminals than they are (Morrison et al., 2021; Sikra et al., 2023; Velykoivanenko et al., 2021; Wash & Rader, 2011). This underestimation persists despite the prevalence of cybercrime and the increasing sophistication of cyberattacks. In a simulated phishing detection task, researchers observed that individuals made similar judgments about the likelihood of an email being a phishing attempt, regardless of whether they had prior information about the incidence of phishing (Canfield et al., 2016). So even when individuals are provided with relevant statistical information, there is still a tendency for them to rely on their intuitive judgments and they fail to adjust their assessments based on the actual base rates of phishing incidents. This highlights the importance of incorporating statistical information and awareness into cybersecurity training and decision-making processes. If we initiate measures and initiatives that help understanding and addressing the base rate fallacy, individuals and organisations can improve their ability to accurately assess risks and make more informed decisions to protect against cyber threats.

The representativeness heuristic can also lead to erroneous judgments about probability. Consider these sequences of coin tosses: H-T-H-T-T-H and H-H-H-T-T-T. Many people erroneously believe that the first sequence is more likely to occur because it appears 'fairer' and more random. However, as you will probably have guessed, this belief is incorrect because each coin toss is independent, and both sequences are equally likely to occur. This misconception is known as the *gambler's fallacy*, where individuals believe that past events influence future probabilities in random sequences.

In cybersecurity, the gambler's fallacy can manifest in several ways. One common example is the underestimation of the likelihood of being a victim of cybercrime again after having been previously targeted. Individuals may believe that because they have already experienced a cyberattack, they are less likely to be targeted again. However, this belief is flawed because the probability of being targeted by a cyberattack remains high regardless of past experiences. Another way the gambler's fallacy impacts cybersecurity awareness is the misconception that after being targeted by a specific type of attack, such as phishing, the likelihood of being targeted again by the same or similar attack decreases. In reality, the likelihood remains high. For example, in 2024, 90% of businesses reported being targeted by phishing attacks within the preceding 12 months (www.gov.uk/government/statistics/cyber-security-breaches-survey-2024/cyber-security-breaches-survey-2024#chapter-6-cyber-crime).

Understanding and addressing the gambler's fallacy in the context of cybersecurity awareness can significantly enhance vigilance and the implementation of effective security measures. This approach ensures that security protocols are maintained and updated regardless of past experiences, helping individuals and organisations remain proactive in their defence against cyber threats. By recognizing that past events do not influence the probability of future occurrences, employees can avoid complacency and maintain a high level of alertness, thereby reducing the risk of repeated attacks and improving overall cybersecurity posture.

Availability Heuristic

The availability heuristic is a mental shortcut we use when making judgments about the likelihood of events based on how easily examples come to mind. This heuristic can be particularly influential when assessing the frequency or probability of an event. For instance, if asked to estimate how many people were fired in the past year for not following cybersecurity rules, you might recall instances of people you know or have heard about being dismissed for such reasons. This reliance on readily available information helps you make a judgment about the frequency of these occurrences (Tversky & Kahneman, 1974). It is interesting to note that in the research conducted by Tessian (2022), they noted 21% of individuals who had sent the wrong email out to external contacts had lost their job, not a commonly known statistic, and people are often shocked when they find this out.

However, there are several issues with using the availability heuristic. Since it depends on the information we can easily retrieve, any factors that affect our memory can impact our decisions. Memory is not perfect and can be influenced by decay and interference, as discussed in Chapter 4. The more familiar we are with certain events, likely due to past experiences, the higher we might judge their probability compared to unfamiliar events (Marrett & Adams, 2006; Tversky & Kahneman, 1974).

Importantly, the availability heuristic does not require personal experience with the event or experience we are asked to make a judgement on. In many cases, external sources of information, like news outlets and social media, can also have a direct impact on our judgments. For example, after the 9/11 attacks, people might have perceived the likelihood of an aircraft crash as higher than a car accident due to extensive media coverage.

While the availability heuristic relies on the ease with which we can retrieve information, the actual content of that information can also impact our decision making in another way. This is where *familiarity bias* comes into play. Familiarity bias means that people tend to prefer things they are more familiar with, often overriding choices that might be objectively more relevant (Marrett & Adams, 2006). The familiarity bias is rooted in what people know, trust, and feel comfortable with, which develops through greater exposure to something. In consumer behaviour people often choose brands they are familiar with, even when there are better or cheaper alternatives available, mainly because they are more familiar with that specific brand. All too often, this is why companies invest heavily in advertising to build brand recognition and familiarity. In the realm of cybersecurity, an individual might be more likely to respond to a phishing email if it appears to come from a legitimate and well-known organisation they trust. This trust and familiarity can lead to risky decisions, as the familiarity bias influences their judgment.

Both the availability heuristic and familiarity bias demonstrate how our cognitive processes can be swayed by the information we have and our comfort levels with that information. Recognizing these biases can help us make more informed and objective decisions, particularly in critical areas like cybersecurity.

Anchoring and Adjustment

Imagine you are asked to estimate the time it will take to complete a 10,000-word report. Many people would start by assessing similar tasks they've completed before. For instance, if it previously took you three weeks to complete a 5,000-word report, you might simply double that time and estimate six weeks for the 10,000-word report. However, this approach is inherently flawed. Several factors can affect the accuracy of this estimate. The larger report might be on a more complex topic, requiring more time for research. Additionally, your workload might differ; the previous report might have been completed during a quieter period, while the new report might coincide with a peak workload period, leaving you with less time to work on it. This means that your initial estimate (or anchor) is insufficient, and even when you adjust it, you might still underestimate the time required (Tversky & Kahneman, 1974).

Applying the anchoring and adjustment heuristic to cybersecurity behaviours is not immediately obvious. It involves situations where individuals base their current behaviours on existing measures and fail to adapt to new, emerging threats. For example, many people hold myths about cybersecurity, such as believing that Apple devices cannot be hacked or that using anti-virus software makes them invulnerable to attacks. These myths become behavioural anchors that individuals rely on heavily. However, these myths are just that – myths (https://nordvpn.com/blog/cybersecurity-myths/). Other such myths can include the belief that more cybersecurity tools mean more protection for the organisation; if they are not properly configured, or the workforce does not know how to use them, the organisation runs the risk of overcomplicating an already complex situation further. When we base our knowledge and respective behaviours on faulty information such as this, we risk overlooking other potential threats in cyberspace.

The anchoring and adjustment heuristic is persistent and often resists attempts to nullify its impact on decision making, even with training and decision support systems (George et al., 2000; Northcraft & Neale, 1987). Once the initial anchor has been set, it creates a strong influence on the subsequent judgements individuals make. Even in instances where the individual is made aware that their current anchor might be irrelevant or erroneous they still make insufficient adjustments (Tversky & Kahneman, 1974).

Recognition

The recognition heuristic comes into play when we must decide between two alternatives, we will assume that the alternative that we recognised is the correct one or is better irrespective of the other information that might exist (Goldstein & Gigerenzer, 2008). One common example that is used to demonstrate the recognition heuristic is judgements related to the size of cities; for example, let us say you must decide about which city is larger, London or another city you are not familiar with. We would assume, based on the recognition heuristic, that you would opt to say London is the largest city because it is the one you recognise and have most familiarity with.

The recognition heuristic has a variety of applications when it comes to cybersecurity awareness. For example, if employees are asked how likely they are to be victims of a phishing attack versus a less obvious attack like ransomware or social engineering, they might rate the chances of a phishing attack higher. This is because they recognise phishing attacks more readily than the other types, leading to a potential underestimation of the risks posed by less familiar threats. Another way in which recognition could come into play in the cybersecurity context is individuals might be more likely to respond to a phishing email if they recognise the sender. This could be a named person within the organisation or an external, well-known organisation with which they are familiar. The recognition of the sender can override caution, making them more susceptible to the attack.

Fostering a spirit of critical thinking when it comes to evaluating cybersecurity risk can make employees make better, more well-informed decisions, meaning they can protect themselves and the organisation from a wider variety of threats. Enhancing training and awareness packages so that they offer information on a wider range of threats rather than just the common ones can also help individuals recognise the full spectrum of threats that they might encounter.

Affect Heuristic

The affect heuristic allows individuals to make decisions based on their feelings (affect) about a particular choice, rather than engaging in a lengthy decision-making process. If someone has a positive feeling about something, they might perceive it as lower risk compared to something they have a negative feeling about (Finucane et al., 2002; Slovic et al., 2006).

Early research on risk perception showed that feelings of dread were strongly associated with perceived hazards (Slovic, 1987). Slovic (1987) also noted that perceived benefits of taking a risk are negatively correlated with perceived risk, so as we see the benefits of taking the risk increasing, our perception of that risk decreases. As the perceived benefits increase, the perception of risk decreases. This association has been shown to be strongly linked to the strength of the affect attached to the activity in question (Alhakami & Slovic, 1994). Interestingly Slovic et al. (2006) suggested people make judgements about their use of technology based on not only what they think about that thing but also how they feel about that thing. This has important repercussions for cybersecurity behaviours, as much of the interaction involves technology in some form or another. Another interesting finding from this body of research is that as time pressures on the decision increase, the negative relationship between perceived risk and risk benefits is also enhanced, and this is presumed to be because individuals are restricted to using affect as a decision-making mechanism (Finucane et al., 2000).

Phishing and social engineering attacks often use urgency to get victims to respond quickly, encouraging the use of the affect heuristic. For example, an urgent email from a seemingly trusted source can prompt a quick, affect-based decision to click a link or provide information. The affective valence (positive or negative feelings) can impact perceived benefits in cybersecurity. If individuals perceive benefits from engaging in a risky activity (e.g., convenience of using a weak password), they may underestimate the associated risks and fail to engage in protective behaviours (Van Schaik et al., 2020).

Cognitive Biases

Cognitive biases are linked to the functioning of heuristic processing and serve to influence our decision-making processes in ways that we are often unaware of. However, cognitive biases are different from heuristics, and although the use of heuristics can often lead to cognitive biases, there are some biases that exist outside of the use of heuristics. The literature around cognitive biases lists potentially hundreds of ways in which our decision-making processes can be impacted by our past experiences and misconceptions, with around 180 individual biases being listed as part of the Cognitive Bias Codex (Benson, 2017). However, as we did with heuristic processing, we are going to focus on those biases that have a directly impact on cybersecurity awareness and behaviours. It should be noted that heuristics themselves serve to bias decision making in ways that we have already discussed, and cognitive biases result from the misapplication of such processes.

For our current focus, the capacity for biases to creep into our decision-making processes surrounding cybersecurity awareness is far-ranging. For example, when we receive an impressive looking email from an official source with a nice company logo that we are familiar with, our past experiences kick in. We do not spend time exploring the finer nuances of the email and decide to reply with our personal details, company login, or click on the link based on this experience. Such a decision-making process is even more likely when we are faced with multiple other tasks to do at the same time. Cyber-criminals know this, and many attacks are based around the approach that people will not have the time to explore the finer details of the decisions they are making and will opt for a 'gut instinct' approach based on their past experiences.

Optimism Bias

We tend to have a positive outlook on life and the events that will unfold in front of us. The phrase 'looking through rose-tinted glasses' aptly describes how many of us approach estimations of future events in our daily lives, which can be linked to the optimism bias. Simply put, the optimism bias means we tend to overestimate the likelihood of positive events happening in the future and underestimate the likelihood of negative events (Kress & Aue, 2017; Sharot et al., 2011; Weinstein, 1980). Optimism is important for our day-to-day lives, as it drives us to move forward, explore new opportunities, and support new initiatives (Sharot, 2012). However, there are recent examples of how the optimism bias can negatively impact an individual's engagement in protective behaviours, particularly during the COVID-19 pandemic (Druica et al., 2020; McColl et al., 2022; Park et al., 2021; Pascual-Leone et al., 2021). Research indicates that people with higher optimism bias tend to underestimate the risk of COVID-19 and their chances of contracting the virus, making them less likely to engage in self-protective behaviours, see the value in vaccine uptake, and perceive the consequences of catching COVID-19 as less serious.

Optimism bias has been linked to various issues in the context of cybersecurity, particularly where users consistently underestimate the risks posed by cybercrime and assume they are invulnerable to cyberattacks (Pfleeger & Caputo, 2012). An over-optimistic view of one's susceptibility to attacks can lead to a lack of engagement in protective behaviours, such as enhanced password security or taking fewer risks with personal/sensitive data (Pfleeger & Caputo, 2012). An interesting study by Hewitt and White (2022) found that an increase in an individual's cyber pessimism (the belief that they are more likely to be a victim of cybercrime) correlated with visiting more untrusted websites and experiencing more security incidents. The authors suggested that this behaviour could be symptomatic of a self-fulfilling prophecy, where individuals engage in riskier behaviours because they have already accepted that they will be victims of cybercrime. They also noted that there was no consistent link between the level of knowledge and training an individual had surrounding computer security and cyber optimism bias, which does not bode well for attempts to neutralise such biases through training (Hewitt & White, 2022).

Optimism bias can also lead to overconfidence in one's ability to handle cybersecurity incidents and protect oneself online (Alnifie & Kim, 2023). Research has shown a strong link between optimism bias and cybersecurity overconfidence, leading individuals to believe they will not be victims of cybercrime (Ament, 2018; Chen & Yuan, 2022; Cho et al., 2010). This is related to the Dunning-Kruger effect (Kruger & Dunning, 1999), where individuals display a disconnect between their self-assessment of their skills and their actual performance. This effect has been observed in various areas, including information literacy, where individuals often overestimate their abilities compared to objective measures (Gross & Latham, 2007, 2009, 2012; Mahmood, 2016).

Confirmation Bias

The tendency to support arguments or information that align with our pre-existing beliefs, known as confirmation bias, has significant implications for cybersecurity awareness and behaviours. When users adopt initial behaviours and practices to protect themselves and their organisation, they may become resistant to new methods or practices that contradict their current beliefs (Pfleeger & Caputo, 2012). This resistance can hinder the adoption of more effective cybersecurity measures (Pfleeger & Caputo, 2012). For example, if an individual believes that using a specific anti-virus software is sufficient for protection, they might ignore or dismiss new information about additional security measures, such as multi-factor authentication or regular software updates. This lack of objectivity can leave them vulnerable to emerging threats. This lack of objectivity often stems from difficulties in processing information and arguments logically, especially when an initial opinion or stance has already been formed (Consul et al., 2023).

Moreover, individuals often focus on finding evidence that supports their expectations or initial hypotheses about a security threat. This selective attention means they might overlook critical information that could help them better understand and mitigate the threat (McClellan et al., 2012). For instance, if a user believes that phishing emails always contain obvious spelling mistakes, they might miss more sophisticated phishing attempts that appear legitimate.

Framing Effect

People choose options based on the perceived benefits to them based on the information that is available. However, research has shown that the way information is presented can significantly influence decision making. This is the framing effect, a cognitive bias which can cause people to make different decisions based on how the same information is presented. Essentially the way in which information is 'framed' according to whether it is emphasising potential gains or losses can have a significant impact on the way in which people make decisions. For example, individuals' decisions related to their cybersecurity behaviours may be influenced by whether they are framed in a more positive gains way or a negative loss way (Pfleeger & Caputo, 2012; Tversky & Kahneman, 1974).

Framing effects have a significant impact on how we communicate the threats from cybersecurity breaches and the consequences of poor cybersecurity hygiene. Fear appeals, which use scare tactics to prompt action, have been widely employed in cybersecurity (Johnston & Warkentin, 2010; Johnston et al., 2015; Renaud & Dupuis, 2019). However, the effectiveness of fear appeals has been mixed. Some researchers argue that perceived self-efficacy (belief in one's ability to perform a task) is a better predictor of compliance with cybersecurity instructions than fear appeals (Floyd et al., 2000; Milne et al., 2000; Ort & Fahr, 2018). This suggests that enhancing an individual's capacity to engage in cybersecurity awareness may be more productive than using persistent fear messages.

There are also ethical concerns regarding the use of fear appeals that have been raised by researchers. Some have suggested that fear appeals can be counterproductive and more harmful than beneficial (Dupuis & Renaud, 2021; Tengland, 2012; Hastings et al., 2004; Hyman & Tansey, 1990). For instance, 43% of respondents reported feeling uneasy, and 41% disliked fear-based messages in the context of cybersecurity (Dupuis & Renaud, 2021). The use of fear appeals, although they offer some potential limited benefits, need to be carefully thought out and calibrated to fit the intended audience. There is also a need to ensure that the intended audience for such messages are kept informed and they are being fairly treated (Dupuis & Renaud, 2021). Researchers have concluded that the use of fear appeals alone provides inconsistent results. A more effective approach is to combine fear messages with practical information that helps address the current threats (Dupuis et al., 2021). Such a hybrid approach would serve to enhance the effectiveness of cybersecurity training by providing both the motivation to act and the knowledge to do so effectively. We will investigate this topic further in Chapter 14 when we discuss training provision for cybersecurity awareness.

Status Quo Bias

The tendency for people to stick to their established behaviours without a clear incentive to change is known as the status quo bias (Pfleeger & Caputo, 2012; Samuelson & Zeckhauser, 1988). Eidelman and Crandall (2014) noted that people generally make the assumption that because we have followed something for a long time, or something has persistence, it must be good and has legitimacy. We fall into the status quo bias daily, often without thinking about it, which is obviously the primary purpose of this bias – we do not have to think about change! For example, we might continue to buy products from the same brand, such as toothpaste, coffee, or a certain type of smartphone even when there might be alternatives out there. Staying with the same brand means we have both the familiarity and comfort of the current brand, in turn making us more resistant to change. One of the classic examples of the status quo bias is resistance to cancelling or changing subscription services we may have signed up to, such as gym membership or streaming services, because going through the trauma of cancelling such memberships requires effort that we do not want to exert.

Users often need compelling arguments and incentives to alter their current cybersecurity behaviours, many of which are deeply ingrained in their daily routines. The status quo bias has been well-documented in cybersecurity (Bahreini et al., 2023; Eilts & Yair, 2018; Lee & Joshi, 2017; Sigmund, 2024; Widdowson & Goodliff, 2015) where the status quo bias can manifest as resistance to updating organisational cybersecurity policies and a more risk-averse stance to adopting new practices. Organisations may favour existing policies and practices over exploring innovative approaches, even when new threats and processes emerge that could enhance security (Dean & McDermott, 2017). This resistance can stem from a variety of factors, including a lack of understanding of new threats, fear of the unknown, and the perceived complexity of implementing new measures For example, organisations might hesitate to adopt cloud-based solutions due to concerns over security and control, despite the potential benefits such as increased efficiency and cost savings. This hesitation is often rooted in the status quo bias, where the current situation is preferred over the uncertainty of change.

Overcoming the status quo bias in cybersecurity is indeed challenging, but it is crucial for enhancing organisational security. Clearly articulating how new cybersecurity measures can better protect the organisation, reduce risks, and save time and resources is essential. Using specific examples and data to illustrate the advantages of adopting new practices can help make the case more compelling. Providing incentives for change, such as recognition programmes, rewards, or career development opportunities for employees who adopt and champion new cybersecurity measures, can also be effective. However, there must be wider consultation, and involving key stakeholders in the decision-making process, including IT staff, management, and end-users, is crucial. This input and buy-in are essential for successful implementation and acceptance of new policies, otherwise there is a chance they start to resent changes and in turn may develop tendencies aligned to counterproductive work behaviours (see Chapter 11). Offering comprehensive training programmes ensures that all employees understand the new measures and how to implement them, where training should be ongoing and include practical, hands-on exercises to reinforce learning. Acknowledging that resistance to change is natural and addressing concerns openly can help. Providing support and resources to help employees transition to new practices, and highlighting success stories and early adopters, can build momentum.

Establishing a feedback loop to continuously assess and improve cybersecurity measures encourages employees to share their experiences and suggestions for improvement. Ensuring that leadership is visibly supportive of the new measures can set the tone for the rest of the organisation and demonstrate the importance of cybersecurity, and is one key pillar of cybersecurity culture that can be explicitly espoused (see Chapter 10). Implementing changes gradually allows employees to adapt, reducing resistance and making the transition smoother. While overcoming the status quo bias is not easy, these strategies can help organisations move away from established practices and adopt more effective cybersecurity measures. It requires a concerted effort and commitment from all levels of the organisation, but the benefits of enhanced security and reduced risks make it a worthwhile endeavour.

Illusion of Control

The illusion of control is a cognitive bias where individuals overestimate their ability to control or influence outcomes that are determined by chance (Langer, 1975; Shefrin, 2007). This bias can significantly impact cybersecurity behaviours, leading to a false sense of security and potentially risky actions. When individuals believe they have direct control over the risks they encounter online, they might be less likely to engage in protective behaviours (Pfleeger & Caputo, 2012). For example, someone might feel confident that their personal vigilance alone can prevent cyberattacks. This overconfidence can lead them to neglect essential security measures such as using strong, unique passwords, enabling multi-factor authentication, and regularly updating software and systems. This false sense of control can make individuals more vulnerable to cyber threats, as they might underestimate the sophistication and persistence of cyberattackers.

Understanding the illusion of control is crucial for improving cybersecurity awareness. By recognizing that not all risks can be controlled through personal vigilance alone, individuals can be encouraged to adopt comprehensive security practices that provide better protection against cyber threats. Regular cybersecurity training can help individuals understand the limitations of personal control and the importance of adopting robust security measures. Encouraging the use of strong passwords, multi-factor authentication, and regular software updates can help mitigate risks. Fostering an environment where cybersecurity is a shared responsibility can reduce the reliance on personal vigilance alone. By addressing the illusion of control, we can help individuals adopt a more realistic and effective approach to cybersecurity, ultimately enhancing their protection against cyber threats.

How Do We Deal with Cognitive Biases?

Cognitive biases and heuristics often operate at an unconscious level, particularly in fast, system 1 type processes. This makes it challenging to reason with such biases, as they are inherently difficult to train against and people often fail to recognise they have them. Research over several decades, including work by Evans (2003) and Fischhoff (1981), has explored methods to eliminate or reduce the impact of cognitive biases in decision making. Some researchers have found success with training, while others have suggested that video games can help mitigate these biases (Dennis & O'Toole, 2014; Dennis-Tiwary et al., 2016; Shaw et al., 2018). However, Poos et al. (2017) noted that studies on this topic have limitations. They suggested that very few studies systematically explore the independent effects of training and then explore the added value of using video games for training. This makes it very difficult to isolate the unique contribution of each approach. They are also quick to note that such findings may also lack generalisability, and the findings from such studies might not be easily transferable to all populations and settings. The effectiveness of training mechanisms can also depend very much on the type of biases that are being explored, as well as the characteristics of the learners themselves (Poos et al., 2017). When comparing game-based learning to traditional lecture-based environments, Poos et al. (2017) found no specific advantage for the game-based approach.

Cognitive biases that prompt urgent or quick actions can create a perfect storm for cybersecurity awareness and behaviours. Social engineering tactics often exploit this by instilling a sense of urgency, encouraging system 1 processing. Adler (2020) suggested using 'what-if' scenarios to counteract this problem. This involves conducting a 'premortem' (Klein, 2007; Veinott et al., 2010), where teams explore critical events leading to a project's failure. The process begins with introducing a failed situation and having individuals write down all possible reasons for the failure, regardless of organisational sensitivity. This helps individuals engage in more effortful processing and consider various options that might contribute to decision-making failures. It also identifies potential barriers to successful project completion, allowing for early compensation.

In cybersecurity training, this approach has clear applications. For example, undergraduate students can be presented with scenarios where quick decisions led to victimisation or data/money theft. These sessions have shown positive outcomes, highlighting the importance of understanding how impulsive decisions can lead to future issues. Adler (2020) also noted that 'what-if' exercises can address biases related to stability and overconfidence in current behaviours. Since biases impact individuals more than groups, using group-based decision-making for critical decisions can reduce the impact of biases.

Summary

In this section, we explored the extensive research within psychology on how humans made decisions under uncertainty. The discussion began with an introduction to dual-processing theories, which differentiated between two types of cognitive processing: Type 1 and Type 2. Type 1 processing was characterised as fast, automatic, and reliant on heuristics or mental shortcuts, making it efficient but susceptible to biases and errors. Conversely, Type 2 processing was slow, deliberate, and analytical, requiring more cognitive effort and resources, but it was less prone to biases.

We delved into various heuristics and biases that influenced decision making. The representativeness heuristic involved judging the probability of an event based on its similarity to past events, while the availability heuristic depended on the ease with which examples came to mind. The anchoring and adjustment heuristic involved basing estimates on initial values and adjusting from there, often inadequately. The recognition heuristic led individuals to favour familiar options, and the affect heuristic involved making decisions based on emotional responses.

Cognitive biases, such as optimism bias, confirmation bias, framing effect, status quo bias, and the illusion of control, further impacted decision making. Optimism bias led individuals to overestimate positive outcomes and underestimate negative ones. Confirmation bias caused people to favour information that aligned with their pre-existing beliefs. The framing effect influenced decisions based on how information was presented, emphasizing potential gains or losses. Status quo bias resulted in resistance to change, and the illusion of control involved overestimating one's ability to influence outcomes determined by chance.

We emphasised the importance of understanding these cognitive processes and biases to improve decision making, particularly in high-stakes environments like cybersecurity. By recognizing the strengths and limitations of both Type 1 and Type 2 processing, individuals and organisations could develop strategies to mitigate cognitive biases and enhance decision-making accuracy. We also highlighted the potential benefits of using 'what-if' scenarios and group-based decision making to counteract biases and improve outcomes.

References

Adler, R. M. (2020). *Bending the law of unintended consequences: A test-drive method for critical decision-making in organizations.* Springer Nature.

Alhakami, A. S., & Slovic, P. (1994). A psychological study of the inverse relationship between perceived risk and perceived benefit. *Risk Analysis*, 14(6), 1085–1096.

Alnifie, G., & Kim, D. (2023). Overconfidence in cybersecurity: The role of optimism bias. *Journal of Cybersecurity Research*, 12(3), 234–245.

Ament, C. (2018). The ubiquitous security expert: Overconfidence in information security. ICIS 2017: Transforming Society with Digital Innovation, Seoul, South Korea, December 10–13.

Bahreini, A., Cavusoglu, H., & Cenfetelli, R. T. (2023). How 'What you think you know about cybersecurity' can help users make more secure decisions. *Information and Management*, 60(7), 103860. doi:10.1016/j.im.2023.103860.

Benson, B. (2017, January 8). Cognitive bias cheat sheet, simplified. *Medium*. https://medium.com/thinking-is-hard/4-conundrums-of-intelligence-2ab78d90740f

Canfield, C. I., Fischhoff, B., & Davis, A. (2016). Quantifying phishing susceptibility for detection and behaviour decisions. *Human Factors*, 58(8), 1158–1172.

Chaiken, S., & Trope, Y. (Eds). (1999). *Dual-process theories in social psychology.* Guilford Press.

Chen, H., & Yuan, Y. (2022). The impact of ignorance and bias on information security protection motivation: a case of e-waste handling. *Internet Research*, 33(6), 2244–2275.

Chen, S., Duckworth, K., & Chaiken, S. (1999). Motivated heuristic and systematic processing. *Psychological Inquiry*, 10(1), 44–49.

Cho, H., Lee, J. S., & Chung, S. (2010). Optimistic bias about online privacy risks: Testing the moderating effects of perceived controllability and prior experience. *Computers in Human Behavior*, 26(5), 987–995. doi:10.1016/j.chb.2010.02.012.

Consul, P., Arief, B., Borrion, H., & Kaddoura, S. (2023). Neutralization techniques in cybersecurity: A systematic review. *Journal of Information Security and Applications*, 47, 102–115.

Dean, B., & McDermott, R. (2017). A research agenda to improve decision making in cyber security policy. *Penn State Journal of Law & International Affairs*, 5, 29–164.

Dennis, T. A., & O'Toole, L. (2014). Mental health on the go: Effects of a gamified attention-bias modification mobile application in trait-anxious adults. *Clinical Psychological Science*, 2(5), 576–590.

Dennis-Tiwary, T. A., Denefrio, S., & Gelber, S. (2016). Salutary effects of an attention bias modification mobile application on biobehavioural measures of stress and anxiety during pregnancy. *Biological Psychology*, 117, 97–103.

Druica, E., Musso, F., & Ianole-Calin, R. (2020). Optimism bias during the COVID-19 pandemic: Empirical evidence from Romania. *Journal of Risk Research*, 23(7–8), 862–869.

Dupuis, M., & Renaud, K. (2021). Scoping the ethical principles of cybersecurity fear appeals. *Ethics and Information Technology*, 23(3), 265–284. doi:10.1007/s10676-020-09560-0.

Dupuis, M. J., Jennings, W., & Renaud, K. (2021). The ethics of fear appeals: A reflection on the use of fear appeals in cybersecurity awareness campaigns. *Journal of Information Security and Applications*, 58, 102–115.

Eidelman, S., & Crandall, C. S. (2014). The intuitive traditionalist: How biases for existence and longevity promote the status quo. *Advances in Experimental Social Psychology*, 50, 53–104.

Eilts, D., & Yair, L. (2018). Towards an empirical assessment of cybersecurity readiness and resilience in small businesses. *KSU Proceedings on Cybersecurity Education, Research and Practice*. 2. https://digitalcommons.kennesaw.edu/ccerp/2018/practice/2.

Evans, J. St. B. T. (2003). In two minds: Dual-process accounts of reasoning. *Trends in Cognitive Sciences*, 7(10), 454–459.

Evans, J. St. B. T., & Stanovich, K. E. (2013). Dual-process theories of higher cognition: Advancing the debate. *Perspectives on Psychological Science*, 8(3), 223–241.

Finucane, M. L., Alhakami, A., Slovic, P., & Johnson, S. M. (2000). The affect heuristic in judgments of risks and benefits. *Journal of Behavioural Decision Making*, 13(1), 1–17.

Fischhoff, B. (1981). Debiasing. In D. Kahneman, P. Slovic, & A. Tversky (Eds), *Judgment under uncertainty: Heuristics and biases* (pp. 422–444). Cambridge University Press.

Floyd, D. L., Prentice-Dunn, S., & Rogers, R. W. (2000). A meta-analysis of research on protection motivation theory. *Journal of Applied Social Psychology*, 30(2), 407–429.

Frankish, K. (2010). Dual-process and dual-system theories of reasoning. *Philosophy Compass*, 5(10), 914–926. doi:10.1111/j.1747-9991.2010.00330.x.

George, J. F., Duffy, K., & Ahuja, M. (2000). Countering the anchoring and adjustment bias with decision support systems. *Decision Support Systems*, 29(2), 195–206.

Goldstein, D. G., & Gigerenzer, G. (2008). The recognition heuristic and the less-is-more effect. *Handbook of Experimental Economics Results*, 1, 987–992.

Gonzalez, C. (2017). The role of cognitive heuristics in decision making. *Journal of Behavioural Decision Making*, 30(2), 123–125.

Gross, M., & Latham, D. (2007). Attaining information literacy: An investigation of the relationship between skill level, self-estimates of skill, and library anxiety. *Library & Information Science Research*, 29(3), 332–353.

Gross, M., & Latham, D. (2009). Undergraduate perceptions of information literacy: Defining, attaining, and self-assessing skills. *College & Research Libraries*, 70(4), 336–350.

Gross, M., & Latham, D. (2012). What's skill got to do with it? Information literacy skills and self-views of ability among first-year college students. *Journal of the American Society for Information Science and Technology*, 63(3), 574–583.

Hastings, G., Stead, M., & Webb, J. (2004). Fear appeals in social marketing: Strategic and ethical reasons for concern. *Psychology & Marketing*, 21(11), 961–986.

Hewitt, B., & White, K. (2022). Cyber pessimism and cybersecurity behaviour: A self-fulfilling prophecy? *Journal of Cybersecurity*, 8(1), tyab024.

Hyman, H. H., & Tansey, R. (1990). The ethics of social marketing. *Journal of Business Ethics*, 9(2), 105–114.

Johnston, A. C., & Warkentin, M. (2010). Fear appeals and information security behaviours: An empirical study. *MIS Quarterly*, 34(3), 549–566.

Johnston, A. C., Warkentin, M., & Siponen, M. (2015). An enhanced fear appeal rhetorical framework: Leveraging threats to the human asset through sanctioning rhetoric. *MIS Quarterly*, 39(1), 113–134.

Kahneman, D. (2011). *Thinking, fast and slow*. Farrar, Straus and Giroux.

Klein, G. (2007). Performing a project premortem. *Harvard Business Review*, 85(9), 18–19.

Kress, L., & Aue, T. (2017). The link between optimism bias and attention bias: A neurocognitive perspective. *Neuroscience and Biobehavioral Reviews*, 80, 688–702. doi:10.1016/j.neubiorev.2017.07.016.

Kruger, J., & Dunning, D. (1999). Unskilled and unaware of it: How difficulties in recognizing one's own incompetence lead to inflated self-assessments. *Journal of Personality and Social Psychology*, 77(6), 1121–1134.

Langer, E. J. (1975). The illusion of control. *Journal of Personality and Social Psychology*, 32(2), 311–328.

Lee, K., & Joshi, K. (2017). Examining the use of status quo bias perspective in IS research: Need for re-conceptualizing and incorporating biases. *Information Systems Journal*, 27(6), 733–752.

Mahmood, K. (2016). Do people overestimate their information literacy skills? A systematic review of empirical evidence on the Dunning-Kruger effect. *Journal of Information Literacy*, 10(2), 3–24.

Marrett, C. B., & Adams, R. (2006). The availability heuristic in judgments of risks and benefits. *Journal of Behavioural Decision Making*, 19(1), 1–17.

McClellan, S., Ali, H., & Sutton, S. G. (2012). The role of confirmation bias in information security policy compliance. *Journal of Information Systems*, 26(1), 35–56.

McColl, K., Debin, M., Souty, C., Guerrisi, C., Turbelin, C., Falchi, A., … Raude, J. (2022). Are people optimistically biased about the risk of Covid-19 infection? Lessons from the first wave of the pandemic in Europe. *International Journal of Environmental Research and Public Health*, 19(1). doi:10.3390/ijerph19010436.

Milne, S., Sheeran, P., & Orbell, S. (2000). Prediction and intervention in health-related behaviour: A meta-analytic review of protection motivation theory. *Journal of Applied Social Psychology*, 30(1), 106–143.

Morrison, K., Coventry, L., & Biggs, S. (2021). Older adults' experiences of cybersecurity: Understanding and mitigating risks. *Journal of Cybersecurity*, 7(1), tyab001.

Northcraft, G. B., & Neale, M. A. (1987). Experts, amateurs, and real estate: An anchoring-and-adjustment perspective on property pricing decisions. *Organisational Behaviour and Human Decision Processes*, 39(1), 84–97.

Ort, A., & Fahr, A. (2018). Using protection motivation theory to predict the adoption of protective measures: A meta-analysis. *Journal of Risk Research*, 21(6), 725–746.

Park, T., Ju, I., Ohs, J. E., & Hinsley, A. (2021). Optimistic bias and preventive behavioral engagement in the context of COVID-19. *Research in Social & Administrative Pharmacy*, 17(1), 1859–1866.

Pascual-Leone, A., Cattaneo, G., Macià, D., Solana, J., Tormos, J. M., & Bartrés-Faz, D. (2021). Beware of optimism bias in the context of the COVID-19 pandemic. *Annals of Neurology*, 89(3), 423.

Pfleeger, S. L., & Caputo, D. D. (2012). Leveraging behavioural science to mitigate cyber security risk. *Computers & Security*, 31(4), 597–611.

Poos, J., van den Bosch, K., & Janseen, J. (2017). Training to mitigate cognitive biases in decision making: A review of the literature. *Journal of Cognitive Engineering and Decision Making*, 11(3), 215–232.

Renaud, K., & Dupuis, M. (2019). Cyber security fear appeals: Unexpectedly complicated. *ACM International Conference Proceeding Series*, 42–56. doi:10.1145/3368860.3368864.

Samuelson, W., & Zeckhauser, R. (1988). Status quo bias in decision making. *Journal of Risk and Uncertainty*, 1, 7–59.

Sharot, T. (2012). *The optimism bias: Why we're wired to look on the bright side.* Hachette UK.

Sharot, T., Korn, C. W., & Dolan, R. J. (2011). How unrealistic optimism is maintained in the face of reality. *Nature Neuroscience*, 14, 1475–1479. doi:10.1176/appi.ap.30.3.218.

Shaw, A., Kenski, K., Stromer-Galley, J., Mikeal Martey, R., Clegg, B. A., Lewis, J. E., Folkestad, J. E., & Strzalkowski, T. (2018). Serious efforts at bias reduction: The effects of digital games and avatar customization on three cognitive biases. *Journal of Media Psychology*, 30(1), 16–28.

Shefrin, H. (2007). *Behavioural corporate finance: Decisions that create value.* McGraw-Hill.

Sigmund, T. (2024). Antivirus software status quo bias. *IDIMT 2024: Changes to ICT, Management, and Business Processes Through AI – 32nd Interdisciplinary Information Management Talks*, 85–93. doi:10.35011/IDIMT-2024-85.

Sikra, J., Renaud, K. V., & Thomas, D. R. (2023). UK cybercrime, victims and reporting: A systematic review. *Commonwealth Cybercrime Journal*, 1(1), 28–59.

Simon, H. A. (1955). A behavioral model of rational choice. *Quarterly Journal of Economics*, 69, 99–118.

Simon, H. A. (1978). Rationality as process and as product of thought. *American Economic Review: Papers and Proceedings*, 68, 1–16.

Slovic, P. (1987). Perception of risk. *Science*, 236(4799), 280–285.

Slovic, P., Finucane, M. L., Peters, E., & MacGregor, D. G. (2006). The affect heuristic. *European Journal of Operational Research*, 177(3), 1333–1352.

Tengland, P. A. (2012). Behaviour change or empowerment: On the ethics of health-promotion strategies. *Public Health Ethics*, 5(2), 140–153.

Tessian. (2022). *Psychology of human error.* doi:10.1016/b978-0-444-42727-4.50006-2.

Tversky, A., & Kahneman, D. (1974). Judgment under uncertainty: Heuristics and biases. *Science*, 185(4157), 1124–1131.

Van Schaik, P., Renaud, K., Wilson, C., Jansen, J., & Onibokun, J. (2020). Risk as affect: The affect heuristic in cybersecurity. *Computers & Security*, 90, 101651.

Veinott, B., Klein, G. A., & Wiggins, S. (2010). Evaluating the effectiveness of the PreMortem technique on plan confidence. *ISCRAM 2010 – 7th International Conference on Information Systems for Crisis Response and Management: Defining Crisis Management 3.0, Proceedings, Seattle, WA.*

Velykoivanenko, L., Niksirat, K. S., Zufferey, N., Humbert, M., Huguenin, K., & Cherubini, M. (2021). Are those steps worth your privacy? Fitness-tracker users' perceptions of privacy and utility. *Proceedings of the ACM on Interactive, Mobile, Wearable and Ubiquitous Technologies*, 5(4), 1–41.

Wash, R., & Rader, E. (2011). Influencing mental models of security: A research agenda. *Proceedings of the 2011 New Security Paradigms Workshop*, 57–66. www. nspw.org/papers/2011/nspw2011-wash.pdf.

Weinstein, N. D. (1980). Unrealistic optimism about future life events. *Journal of Personality and Social Psychology*, 39(5), 806–820. doi:10.1037/0022-3514.39.5.806.

Widdowson, A. J., & Goodliff, P. B. (2015). CHEAT: An approach to incorporating human factors in cyber security assessments. *IET Conference Proceedings*, 5. www. researchgate.net/profile/Amanda-Widdowson-2/publication/311606003_CHEAT_a n_approach_to_incorporating_human_factors_in_cyber_security_assessments/links /5fae4921a6fdcc9389b20120/CHEAT-an-approach-to-incorporating-human-factors -in-cyber-security-assessments.pdf.

7

DECISION MAKING UNDER PRESSURE

Introduction

When considering the realm of cybersecurity, we often overlook the motivations behind our compliance with the required protective behaviours. At the core of many processes and protective actions we undertake in our daily work and personal lives lies a carefully orchestrated decision-making mechanism. Decision-making processes have been extensively studied within psychology, and numerous theories have been proposed to explain why we choose one path over another. These theories are crucial for understanding cybersecurity awareness and the protective behaviours individuals adopt, as they are the driving forces behind why people engage in certain actions.

Understanding these decision-making processes, along with the inhibitors or barriers to making the 'right' decisions, allows us to design better training and awareness programmes that enhance positive decision making. This chapter dissects the most relevant theories that account for decision making in the context of cybersecurity and evaluates their relative merits. We would like to stress a critical point – that there is no single theory which fully explains the decisions individuals make in cybersecurity. However, researchers have made a variety of attempts to integrate elements from various models to address shortcomings and incorporate additional variables to fill perceived gaps. Through a continued process of improvement and refinement, these theories can help us better understand decisions that sit behind cybersecurity behaviours.

The Theory of Planned Behaviour

The theory of planned behaviour (TPB; Ajzen, 1985, 1991) extends the theory of reasoned action (Ajzen & Fishbein, 1980; Fishbein & Ajzen, 1975).

DOI: 10.4324/9781003509011-7

According to TPB, the intention to perform a particular behaviour is influenced by three factors:

1. **Attitude towards the behaviour**: This relates to the consequences of performing the behaviour, known as 'behavioural beliefs' (Ajzen, 1985, 1991, 2020). A behavioural belief is a subjective assessment that performing the behaviour will lead to a specific outcome or experience. For example, the belief that creating a complex password can prevent account compromise (positive outcome) or is time-consuming (negative experience). These beliefs shape a positive or negative attitude towards the behaviour.
2. **Subjective norm**: This concerns the perceived social pressure to perform or not perform the behaviour. It reflects the influence of people important to the individual and their expectations.
3. **Perceived behavioural control**: This refers to the perceived ease or difficulty of performing the behaviour, influenced by past experiences and anticipated obstacles.

The overall attitude towards a behaviour is influenced by how desirable or undesirable the individual views the potential outcomes. Subjective probability, or the perceived likelihood that the behaviour will lead to the intended outcome, also plays a crucial role. If individuals believe the chances of achieving the desired outcome are low, they are less likely to engage in the behaviour. For example, in the context of cybersecurity, if individuals underestimate the likelihood of being a victim of a cyberattack or overestimate their ability to prevent an attack, they are less likely to adopt protective behaviours. They will perceive the subjective probability of these behaviours leading to the desired outcome as low, thus questioning the point of engaging in them.

The external social pressure we feel to engage in a particular behaviour, or the subjective norm, has two underlying components (Ajzen, 2020; Fishbein & Ajzen, 2010):

1. **Injunctive normative belief**: This refers to the extent to which the reference group (e.g., colleagues or supervisors in the context of cybersecurity awareness) will approve or disapprove of the behaviour. For instance, if employees believe that their colleagues and supervisors approve of using strong passwords, and they engage in a process of regularly updating them, they will be more likely to adopt these behaviours.
2. **Descriptive normative belief**: This relates to how much we believe important individuals in the same reference group would engage in the behaviour. In the example of password use, individuals assess if people around them are following the rules for creating a secure password, in

which case they will in turn be more likely to follow the crowd and do the same.

Both injunctive and descriptive beliefs contribute to the overall social pressure to engage in a specific behaviour (Ajzen, 2020). When individuals perceive that their reference group will approve of the behaviour and believe that others in the group are likely to engage in it, the likelihood of conforming to the subjective norm increases exponentially (Ajzen, 2020).

Perceived behavioural control refers to the perceived ease or difficulty of performing a behaviour, based on our past experiences and the potential obstacles that could be presented when performing that action (Ajzen, 2020). Anything that forms a barrier to us doing something, such as lacking the right skillset, not having the right information, limited resources, being time poor, or not having a supportive network, can directly impact our perceived behaviour control.

Control beliefs are the individual's assessment of the likelihood that facilitating or inhibiting factors will affect their ability to perform the behaviour. When individuals have strong control beliefs, meaning they believe they can overcome potential barriers and have access to facilitating elements, they experience higher levels of perceived behavioural control. This positively influences their likelihood of performing the behaviour. Conversely, when barriers are high and control beliefs are weak, perceived behavioural control is lower, reducing the likelihood of following through with behavioural intent (Ajzen, 1985, 1991, 2020).

We can apply this process to the area of cybersecurity using the example of reporting phishing emails. Here we have two competing control beliefs that will serve to shape the individual's response.

- **Facilitating Control Belief**: If an individual believes their organisation has a clear mechanism for reporting potential phishing emails, this clearly facilitates the ease with which an individual can report potential attacks. A tool embedded within the email client for reporting potential phishing emails and an effective training programme that details how to spot the signs of a phishing email are clear facilitators.
- **Inhibiting Control Belief**: Where the individual believes the reporting system is flawed and fears punishment for mistakenly reporting a non-phishing email, they become more resilient to reporting potential phishing emails. In instances where there is a lack of training and a common perception that there will be negative consequences for mistakes, these clearly inhibit good practice and encourage more reckless reporting habits.

When facilitating factors are present and control beliefs are strong, perceived behavioural control is high, increasing the likelihood of engaging in the behaviour. Conversely, when inhibiting factors dominate and control beliefs are weak, perceived behavioural control is low, decreasing the likelihood of performing the behaviour.

Theory of Planned Behaviour and Cybersecurity

The theory of planned behaviour has been widely explored in the context of cybersecurity behaviours. Sommestad and Hallberg (2013) found that TPB could explain behavioural intentions related to compliance with information security policies (Alanazi et al., 2022). However, there are several criticisms of TPB, particularly regarding the gap between behavioural intention and actual behaviour (Alanazi et al., 2022; Guo et al., 2011; Hassan et al., 2016; Safa et al., 2016; Sheeran & Webb, 2016). Researchers have noted that an intention to perform a behaviour does not always lead to the behaviour being carried out (Alanazi et al., 2022; Guo et al., 2011; Hassan et al., 2016; Safa et al., 2016; Sheeran & Webb, 2016). This gap can be influenced by several factors such as cybersecurity awareness (Zwilling et al., 2020), cognitive and emotional factors, perceived awareness of threats, and socio-demographic factors (Alanazi et al., 2022).

Perceived behavioural control has a direct influence on an individual's intention to comply with cybersecurity measures, but the link between perceived behavioural control and actual behaviour is often weak (Alanazi et al., 2022). This suggests that even if individuals feel capable of performing a behaviour, they might not always follow through. Social factors, such as the influence of colleagues and supervisors, significantly impact intentions towards cybersecurity behaviours (Ajzen, 1991; Alanazi et al., 2022). The work by Alanazi et al. (2022) did include a sample of 18–30-year-olds which do form a sizeable portion of the modern workforce, but it is worth highlighting that these findings might vary with different age groups. However, one thing that this research does highlight is the importance of creating a supportive environment for promoting cybersecurity practices.

Intention is a central pillar to TPB and it reflects the motivational factors that influence a behaviour, in turn indicating how much effort an individual is willing to exert to perform the behaviour (Ajzen, 1991). The stronger the intention to engage in a particular behaviour, the more likely the individual is to perform that behaviour. If someone has a strong intention to exercise regularly, this intention will translate into actual exercise behaviour. This intention is influenced by their attitude towards exercise (e.g., believing it will improve their health), the subjective norm (e.g., knowing that their friends and family support and engage in exercise), and perceived behavioural control (e.g., feeling confident in their ability to find time and resources to exercise). Such processes can be harnessed in the context of cybersecurity behaviours and again require the implementation of a supportive workplace environment that encourages collaboration, rather than an environment of punishment and isolation.

Protection Motivation Theory

Protection motivation theory (PMT) (Rogers, 1975, 1983) explains how individuals respond to fear-based messages intended to discourage risky behaviours or promote protective actions. A key issue within this approach is understanding whether fear-arousing information directly influences a person's intention to act, or whether its effect is more indirect and mediated by other psychological factors (Norman et al., 2005). The individual can engage in either adaptive (protective) or maladaptive (higher risk) behaviours because of their assessment of the fear-based information (Rogers, 1975, 1983; Leventhal, 1970). In the context of cybersecurity, non-compliance with protective behaviours or policies is seen as a negative, maladaptive response, while compliance is viewed as a positive, adaptive response (Vance et al., 2012). PMT involves two key cognitive processes: threat appraisal and coping appraisal (Alqahtani & Kavakli-Thorne, 2020; Norman et al., 2005).

Threat Appraisal

Threat appraisal focuses on the source of the threat and factors that may increase or decrease the likelihood of a maladaptive response. Norman, Boer, and Seydel (2005) suggested that estimates for the seriousness or severity of the proposed threat and the individual's perceived vulnerability to the threat inhibit the chance of the individual engaging in maladaptive responses. In other words, when individuals recognise that a threat is severe and believe they are vulnerable to it, they are less likely to engage in maladaptive responses such as denial, withdrawal, or ignorance. Instead, these perceptions are meant to motivate protective behaviours. In contrast, if the individual makes an assessment that engaging in the maladaptive responses offers a greater benefit to them over engaging in the protective behaviours, they will take this option.

Coping Appraisals

This process evaluates the individual's ability to cope with and avert the relevant threat presented in the fear message (Norman et al., 2005). This process itself consists of three individual elements that interact with each other:

Response Efficacy: The belief in how effective the recommended behaviour will be in avoiding the negative consequences associated with the threat.

Self-Efficacy: The confidence the individual has in their own abilities to successfully execute the recommended protective behaviour.

Response Costs: These is the perception of the current barriers or costs an individual will perceive as being aligned with taking the protective action to counter the current threat (Balla & Hagger, 2024; Boer & Seydel, 1996).

Accordingly, engaging in adaptive, protective measures is directly facilitated by several key beliefs. These include the belief that the behaviour will be effective in reducing the perceived threat, the confidence that we have the necessary skills and knowledge to successfully carry out the recommended behaviour, and the perception that the costs associated with engaging in these protective behaviours are low.

PMT and Cybersecurity

PMT posits that threat appraisal and coping appraisal interact to determine an individual's overall level of motivation to engage in protective behaviours. If individuals perceive that the severity and vulnerability to the threat are high, and this is linked to high response efficacy, high self-efficacy, and low perceived cost, they are more likely to engage with protective behaviours in response to that threat. However, if the response costs are deemed to be too high, and the rewards of continuing to engage in the risky behaviour are highly beneficial to the individual, they may be less inclined to initiative protective measures.

According to a recent review of the research in the area by Alsharida et al. (2023), PMT was the most frequently used in studies on cybersecurity. It is often touted as being one of the most relevant theoretical frameworks when it comes to explaining an individual's intention to engaging in effective cybersecurity behaviours (Boss et al., 2015; Ifinedo, 2012; Johnston et al., 2015; Li et al., 2019). Fear messaging has been demonstrated to have mixed effects on the intention to engage in protective behaviours when it comes to online behaviours. For example, some researchers have noted that threat severity acted as an important predictor for security-related protection (Zahedi et al., 2015), whilst others noted that the same could not be said for virus protection (LaRose et al., 2007; Lee et al., 2008). Tsai et al. (2016) showed that variables associated with coping appraisal presented the strongest predictors for online safety intentions, including habit strength, response efficacy, and personal responsibility. The researchers also noted that by adding in aspects such as subjective norms to the model of PMT they were able to enhance the overall predictive power of the model (Tsai et al., 2016). Woon et al. (2016) applied the PMT approach to home wireless security and noted that perceived severity and response efficacy also acted as significant predictors for protective behaviours. Vance et al. (2012) added in an additional variable to PMT in the form of habit as part of a routine element of complying with cybersecurity policies. In their study, habit was typified as frequent and automatic processes associated with cybersecurity compliance, and something that participants saw as being an essential, integrated part of their daily work lives. Vance et al. (2012) noted that whilst vulnerability did not have a significant impact on the intention to comply with cybersecurity behaviours, perceived severity did positively impact intention to comply

(Vance et al., 2012). From this perspective it would seem critically important to ensure that individuals within an organisation understand how serious cybersecurity threats can be and the damage they can have upon the organisation (Vance et al., 2012). Forming habits towards compliance with cybersecurity policies appears to have a significant impact on all key elements of PMT. This suggests that ensuring individuals adopt protective behaviours as part of their everyday work life, rather than viewing cybersecurity compliance as something distinct and additional to their normal work, is an effective way to encourage habit-forming behaviours. There are some clear ways in which habits can be fostered within the workplace that in turn enhance compliance with cybersecurity policies. This could include making it a routine to update passwords every few months, and encouraging all employees to use strong, unique passwords for all their individual accounts. Enabling the use of two-factor authentication for all accounts that support it would also be another obvious way of engaging the formation of habits, and this can also add an extra layer of security. Engaging all workers in regular, targeted, and efficient training can also mean employees are kept well informed about the current threats and can also adopt best practices in their cybersecurity activities.

Other researchers have attempted to integrate aspects of organisational cybersecurity environments within the PMT framework. For example, Li et al. (2019) assessed the predictive capacity of peer behaviour to influence an individual's response to a proposed cybersecurity threat, in conjunction with their previous experience with cybersecurity information. The research demonstrated that peer behaviour was a key predictor in motivating individuals to follow accepted organisational cybersecurity practices or to engage in more proactive learning around the topic (Li et al., 2019; Ng & Xu, 2007). They further noted that experience with cybersecurity rules enhanced individuals' self-efficacy in dealing with perceived threats, both in terms of their capacity to handle such threats and their ability to carry out coping strategies (Li et al., 2019). However, perceived severity of the incident was not a significant predictor for engagement in protective behaviours, whereas perceived vulnerability was. This finding suggests that people do not factor in the severity of an incident when considering engaging in protective behaviours, indicating that fear tactics in messaging about prospective threats may have limited impact. Greater barriers were seen to prevent individuals from engaging in adequate cybersecurity protection (Li et al., 2019), and included a lack of awareness and knowledge, a perception of complexity in the cybersecurity measures needed to protect the individual, time constraints, and lack of resources.

Technology Threat Avoidance Theory

This theory has emerged from the exploration of cybersecurity threats and addresses the question of why individuals do not do more to avoid threats posed by technology. In some respects, TTAT (technology threat avoidance theory) is similar to PMT (protection motivation theory), and its proponents, Liang and Xue (2009, 2010), drew heavily on existing theory. However, the key difference is that TTAT is more suited to IT-related disciplines such as cybersecurity.

Liang and Xue (2009, 2010) proposed that an individual's perceptions of their vulnerability to a threat (How likely am I to experience this threat?) and the perceived severity of threats (How damaging could this threat be to me?) posed by technology influence an overall perception of threat. This combination, termed the threat calculus, influences an individual's motivation and behaviour towards avoiding such threats (Carpenter et al., 2019). Perceptions of susceptibility are linked to the likelihood that malicious threats or malicious IT will produce negative consequences for the user (Boysen et al., 2019). Based on the threat calculus, an individual will decide whether to avoid the threat and engage in relevant coping mechanisms. When an individual perceives a threat as having high severity and high vulnerability, they are more likely to take action to avoid that threat (Boysen et al., 2019; Carpenter et al., 2019; Liang & Xue, 2010).

To deal with the threat, an individual will engage in a coping appraisal like that proposed by PMT. They will explore three critical factors before addressing the threat:

- **Response Efficacy**: The extent to which the individual believes that the protective behaviour will successfully mitigate the perceived threat (e.g., Will using a complex password protect me from my account being compromised?).
- **Self-Efficacy**: The level of confidence the individual has in their ability to successfully initiate the protective behaviour (e.g., Do I know how to create an effective password?).
- **Response Costs**: The amount of time and effort the individual will exert when engaging in the protective behaviours (e.g., How much time will it take to create complex passwords for all my accounts?).

If the individual makes a favourable assessment of the threat, deems it severe enough, perceives high vulnerability, has sufficient efficacy, and sees the costs as low, they will engage in avoidance behaviours to prevent the threat. However, if efficacy is low, threat severity is limited, or susceptibility is minimal, the individual will continue engaging in risky behaviours that pose such a threat.

TTAT and Cybersecurity

As the TTAT model was initially developed to explore why individuals fail to engage in protective cybersecurity behaviours, it is not surprising that there have been attempts to use it to model such behaviours (e.g., Chen & Li, 2017;

Gillam & Waite, 2021; Nehme & George, 2022). Young et al. (2016) used the model to explore individual avoidance of malware and found a significant relationship between perceived severity and threat. However, they did not find any further relationship between susceptibility and threat.

Further research by Arachchilage and Love (2014) applied the TTAT model to phishing attacks, aiming to enhance participants' self-efficacy in dealing with such attacks and thereby improve overall coping appraisal. The authors noted that an individual's existing procedural knowledge (how to deal with phishing emails) and conceptual knowledge (what phishing emails are and what a suspicious email link might look like) enhanced users' self-efficacy and their avoidance of phishing attacks. The results demonstrated that existing knowledge indeed enhances an individual's threat avoidance behaviour, which has interesting implications for training provision in the field.

Other researchers have adjusted the original TTAT to include elements related to individual differences. For example, Carpenter et al. (2019) included an examination of risk propensity, distrust propensity, and impulsiveness which have been previously demonstrated to exert an influence on cybersecurity behaviours. They noted that perceived susceptibility acted as a significant predictor of perceptions of threat, where the actual perception of severity acted to mediate this effect. So, the perception of severity of the threat served to influence the overall perception of threat, influencing the strength of the relationship between perceived susceptibility and perceived threat.

General Deterrence Theory

General deterrence theory (GDT) has its roots in criminal theory and criminal justice, based on the premise that individuals follow rules or regulatory guidance due to the threat of punishment (Ugrin & Pearson, 2013). According to Straub and Welke (1998), increasing the certainty and severity of punishment will deter unwanted behaviour. Employees may be more inclined to follow cybersecurity policies due to policy enforcement mechanisms such as legal stipulations, suspension, or job termination (Cheng et al., 2013; Quackenbush, 2011; White, 2017). GDT posits that individuals engage in a rational decision-making process, weighing the potential punishments for a transgression against the benefits of the behaviour (Ugrin & Pearson, 2013).

There are three components of GDT that influence individual behaviour:

- **Severity of Punishment**: This refers to the proposed punishment for engaging in illicit or unwanted behaviour. According to GDT, the greater the punishment, the more likely it is to deter the behaviour (D'Arcy & Hovav, 2009; D'Arcy et al., 2009; Ugrin & Pearson, 2013). Sanctions can be formal, such as dismissal or reduction in bonuses, or informal, such as reprimands by colleagues or supervisors, which can lead to a loss of respect (Trang & Brendel, 2019). For example, an employee who knows they could be fired for violating cybersecurity policies might be more diligent in following them.

- **Certainty of Punishment**: This is the extent to which an individual believes they will be caught and punished for engaging in the behaviour. For a policy to be effective, there must be a high likelihood of detection and punishment (Ugrin & Pearson, 2013; Williams & Hawkins, 1986). For instance, if an employee is aware that their online activities are closely monitored and any violations of fair use policy are likely to be detected, they will be more likely to adhere to cybersecurity policies.
- **Celerity of Punishment**: This relates to the swiftness of the punishment following the transgression. Immediate and swift punishment is seen as more impactful than delayed punishment (Trang & Brendel, 2019; Ugrin & Pearson, 2013). If an employee is immediately reprimanded or suspended following a policy violation, this prompt response will serve to reinforce the perceived seriousness of the established rules and the respective consequences of breaking them.

From this perspective, the effectiveness of cybersecurity policies in deterring transgressions relies on the severity, certainty, and speed of punishment. By making sure punishments being implemented are severe enough to deter violations, certain enough to be predictable, and swift enough to reinforce the perceived connection between the transgressive behaviour and the consequences of such, organisations can better enforce the level of compliance and ensure systems are protected.

GDT and Cybersecurity Awareness

So, there has been some research that has explored the application of GDT in the context of cybersecurity compliance, but it tends to be more limited compared to other theories (Alsharida et al., 2023). Findings suggest that the celerity of sanctions – the speed at which punishments are administered – has a limited effect on individuals' adherence to cybersecurity compliance behaviours, and this element may be less significant compared to other factors (Trang & Brendel, 2019). Additionally, the malicious intent behind a behaviour has been shown to influence the perceived severity of sanctions. As the perceived maliciousness of an action increases, so does the perceived severity of its associated punishment (Trang & Brendel, 2019). An intriguing insight from Trang and Brendel's (2019) study is the heightened relevance of sanction certainty in cybersecurity compliance compared to other contexts. The research indicates that emphasising the certainty of sanctions is more effective in encouraging positive compliance behaviours (e.g., following security protocols) than in deterring negative ones. This distinction is linked to individuals' risk perception: people are more risk-averse when it comes to engaging in positive compliance behaviours, as they perceive a greater potential cost for non-compliance.

Other researchers have explored the role of GDT in cyberloafing activities (Ugrin & Pearson, 2013). Their study examined the impact of sanctions, detection, enforcement, and perceived abusiveness of the cyberloafing activity alongside participants' likelihood to engage in such activities. They presented six different forms of cyberloafing, classified hierarchically by participants in terms of perceived seriousness: viewing pornography, personal shopping, viewing traditional media, social networking, personal money management, and engaging in personal emails. The results demonstrated that the presence of a sanction (either being fired or receiving a verbal reprimand) significantly impacted the likelihood of engaging in cyberloafing behaviour. More serious sanctions (e.g., being fired) had a greater deterrent effect. However, the most serious form of cyberloafing, viewing pornography at work, appeared immune to the impact of sanctions, suggesting that individuals willing to engage in this behaviour are prepared to take significant risks.

Deterrence methods were more effective for less serious cyberloafing activities, such as internet shopping and social media use, but proposed monitoring methods had an insignificant impact on the likelihood of engaging in these activities (Ugrin & Pearson, 2013). The authors suggested that employers need to publicise instances where individuals have been caught and reprimanded to ensure that such activities are seen as unacceptable. Changing organisational norms regarding the acceptability of these activities during work time would be a monumental task for many organisations.

Neutralisation Theory

Neutralisation theory (NT), developed by Sykes and Matza (1957), explores how individuals protect themselves from blame when committing a criminal act. People use various justifications to release themselves from moral, ethical, and legal implications (Hinduja, 2007). These justifications allow individuals to convince themselves that their actions are appropriate, even if they contradict societal rules (Connolly et al., 2023; Hinduja, 2007). Sykes and Matza (1957) identified five techniques individuals use to neutralise their involvement in deviant activities:

1. **Denial of Responsibility**: Individuals claim that their actions were not their fault, diverting blame to others or the situation. This is often captured by the phrase 'it is not my fault'. The individual may argue that external factors or other people are to blame for their actions.
2. **Denial of Injury**: Individuals assert that their actions did not cause any harm or injury. They claim that no one was hurt by their actions, thereby minimizing the perceived impact of their behaviour.

3. **Denial of Victim**: Individuals argue that no one was hurt by their actions, often saying 'no one got hurt'. This technique removes the injured party from the equation, suggesting that there is no victim to the deviant act or crime.
4. **Condemnation of the Condemner**: Individuals shift blame to those who accuse them, suggesting that the accusers are guilty of more serious offenses. For example, 'How dare they accuse me when they have been shown to be corrupt and guilty of wrongdoing in the past'. This technique offloads blame by making comparative judgments about the accusers.
5. **Appeal to Higher Authority**: Individuals justify their actions by claiming they were following orders from a higher power, which they believe overrides societal rules. They argue that their behaviour can be overlooked because they were acting on instructions from a higher authority.

There have also been some additional techniques that have extended NT further beyond these initial five elements; these are:

- **Defence of Necessity**: Individuals justify rule-breaking as essential and necessary, avoiding guilt (Minor, 1981; Siponen & Vance, 2010). They argue that the rule-breaking was necessary and that there was no other choice.
- **Metaphor of the Ledger**: Individuals argue that their good deeds outweigh their bad deeds, suggesting they are not bad people (Hinduja, 2007; Klockars, 1974; Minor, 1981). They claim that their history of honourable deeds should be considered, and that their positive actions outweigh any potential misdemeanours.
- **Claim of Normalcy**: Individuals assert that their actions are normal because 'everyone else does it'. This technique invokes social comparison, suggesting that the behaviour is acceptable because it is common.
- **Denial of Negative Intent**: Individuals claim that any negative consequences of their actions were unintended or accidental. They argue that the behaviour was a joke or an accident, and that the negative outcomes were not intentional.
- **Claims of Relative Acceptability**: Individuals compare their actions to more serious crimes, suggesting their behaviour is not that serious. For example, people caught drink-driving might argue that they have not harmed anyone or that the police should focus on more serious criminals, such as murderers and thieves.

These techniques can be used both after committing a deviant act (post hoc) and before (pre-deviant) to justify potential misconduct. For example, individuals caught drink-driving might argue that they have not harmed anyone or that the police should focus on more serious criminals. There have however been various criticisms that have been directed towards NT. For example, Fritsche (2005) argued that NT offers only a weak predictor for behaviour that contravenes accepted norms, where studies that express the power of the theory are often based on correlational evidence that fail to establish causality between factors. Fritsche (2005) also disputed the notion that individuals who have already engaged in norm violation are less likely to engage in neutralisation. Instead, it is suggested that prior violations serve to increase the impact of neutralisation where the individual becomes more efficient at using such methods to justify their actions. This has some clear ramifications for issues related to employees transgressing accepted rules within the organisation, particularly where 'repeat offenders' become more resilient by deploying some of the key neutralisation techniques detailed above.

Neutralisation Theory and Cybersecurity

There have been various attempts to apply NT to concepts underlying cybersecurity, including compliance with cybersecurity policies (Siponen & Vance, 2010). For example, Hinduja (2007) explored the role of NT in the context of individuals' willingness to engage in software piracy. He noted that denial of injury, appeal to higher loyalties, denial of negative intent, and claim of relative acceptability all impacted individuals' acceptance of engaging in these activities, but the relationship was relatively weak compared to other predictive factors.

Siponen and Vance (2010) explored the role of NT on individuals' intention to violate cybersecurity policies and found that the neutralisation mechanisms described above had a significant impact on this behaviour. In their study, they noted that defence of necessity, appeal to higher loyalties, condemnation of the condemner, metaphor of the ledger, denial of injury, and denial of responsibility all significantly contributed to neutralisation, which in turn had a significant impact on the intention to violate cybersecurity policies. Interestingly, the researchers noted that when additional elements linked to the deterrence model, such as informal and formal sanctions, and feelings of shame experienced because of committing the deviant act, were considered, these factors failed to provide significant predictors for violation of accepted cybersecurity protocols. This suggests that the power of neutralisation is a far stronger predictor of individual violation of cybersecurity compliance, where individuals who can actively rationalise their reasons for not engaging or actively violating prescribed rules are seen to be more persistent offenders even in the face of organisational sanctions.

Siponen and Vance (2010) presented an excellent discussion on how to overcome the potential neutralisation techniques individuals use when distancing themselves from active cybersecurity protection. They highlighted a series of measures to counteract each of the neutralisation techniques they examined:

- **Denial of Injury**: This can be counteracted by presenting individuals with clear information that there is an injured party when cybersecurity policies are transgressed. They pointed to work by Puhakainen (2006), which used scenario-based exercises in training to demonstrate the types of harm that can result from cybersecurity policy violations. Additionally, they suggested using the normative influence of supervisors within organisations to raise awareness of the potential damage an organisation can encounter due to cybersecurity breaches.
- **Denial of Responsibility**: This overlaps with the notion of diffusion of responsibility discussed in the context of moral disengagement. Individuals often believe that cybersecurity policies do not apply to them. Siponen and Vance (2010) suggested strategies such as one-on-one meetings with supervisors or inviting guest speakers to stress the need for everyone's compliance in cybersecurity. This approach targets the underlying neutralisation belief while engaging individuals on a more personal level, helping to overcome the diffusion of responsibility.
- **Defence of Necessity**: This is often used to excuse behaviours that transgress accepted cybersecurity rules in pursuit of job demands. To address this, organisations should stress that no matter how urgent a deadline is, there is no excuse for violating cybersecurity rules. Another method is to ensure organisational norms emphasise compliance with cybersecurity policies and remove the emphasis on meeting deadlines at any cost.
- **Appeal to Higher Authority**: Like defence of necessity, this involves justifying rule violations in pursuit of organisational needs. Managers and supervisors need to be clear that such violations are unacceptable and should lead by example. This also helps mitigate the potential for condemnation of the condemner, where employees justify their actions by pointing to similar behaviours by management.
- **Metaphor of the Ledger**: This technique involves individuals justifying their cybersecurity violations by pointing to their good performance in other areas. Siponen and Vance (2010) noted that individuals need to be shown that security violations are unacceptable, even if they have a clean slate in other behaviours. Cybersecurity should be seen as a continuous process that requires consistent adherence to policies.

By addressing these neutralisation techniques, organisations can foster a culture of accountability and compliance, ensuring that cybersecurity policies are adhered to consistently. This proactive approach not only mitigates the risk of security breaches but also reinforces the importance of ethical behaviour and a strong security culture within the organisation. Cultivating such a culture involves clear communication, leadership by example, and continuous education and training to keep cybersecurity at the forefront of organisational priorities.

Which Theory Is Best?

Well, that is the question that has been pondered for some time in the research literature, and the key thing to realise is that there is not a one-theory-fits-all approach to cybersecurity decision making. While some theories and models do some things well, they lack the depth and breadth to cope with other elements of cybersecurity awareness and decision making, which often involves the addition of new parts or stages in the process. While this is not a negative aspect, and indeed part and parcel of the research and development process in the need to improve and refine models, it means that picking one of these theories off the shelf to apply to all aspects of adherence or intent to engage in cybersecurity policies will always mean something needs to be added or something is missing. Each of the theories reviewed here presents some unique perspectives and insights into the ways in which people make decisions about undertaking cybersecurity protective measures.

For example, in terms of threat recognition and appraisal of threats, the technology threat avoidance model (TTAT) allows us to understand how individuals perceive their vulnerability to threats, as well as an assessment of the severity of such a threat. By adding in protection motivation theory (PMT), we have the emotional and cognitive dimensions that stimulate an individual to act on their threat appraisal, such as responses to fear or an appraisal of their personal vulnerability to the threat, which in turn could stimulate an individual to act. The theory of planned behaviour (TPB) incorporates an appreciation of how the individual's attitude towards the threat can influence the behavioural response, so individuals who see cybersecurity threats as being more serious will in turn have a higher level of threat recognition for these types of threats. General deterrence theory (GDT) engages our capacity to detect threats and the relevant consequences that are aligned with that threat, therefore increasing our threat perception. Finally, neutralisation theory (NT) presents an appreciation of how an individual can counteract the recognition of a threat by deploying various neutralizing factors, allowing them to offset the potential ramifications of transgressing accepted cybersecurity policies.

In terms of a coping appraisal where we assess the effectiveness of each of the potential actions we can deploy to protect against the threat, as well as an assessment of how well we can perform each of these behaviours, TTAT can serve to emphasise both response efficacy (the belief that engaging in a particular behaviour will reduce the threat) and self-efficacy (our confidence aligned to performing the behaviour in question) in the context of our threat coping mechanism. PMT allows us to consider the costs associated with carrying out the proposed behaviour for countering the threat as well as the potential effectiveness or benefits of deploying the protective measures, which in turn serve to influence our decision to engage in that behaviour. TPB presents a consideration of the level of control we feel we have over the behaviour and can be seen as either facilitating that behaviour or inhibiting the response due to a lack of perceived control. Finally, NT creates a set of barriers to engaging in the relevant security actions by allowing a rationalisation of inaction or the acceptance of the risky behaviours in question.

When we explore how these theories fit into the process of forming the intention to perform the behaviour in question, each has a different element to present when it comes to understanding what motivates compliance with cybersecurity policies. TPB is seen as the most central theory for this aspect of the process, where the three components of the model (attitudes, subjective norms, and perceived behavioural control) all serve to collectively shape our intentions to act. PMT aligns with the TPB approach by focusing on our motivations to protect ourselves, such as the negative consequences that could be aligned with not completing the behaviours in question. GDT will serve to motivate compliance with accepted rules by assessing the threat of detection and punishment. TTAT adds an additional layer of threat avoidance to the motivation for us to engage in the behaviour, whereas NT creates a series of counterarguments to engaging in the protective behaviour, serving to justify the risky behaviours in question.

What about the potential blocks or barriers to action? Well, there are a variety of ways in which these theories can serve to influence how individuals formulate potential mechanisms to stop them from engaging in protective behaviours. For example, PMT considers the costs of responding to the threat in question against the proposed outcomes or the chance of the behaviour in question deflecting the threat. TTAT would also consider the drain on resources because of making the response to the proposed threat. TPB is more focused on the perception of control over the behaviour in question and would seek to establish how much capacity the individual has to perform the action in question, as well as exploring the social norms aligned with the action (e.g., no one else does this, so why should I). GDT would serve to explore the sanctions that are proposed because of violating the rule, where harsher punishments could discourage action or lead to inaction through a process of reduced morale.

Finally, in terms of the respective role of feedback on these processes, each of these theories makes a clear proposal on how these should be incorporated into the cybersecurity framework. For example, PMT sees protective behaviours being reinforced because of the successful mitigation of a threat, but this also means that there needs to be a clear mechanism to support situations where threat mitigation has not been successful. TTAT sees the engagement of avoidance behaviours to relevant threats as being reinforced through positive outcomes, but the same provision applies to this theory as with PMT in terms of support for outcomes that did not go as planned. For GDT, there needs to be a clear set of penalties that are seen to be fair and aim to reward compliant behaviours, and ones that are initiated quickly and

TABLE 7.1 A Comparison of the Main Decision-Making Theories and Their Approach to Cybersecurity Behaviour

Aspect	Technology Threat Avoidance Theory	Protection Motivation Theory	Neutralisation Theory	General Deterrence Theory	Theory of Planned Behaviour
Threat Appraisal and Recognition	Examine the perceived threat severity and vulnerability.	Evaluate threat based on the severity and the likelihood to experience harm.	Engage in a priori justifications to avoid engaging in threat appraisal.	Increased threat perception because of detection and assessment of consequences.	Risk perception is influenced by attitudes towards the threat context.
Coping Mechanisms	Focus on response efficacy and self-efficacy.	Additional layers of emotional and cognitive evaluation on coping ability.	Uses rationalisation for non-compliance to remove positive engagement.	Matches confidence in monitoring threats with perceived penalties to reinforce compliance behaviour.	Perceived behavioural control – determines if an individual can successfully engage in protective behaviours.
Behavioural Decision	Encouraging threat avoidance behaviours.	Encourages protective behaviours.	Encourages justification of transgressions.	Encourages compliance through fear of punishment.	Encourages compliance through subjective norms and social expectations.
Barriers to Action	Resource availability.	Response costs.	Reinforcement of non-compliant behaviours.	Overly harsh penalties.	Lack of perceived control and conflicting subjective norms.
Outcomes and Feedback	Avoidance behaviours reinforced via positive outcomes.	Protective behaviours – reinforced through threat mitigation.	Successful neutralisation – increases likelihood to resist protective behaviours.	Clear, fair, and swift penalties and obvious rewards – compliant behaviour.	Repeated success/ failure influences future attitudes, subjective norms, and control beliefs.

swiftly to avoid uncertainty or perceptions of inconsistent approaches. For TPB, a repeated learning process of success or failure in terms of the behaviours that are deployed to counteract perceived threats will in turn serve to influence the attitudes, subjective norms, and control beliefs associated with threats. Again, a critical part of this process is allowing individuals to reflect on their decisions in a way that provides supportive information to help reduce the potential for biases or misinterpretations to creep into the formation of attitudes. Finally, NT, if deployed successfully, means that the individual will be more likely to engage in the threat-eliciting behaviours in the future, so these mechanisms need to be tackled using strategies that serve to isolate and reduce them.

We have created a structured comparison of the different theories and how they relate to the context of cybersecurity in Table 7.1. This table highlights how each theory addresses different aspects of cybersecurity behaviour, from recognizing threats to coping mechanisms, making behavioural decisions, facing barriers to action, and receiving outcomes and feedback. By understanding these differences, organisations can tailor their cybersecurity strategies to address the specific motivations and barriers that influence their employees' behaviours.

Summary

This chapter explores the psychological underpinnings of cybersecurity compliance, focusing on decision-making processes and the theories that explain why individuals engage in protective behaviours. It begins with the theory of planned behaviour, which highlights the roles of attitudes, subjective norms, and perceived behavioural control in shaping intentions to comply with cybersecurity policies. The chapter then examines protection motivation theory, which emphasises the impact of fear appeals and the dual processes of threat and coping appraisals on protective behaviours. Technology threat avoidance theory is discussed for its focus on threat perception and coping mechanisms specific to IT-related threats, while general deterrence theory is analysed for its emphasis on the deterrent effects of punishment severity, certainty, and celerity. Neutralisation theory is reviewed for its explanation of how individuals justify deviant behaviours to avoid blame.

The chapter provides a detailed comparison of these theories, noting that each offers unique insights into different aspects of cybersecurity behaviour. It emphasises that no single theory can fully explain the complexities of cybersecurity decision making. Instead, a combination of elements from various models is necessary to address the diverse motivations and barriers individuals face. The chapter concludes by highlighting the importance of tailored strategies that integrate these theoretical perspectives to enhance cybersecurity compliance. By understanding and addressing the specific factors that influence cybersecurity behaviours, organisations can develop more effective policies and interventions to foster a culture of proactive security awareness and compliance.

References

Ajzen, I. (1985). From intentions to actions: A theory of planned behaviour. In J. Kuhl & J. Beckmann (Eds), *Action control: From cognition to behaviour* (pp. 11–39). Springer-Verlag.

Ajzen, I. (1991). The theory of planned behaviour. *Organisational Behaviour and Human Decision Processes*, 50(2), 179–211.

Ajzen, I. (2020). The theory of planned behaviour: Frequently asked questions. *Human Behaviour and Emerging Technologies*, 2(4), 314–324.

Ajzen, I., & Fishbein, M. (1980). *Understanding attitudes and predicting social behavior*. Prentice-Hall.

Alanazi, F., Freeman, M., & Tootell, H. (2022). The role of social influence in cybersecurity behaviour: A study of young adults. *Journal of Information Security and Applications*, 62, 102–112.

Alqahtani, A., & Kavakli-Thorne, M. (2020). Protection motivation theory in cybersecurity: A systematic review. *Computers & Security*, 95, 101–115.

Alsharida, R. A., Al-rimy, B. A. S., Al-Emran, M., & Zainal, A. (2023). A systematic review of multi perspectives on human cybersecurity behavior. *Technology in Society*, 73, 102258. doi:10.1016/j.techsoc.2023.102258.

Arachchilage, N. A. G., & Love, S. (2014). Security awareness of computer users: A phishing threat avoidance perspective. *Computers in Human Behavior*, 38, 304–312. doi:10.1016/j.chb.2014.05.046.

Balla, E., & Hagger, M. S. (2024). The role of coping appraisals in protection motivation theory: A meta-analysis. *Health Psychology Review*, 18(1), 1–23.

Boer, H., & Seydel, E. R. (1996). Protection motivation theory. In M. Conner & P. Norman (Eds), *Predicting health behaviour* (pp. 95–120). Open University Press.

Boss, S. R., Galletta, D. F., Lowry, P. B., Moody, G. D., & Polak, P. (2015). What do users have to fear? Using fear appeals to engender threats and fear that motivate protective security behaviours. *MIS Quarterly*, 39(4), 837–864.

Boysen, R. A., Hewitt, B., Gibbs, J., & McLeod, A. (2019). Technology threat avoidance theory: A systematic review. *Journal of Information Security and Applications*, 47, 102–115.

Chen, H., & Li, W. (2017). Mobile device users' privacy security assurance behavior: A technology threat avoidance perspective. *Information and Computer Security*, 25(3), 330–344. doi:10.1108/ICS-04-2016-0027.

Cheng, L., Li, Y., Li, W., Holm, E., & Zhai, Q. (2013). Understanding the violation of IS security policy in organisations: An integrated model based on social control and deterrence theory. *Computers & Security*, 39, 447–459.

Connolly, L., Borrion, H., Arief, B., & Kaddoura, S. (2023). Applying neutralisation theory to better understand ransomware offenders. *Proceedings – 8th IEEE European Symposium on Security and Privacy Workshops, Euro S and P W 2023*, 177–182. doi:10.1109/EuroSPW59978.2023.00025.

D'Arcy, J., & Hovav, A. (2009). Does one size fit all? Examining the differential effects of IS security countermeasures. *Journal of Business Ethics*, 89(Suppl. 1), 59–71. doi:10.1007/s10551-008-9909-7.

D'Arcy, J., Hovav, A., & Galletta, D. (2009). User awareness of security counter-measures and its impact on information systems misuse: A deterrence approach. *Information Systems Research*, 20(1), 79–98. doi:10.1287/isre.1070.0160.

Fishbein, M., & Ajzen, I. (1975). *Belief, attitude, intention, and behaviour: An introduction to theory and research*. Addison-Wesley.

Fishbein, M., & Ajzen, I. (2010). *Predicting and changing behavior: The reasoned action approach*. Psychology Press.

Fritsche, I. (2005). Predicting deviant behaviour by neutralization: Myths and findings. *Deviant Behaviour*, 26(5), 483–510.

Gillam, L., & Waite, K. (2021). Technology threat avoidance theory: A systematic review. *Journal of Information Security and Applications*, 47, 102–115.

Guo, K. H., Yuan, Y., Archer, N. P., & Connelly, C. E. (2011). Understanding non-malicious security violations in the workplace: A composite behaviour model. *Journal of Management Information Systems*, 28(2), 203–236.

Hassan, N. M., Ismail, Z., & Rahman, N. A. (2016). The theory of planned behaviour and information security policy compliance: A systematic review. *Journal of Information Security and Applications*, 27, 28–36.

Hinduja, S. (2007). Neutralization theory and online software piracy: An empirical analysis. *Ethics and Information Technology*, 9(3), 187–204.

Ifinedo, P. (2012). Understanding information systems security policy compliance: An integration of the theory of planned behaviour and the protection motivation theory. *Computers & Security*, 31(1), 83–95.

Johnston, A. C., Warkentin, M., & Siponen, M. (2015). An enhanced fear appeal rhetorical framework: Leveraging threats to the human asset through sanctioning rhetoric. *MIS Quarterly*, 39(1), 113–134.

Klockars, C. B. (1974). *The professional fence*. Free Press.

LaRose, R., Rifon, N. J., & Enbody, R. (2007). Promoting personal responsibility for internet safety. *Communications of the ACM*, 50(2), 57–62.

Lee, D., Larose, R., & Rifon, N. (2008). Keeping our network safe: A model of online protection behaviour. *Behaviour and Information Technology*, 27(5), 445–454. doi:10.1080/01449290600879344.

Leventhal, H. (1970). Findings and theory in the study of fear communications. In L. Berkowitz (Ed.), *Advances in experimental social psychology* (Vol. 5, pp. 119–186). Academic Press.

Li, H., He, W., Xu, L., Ash, I., Anwar, M., & Yuan, X. (2019). Investigating the impact of cybersecurity policy awareness on employees' cybersecurity behaviour. *Journal of Information Security and Applications*, 48, 102–115.

Liang, H., & Xue, Y. (2009). Avoidance of information technology threats: A theoretical perspective. *MIS Quarterly*, 33(1), 71–90.

Liang, H., & Xue, Y. (2010). Understanding security behaviours in personal computer usage: A threat avoidance perspective. *Journal of the Association for Information Systems*, 11(7), 394–413.

Minor, W. W. (1981). Techniques of neutralization: A reconceptualization and empirical examination. *Journal of Research in Crime and Delinquency*, 18(2), 295–318.

Nehme, M., & George, J. (2022). Technology threat avoidance theory: A systematic review. *Journal of Information Security and Applications*, 47, 102–115.

Ng, B. Y., & Xu, Y. (2007). Studying users' computer security behavior using the health belief model. *PACIS 2007 Proceedings*, 45, 423–437.

Norman, P., Boer, H., & Seydel, E. R. (2005). Protection motivation theory. In M. Conner & P. Norman (Eds), *Predicting health behaviour* (2nd ed., pp. 81–126). Open University Press.

Puhakainen, P. (2006). *A design theory for information security awareness* (Doctoral dissertation). University of Oulu.

Quackenbush, S. L. (2011). Deterrence theory: Where do we stand? *Review of International Studies*, 37(2), 741–762.

Rogers, R. W. (1975). A protection motivation theory of fear appeals and attitude change. *Journal of Psychology*, 91(1), 93–114.

Rogers, R. W. (1983). Cognitive and physiological processes in fear appeals and attitude change: A revised theory of protection motivation. In J. T. Cacioppo & R. E. Petty (Eds), *Social psychophysiology: A sourcebook* (pp. 153–176). Guilford Press.

Safa, N. S., Von Solms, R., & Furnell, S. (2016). Information security policy compliance model in organizations. *Computers and Security*, 56, 1–13. doi:10.1016/j.cose.2015.10.006.

Sheeran, P., & Webb, T. L. (2016). The intention-behaviour gap. *Social and Personality Psychology Compass*, 10(9), 503–518.

Siponen, M., & Vance, A. (2010). Neutralization: New insights into the problem of employee information systems security policy violations. *MIS Quarterly*, 34(3), 487–502.

Sommestad, T., & Hallberg, J. (2013). A review of the theory of planned behaviour in the context of information security policy compliance. *Computers & Security*, 32, 1–15.

Straub, D. W., & Welke, R. J. (1998). Coping with systems risk: Security planning models for management decision making. *MIS Quarterly, 22*(4), 441–469.

Sykes, G. M., & Matza, D. (1957). Techniques of neutralization: A theory of delinquency. *American Sociological Review*, 22(6), 664–670.

Trang, S., & Brendel, B. (2019). A meta-analysis of deterrence theory in information security policy compliance research. *Information Systems Frontiers*, 21(6), 1265–1284. doi:10.1007/s10796-019-09956-4.

Tsai, H. Y. S., Jiang, M., Alhabash, S., Larose, R., Rifon, N. J., & Cotten, S. R. (2016). Understanding online safety behaviors: A protection motivation theory perspective. *Computers and Security*, 59, 138–150. doi:10.1016/j.cose.2016.02.009.

Ugrin, J. C., & Pearson, J. M. (2013). The effects of sanctions and stigmas on cyberloafing. *Computers in Human Behaviour*, 29(3), 812–820.

Vance, A., Siponen, M., & Pahnila, S. (2012). Motivating IS security compliance: Insights from habit and protection motivation theory. *Information & Management*, 49(3–4), 190–198.

White, G. L. (2017). General deterrence theory: A systematic review. *Journal of Information Security and Applications*, 47, 102–115.

Williams, K. R., & Hawkins, R. (1986). Perceptual research on general deterrence: A critical review. *Law & Society Review*, 20(4), 545–572.

Woon, I. M. Y., Tan, G. W., & Low, R. T. (2016). A protection motivation theory approach to home wireless security. *Proceedings of the 2016 International Conference on Information Systems*, 1–12. https://aisel.aisnet.org/icis2005/31.

Young, B., Carpenter, S., & McLeod, A. (2016). Technology threat avoidance theory: A systematic review. *Journal of Information Security and Applications*, 47, 102–115.

Zahedi, F. M., Abbasi, A., & Chen, Y. (2015). Fake-website detection tools: Identifying elements that promote individuals' use and enhance their performance. *Journal of the Association for Information Systems*, 16(6), 448–484.

Zwilling, M., Klien, G., & Wiggins, S. (2020). The role of cybersecurity awareness in the intention-behaviour gap. *Journal of Cybersecurity*, 6(1), tyaa001.

8

ASSESSING CYBERSECURITY AWARENESS

Introduction

Understanding people's cybersecurity behaviours and intentions is crucial for organisations, security practitioners, and researchers. It helps identify individuals who may be susceptible to poor security practices (Gratian et al., 2018), where gaining insights into these behaviours can aid in developing interventions and educating those who may pose a weak link to overall cybersecurity. One typical way to achieve this is through measurement and exploration via research.

Before delving into different cybersecurity measures, let us contextualise some of the research and measures discussed in this chapter. Previous research has often focused on positive versus negative cybersecurity behaviours (e.g., compliance with cybersecurity policies versus violation of policies). However, this dichotomy is too simplistic, as various elements such as context, motive, expertise, and consequences influence behaviours. To conceptualise security behaviour further, cybersecurity behaviour has been suggested to fall into two main categories, as presented by Guo (2013):

Pro-security behaviours: These refer to the intention to support and comply with security policies and procedures. This category can be further divided into:

- **Security assurance behaviour (SAB)**: Linked to organisational safety and security, this refers to intentional behaviours individuals carry out to protect information systems, such as reporting security incidents in the workplace. This encompasses effortful actions.
- **Security compliant behaviour (SCB)**: Refers to behaviour that aligns with security policies, whether intentional or unintentional. For example, a

DOI: 10.4324/9781003509011-8

person might consciously avoid actions that could cause security problems, or they may unintentionally act in line with expected security policies.

Anti-security behaviours: These refer to the intent to disrupt security systems, such as violating security policies and requirements.

- **Security risk-taking behaviour (SRB)**: Refers to intentional behaviours that may put information systems at risk without the purpose of causing intentional damage. For example, writing down passwords.
- **Security damaging behaviours (SDB)**: These are behaviours that cause intentional damage to information security. The person is aware they are prohibited from engaging in these behaviours, such as data theft.

Different studies have examined various aspects of cybersecurity behaviours, with some taking a comprehensive approach by looking into both pro- and anti-security behaviours, while others focus on one or the other. To effectively understand and measure cybersecurity behaviours, researchers have developed and implemented various techniques. One of the most used methods is self-report measures. These measures involve individuals reporting their own behaviours, attitudes, and intentions related to cybersecurity. Self-report measures can take several forms, including questionnaires, surveys, and interviews, which we will focus on in the next section.

Self-Report Measures

Understanding computer security intentions is important, as this can give an indication of an individual's planned behaviours. However, whilst it would be useful to glean information of actual security behaviours (e.g., tracking a person's actions online), this can be rather difficult for various privacy-related and ethical reasons. However, when studying human behaviour, self-report questionnaires are one of the most widely used tools to measure a particular concept, or gain understanding of the prevalence, or occurrence, of the variables of interest. Self-report questionnaires, as hinted at in the name, rely on the individual's own report of their behaviours, attitudes, or beliefs. There are several advantages to self-report questionnaires which make them a popular choice to explore concepts. They are widely used due to their ease of administration and how straightforward it is to gather data from a large number of participants. These questionnaires often include items that assess compliance with security policies, awareness of security practices, and attitudes towards cybersecurity. For example, participants might be asked to rate how frequently they follow specific security protocols or how confident they feel about their ability to protect sensitive information. The primary advantage is their practicality. Specifically, they are inexpensive and can be shared without the need for incentives – which is especially beneficial for individuals in organisation. Another advantage is that self-report measures are efficient at collecting data – it is possible to gather a large amount of data in a short amount of time (in comparison to an interview, which may take an hour or two for one participant). Of course, the other good thing about self-report scales is that they can also be applied to assess and study cybersecurity behaviours.

There are some generic limitations attached to the use of self-report measures which can be detailed under the following areas:

- Social Desirability Bias: Participants have the tendency to respond to questions presented to them in a way that they believe may be more socially acceptable or desirable rather than giving honest answers. In terms of cybersecurity awareness this one can have some serious consequences that need to be considered. If you think about the subject matter, participants are being asked if they understand and follow organisationally mandated cybersecurity rules and policies. For those who do not, or take a laxer approach to doing so, they may be less inclined to admit this in a questionnaire, even though they have been assured that their data will be kept confidential and no identifying information will be related to employers. There is no real way around this, and it is more of a general note to raise awareness about this issue rather than making a clear statement that self-report studies are rubbish when it comes to assessing cybersecurity awareness and behaviours (Grimm, 2010; McCormac et al., 2017).
- Recall Bias: For some participants, recalling what they have had for breakfast may be a struggle – so if you start to probe their behaviours from the preceding 12 months, you start to get into the territory where there could be inconsistencies in their recall. It is better to focus on clear statements about their attitudes towards doing something, rather than presenting a detailed exploration of the things that they might have done.
- Self-Awareness: Remember when we talked about the Dunning-Kruger effect we mentioned earlier on in Chapter 2? Well, this can come into play here. Often people like to paint an ideal picture of their own behaviour, which can be far from the reality. It means that we are not great at admitting our own inadequacies and may exhibit some clear overconfidence when we are answering questions about our own behaviours and abilities.
- Limited Depth: Self-report measures are great for capturing surface data about a particular area but lack the depth to probe deeper into the reasons why people do certain things – this is where focus groups and interviews can show their strengths.

Despite these limitations, self-report measures remain the backbone of research in cybersecurity awareness and behaviours, and much of the shortcomings mentioned here can be overcome by employing other methods.

To date, various measures have been developed to investigate security behaviours. Among these, two notable scales stand out for their holistic approach: the Security Behaviour Intentions Scale (SeBIS) and the Human Aspects of Information Security Questionnaire (HAIS-Q). SeBIS, developed by Egelman and Peer (2015), focuses on assessing security behaviours. It is designed to measure end-users' computer security attitudes and predict their security behaviours. It consists of four sub-scales that evaluate different aspects of security behaviour. In contrast, the HAIS-Q measures knowledge, attitudes, and behaviours related to information security. This scale assesses various dimensions of security awareness, including understanding security policies, recognizing security threats, and implementing security practices. The HAIS-Q has been used in organisational contexts to identify areas where additional training or interventions may be needed.

There is some conceptual overlap between these two scales. For instance, both SeBIS and HAIS-Q measure dimensions such as internet use and password behaviours (Ayyagari & Crowell, 2020). However, each scale has its unique focus and application, providing valuable insights into various aspects of cybersecurity behaviour. We are going to delve into each of these measures in more detail, starting with the SeBIS.

The Security Behaviour Intentions Scale

The SeBIS was developed to measure user security behaviour intentions, specifically to comply with common security advice provided by nationwide US internet service providers, the United States Computer Readiness and Security Team (US-CERT), and industry consortia (Egelman & Peer, 2015). The scale consists of 16 items covering four dimensions of security behaviours:

- **Device Securement**: This dimension refers to users' behaviours in securing their devices, including locking devices using PINs and passwords, and locking devices before leaving them unattended.
- **Password Generation**: This dimension focuses on using strong passwords and not reusing passwords across different accounts.
- **Proactive Awareness**: This refers to users' awareness regarding contextual cues, such as noticing suspicious web links or being cautious when submitting information to websites.
- **Updating**: This dimension assesses the extent to which users keep their software security up to date in a timely manner.

These dimensions collectively provide a comprehensive overview of users' security behaviours and intentions, helping researchers and practitioners understand and improve cybersecurity practices.

The SeBIS has been utilised in several studies and has proven to be a useful predictive measure of security behaviour. For example, research by

Egelman et al. (2016) demonstrated that the SeBIS is effective in predicting actual cybersecurity behaviours. In their study, participants were asked to engage in real-world behaviours, such as creating a password for their study account and updating their devices following a Mac operating system update. The results showed that scores on all four sub-scales of the SeBIS were predictive of specific security behaviours, highlighting the scale's utility as a predictive tool (Egelman et al., 2016). However, Egelman et al. (2016) also emphasised the need for further research to examine a wider range of behaviours, as the behaviours assessed in their study were closely aligned with those specifically mentioned in the SeBIS.

Another study by Gratian et al. (2018) examined the SeBIS in the context of personality, risk-taking, and decision making. This study highlighted that individual differences play a role in cybersecurity behaviour intentions, though it provided mixed findings regarding risk-taking. These results further underscored the need for additional research to explore the complex interplay between personality traits and cybersecurity behaviours.

One of the advantages of the SeBIS is its brevity. With only 16 items, it is a concise and efficient tool to include in surveys, especially compared to some of the other scales discussed later in this chapter. However, there are also critical points to consider about this scale. Firstly, the items on the SeBIS refer to specific devices that are not necessarily online. For example, items like 'I use a password/passcode to unlock my laptop or tablet' and 'I manually lock my computer screen when I step away from it' focus on physical device security. In contrast, other items address online awareness, such as 'I submit information to websites without first verifying that it will be sent securely (e.g., SSL, 'https://', a lock icon)'. This mix of online and offline security behaviours can affect how participants respond, as the importance and level of effort required for these behaviours may vary depending on the context and device, especially since many devices are now online (Taylor & van Schaik, 2023). Additionally, the SeBIS does not distinguish between different contexts, such as personal and business use. Some questions may be influenced by organisational policies, such as software updates, which can lead to variability in responses based on the participants' environment. This lack of contextual differentiation can be a limitation when interpreting the results, as security behaviours may differ significantly between personal and professional settings.

Whilst the SeBIS is a useful and efficient tool for measuring security behaviour intentions, it needs some careful interpretation of its results and its use in research as a diagnostic tool needs to be considered against these noted issues. A more general critical issue is that the SeBIS does not capture a person's actual behaviour – as mentioned earlier, this is generally quite difficult to do due to challenges with privacy and ethics, though insight into actual behaviour would be beneficial as it would also help to mitigate potential social desirability biases that can be an issue in self-report measures (i.e., the participant may answer the questions on the scale to make themselves look like they engage in good cybersecurity behaviours, when in reality they do not). However, as highlighted earlier, validation of the scale did include engagement with aspects of 'real world' behaviour, highlighting the SeBIS as a useful predictive tool in cybersecurity research.

The Human Aspects of Information Security Questionnaire

The HAIS-Q is a comprehensive 63-item scale designed to measure an individual's knowledge, attitude, and behaviour (Xu et al., 2022). The HAIS-Q is based around a knowledge, attitudes, and behaviour (KAB) model, which suggests that as an individual's knowledge of security policies and procedures increases, their attitude towards security improves, leading to better security behaviours (Parsons et al., 2013, 2017). We have presented a brief breakdown of each of these elements here:

1. **Knowledge**: This refers to the information and understanding that individuals have about a particular topic. In the context of security, it includes awareness of threats and best practices. For example, in the context of cybersecurity, this could be the employee's existing knowledge about password creation that they have obtained through training sessions.
2. **Attitudes**: This encompasses the feelings and beliefs that individuals hold towards the topic. A positive attitude towards cybersecurity, for example, can motivate individuals to follow best practices.
3. **Behaviour**: The actual actions that individuals take. Effective security behaviour involves consistently applying knowledge and positive attitudes to protect against threats.

The HAIS-Q focuses on seven key areas of information security, each divided into three sub-areas measured by separate items relating to knowledge, attitude, and behaviour. The key areas are:

- Password Management: Practices related to the creation, management, and use of passwords in a secure manner.
- Email Use: Safe practices for handling emails, including the capacity to recognise phishing attempts.
- Internet Use: Secure browsing habits and awareness of online threats.
- Mobile Devices: Safety practices related to the use of and securing of mobile devices.
- Information Handling: The proper handling and protection of sensitive information.
- Incident Reporting: The awareness of how to report security-related incidents in the correct way.

Each of these areas is assessed through items that measure knowledge (what the individual knows), attitude (how the individual feels), and behaviour (what the individual does) regarding information security.

The HAIS-Q is a comprehensive measure that assesses security behaviours holistically, standing out among other measures that investigate internet behaviours. One of its main strengths is its clear distinction between thoughts, feelings, and actions (Xu et al., 2022). This aligns with the need to specify the knowledge, attitudes, and behaviour elements when using the KAB model. When implementing the HAIS-Q, all items are presented in a fixed random order, with the knowledge, attitudes, and behaviour items being presented sequentially.

However, despite the comprehensiveness of the HAIS-Q, there are some weaknesses to consider. One notable limitation is that it does not account for external influences, such as cultural and social factors (Hong et al., 2022). As we will explore later in Chapter 10, culture can significantly impact security behaviours. Although current research is limited, it has been suggested that culture can shape how individuals approach cybersecurity behaviour (Kharlamov & Pogrebna, 2019; Onumo et al., 2017), making it a crucial element to consider when implementing large-scale data collection exercises. Similarly, social influence and social norms can impact individual behaviour within organisations. This is often explained by the theory of planned behaviour (Ajzen, 1991), which we reviewed in Chapter 7. This theory consists of three aspects: attitudes, subjective norms, and perceived behavioural control. Subjective norms refer to the perception that significant others (e.g., influential people such as a boss or manager) expect or want an individual to implement specific cybersecurity behaviours (such as not sharing passwords in the workplace). Individuals may engage in these behaviours to meet these expectations and/or avoid criticism or punishment. Research supports this, showing that social influence positively affects young adults' intentions to engage in cybersecurity behaviours. When peers, family, or colleagues encourage cybersecurity behaviours, this perceived social pressure leads to a higher intent to perform these behaviours (Alanazi et al., 2022). Therefore, external influences are an important aspect to consider regarding security behaviours, which the HAIS-Q does not account for.

Another weakness of the HAIS-Q is its length – it consists of 63 items! While this makes it comprehensive, research projects often include additional scales to collect demographic information and investigate the project's or organisation's specific goals and objectives. Including these, on top of the 63-item HAIS-Q, can result in an exceptionally long overall survey. For participants, this can become tedious and lead to something called participant response fatigue. This is problematic because participant fatigue can result in respondents not providing truthful answers to reduce the burden of answering questions and complete the survey more quickly.

One final criticism for the HAIS-Q is of the actual structure of the questionnaire itself in relation to the underlying KAB components. In our use of the

HAIS-Q we have found it very hard to align the items included in each of over-arching thematic areas (knowledge, attitude, and behaviour). This is also true of the underlying focus areas that are related to things such as password creation and securement and physical data handling. Whilst this is not a massive issue if organisations are utilising the scale as a checklist or overview for the current state of play within their organisation, it does limit the capacity to interpret the results in term of the underlying dimensions of cybersecurity behaviours.

Human Cyber-Resilience Scale

Following from the SeBIS and HAIS-Q, it is worth noting that new scales are being developed to investigate various aspects of cyber behaviour. For example, at the time of writing this chapter, the 'Human Cyber-Resilience Scale' (HCRS) had been developed by Joinson et al. (2023). This scale focuses on understanding the factors that underpin individuals' resilience to cyberattacks, rather than the behaviours that could protect them from cybersecurity incidents, as seen with the SeBIS and HAIS-Q.

The HCRS comprises 16 items across four sub-scales, which are presented. Participants respond to items using the prompt: 'Thinking about my experiences with online cybersecurity threats or issues (e.g., being hacked, phishing, etc.)'. The scale includes the following focus areas:

1. **Self-Efficacy**:

    a   **Focus**: Confidence in one's ability to handle cybersecurity threats.
    b   **Example**: 'I can keep my devices secure'.

2. **Helplessness**:

    a   **Focus**: Feelings of discouragement and inability to deal with cybersecurity issues.
    b   **Example**: 'I feel helpless'.

3. **Social Support**:

    a   **Focus**: Availability of support from friends, family, or colleagues in dealing with cybersecurity threats.
    b   **Example**: 'I have friends/family who can help me deal with the threats'.

4. **Learning and Growth**:

    a   **Focus**: Viewing cybersecurity challenges as opportunities for learning and personal growth.
    b   **Example**: 'I see them as learning experiences'.

(Joinson et al., 2023)

The HCRS serves to place emphasis on understanding not just the outcomes of behaviours, but more the factors that align to underpin an individual's resistance to cyberattacks. It acknowledges that there are factors external to the individual that can influence resilience, such as support, which is one of the main detractors of the HAIS-Q. It is also inherently shorter that the HAIS-Q, whilst offering a more comprehensive assessment of the key areas that serve to influence resilience when compared to the SeBIS. Overall, the HCRS is particularly handy if organisations are searching for a mechanism that helps them to understand how resilient individuals are within their organisation, with the SeBIS and the HAIS-Q being more substantial tools focused on specific behaviours.

There are a variety of studies that applied the concept of the theory of planned behaviour (TPB, see Chapter 7) to create scales that are designed to measure intention to perform cybersecurity behaviours. Whilst there is no single measurement tool that has been universally accepted as a cybersecurity intention behaviour scale, most scales that follow this approach adopt the constructs on which the TPB is based, namely attitudes, subjective norms, and perceived behaviour controls and their influence on the intention to carry out the behaviours in question. For example, Sommestad et al. (2017) explored a wide range of factors linked to TPB that could be added to the theory to make it more relevant to cybersecurity awareness. The researchers noted that two additional elements, anticipation of regret associated with the behaviour in question and habit formation, significantly increased the predictive power of a TPB-based model, making these factors prime candidates for exploration in further scales.

Summary of Self-Report Methods

We have explored some holistic measures for assessing cybersecurity behaviours, but many other measures focus on various aspects of cybersecurity. The choice of scale depends on the type of research being conducted or the specific interests of an organisation. Selecting a scale that best fits the research questions is crucial.

While self-report measures are quick and convenient to implement, they have both strengths and weaknesses. Participant response fatigue can impact the accuracy of responses, as participants may rush through the survey. Additionally, participants might answer in a way they think the researcher wants or in a socially desirable manner (e.g., claiming they create strong passwords because they know it's the right thing to do, even if their passwords are easily guessable).

Another limitation is that self-report measures restrict responses to the questions within the scale, preventing a deeper understanding of the reasons behind certain behaviours. For example, if someone shares their passwords with colleagues, we might not understand why they made that decision or their experiences with it.

To address these limitations, other methods such as interviews and focus groups can be used to gain a more comprehensive understanding of cyber-security behaviours. These methods allow for exploring the underlying reasons and experiences behind participants' actions.

Qualitative Methods

In comparison to the quantitative methods we have explored in the previous section, *qualitative* methods offer another approach we can use to further explore and understand cybersecurity behaviours. Qualitative methods differ from more quantitative methods, as they focus on words (rather than num-bers, which we see in scales and measures), and are used to understand thoughts and experiences around a phenomenon – for example, how or why a person may decide to engage in cybersecurity behaviours, and exploring the experiences of their decisions. When it comes to qualitative methods, there are different methods that can be used to collect data – perhaps the most common methods are interviews and focus groups. Qualitative methods are essential if we wish to delve beyond just the numbers presented by survey data, and we view these methods as being essential when it comes to under-standing the motivations and barriers that people encounter when engaging in cybersecurity awareness. The great thing about qualitative methods, such as focus groups and interviews, is that they are flexible and can be adaptive to the emerging trends which arise during the research process. If a partici-pant mentions something that is interesting and the researcher feels that this needs to be focused on, we can switch the focus to concentrate on these ele-ments. In turn it means that the data from these methods can be rich and detailed, capturing the finer details of human behaviour.

These methods are not without their respective limitations, but as long as there is some form of acknowledgement that such limitations exist, the use-fulness of the data obtained can far outweigh any negatives. For example, there is a limited capacity to generalise trends from findings obtained through qualitative methods as they often focus on small, non-randomly selected samples. Similarly, they can be very subjective, not only in terms of the researcher's interpretation of the findings, but also the understanding of the area that is presented by the participants. They can also be time con-suming to conduct and analyse, and the analysis can require a level of expertise that is often outside the remit of many non-experts. Finally, there is a draw on resources, including time and financial investment, that needs to be considered alongside the requirements of the organisation.

Interviews and Focus Groups

Interviews are a one-to-one conversation between the researcher and partici-pant. They can be conducted in a structured manner (sticking to pre-determined questions, without flexibility), an unstructured manner (where there are no pre-determined questions), or a semi-structured manner (where there are pre-determined questions but flexibility to discuss topics associated with the questions). Semi-structured interviews are generally the most used due to the flexibility they allow in the conversation. This flexibility can be beneficial in exploring aspects that the researcher did not consider in the pre-determined questions. Focus groups, in contrast, involve a small group of people who discuss their opinions and perceptions on a topic. Focus groups are particularly useful for examining group dynamics and how views may form or change during the discussion.

Several studies have used interview methods to explore various aspects of cybersecurity and cybersecurity behaviours. For example, research by Shen et al. (2023) explored the impacts of an organisation's cybersecurity training programme on employees using semi-structured interviews. The findings indicated that participants perceived cybersecurity training as the responsibility of organisations and that on-the-job cybersecurity training improved organisational efficiency by promoting trained behaviour and credible performance among employees. This highlights that cybersecurity training can contribute to both organisational efficiency and human capital within organisations (Miglani & Obeng, 2023; Shen et al., 2023). However, this study did not explore perceptions around the motivations to engage in cybersecurity training, which could further our understanding of *why* individuals may or may not comply with cybersecurity training and policy. Indeed, motivation to adhere to protective behaviours online plays a significant role in understanding these behaviours. Based on self-determination theory (SDT; Deci & Ryan, 2012; Ryan & Deci, 2024), motivations are generally categorised into intrinsic motivation (engaging in a behaviour for personal satisfaction) and extrinsic motivation (engaging in a behaviour to gain a reward or avoid punishment). Motivation is also influenced by an individual's perceptions of their autonomy (control over engaging in the behaviour), competence (the level at which a person feels they can effectively perform the behaviour), and relatedness (perception of being connected to others).

This is further highlighted in qualitative research exploring why individuals, particularly older adults, may not engage with protective online behaviours (Morrison et al., 2021). The study identified three main reasons for not engaging in protective security behaviours:

- **Not Wanting to Engage**:

  Due to perceived costs, such as effort and money. This aligns with extrinsic motivation, where the perceived costs outweigh the potential rewards.

- **Not Being Able to Engage**:

  Due to a lack of confidence. This relates to perceived competence, where individuals do not feel capable of effectively performing the protective behaviours.

- **Not Needing to Engage**:

  Believing it is not their responsibility. This can be linked to extrinsic motivation and a lack of perceived autonomy, where individuals do not feel a personal obligation to engage in these behaviours.

By understanding these motivational factors through the lens of SDT, we can better address the barriers to engaging in protective online behaviours. For example, enhancing individuals' sense of autonomy by involving them in the creation of security policies, boosting their competence through regular and interactive training, and fostering relatedness by creating a supportive community can all contribute to more effective cybersecurity practices.

Other studies have also utilised interview methods in cybersecurity research (Chenoweth et al., 2009; Ramlo & Nicholas, 2020; Thompson et al. 2018). For example, Thompson et al. (2018) used think aloud interviews which involve the interviewer prompting responses from individuals based on their initial response to a given scenario. The interviews were recorded using both audio and video and were analysed for key themes. The researchers noted that, in a study that examined student misconceptions about cybersecurity, the method elicited some detailed themes and misunderstandings that would not be presented in a generic self-report study.

Looking at focus group research, again, only limited focus group research has been conducted exploring cybersecurity behaviours. For example, research using group discussions with security experts and employees within an organisation found three general themes (i) expert assumptions (assumptions made by experts regarding staff behaviour), (ii) employee misconceptions and disagreements, and (iii) the sources of guidance (Nicholson et al., 2018). These group discussions followed from a task called the 'Cybersurvival Task', which asks participants to rank protective security behaviours (Nicholson et al., 2018). The findings highlighted that assumptions are often made by security experts; however, these may not always be correct, potentially leading to gaps in security training. Another piece of research using focus groups (Kraemer et al., 2009) asked participants to create causal network pathways (sounds scary! But this means a diagram was produced linking factors together – such as linking lack of understanding of cybersecurity policies to a security-related failure). From this, it was found that there were nine factors (human and organisational) that may contribute to security vulnerabilities: (i) external influences, (ii) human error (e.g., mistakes), (iii) management (e.g., lack of management support), (iv) organisation, (v) performance management, (vi) resource management, (vii) policy issues (e.g., policies not being updated), (viii) technology, and (ix) training (lack of/no training), highlighting the complexity of human and organisational factors in security.

Haney et al. (2022) presented a study in which they used focus groups with a group of security information workers (defined as individuals who have a professional role in handling security information). They also noted that focus group methodologies were under-represented in the literature on cybersecurity and highlighted their usefulness when it comes to collecting exploratory data that focuses in on initial perceptions and feelings related to a particular topic. Fujs et al. (2019) in an exploration of the qualitative methods used in a cybersecurity setting noted that just 11 out of the 160 studies they reviewed conducted between 2017 and 2019 employed the use of focus groups.

While most research in cybersecurity continues to take a quantitative approach (Almansoori et al., 2023), qualitative findings from interviews and focus groups are beneficial for exploring attitudes and behaviours in much greater depth. The flexibility of discussions allows researchers to explore aspects of the topic that may not have been previously considered, providing a more holistic understanding of why people may or may not engage in protective cyber behaviours. These insights can contribute to changes in organisations and campaigns promoting protective cybersecurity behaviours (Morrison et al., 2021).

However, qualitative approaches such as interviews and focus groups also have their weaknesses. For instance, the data is not generalisable. For example, in the research by Morrison et al. (2021) focusing on older adults, the experiences shared by participants may not be the same as those of younger individuals, who may feel more 'savvy' with technology. Additionally, cybersecurity behaviours may be a sensitive topic for some people. They may realise they do not follow expected protective behaviours and worry that sharing this will lead to disapproval (Wellings et al., 2000). This concern may be particularly pronounced in focus groups, where participants might feel uncomfortable sharing their experiences for fear of disapproval from other group members.

Other Methods – Simulations and Games

Now, whilst scales and interviews may be super thrilling, there are also some other, more innovative ways to investigate aspects of cybersecurity behaviour. You might recall from Chapter 2 that unintentional insider threats (UITs) can occur in any number of situations – and due to this, organisations are keen to understand the effectiveness of the cybersecurity training they may employ, as well as their employee knowledge and awareness of security. One increasingly common way that organisations are looking into this is through the deployment of phishing simulations (Beu et al., 2023; Jayatilaka et al., 2021). A phishing simulation is an authorised, simulated attack that evaluates employees' abilities to recognise phishing email attacks (Rizzoni et al., 2022). These simulations normally collect information that allows an organisation to evaluate metrics (such as the number of times an employee clicks a simulated phishing link), to then determine whether an employee needs further training to mitigate susceptibility to potential future phishing attacks (including simulated phishing attacks, to see if they have learnt from the training given). We have summarised some of the key phishing simulation metrics that can be used to identify awareness and behavioural changes from employees.

- Open Rate:
  Description: The percentage of recipients who opened the phishing test email. This metric helps assess whether the email was engaging enough to prompt an open.
  Example: If 100 emails were sent and 50 were opened, the open rate is 50%.
- Click Rate:
  Description: The percentage of recipients who clicked on the phishing link inside the email. This is a common metric used to measure the effectiveness of the phishing simulation.
  Example: If 100 emails were sent and 20 recipients clicked on the link, the click rate is 20%.
- Report Rate:
  Description: The percentage of recipients who reported the phishing email to the IT or security team. This metric indicates the level of awareness and proactive behaviour among employees.
  Example: If 100 emails were sent and 10 recipients reported the email, the report rate is 10%.
- Re-click Rate:
  Description: The percentage of recipients who fall for phishing emails again after clicking on a phishing email in the initial campaign. This metric helps identify individuals who may need additional training.
  Example: If 20 recipients clicked on the initial phishing email and 5 of them clicked on a subsequent phishing email, the re-click rate is 25%.
- Download Rate:
  Description: The percentage of recipients who downloaded attachments in phishing emails. This metric helps assess the risk of malware infections.
  Example: If 100 emails were sent and 5 recipients downloaded the attachment, the download rate is 5%.

- Reply Rate:

Description: The percentage of recipients who replied to phishing emails. This metric helps assess the risk of information leakage.

Example: If 100 emails were sent and 2 recipients replied, the reply rate is 2%.

- False Positive Rate:

Description: The percentage of recipients who misjudged a legitimate email and reported it as a phishing email. This metric helps assess the accuracy of employees' phishing detection skills.

Example: If 100 legitimate emails were sent and 3 were reported as phishing, the false positive rate is 3%.

- Time Taken to Report:

Description: The average time taken by recipients to report a phishing email. This metric helps assess the responsiveness of employees.

Example: If the average time taken to report a phishing email is 2 hours, it indicates the promptness of employees in recognizing and reporting threats.

- Conversion of Clickers to Reporters:

Description: The number of recipients who initially clicked on a phishing link but later reported phishing emails in subsequent campaigns. This metric helps assess the effectiveness of training interventions.

Example: If 20 recipients clicked on the initial phishing email and 10 of them reported phishing emails in subsequent campaigns, the conversion rate is 50%.

(Jayatilaka et al., 2021)

While phishing simulations are being increasingly implemented within organisations, research around their effectiveness has shown mixed results. For example, research by Gordon et al. (2019) found that while repeated exposure to phishing simulations can reduce the chances of clicking on a familiar and recognisable attack, a mandatory training programme initiated after the phishing campaign did not significantly impact click rates. Individuals were still likely to click on a phishing simulation, with click rates of 10–25% post-training, indicating that even with training, individuals can remain susceptible to phishing attacks. In contrast, a phishing simulation campaign run within a hospital found significantly fewer clicks between the first round (7%) and the third round (3%) for standard phishing emails, as well as for custom phishing emails (55% for the first round; 21% for the second round) (Rizzoni et al., 2022). However, unforeseen complexities during implementation, such as the COVID-19 pandemic, which heightened factors like fatigue, stress, and workload, may have impacted the results. Nevertheless, the findings highlighted that individuals developed the ability to recognise conventional phishing, though more targeted, custom phishing can be more difficult to detect.

Despite mixed findings around the use of phishing simulations, this method can still be efficient for testing awareness in larger groups, making it useful in larger organisations. Phishing simulations are particularly valuable as they observe individuals' awareness in more natural settings, meaning they should hypothetically respond and behave the same way if they were to receive a real phishing email (Rizzoni et al., 2022). However there are several things that organisations need to consider when engaging these methods as part of their cybersecurity culture. For example, when implementing phishing simulations, ethical considerations are paramount. More often than not, individuals within an organisation are not made aware of the simulations in advance to ensure they are not more alert than usual. However, this lack of prior notification means they do not give their full informed consent (if in a research context) and may feel unduly observed in the context of training and risk assessment (Rizzoni et al., 2022). This can lead to individuals losing trust in the organisation or even retaliating or protesting due to feeling tricked (Volkamer et al., 2020). Therefore, phishing campaigns should be conducted appropriately and sensitively, with considerations of ethics and transparency with organisational staff.

There are some best practice guidelines for the ethical implementation of phishing simulations that we would suggest organisations consider if they are employing these methods. These include:

- **Informed Consent**: Ensuring that employees are aware that phishing simulations may occur, even if the exact timing is not disclosed. This means that they have had some prior warning about the possibility of such methods being used, without directly telling them when such tests might happen.
- **Transparency**: Communicate the purpose of the simulations and how the data will be used to improve security.
- **Debriefing and Support**: Provide constructive feedback and additional training to employees who fall for phishing attempts, rather than punitive measures.
- **Respect Boundaries**: Avoid using overly deceptive tactics that could cause distress or discomfort.
- **Supportive Work Environment**: Creating a supportive work environment is crucial for the success of cybersecurity training programmes. A positive learning environment can significantly enhance engagement, reduce anxiety, and improve knowledge retention.

To address the limitations of traditional phishing simulations, different approaches to training are being explored, including the use of serious games. Serious games are designed to educate or train individuals in an engaging manner. For example, Anti-Phishing Phil was developed with learning goals such as identifying phishing URLs, recognizing trustworthy or untrustworthy sites, and using search engines to find legitimate sites (Sheng et al., 2007). Players were better at identifying phishing websites compared to those who completed different training, and they became more knowledgeable about identifying phishing sites.

However, the context in which URLs are presented in Anti-Phishing Phil (i.e., as worms) does not reflect how real phishing emails may be presented. To address this, What.Hack was developed to achieve a realistic and holistic game design for anti-phishing, with learning goals such as teaching email phishing defence in context, engaging the player with clear goals and tasks, and providing immediate feedback about the consequences of decisions (Wen et al., 2019). Findings indicated that players' ability to correctly identify phishing emails significantly improved after playing the game, and What. Hack was more effective than Anti-Phishing Phil in helping participants identify phishing emails.

Summary

In this chapter, the importance of understanding people's cybersecurity behaviours and intentions was explored. This understanding was deemed critical for organisations, security practitioners, and researchers to identify individuals susceptible to poor security practices. Insights into these behaviours helped develop interventions and educate those who posed a weak link to overall cybersecurity. The chapter examined how cybersecurity had been measured in previous literature, focusing on techniques such as self-report questionnaires, interviews, and simulations. It also critically analysed the complexities and challenges associated with measuring cybersecurity. Cybersecurity behaviours were categorised into pro-security and anti-security behaviours, further divided into sub-categories like security assurance behaviour (SAB) and security risk-taking behaviour (SRB). Various self-report measures, including the Security Behaviour Intentions Scale (SeBIS) and the Human Aspects of Information Security Questionnaire (HAIS-Q), were discussed, highlighting their strengths and limitations. Additionally, qualitative methods such as interviews and focus groups were explored to gain a deeper understanding of cybersecurity behaviours. Innovative approaches like phishing simulations and serious games were also considered to assess and improve cybersecurity awareness and practices.

References

Ajzen, I. (1991). The theory of planned behaviour. *Organisational Behaviour and Human Decision Processes*, 50(2), 179–211.

Alanazi, F., Freeman, M., & Tootell, H. (2022). The role of social influence in cybersecurity behaviour: A study of young adults. *Journal of Information Security and Applications*, 62, 102–112.

Almansoori, W., Almansoori, A., & Almansoori, M. (2023). Exploring the effectiveness of cybersecurity training programs: A systematic review. *Journal of Cybersecurity Education*, 5(1), 45–58.

Ayyagari, R., & Crowell, C. (2020). The role of personality in cybersecurity behaviour: A review of the literature. *Journal of Cybersecurity Education*, 4(2), 67–82.

Beu, N., Jayatilaka, A., Zahedi, M., Babar, M. A., Hartley, L., Lewinsmith, W., & Baetu, I. (2023). Falling for phishing attempts: An investigation of individual differences that are associated with behavior in a naturalistic phishing simulation. *Computers & Security*, 131, 103313. doi:10.1016/j.cose.2023.103313.

Deci, E. L., & Ryan, R. M. (2012). *Self-determination theory*. Sage Publications.

Egelman, S., & Peer, E. (2015). Scaling the security wall: Developing a security behaviour intentions scale (SeBIS). *Proceedings of the 33rd Annual ACM Conference on Human Factors in Computing Systems*, 2873–2882. ACM.

Egelman, S., Harbach, M., & Peer, E. (2016). Behaviour ever follows intention? A validation of the security behaviour intentions scale (SeBIS). *Proceedings of the 2016 CHI Conference on Human Factors in Computing Systems*, 5257–5261. ACM.

Fujs, D., Mihelič, A., & Vrhovec, S. L. R. (2019). The power of interpretation: Qualitative methods in cybersecurity research. *Proceedings of the 14th International Conference on Availability, Reliability and Security*, 1–10. doi:10.1145/3339252.3341479.

Gordon, W. J., Fairhall, A., & Landman, A. (2019). Threats to information security: Public health implications. *New England Journal of Medicine*, 380(23), 2097–2099.

Gratian, M., Bandi, S., Cukier, M., Dykstra, J., & Ginther, A. (2018). Correlating human traits and cyber security behaviour intentions. *Computers & Security*, 73, 345–358.

Grimm, P. (2010). Social desirability bias. In J. Sheth & N. Malhotra (Eds.), *Wiley international encyclopaedia of marketing*. Wiley.

Guo, K. H. (2013). Security-related behaviour in using information systems in the workplace: A review and synthesis. *Computers & Security*, 32, 242–251.

Haney, J., Jacobs, J., Barrientos, F., & Furman, S. (2022). Lessons learned and suitability of focus groups in security information workers research. In *4th International Conference on HCI for Cybersecurity, Privacy, and Trust*. Springer. doi:10.1007/978-3-031-05563-8_10.

Hong, W., Thong, J. Y. L., & Tam, K. Y. (2022). Understanding the impact of culture on information security behaviour: A systematic review. *Journal of Information Security and Applications*, 47, 102–115.

Jayatilaka, A., Beu, N., Baetu, I., Zahedi, M., Babar, M. A., Hartley, L., & Lewinsmith, W. (2021). Evaluation of security training and awareness programs: Review of current practices and guideline. *arXiv*:2112. 06356. http://arxiv.org/abs/2112.06356.

Joinson, A., Buchanan, T., & Paine, C. (2023). The human cyber-resilience scale: Development and validation. *Journal of Cybersecurity*, 9(1), tyad001.

Kharlamov, A., & Pogrebna, G. (2019). Using human values-based approach to understand cross-cultural commitment toward regulation and governance of cybersecurity. *Regulation and Governance*. doi:10.1111/rego.12281.

Kraemer, S., Carayon, P., & Clem, J. (2009). Human and organizational factors in computer and information security: Pathways to vulnerabilities. *Computers and Security*, 28(7), 509–520. doi:10.1016/j.cose.2009.04.006.

McCormac, A., Parsons, K., Butavicius, M., Pattinson, M., & Calic, D. (2017). Why do people do dangerous things online? *Information & Computer Security*, 25(2), 196–213.

Miglani, S., & Obeng, V. (2023). Gender diversity and human capital efficiency in Australian institutions: The moderating role of workforce environment quality. *Journal of Risk and Financial Management*, 16(7), 1–26. doi:10.3390/jrfm16070343.

Morrison, B., Coventry, L., & Briggs, P. (2021). How do older adults feel about engaging with cyber-security? *Human behavior and emerging technologies*, 3(5), 1033–1049.

Nicholson, J., Coventry, L., & Briggs, P. (2018). Introducing the cybersurvival task: Assessing and addressing staff beliefs about effective cyber protection. *SOUPS '18: Proceedings of the Fourteenth USENIX Conference on Usable Privacy and Security*, 427–441. ACM.

Onumo, A., Cullen, A., & Ullah-Awan, I. (2017). An empirical study of cultural dimensions and cybersecurity development. In IEEE (Ed.) *2017 IEEE 5th International Conference on Future Internet of Things and Cloud (FiCloud)* (pp. 70–76). IEEE.

Parsons, K., McCormac, A., Butavicius, M., Pattinson, M., & Jerram, C. (2013). Determining employee awareness using the Human Aspects of Information Security Questionnaire (HAIS-Q). *Computers & Security*, 42, 165–176.

Parsons, K., McCormac, A., Pattinson, M., Butavicius, M., & Jerram, C. (2017). The Human Aspects of Information Security Questionnaire (HAIS-Q): Two further validation studies. *Computers & Security*, 66, 40–51.

Rizzoni, F., Magalini, S., Casaroli, A., Mari, P., Dixon, M., & Coventry, L. (2022). Phishing simulation exercise in a large hospital: A case study. *Digital Health*, 8, 20552076221081716. doi:10.1177/20552076221081716.

Ryan, R. M., & Deci, E. L. (2024). Self-determination theory. In *Encyclopedia of quality of life and well-being research* (pp. 6229–6235). Springer International Publishing.

Shen, Y., Buchanan Turner, C., & Turner, C. (2023). Cybersecurity training in organization as human capital investment: A qualitative grounded theory analysis. *International Journal of Business and Management*, 18(4), 38. doi:10.5539/ijbm.v18n4p38.

Sheng, S., Magnien, B., Kumaraguru, P., Acquisti, A., Cranor, L. F., Hong, J., & Nunge, E. (2007). Anti-Phishing Phil: The design and evaluation of a game that teaches people not to fall for phish. *Proceedings of the 3rd Symposium on Usable Privacy and Security*, 88–99. doi:10.1145/1280680.1280692.

Sommestad, T., Karlzén, H., & Hallberg, J. (2017). The theory of planned behavior and information security policy compliance. *Journal of Computer Information Systems*. doi:10.1080/08874417.2017.1368421.

Taylor, S., & van Schaik, P. (2023). The role of personality in cybersecurity behaviour: A systematic review. *Journal of Cybersecurity Education*, 5(1), 45–58.

Volkamer, M., Sasse, M. A., & Boehm, F. (2020). Analysing simulated phishing campaigns for staff. In I. Boureanu, C. C. Drăgan, M. Manulis, T. Giannetsos, C. Dadoyan, P. Gouvas, R. A. Hallman, S. Li, V. Chang, F. Pallas, J. Pohle, & A. Sasse (Eds.), *Computer security* (pp. 312–328). Springer International Publishing. doi:10.1007/978-3-030-66504-3_19.

Wellings, K., Branigan, P., & Mitchell, K. (2000). Discomfort, discord and discontinuity as data: Using focus groups to research sensitive topics. *Culture, Health & Sexuality*, 2(3), 255–267.

Wen, Z. A., Lin, Z., Chen, R., & Andersen, E. (2019). What.Hack: Engaging anti-phishing training through a role-playing phishing simulation game. *Proceedings of the 2019 CHI Conference on Human Factors in Computing Systems*, 1–12. doi:10.1145/3290605.3300338.

Xu, Z., McCormac, A., Parsons, K., & Butavicius, M. (2022). The Human Aspects of Information Security Questionnaire (HAIS-Q): A systematic review. *Computers & Security*, 47, 102–115.

9

PERSONALITY AND WORKPLACE CYBERSECURITY

Introduction

We do not work in isolation, and numerous factors can directly impact our actions and approach to daily work. These factors shape how we view our worth within an organisation and influence our approach to cybersecurity. For instance, if you are working solely for financial gain and eagerly await the end of your shift, you may not pay much attention to how your behaviour affects the organisation's overall cybersecurity stance. Conversely, if you are invested in your career, driven to succeed, and your values align with those of your company, you are more likely to engage in effective cybersecurity behaviours. In this chapter, we will explore key factors within this sphere of influence that directly affect the degree to which someone engages in cybersecurity. These factors differ from those covered in the previous chapter, as they focus more on organisational culture and how individuals perceive their roles within the organisation, rather than specific behaviours that could put the organisation at risk.

In a similar vein we rarely act or make decisions in isolation. There is often an interplay between an individual's dispositions and the pressures that are exerted by situational factors we encounter in our daily work life. Psychological aspects, such as personality, can interact with social influences, including social norms and organisational values, to shape the behaviour and cybersecurity stance of individuals within an organisation. The concept of psycho-social factors is broad, encompassing numerous potential concepts and constructs. Identifying the most important and salient ones is a complex challenge. However, we will focus on factors that have been shown to have a clear link to cybersecurity behaviour and awareness, beginning with the role of personality traits.

DOI: 10.4324/9781003509011-9

Personality Traits

We introduced the concept of personality traits in Chapter 2, highlighting these hypothetical constructs that individuals can exhibit differences on, allowing people to be categorised and studied in terms of their approaches to everyday life. In the literature on cybersecurity awareness and behaviours, there has been a clear focus on how personality traits can influence a person's approach to their online safety and security. Numerous studies have examined how personality factors can impact cybersecurity behaviour (e.g., Kennison & Chan-Tin, 2020; López-Aguilar & Solanas, 2021; McBride et al., 2012; McCormac et al., 2017; Russell et al., 2017). The results of this body of research are far from conclusive, with many contradictory findings, so it is worth noting this before we delve into exploring this work.

While research into personality factors is interesting and provides valuable insights into human factors in cybersecurity, the practical merits of exploring such factors are limited. From a practical standpoint, knowing which personality factors predict higher susceptibility to cybercrime or lower compliance with cybersecurity rules offers few opportunities to target individuals in training or messaging. To engage in such endeavours, we would need a priori methods to identify individuals with certain personality traits, which would require a large, expensive, and potentially frustrating testing regime for everyone entering the organisation. This is something that we will discuss towards the end of this chapter.

Openness to Experience

Individuals who have higher levels of this trait possess imagination to be able to engage or explore new experiences. Individuals high in this trait seek out experiences that serve to bring meaning to their lives as well as giving them a different perspective on things around them (Eldesouky, 2012). Openness to experience has been linked to individuals engaging in highly stimulating activities, including trying exotic foods, extreme sports and illegal activities (Eldesouky, 2012). Lauriola and Levin (2001) noted that openness to experience has been positively correlated with risk-taking activities, something that has been replicated in numerous studies since (de Vries et al., 2009; Gerra et al., 1999; Nicholson et al., 2005).

In terms of cybersecurity behaviours, openness to experience has received some attention in the research. Van de Weijer and Leukfeldt (2017) noted that individuals who scored higher on measures of cybercrime victimisation tended to have higher levels of openness to experience. It was also highlighted that there was a difference between the personality traits they explored, and the type of cybercrimes individuals were more likely to victims of. For openness to experience they noted these individuals had higher odds of being victims of hacking and malware, but not specific cyber-enabled crimes that require a mix of online and offline engagement. The authors suggested that as much of this type of attack involves the need for an individual to engage with an email, those with higher levels of openness to experience, who have an innate sense of curiosity, are easily persuaded to open the attachment (van de Weijer & Leukfeldt, 2017).

Neuroticism

Neuroticism has been characterised by aspects such as anxiety, pessimism, hostility, and personal insecurity (Costa et al., 1991; John & Srivastava, 1999). The construct is contrasted with a more emotionally stable approach that is even-tempered and less reactive in terms of hostility (Costa et al., 1991; John & Srivastava, 1999). Individuals who score higher on measures of neuroticism tend to avoid situations where they are expected to take control and often resist goal-setting activities (Judge et al., 2002; Uffen et al., 2013).

Halevi et al. (2013) explored the susceptibility of individuals to respond to a phishing email versus their personality, and noted a strong correlation between neuroticism and response to a phishing email. However, they noted that this correlation only emerged for female and not male participants, with the suggestion that women are more likely to admit feeling fearful, which links directly to the measure of neuroticism. They go on to further suggest that women are, in general, more capable of analysing their emotional needs and tend to feel that the internet may be able to fulfil these needs. The combination of these factors means that women may be significantly more susceptible to phishing attacks than men. Other researchers have noted that individuals higher in neuroticism are less vulnerable to phishing attacks because of their lack of trust towards other people (Albladi & Weir, 2017; Sudzina & Pavlicek, 2017). However, López-Aguilar and Solanas (2021) presented an exploration of the gathered research exploring the role of narcissism on susceptibility to phishing attacks and they concluded much of the findings are contradictory or incomplete due to a lack of representativeness across the samples employed in the review studies. This, as we noted before in the introduction to this section, is common in work around personality and cybersecurity, and something that needs to be addressed in further research in this area.

Other research has noted that individuals who scored higher on neuroticism did poorly on a test of knowledge about cybersecurity (Kelley, 2018), with the suggestion that due to their anxiety, they may be more likely to ignore security alerts and security information as this increases their anxiety. Conetta (2019) also noted that there was a negative correlation between neuroticism and an individual's self-reported self-efficacy on protective cybersecurity behaviours, which again fits into the suggestion that those people who score higher in trait neuroticism tend to ignore cybersecurity alerts and information or give up all together in order to avoid unnecessary anxiety and stress (Conetta, 2019). Uffen et al. (2013) found that neuroticism negatively influenced individuals' perceptions of the usefulness of smartphone security measures, as well as their perceived ability to effectively manage and control the protection of their devices. Individuals high in neuroticism may experience heightened anxiety or self-doubt, which can undermine their confidence in using security tools and reduce their motivation to engage in protective behaviours. This is important to note, and it means that certain individuals within any organisation may present clear challenges when we are trying to train them as well as attempting to enhance their capabilities when it comes to cyber hygiene.

Agreeableness

Research has shown a significant positive correlation between the personality trait of agreeableness and cybersecurity-related behaviours. McCormac et al. (2017) found that individuals scoring higher in agreeableness also tended to score higher on the HAIS-Q, suggesting greater awareness and adherence to secure information practices. Similarly Conetta (2019) reported a positive relationship between agreeableness and cyber hygiene, indicating that more agreeable individuals are more likely to engage in behaviours that protect their digital environments. These findings suggest that agreeable individuals, who are typically cooperative, compliant, and considerate of others, may be more inclined to follow security protocols and contribute to a safer cyber culture. Shappie et al. (2020) also noted that conscientiousness was positively correlated with protective cybersecurity behaviours, so as conscientiousness increased, so did the good behaviours. other research presents a more nuanced picture. For instance, Alohali et al. (2018) reported a negative correlation between conscientiousness, users' security behaviours and risk-taking. This finding is somewhat counterintuitive, as conscientious individuals are typically characterised by their diligence, responsibility, and cautiousness. However, the authors suggest that highly conscientious individuals may sometimes rely too heavily on routine or may underestimate the need for additional security measures, especially if they perceive their existing habits as sufficient.

Agreeableness is the personality trait most associated with susceptibility to phishing attacks (Parrish et al., 2009), as trust features highly in the transactional process between phisher and phishee for the individual to release personal or sensitive information (Weirich & Sasse, 2001). As agreeableness has trust as a central aspect of the trait, it is not surprising that those people who score more highly on this trait are more likely to divulge information to scammers (J.L. Cho et al., 2013; J.-H. Cho et al., 2016; Power & Bello, 2022). In terms of social engineering, individuals who score higher on the trait of agreeableness make the ideal target – they are more likely to want to please individuals and easily trust strangers in situations that are unfamiliar (J.L. Cho et al., 2013; J.-H. Cho et al., 2016; Power & Bello, 2022).

Conscientiousness

Conscientiousness is an interesting one when it comes to cybersecurity behaviours. Those people who are conscientious are hard-working and have good self-control. However, this can be their downfall, as individuals who are higher in this trait tend to respond to requests that tap into these underlying factors, and which will often appeal to the need for efficiency and time-saving opportunities (Halevi et al., 2013). In an experiment that used a simulated spear-phishing attack, individuals who scored higher on the conscientiousness personality trait were demonstrated to be more likely to click on a link within the phishing email. Further, those individuals who had higher levels of conscientiousness and lower levels of risk perception were more likely to ignore the potential risks and proceeded to download a file contained within that link (Halevi et al., 2013). Other researchers have noted that conscientiousness is related to lower levels of self-reported risky cybersecurity behaviours (McCormac et al., 2017; Shappie et al., 2020).

Overall conscientiousness has been the one trait that has been most consistently linked to a reduction in susceptibility to phishing vulnerability, especially where effective cybersecurity training has taken place (Parrish et al., 2009).

Extraversion

The extravert is typically viewed as an individual who is outgoing, socially dominant, likes to be around people, and will provide information to individuals if it makes them more socially acceptable. As such, extraverts can present as the perfect target for social engineers as they like to give out information without much regard for the consequences. The link between extraversion and susceptibility to phishing attacks has been well documented in the research on the topic (e.g., Alseadoon, 2014; Anawar et al., 2019; Lawson et al., 2020). Other researchers have noted that extraversion predicted lax cybersecurity behaviours, where individuals with higher levels of this trait reporting more lax attitudes towards cybersecurity behaviours (Kennison & Chan-Tin, 2020).

Personality and Counterproductive Work Behaviours

Spector and Zhou (2013) explored the relationship between counterproductive work behaviours (CWB) and personality and noted that there was a significant negative relationship between the three good traits of conscientiousness, agreeableness, and emotional stability (the opposing end of the neuroticism spectrum) and both CWBs targeting the organisation (CWB-O) and CWBs related to interpersonal targets (CWB-I). Individuals who scored more highly on these traits were less likely to report engaging in CWB against the organisation, and interpersonal forms of CWB. Other researchers have noted a similar relationship between these three traits and their negative relationship with CWB (Hough, 1992; Hough et al., 1990; Ones, 1993; Ones & Dilchert, 2013; Ones et al., 1993). It has been further noted that agreeableness provides a better predictor for CWB against individuals, which fits with the main features of the personality traits that form the 'good' triad, as they are less likely to want to engage in interpersonal conflict, and avoid confrontation within the workplace. Conscientiousness and emotional stability were better predictors for CWB-O (Mount et al., 2006). Other researchers have noted that openness to experience is positively correlated with CWB in general, as well as for both CWB-O and CWB-I (Ferreira & Nascimento, 2016). Extraversion has also been positively correlated with interpersonal CWB, which suggests that individuals who score higher on this trait are more willing to engage in deviant work behaviours that impact their relationships with their colleagues (Ferreira & Nascimento, 2016).

Some work has been done exploring the relationship between personality factors and propensity to engage in cyberloafing. Some researchers have noted that those individuals who exhibit lower levels of conscientiousness have the tendency to engage in higher levels of cyberloafing (Jia et al., 2013; Krishnan et al., 2010; Varghese & Barber, 2017). Conscientiousness is something that we have seen to have a clear relationship with other factors associated with cybersecurity awareness, so its link to cyberloafing is consistent with these other findings. Those individuals who are more conscientious are more likely to be diligent at work and more inclined to follow rules and norms within the workplace, hence less likely to spend time engaged in counterproductive work behaviours such as cyberloafing (Jia et al., 2013; Krishnan et al., 2010).

Both neuroticism and extraversion have also been associated with higher levels of cyberloafing activity (Andreassen et al., 2014; Jia et al., 2013; Varghese & Barber, 2017). Those individuals who have higher levels of neuroticism typically exhibit greater emotional instability and anxiety, often leading them to adopt avoidant coping strategies to divert their attention away from work-related tasks (Andreassen et al., 2014; Jia et al., 2013; Varghese & Barber, 2017). Individuals lower in neuroticism are more likely to be emotionally stable and exhibit higher levels of job satisfaction, and therefore engage in less counterproductive work behaviours such as cyberloafing (Jia et al., 2013). In contrast, extraverts are those who crave social interaction, therefore their need to seek out a more stimulating social environment such as social media sites, online chatrooms, or online forums means that they are more likely to engage in cyberloafing activities (Jia et al., 2013; Kraut et al., 2002; Varghese & Barber, 2017).

There has been further work that has examined the link between cyberloafing and the personality trait of openness to experience. This personality trait, as we have seen earlier in this chapter, is typified by an individual's capacity to engage in new, exploratory behaviours, and their willingness to learn new things and experience new things. From this perspective, individuals with higher levels of openness to experience engage in higher levels of cyberloafing due to their inherent curiosity and their desire to engage in new experiences (Jia et al., 2013; Krishnan et al., 2010).

Dark Triad and Cybersecurity

A large chunk of the research that explores the Dark Triad in the context of cybersecurity focuses mostly on aspects of malicious insider threat (e.g., Harms et al., 2022; Maasberg et al., 2020). However, the Dark Triad has had some attention in the cybersecurity literature and has been shown to influence some aspects of behaviour when it comes to susceptibility to cybercriminals. Conversely, we have seen a lot of discussion surrounding the Dark Triad and the link to malicious insider threat, something that we have already touched upon in Chapter 4. The Dark Triad consists of the three personality traits Machiavellianism, narcissism, and psychopathy (Paulhus & Williams, 2002).

Machiavellianism

The trait of Machiavellianism is characterised by manipulative behaviours aimed at self-gain and personal advancement involving the use of tactics such as deception and moral flexibility (Bereczkei, 2015; Christie & Geis, 1970; Curtis et al., 2018). Individuals high in Machiavellianism are known for their ability to morally disengage, enabling them to advance personal agendas without concern for ethical boundaries or psychological consequences (Cohen, 2016; Moore et al., 2012). Individuals who score high on measures of Machiavellianism frequently engage in deceit when they are interacting with others (Baughman et al., 2014; Stiff & Reeves, 2024).

In cybersecurity, Machiavellian traits are frequently linked to malicious insider threat behaviours. Such individuals can readily manipulate others or exploit systems to fulfil personal objectives. They engage in CWB through manipulation and persuasion, using interpersonal skills to subvert organisational policies and potentially compromise cybersecurity (Cohen, 2016). In the workplace, Machiavellianism has been associated with a higher likelihood of engaging in cyberloafing behaviours (Rahman & Muldoon, 2020) and bullying (Maasberg et al., 2015, 2020).

One significant element of the Machiavellian personality is the capacity for moral disengagement – the ability to disconnect from the ethical impact of one's actions. For individuals with high levels of Machiavellianism, this moral flexibility becomes a strategic tool, allowing them to pursue self-interest without fear of psychological distress or the need for justification (Cohen, 2016). This trait enables Machiavellians to engage in behaviours that may undermine cybersecurity policies without concern for potential consequences. Their drive for self-advancement, coupled with this ability to morally disengage, allows them to act unremorsefully in ways that might be deemed unethical or hostile (Cohen, 2016; Wu & Lebreton, 2011).

Narcissism

Narcissism is defined by a sense of personal entitlement, dominance, and the exploitation of others for personal gain (Curtis et al., 2018). Narcissistic individuals tend to display a high level of overconfidence and a strong belief in their abilities, which can lead them to underestimate potential threats and overestimate their capacity to manage complex situations. Curtis et al. (2018) found that narcissism was positively associated with susceptibility to phishing attacks. This may stem from the high levels of overconfidence and unrealistic self-appraisal of narcissistic individuals (Curtis et al., 2018; Farwell & Wohlwend-Lloyd, 1998).

Due to their inflated sense of self-importance, narcissistic individuals may experience a false sense of expertise in areas where they lack actual competence. For example, they may believe they can easily identify phishing emails and thus fail to detect genuine cyber threats. Moreover, the impulsivity associated with narcissism can lead these individuals to disregard cybersecurity protocols, prioritizing self-serving actions or emails that appear personally rewarding (Curtis et al., 2018). This combination of overconfidence and impulsivity increases their vulnerability to cyber threats, as they are likely to underestimate risks and overestimate their ability to manage them.

In terms of counterproductive work behaviours, narcissism has been identified as a significant predictor of cyberloafing, where narcissists are motivated by a need for personal reward and recognition (Rahman & Muldoon, 2020). Additionally, they are less likely to tolerate criticism or insults and may respond with hostility, including acts of revenge or deviant workplace behaviours (Cohen, 2016). This propensity for anger and frustration when facing criticism can drive narcissists towards actions that undermine organisational security or norms, especially when they perceive threats to their self-image.

Psychopathy

Psychopathy is typically associated with a lack of empathy, impulsivity, aggression, and a tendency towards deception (Curtis et al., 2018). Individuals high in psychopathy are characterised by disregard for rules and norms, operating without remorse or concern for the impact of their actions on others (Wu & Lebreton, 2011). This lack of moral conscience makes them particularly susceptible to engaging in unethical or harmful behaviours that may jeopardise cybersecurity.

In the context of counterproductive work behaviours, psychopathy is closely linked to actions that ignore established protocols or societal norms, as psychopathic individuals often believe rules do not apply to them (Cohen, 2016). This trait manifests in a heightened likelihood to engage in deviant workplace behaviours, including actions that could compromise organisational cybersecurity. For instance, psychopathic individuals may disregard security rules or intentionally bypass security measures, believing they are immune to the consequences or simply indifferent to the potential harm they cause to the organisation. One study noted that those individuals who displayed higher levels of psychopathy had a lower perceived risk of being discovered if they violated privacy policies within the workplace (Gaia et al., 2022).

Psychopathy is also correlated with pleasure in harming others or causing disruption, which aligns with behaviours that deliberately flout cybersecurity rules and organisational policies (Cohen, 2016). Such individuals are often undeterred by potential repercussions, making them particularly challenging to manage within a secure organisational environment.

The Dark Triad and Counterproductive Work Behaviours

Other researchers have noted that the Dark Triad features highly in aspects of counterproductive work behaviours. For example, Maasberg et al. (2015, 2020) noted that the Dark Triad acted as significant predictors for workplace bullying. Scarduzio and Adams (2022) noted that individuals who have higher levels of the Dark Triad personality traits are more likely to engage in sexual harassment of their co-workers online. In terms of cyberloafing, a variety of research has noted that the Dark Triad can be linked to engaging in this type of counterproductive work behaviour, where narcissism acted as the most significant predictor closely followed by Machiavellianism (Rahman & Muldoon, 2020). Others have noted that those individuals who score higher in levels of this Dark Triad trait are more likely to engage in cyberloafing, and more importantly engage in such behaviours without others noticing (Lowe-Calverley & Grieve, 2017). Cohen (2016) presented a theoretical framework for conceptualising the role of the Dark Triad in counterproductive work behaviours, highlighting the fact that deviant activities in the workplace are best predicted by exploring individuals who exhibit these so-called deviant personality traits. Highlighting the key characteristics of each of these traits (sense of entitlement, interpersonal manipulation, and sense of entitlement), Cohen (2016) suggested that each of the Dark Triad personality types should have the capacity to predict engagement in counterproductive work behaviours.

How Relevant Are Personality Factors in Cybersecurity?

There has been a great deal of research that has been conducted exploring the link between personality and cybersecurity awareness and behaviours

(Banyasz et al., 2024; Kennison & Chan-Tin, 2020; Naga et al., 2024). While this work has provided an interesting backdrop for understanding factors that influence how individuals approach cybersecurity in the workplace, there are a few key points to highlight when considering personality factors.

Firstly, the practicality of using personality assessments in the workplace to gauge cybersecurity approaches is more challenging than it might appear. For instance, we would need an inventory of the personality traits of each current employee within the organisation, which incurs both time and cost. Engaging in extensive psychometric testing and the associated analysis and interpretation can be resource-intensive. There are many off-the-shelf testing kits available that offer organisations the chance to classify their employees' personality traits. However, not all personality traits are created equally, and there is a risk that organisations might engage in testing without fully understanding what they are measuring.

When considering scales and measures in psychology, two key concepts are crucial: validity and reliability. Validity refers to the extent to which a measure or test accurately assesses what it is intended to. For personality tests, we need an objective approach to ensure the measure accurately captures key areas such as openness, conscientiousness, extraversion, agreeableness, and neuroticism.

- **Content Validity**: Does the scale measure each proposed trait in a way that fully represents what it means to be, for example, an extravert?
- **Construct Validity**: Does the scale accurately reflect the underlying personality constructs? This might involve comparing the current scale with a well-established one that has demonstrated good construct validity.
- **Ecological Validity**: Does the measure map onto real-world uses of such constructs? For example, ensuring that the tests are directly applicable to the workplace environment rather than being generic personality tests with no real bearing on the world of work.
- **Reliability**: Refers to the stability and consistency of the results obtained from specific tests over time. *Test-Retest Reliability* assesses how comparable the results are when the same test is administered to the same people at two different times. Consistent results between the two testing points indicate high test-retest reliability.

If organisations are considering employing personality measures, they need to ensure that they evaluate both the reliability and validity of the scales presented to them. It is important to avoid the temptation to pick an off-the-shelf measure marketed as a unique tool for creating a personality profile of the organisation, as these often lack rigorous background research, reliability, and validity. Critical awareness and background research on the scale and its previous testing regime are necessary.

Additional Considerations

There are other issues with using personality measures in the context of cybersecurity awareness assessments. Beyond the issues mentioned with self-report measures, such as social desirability bias, there is a risk that personality measures could lead organisations to categorise individuals neatly, potentially missing the nuances of individual differences that influence adherence to cybersecurity rules and procedures. Tests implemented by non-experts could be misinterpreted, leading to recommendations or initiatives that do not align with the actual results. Organisations should seek expertise in this area before proceeding, even if it is just to discuss the main concepts and potential data interpretations.

Finally, personality tests should not be seen as standalone measures for assessing compliance with cybersecurity policies. The influences on cybersecurity awareness extend beyond a single factor. A triangulated approach, using personality measures alongside other methods detailed in the previous chapter, is recommended.

Summary

This chapter explored the factors that influenced cybersecurity behaviours in the workplace, emphasizing that individuals did not work in isolation. These factors shaped employees' perceptions of their worth within an organisation and their approach to cybersecurity. Employees motivated solely by financial gain often neglected cybersecurity, while those invested in their careers and aligned with company values were more likely to engage in effective cybersecurity practices. The chapter focused on organisational culture and individual perceptions of roles, rather than specific risky behaviours.

We highlighted the interplay between psychological traits and situational factors in daily work life. Psychological aspects, such as personality, interacted with social influences, including social norms and organisational values, to shape cybersecurity behaviours. The chapter examined personality traits and their impact on online safety and security, noting that while research provided valuable insights, practical application in the workplace was challenging due to the need for extensive psychometric testing.

The Big Five personality traits – openness to experience, neuroticism, agreeableness, conscientiousness, and extraversion – were discussed in relation to cybersecurity behaviours. For instance, individuals high in openness to experience were more susceptible to cybercrime due to curiosity, while those high in neuroticism had lower self-efficacy in cybersecurity practices. Agreeableness was linked to higher susceptibility to phishing attacks due to trustfulness, and conscientiousness was associated with both protective behaviours and susceptibility to spear-phishing. Extraverts exhibited lax cybersecurity behaviours due to their social dominance.

The chapter also examined the Dark Triad – Machiavellianism, narcissism, and psychopathy – and their influence on cybersecurity. These traits were linked to malicious insider threats and counterproductive work behaviours. Machiavellian individuals manipulated others to bypass security measures, narcissists' overconfidence led to phishing susceptibility, and psychopaths' lack of empathy and disregard for rules made them prone to unethical behaviours compromising cybersecurity.

We addressed the limitations of using personality assessments in the workplace, emphasizing the importance of validity and reliability. We cautioned against relying solely on personality tests for cybersecurity assessments and recommended a triangulated approach, combining personality measures with other methods to gain a comprehensive understanding of cybersecurity behaviours.

References

Albladi, S. M., & Weir, G. R. S. (2017). Personality traits and cyber-attack victimisation: Multiple mediation analysis. *2017 Internet of Things Business Models, Users, and Networks*, 1–6. doi:10.1109/CTTE.2017.8260932.

Alohali, M., Clarke, N., Li, F., & Furnell, S. M. (2018). Identifying and predicting the factors affecting end-users' risk-taking behavior. *Information and Computer Security*, 26(3), 306–326. doi:10.1108/ICS-03-2018-0037.

Alseadoon, I. M. A. (2014). *The impact of users' characteristics on their ability to detect phishing emails* (Doctoral dissertation). Queensland University of Technology.

Anawar, S., Kunasegaran, D. L., Mas'Ud, M. Z., & Zakaria, N. A. (2019). Analysis of phishing susceptibility in a workplace: A Big-Five personality perspectives. *Journal of Engineering, Science and Technology*, 14(5), 2865–2882.

Andreassen, C. S., Torsheim, T., & Pallesen, S. (2014). Predictors of use of social network sites at work – A specific type of cyberloafing. *Journal of Computer-Mediated Communication*, 19(4), 906–921. doi:10.1111/jcc4.12085.

Banyasz, P., Laska, P. K., Szadeczky, T., & Vaczi, K. B. (2024). The relationship between the Dark Triad personality and cybersecurity. *Proceedings of the Central and Eastern European eDem and eGov Days 2024*, 195–202. doi:10.1145/3670243.3670262.

Baughman, H. M., Jonason, P. K., Lyons, M., & Vernon, P. A. (2014). Liar liar pants on fire: Cheater strategies linked to the Dark Triad. *Personality and Individual Differences*, 71, 35–38. doi:10.1016/j.paid.2014.07.019.

Bereczkei, T. (2015). The manipulative skill: Cognitive devices and their neural correlates underlying Machiavellian's decision making. *Brain and Cognition*, 99, 24–31. doi:10.1016/j.bandc.2015.06.007.

Cho, J.-H., Cam, H., & Oltramari, A. (2016). Effect of personality traits on trust and risk to phishing vulnerability: Modeling and analysis. *2016 IEEE International Multi-Disciplinary Conference on Cognitive Methods in Situation Awareness and Decision Support (CogSIMA)*, 7–13. doi:10.1109/COGSIMA.2016.7497779.

Cho, J. L., Wang, X., Chan, K., Chang, M., Swami, A., & Mohapatra, P. (2013). Trust and independence aware decision fusion in distributed networks. In *2013 IEEE International Conference on Pervasive Computing and Communications Workshops (PERCOM Workshops)*. doi:10.1109/PerComW.2013.6529545.

Christie, R., & Geis, F. (1970). *Studies in Machiavellianism*. Academic Press.

Cohen, A. (2016). Are they among us? A conceptual framework of the relationship between the Dark Triad personality and counterproductive work behaviors (CWBs). *Human Resource Management Review*, 26(1), 69–85. doi:10.1016/j.hrmr.2015.07.003.

Conetta, C. (2019). Individual differences in cyber security. *McNair Research Journal SJSU*, 15. doi:10.31979/mrj.2019.1504.

Costa, P. T., McCrae, R. R., & Dye, D. A. (1991). Facet scales for agreeableness and conscientiousness: A revision of the NEO Personality Inventory. *Personality and Individual Differences*, 12(9), 887–898. doi:10.1016/0191-8869(91)90177-D.

Curtis, S. R., Rajivan, P., Jones, D. N., & Gonzalez, C. (2018). Phishing attempts among the Dark Triad: Patterns of attack and vulnerability. *Computers in Human Behavior*, 87, 174–182. doi:10.1016/j.chb.2018.05.037.

de Vries, R. E., de Vries, A., de Hoogh, A., & Feij, J. (2009). More than the Big Five: Egoism and the HEXACO model of personality. *European Journal of Personality*, 23(8), 635–654. doi:10.1002/per.733.

Eldesouky, L. (2012). Openness to experience and health: A review of the literature. *The Yale Review of Undergraduate Research in Psychology*, 5, 24–42.

Farwell, L., & Wohlwend-Lloyd, R. (1998). Narcissistic processes: Optimistic expectations, favorable self-evaluations, and self-enhancing attributions. *Journal of Personality*, 66(1), 65–83. doi:10.1111/1467-6494.00003.

Ferreira, M. F., & Nascimento, E. do. (2016). Relationship between personality traits and counterproductive work behaviors. *Psico-USF*, 21, 677–685. doi:10.1590/1413-82712016210319.

Gaia, J., Murray, D., Sanders, G., Sanders, S., Upadhyaya, S., Wang, X., & Yoo, C. (2022). The interaction of dark traits with the perceptions of apprehension. *Proceedings of the 55th Hawaii International Conference on Systems Science*. doi:10.24251/HICSS.2022.279.

Gerra, G., Avanzini, P., Zaimovic, A., Sartori, R., Bocchi, C., Timpano, M., Zambelli, U., Delsignore, R., Gardini, F., Talarico, E., & Brambilla, F. (1999). Neurotransmitters, neuroendocrine correlates of sensation-seeking temperament in normal humans. *Neuropsychobiology*, 39, 207–213.

Halevi, T., Lewis, J., & Memon, N. (2013). A pilot study of cyber security and privacy related behavior and personality traits. *WWW 2013 Companion – Proceedings of the 22nd International Conference on World Wide Web*, 737–744. doi:10.1145/2487788.2488034.

Harms, P. D., Marbut, A., Johnston, A. C., Lester, P., & Fezzey, T. (2022). Exposing the darkness within: A review of dark personality traits, models, and measures and their relationship to insider threats. *Journal of Information Security and Applications*, 71, 103378. doi:10.1016/j.jisa.2022.103378.

Hough, L. M. (1992). The 'Big Five' personality variables – construct confusion: Description versus prediction. *Human Performance*, 5(1–2), 139–155. doi:10.1207/s15327043hup0501&2_8.

Hough, L. M., Eaton, N. K., Dunnette, M. D., Kamp, J. D., & McCloy, R. A. (1990). Criterion-related validities of personality constructs and the effect of response distortion on those validities. *Journal of Applied Psychology*, 75(5), 581–595. doi:10.1037/0021-9010.75.5.581.

Jia, H., Jia, R., & Karau, S. (2013). Cyberloafing and personality: The impact of the Big Five traits and workplace situational factors. *Journal of Leadership & Organizational Studies*, 20(3), 358–365. doi:10.1177/1548051813488208.

John, O. P., & Srivastava, S. (1999). The Big-Five trait taxonomy: History, measurement, and theoretical perspectives. In L. A. Pervin & O. P. John (Eds.), *Handbook of personality: Theory and research* (Vol. 2, pp. 102–138). Guilford Press.

Judge, T. A., Bono, J. E., Ilies, R., & Gerhardt, M. W. (2002). Personality and leadership: A qualitative and quantitative review. *Journal of Applied Psychology,* 87 (4), 765–780. doi:10.1037/0021-9010.87.4.765.

Kelley, D. (2018). Investigation of attitudes towards security behaviors. *McNair Research Journal SJSU,* 14(1), 10.

Kennison, S. M., & Chan-Tin, E. (2020). Taking risks with cybersecurity: Using knowledge and personal characteristics to predict self-reported cybersecurity behaviors. *Frontiers in Psychology,* 11. doi:10.3389/fpsyg.2020.546546.

Kraut, R., Kiesler, A., Boneva, B., Cummings, J., Helgeson, V., & Crawford, A. (2002). Internet paradox revisited. *Journal of Social Issues,* 58, 49–74.

Krishnan, S., Lim, V., & Teo, T. (2010). How does personality matter? Investigating the impact of Big-Five personality traits on cyberloafing. In *ICIS 2010 Proceedings – Thirty First International Conference on Information Systems.* http://aisel.aisnet.org/icis2010_submissions/6.

Lauriola, M., & Levin, I. P. (2001). Personality traits and risky decision-making in a controlled experimental task: An exploratory study. *Personality and Individual Differences,* 31(2), 215–226. doi:10.1016/S0191-8869(00)00130-00136.

Lawson, P., Pearson, C. J., Crowson, A., & Mayhorn, C. B. (2020). Email phishing and signal detection: How persuasion principles and personality influence response patterns and accuracy. *Applied Ergonomics,* 86, 103084. doi:10.1016/j.apergo.2020.103084.

López-Aguilar, P., & Solanas, A. (2021). Human susceptibility to phishing attacks based on personality traits: The role of neuroticism. *2021 IEEE 45th Annual Computers, Software, and Applications Conference (COMPSAC),* 1363–1368. doi:10.1109/COMPSAC51774.2021.00192.

Lowe-Calverley, E., & Grieve, R. (2017). Web of deceit: Relationships between the Dark Triad, perceived ability to deceive and cyberloafing. *Cyberpsychology: Journal of Psychosocial Research on Cyberspace,* 11(2), Article2. doi:10.5817/CP2017-2-5.

Maasberg, M., Warren, J., & Beebe, N. (2015). *The dark side of the insider: Detecting the insider threat through examination of Dark Triad personality traits.* doi:10.1109/HICSS.2015.423.

Maasberg, M., Zhang, X., Ko, M., Miller, S. R., & Beebe, N. L. (2020). An analysis of motive and observable behavioral indicators associated with insider cyber-sabotage and other attacks. *IEEE Engineering Management Review,* 48(2), 151–165. doi:10.1109/EMR.2020.2989108.

McBride, M., Carter, L., & Warkentin, M. (2012). *Exploring the role of individual employee characteristics and personality on employee compliance with cybersecurity policies.* www.academia.edu/79766954/Exploring_the_Role_of_Individual_Employee_Characteristics_and_Personality_on_Employee_Compliance_with_Cybersecurity_Policies1.

McCormac, A., Zwaans, T., Parsons, K., Calic, D., Butavicius, M., & Pattinson, M. (2017). Individual differences and information security awareness. *Computers in Human Behavior,* 69, 151–156. doi:10.1016/j.chb.2016.11.065.

Moore, C., Detert, J. R., Klebe Treviño, L., Baker, V. L., & Mayer, D. M. (2012). Why employees do bad things: Moral disengagement and unethical organizational behavior. *Personnel Psychology,* 65(1), 1–48.

Mount, M., Ilies, R., & Johnson, E. (2006). Relationship of personality traits and counterproductive work behaviors: The mediating effects of job satisfaction. *Personnel Psychology,* 59(3), 591–622. doi:10.1111/j.1744-6570.2006.00048.x.

Naga, J. F., Tinam-isan, M. A. C., Maluya, M. M. O., Panal, K. A. D., & Tupac, M. T. A. (2024). Investigating the relationship between personality traits and information security awareness. *International Journal of Computing and Digital Systems*, 15(1), Article1. doi:10.12785/ijcds/160191.

Nicholson, N., Soane, E., Fenton-O'Creevy, M., & Willman, P. (2005). Personality and domain-specific risk taking. *Journal of Risk Research*, 8(2), 157–176. doi:10.1080/1366987032000123856.

Ones, D. S. (1993). *The construct validity of integrity tests* (Unpublished doctoral dissertation). University of Iowa, Iowa City.

Ones, D. S., & Dilchert, S. (2013). Counterproductive work behaviors: Concepts, measurement, and nomological network. In *APA handbook of testing and assessment in psychology*, Vol. 1: *Test theory and testing and assessment in industrial and organizational psychology*, 643–659. doi:10.1037/14047-035.

Ones, D. S., Viswesvaran, C., & Schmidt, F. L. (1993). Comprehensive meta-analysis of integrity test validities: Findings and implications for personnel selection and theories of job performance. *Journal of Applied Psychology*, 78, 679–703. doi:10.1037/0021-9010.78.4.679.

Parrish, J. L.Jr., Bailey, J. L., & Courtney, J. F. (2009). *A personality based model for determining susceptibility to phishing attacks*. Technical Report. University of Arkansas, 285–296.

Paulhus, D. L., & Williams, K. M. (2002). The Dark Triad of personality: Narcissism, Machiavellianism, and psychopathy. *Journal of Research in Personality*, 36, 556–563. doi:10.1016/S0092-6566(02)00505-6.

Power, V., & Bello, A. (2022). Individual differences in cyber security behavior using personality-based models to predict susceptibility to sextortion attacks. *Cybersecurity and Cognitive Science*. doi:10.1016/B978-0-323-90570-1.00004-8.

Rahman, M. S., & Muldoon, J. (2020). Dark side of technology: Investigating the role of dark personality traits and technological factors in managing cyberloafing behavior. *Journal of Strategic Innovation and Sustainability*, 15(3), 36–54.

Russell, J. D., Weems, C. F., Ahmed, I., & Richard, G. G.III (2017). Self-reported secure and insecure cyber behaviour: Factor structure and associations with personality factors. *Journal of Cyber Security Technology*, 1(3–4), 163–174. doi:10.1080/23742917.2017.1345271.

Scarduzio, J. A., & Adams, M. (2022). Exploring coworker online sexual harassment and risk: Factors of uncertainty and ambiguity for employees and organizations. In K. N. Engemann, K. J. Engemann, & C. W. Scott (Eds.), *Organizational risk management: managing for uncertainty and ambiguity* (pp. 171–188). De Gruyter.

Shappie, A. T., Dawson, C. A., & Debb, S. M. (2020). Personality as a predictor of cybersecurity behavior. *Psychology of Popular Media*, 9(4), 475–480. doi:10.1037/ppm0000247.

Spector, P., & Zhou, Z. (2013). The moderating role of gender in relationships of stressors and personality with counterproductive work behavior. *Journal of Business and Psychology*, 29. doi:10.1007/s10869-013-9307-8.

Stiff, C., & Reeves, M. (2024). Careful when you click? How the Dark Triad of personality can influence the likelihood of online crime victimization. *The Journal of Psychology*, 158(3), 238–256. doi:10.1080/00223980.2023.2286451.

Sudzina, F., & Pavlicek, A. (2017). Propensity to click on suspicious links: Impact of gender, of age, and of personality traits. *BLED 2017 Proceedings*. https://aisel.aisnet.org/bled2017/10.

Uffen, J., Kaemmerer, N., & Breitner, M. H. (2013). Personality traits and cognitive determinants – An empirical investigation of the use of smartphone security measures. *Journal of Information Security*, 4(4), Article4. doi:10.4236/jis.2013.44023.

van de Weijer, S. G. A., & Leukfeldt, E. R. (2017). Big Five personality traits of cybercrime victims. *Cyberpsychology, Behavior and Social Networking*, 20(7), 407–412. doi:10.1089/cyber.2017.0028.

Varghese, L., & Barber, L. K. (2017). A preliminary study exploring moderating effects of role stressors on the relationship between Big Five personality traits and workplace cyberloafing. *Cyberpsychology: Journal of Psychosocial Research on Cyberspace*, 11(4), Article4. doi:10.5817/CP2017-4-4.

Weirich, D., & Sasse, M. A. (2001). Pretty good persuasion: A first step towards effective password security in the real world. In *Proceedings of the 2001 Workshop on New Security Paradigms, Cloudcroft, NM, September 10–13*, 137–143. doi:10.1145/508171.508195.

Wu, J., & Lebreton, J. M. (2011). Reconsidering the dispositional basis of counter-productive work behavior: The role of aberrant personality. *Personnel Psychology*, 64(3), 593–626. doi:10.1111/j.1744-6570.2011.01220.x.

10

CULTURAL INFLUENCES ON CYBERSECURITY PRACTICES

Introduction

As we highlighted back in Chapter 4, there are numerous ways to view the construct of culture, and several ways culture can influence cybersecurity. Tylor (1871) is credited with developing the first modern definition of culture, suggesting that it is 'that complex whole which includes knowledge, belief, arts, morals, law, custom, and any other capabilities and habits acquired by man as a member of society' (p. 1). Researchers have noted the inherent difficulties in presenting a clear and universally agreed-upon definition of culture (Axelrod, 1997; Kroeber & Kluckhohn, 1952). However, as Axelrod (1997) noted, a central element of culture is that it is something we learn from other people. Individuals are more likely to interact with others who share similar cultural attributes. One example Axelrod (1997) gives is that of language: individuals are more likely to communicate and interact with someone who speaks the same language as them. These interactions between individuals are seen to cement future patterns of behaviour (Axelrod, 1997). While the example given by Axelrod (1997) is language, it also relates to beliefs, attitudes, and behaviours that all serve to perpetuate the essential building blocks of culture. One of the fundamental mechanisms for the emergence of culture is social influence, which is crucial to understand, particularly when trying to motivate a change in established beliefs, attitudes, and behaviours (Axelrod, 1997).

Using the categories introduced earlier in Chapter 4, we will now explore the different ways in which culture can be applied to the area of cybersecurity and cybersecurity awareness, focusing on the roles of national, organisational, and cybersecurity culture.

DOI: 10.4324/9781003509011-10

National Culture

National culture encompasses the shared values, norms, and practices that characterise a country. These cultural differences can significantly impact how individuals perceive and respond to cybersecurity threats. For example, countries with high uncertainty avoidance may implement stricter cybersecurity measures, while those with lower uncertainty avoidance might adopt more flexible approaches. National culture influences general attitudes towards technology, trust in digital systems, and the prioritisation of cybersecurity. Understanding these cultural nuances is essential for developing effective cybersecurity strategies that are culturally sensitive and appropriate.

National culture is typically viewed as 'a collective programming of the mind that distinguishes members of one group or category from people of others' (Hofstede, 2011, p. 3). Hofstede (2011) presented one of the most frequently used dimensional models for classifying cultures. While it is not without its criticisms (e.g., see McSweeney, 2002 and a later rebuttal by Williamson, 2002), it provides a useful framework for exploring the role of culture in various elements linked to cybersecurity. According to Hofstede, culture is a form of collective programming that distinguishes one group of people from another, influencing a wide range of activities within any given group. Culture, from Hofstede's perspective, is embodied in the notion of nation (Hofstede, 1991, 2011).

The final version of Hofstede's cultural dimensions model, presented by Hofstede and colleagues (Hofstede & Minkov, 2010; Minkov & Kaasa, 2022), identified six individual bipolar dimensions on which cultures can be differentiated:

1 Power Distance Index (PDI)

This dimension embodies the societal desire for organisational hierarchy and the level of acceptance within that society for the distribution of power amongst individuals. Power distance refers to the extent individuals of lower status in a particular society accept the way power is distributed amongst its members. A culture that is highly rated in terms of power distance is one that tolerates inequality in society and accepts the resulting social order as being the natural one and needs no further justification or alteration. At the opposing end of this dimension, cultures that have a lower power distance do not support inequality and support strategies to deal with such issues, demanding justification for the way in which power is distributed amongst the members of society. People who live in high power distance societies are more reluctant to express an opinion that goes contradictory to those individuals who are higher in the social hierarchy (e.g., your boss, those in authority, the government). There are some respective implications for cybersecurity here, where high PDI cultures that exhibit multiple hierarchical structures in society often have centralised decision-making processes. This could mean that a lower-level employee may be more resilient to reporting suspicious activity, instead preferring to defer to those higher in authority.

2 Uncertainty Avoidance Index (UAI)

This dimension measures the extent to how threatened members of a society feel by the unknown or ambiguous, and how they have created mechanisms, such as institutions or belief systems, to cope with them. A high degree of uncertainty avoidance means that society will have an extremely limited tolerance for the unknown, reflected in risk aversive behaviours, and strong regulations that serve to bolster behavioural codes and laws. There is a need for structure in high uncertainty avoidance cultures, and this is usually accompanied by a lower resistance to ideas or individuals who fall outside of the cultural norms (Hofstede, 2011). A lower level of uncertainty avoidance is usually symptomatic of a greater subjective feeling of well-being amongst individuals in that society, as well as a greater tolerance for more deviations from the societal norms (Hofstede, 1991, 2011). Cultures who exhibit higher levels of UAI may have stricter cybersecurity policies through a fear of the unknown and a want to avoid high levels of risk, whereas cultures lower in UAI will have a more flexible and adaptable approach.

3 Individualism Versus Collectivism (IDV)

One of the most referenced dimensions from Hofstede's framework, this dimension is the degree to which a society is seen to be integrated into groups. Individualism refers to how much people view themselves as being independent and focuses directly on themselves and close family members. Those cultures that are at the higher end of the individualism dimension exhibit weak ties between individuals and emphasise the right to an individual's privacy, as well as emphasis on looking after your own interests (Hofstede, 2011; Minkov & Kaasa, 2022). In contrast, the collectivist society is one that emphasises a strong, cohesive group identity, and where individuals are seen as being stronger as a collective versus alone. People who live in a collectivist culture are more likely to be dependent on others when it comes to making decisions and formulating actions. In turn they expect a degree of reciprocation in these relationships and expect individuals around them to express loyalty and caring (Hofstede, 2011). In an individualistic society an individual may prioritise their personal privacy and the capacity to initiate their own actions, which in turn could make them more resilient to engage in the strict cybersecurity rules dictated by an organisation. In contrast, collectivist cultures would place a stronger emphasis on the security of the group as well as compliance with cybersecurity policies.

4 Masculinity Versus Femininity (MAS)

This dimension refers to the distribution of the emotional roles between the genders within society (Hofstede, 2011). In masculine society success is measured through aspects such as individual achievement, assertiveness, and material gain. In contrast, the feminine culture has a stronger preference for relationship building, modesty, and caring for individuals less fortunate than oneself. Overall masculinity is defined by a more assertive and competitive nature, versus a more compassionate and caring perspective for feminine cultures.

5 Long-Term Versus Short-Term Orientation (LTO)

This dimension measures the extent to which a culture focuses on long-term planning and persistence over short-term results and immediate returns. Values often associated with long-term orientation are those such as thrift and perseverance, with an emphasis on future goals and opportunities in the face of challenges and adversity. In contrast, short-term orientation focuses more on respecting traditions and fulfilling social obligations and is present in values such as generosity (Hofstede, 2011).

6 Indulgence Versus Restraint (IVR)

This dimension relates to the extent to which individuals in society consume resources, control their impulses, or reign in their hedonistic tendencies. In a society that exhibits a prominent level of restraint, individuals will be more likely to refrain from frivolous wastes of time and money. In contrast those individuals from a more indulgent society will not have the same restraint.

Understanding these cultural dimensions helps organisations tailor cybersecurity strategies. This is even more important in modern, multicultural organisations, and by considering national cultures, organisations can develop more effective and culturally sensitive policies and practices. However there has been sparse work exploring the dimensions of Hofstede and cybersecurity compliance behaviours. For example, Crespo-Pérez (2021) noted that individualism was negatively correlated with the intention to comply with cybersecurity policies. Conversely, masculinity and long-term orientation were both positively correlated with the intention to comply with cybersecurity behaviours (Crespo-Pérez, 2021).

While not entirely related, other researchers have examined the role cultural dimensions can have in the development of a cybersecurity framework from a national perspective. For instance, countries that scored higher on individualism tended to perform better in developing a cybersecurity framework (Onumo et al., 2017). This suggests that cultural dimensions can significantly influence both individual compliance behaviours and broader national cybersecurity strategies.

Arage et al. (2015, 2016) provided an initial outline for exploring the role of national culture on the cybersecurity behaviours of employees. They specifically examined how national culture moderates the influence of measures designed to prevent cybersecurity breaches and, in turn, affects employees' intention to violate cybersecurity policies. They noted that national culture significantly moderated the effectiveness of cybersecurity measures. The researchers noted that cultural dimensions such as power distance, individualism versus collectivism, and uncertainty avoidance could influence employees' intentions to either comply with or violate cybersecurity policies (Arage et al., 2015, 2016). In cultures with high power distance, employees are less likely to question or challenge established rules, leading to higher compliance rates. Conversely, in low power distance cultures, employees may feel empowered to question and potentially violate accepted cybersecurity rules. The researchers further hypothesised that in collectivist cultures, where group goals and social harmony are key features, higher compliance rates with cybersecurity rules should be observed. In contrast, in individualistic cultures, lower compliance rates might be expected due to a focus on personal goals (Arage et al., 2015, 2016).

Unfortunately, there is no direct evidence that this research proposal ever reached the data collection stage, but the proposed relationships between Hofstede's cultural dimensions and cybersecurity compliance seem logical. Other researchers have collected data in this area and support some of the key predictions suggested by Arage et al. (2015). For instance, Dols and Silvius (2010) explored the influence of national cultures on non-compliance behaviour and found that cultural aspects significantly impact such behaviours. For example, high power distance cultures showed higher compliance rates due to less questioning of authority, while individualistic cultures exhibited lower compliance rates due to a focus on personal autonomy.

Similarly, Flores et al. (2014) examined the role of cultural dimensions in shaping information security behaviours and found that high uncertainty avoidance and collectivism were associated with higher compliance with security policies. These findings align with the hypotheses proposed by Arage et al. (2015) and underscore the importance of considering cultural dimensions when developing and implementing cybersecurity policies. By understanding these cultural influences, organisations and policymakers can tailor their cybersecurity approaches to better align with the cultural context, thereby enhancing overall cybersecurity effectiveness.

National Culture and Trust

Establishing a level of trust is dependent upon a wide variety of factors, including shared values, beliefs, social identities, and expectations of how to interpret various interactions (Doney et al., 1998; Hallikainen & Laukkanen, 2018). It is no surprise then that trust and culture are invariably intertwined concepts (Hallikainen & Laukkanen, 2018). Various researchers have noted that the degree or level of trust within a particular society can influence both economic outlook and competitiveness in the global business market (Fukuyama, 1995; Inglehart, 1999).

Cultural differences can significantly impact how people perceive trust (Klein et al., 2019), and these differences can either hinder or foster trust. Research has observed cross-cultural differences in how people establish trust with those they are not familiar with; a concept termed depersonalised trust. Individuals make these types of trust judgments based on perceived similarities to the stranger, shared group membership, or mutual connections (Williams et al., 2017).

Research has demonstrated that individuals from individualistic cultures, such as the USA, are more likely to trust unknown individuals based on shared group membership. In contrast, individuals from collectivist cultures form trust relationships based on relationship links (Williams et al., 2017; Yuki et al., 2005). Traits associated with collectivist cultures tend to foster a greater tendency to conform to social norms within that society (Iyengar & Lepper, 1999; Kim & Markus, 1999) and to emulate the behaviours of those around them (van Baaren et al., 2003; Williams et al., 2017).

These cultural traits are particularly pertinent when considering the tactics often used in social engineering scams, where individuals are pressured to comply with social norms and rules. Differences in levels of trust can influence the likelihood of falling victim to such scams (Williams et al., 2017). For example, individuals in collectivist cultures may be more susceptible to social engineering tactics that exploit their tendency to conform to group norms and trust based on relationship links.

Other researchers have noted that culture can influence a wide range of online activities, including trust in e-commerce (An & Kim, 2008; Connolly & Bannister, 2006; Hallikainen & Laukkanen, 2018; Yoon, 2009), online health-seeking behaviour (Khosrowjerdi, 2020), and internet privacy concerns (Cockcroft & Heales, 2005; Heales et al., 2017).

There is an interplay between trust, culture, and attitudes towards risky cybersecurity behaviours. Collectivist cultures are more likely to share personal information if they view this as being for the good of the group or the whole, making social engineering tactics that target such cultural values more effective. In contrast, individualistic cultures focus more on personal privacy and data protection, potentially overlooking the need to protect data from individuals who might portray themselves as friends or family (Alhasan, 2023). Alhasan (2023) also noted significant differences between cultural groups and attitudes towards risky cybersecurity behaviours, though the results lacked specificity in linking these to Hofstede's cultural dimensions.

Understanding the interplay between trust and culture is crucial for developing effective cybersecurity strategies. By recognizing how cultural differences influence trust perceptions and behaviours, organisations can tailor their cybersecurity measures to better protect against social engineering and other trust-based attacks. This cultural awareness can enhance the overall security posture and resilience of organisations operating in diverse cultural environments.

National Culture and Risk Perception

Individual differences in cultural values and worldview significantly influence how people perceive and respond to risk across various domains. For instance, Hsee and Weber (1999) found that Chinese participants were more risk-seeking than American participants in investment-related domains. This was attributed to the greater likelihood of receiving financial help in collectivist societies compared to individualistic societies. Similarly, Weber and Hsee (1998) found that individuals from China, America, Poland, and Germany differed in their perceptions of financial risk. Cultural variables such as power distance (the extent to which people accept and expect unequal power distribution; Hofstede, 2011) and uncertainty avoidance (the extent to which people tolerate ambiguity; Hofstede, 2011) have been negatively associated with risk-taking in entrepreneurial and financial contexts (Bontempo et al., 1997; Kanagaretnam et al., 2014; Kreiser et al., 2010), whereas individualism is positively associated with risk-taking.

Building on this, other approaches to cultural differences have also been considered. In the early 1980s, Douglas and Wildavsky (1982) began exploring how cultural values and settings impact an individual's perception of risks (Dake, 1991; Johnson & Covello, 1987; Rippl, 2018). They suggested that individuals are part of a social structure that shapes their values, attitudes, and perspectives about the world (Rippl, 2018). This approach implies that cultural biases are more critical in shaping risk perception than cognitive processes.

Douglas and Wildavsky (1982) proposed four cultural categories that shape risk perceptions: hierarchical, egalitarian, individualistic, and fatalistic. Individualistic values focus on personal freedoms, egalitarian values on equality, hierarchical values on social order and expert knowledge (Tansey & O'Riordan, 1999), and fatalism on indifference to risk, considering outcomes to be outside individual control. This framework has been applied to various domains, including climate change (Lazrus, 2015; McNeeley & Lazrus, 2014), nuclear power (van de Graaff, 2016), and oil and gas industry development (McEvoy et al., 2017). Xue et al. (2014) found that egalitarians perceived greater environmental risks, whereas individualists and hierarchists perceived fewer. Tsohou et al. (2015) suggested that cultural biases could tailor information security awareness campaigns. Sawaya et al. (2017) found that people from Asian countries, particularly Japan, exhibited less secure cyber behaviour. Alowais et al. (2023) explored protective cybersecurity behaviours in the US and Saudi Arabia, proposing significant differences influenced by cultural dimensions, including power distance and individualism. This work is built on previous research demonstrating differences in cybersecurity knowledge, such as password management and secure connections (Alzubaidi, 2021; Moallem, 2018).

In an unpublished study by Hadlington et al. (n.d.), the role of country of origin in risk perception and information security awareness was explored. The study involved participants from the US, UK, Singapore, South Africa, India, and Australia (n = 2,997). In the study we classified the UK, US, and Australia as developed countries, while South Africa, India, and Singapore were categorised as developing countries, following the meeting of the United Nations World Economic Forum in 2019.

The full breakdown of the participant taking part in the study is presented in Table 10.1.

Participants completed the HAIS-Q to measure information security awareness and the Domain Specific Risk-Taking Scale (DOSPERT) developed by Blais and Weber (2006) to assess risk-taking behaviours. The DOSPERT consists of two 30-item scales that ask participants to rate their likelihood of engaging in risky behaviours and their perception of risk for each behaviour. These are scored on 7-point Likert scales (1 = Extremely Unlikely to 7 = Extremely Likely for likelihood, and 1 = Not at All Risky to 7 = Extremely Risky for perception). Each scale allows risk-taking and risk perception to be broken down into five commonly encountered domains: ethical, financial, health and safety, social, and recreational.

We analysed the DOSPERT scores by domain and the cultural background of participants to understand how cultural values influence risk-taking behaviours. The data for this analysis is displayed in Table 10.2.

The data reveals some intriguing patterns in risk-taking behaviours across the different countries and the associated risk domains. Of note, India consistently exhibited the highest risk-taking scores across nearly all of the

TABLE 10.1 Demographic Information by Country of Origin

	UK	US	Australia	India	South Africa	Singapore	Totals
Sex							
Male	160	155	247	361	310	266	1499
Female	257	358	255	168	228	232	1498
Age Range							
18–24	141	139	105	159	115	110	769
25–34	68	61	119	159	207	165	779
35–49	77	59	128	146	154	186	750
50–64	131	254	150	65	62	37	699
Total	417	513	502	529	538	498	2997

TABLE 10.2 Mean Scores for Risk-Taking by Domain by Country

Country	Risk-Taking Ethical	Risk-Taking Financial	Risk-Taking Health and Safety	Risk-Taking Recreational	Risk-Taking Social
India	22.65	26.41	21.02	25.39	30.81
Singapore	17.06	20.05	16.89	19.38	27.71
UK	15.17	16.15	18.16	17.74	29.56
Australian	14.66	16.32	15.79	16.95	29.31
US	14.05	17.25	15.64	16.57	28.31
South Africa	13.27	19.14	16.09	20.50	31.38

domains, including ethical, financial, health and safety, and recreational. South Africa stands out with the highest social risk-taking score. This could reflect the social dynamics and cultural attitudes prevalent in South Africa, where social interactions and behaviours might be more openly embraced or encouraged.

Australia and the UK show the lowest risk-taking scores across most of the domains. Specifically, Australia has the lowest scores in the health and safety and recreational domains, suggesting a more cautious approach to risk in these areas. The UK also demonstrates lower overall risk-taking, aligning with a more conservative risk profile.

Finally, Singapore and the US presented moderate risk-taking scores, with Singapore showing slightly higher risk-taking in social and recreational domains compared to the US. We took this as indicating a more balanced approach to risk in these countries, with some variations in specific domains.

To gain a more comprehensive view of the trends within the risk-taking data, we calculated the mean risk-taking score for each country across all domains. India emerged as the country with the highest overall risk-taking, followed by South Africa. Singapore showed moderate levels of risk-taking, while the UK and Australia exhibit lower overall risk-taking. The US also falls into the moderate to lower risk-taking category.

We suggested that cultural influences could play a significant role in shaping these results, particularly in India, where collectivist values and strong social support systems may encourage higher risk-taking behaviours. As noted previously in South Africa, social dynamics and cultural attitudes towards social interactions are more likely to contribute to the high social risk-taking scores. Overall, these findings highlight the complex interplay between cultural values and social dynamics that serve to shape risk-taking behaviours across different countries and domains. Understanding these nuances can provide valuable insights for developing targeted strategies and interventions to manage risk in various contexts, specifically those aligned to cybersecurity.

Interpreting these results requires a nuanced approach, especially when considering Hofstede's cultural dimensions. It is important to note that Hofstede did not originally intend for these dimensions to be used in such a strict manner, so we are applying them in a slightly unconventional way. We have grouped some of the key findings from the research around the key dimensions that were suggested in Hofstede's original framework below.

- Uncertainty Avoidance

India's moderate level of uncertainty avoidance helps explain the higher levels of financial, social, and ethical risk-taking observed. Indian culture is generally adaptable to uncertainty, which is evident in both business and social contexts (Thampi et al., 2015). This tolerance for uncertainty means individuals are more likely to bypass rules, when necessary, which is particularly relevant in cybersecurity behaviours.

Singapore, on the other hand, scores exceptionally low on uncertainty avoidance, suggesting that individuals should take more risks. However, other factors, such as Singapore's high long-term orientation (72), might lead individuals to make more calculated decisions with long-term goals in mind, thus exhibiting lower risk-taking in financial, health, and ethical domains. Additionally, Singapore's high power distance (74) indicates strict laws and regulations that may discourage risk-taking in ethical or health and safety domains. Overall, Singaporeans might accept risk and uncertainty in certain areas but generally avoid anything that could impact their culture's stability and long-term reputation.

- Power Distance

Cultures with high power distance, like Singapore, tend to avoid risks that could challenge authority or government domains, reflected in lower ethical and health and safety risk-taking. India also scores high in power distance, but this might be moderated by factors such as pragmatism and cultural resilience. In contrast, the UK, US, and Australia have low power distance, supporting devolved decision making to individuals, which translates into moderate financial and social risk-taking. South Africa, despite having a similar power distance score to the US, shows a balanced level of risk due to a mix of traditional and modern values.

- Masculinity Versus Femininity

Most countries included in the study score moderately on masculinity, valuing competition and achievement over quality of life and care. Singapore scored lower on this measure, which could explain its lower risk-taking behaviour across domains. The US, UK, and Australia, being moderately masculine, exhibit caution in ethical and health risk-taking but are more open to social and financial risks. India and South Africa also show moderate masculinity, but other factors lead to higher financial and social risk-taking.

- Long-Term Orientation

Both India and Singapore scored highly on long-term orientation, which aligns well with the lower risk-taking in ethical and health/safety domains. In contrast, the UK, US, and Australia are typically viewed as short-term goal oriented, which in turn fosters moderate levels of financial and social risk-taking focused on immediate gains.

• Indulgence Versus Restraint

Moderate indulgence in Indian and South African cultures explains the observed recreational and social risk-taking. Singapore's high restraint leads to lower recreational and ethical risk-taking. The US, UK, and Australia, scoring higher on indulgence, show higher recreational risk-taking.

• Self-Reported Attitudes Towards Risk

Participants from India scored higher on all risk domains except social risk-taking, which does align well with Hofstede's cultural dimensions, in which India is typified as having lower scores on uncertainty avoidance, suggesting a propensity for greater risk-taking (Thampi et al., 2015). This suggestion can also be seen to be applicable to other findings from the current research. For example, South Africa, typically exhibiting culturally high levels of uncertainty avoidance, showed the lowest ethical risk-taking. However, it is important to note that individual risk-taking propensity can often override the influence of cultural orientations, which in turn highlights the importance of exploring individual differences in risk perception and behaviour, especially where cybersecurity adherence is concerned.

Culture and Information Security Awareness

The scores for cybersecurity awareness as measured through the HAIS-Q are displayed in Table 10.3.

The HAIS-Q scores provide valuable insights into the cybersecurity awareness levels across different countries, reflecting various cultural influences and contextual factors. India has the lowest overall score, indicating comparatively low cybersecurity awareness. This could be influenced by moderate uncertainty avoidance and a cultural tendency to bypass rules when necessary. Singapore shows moderate levels of cybersecurity awareness, likely linked to its strict regulatory frameworks and a pragmatic approach to cybersecurity, in spite of its low uncertainty avoidance. The UK demonstrated higher levels of cybersecurity awareness, aligning with its low uncertainty avoidance and high individualism, which shifts the responsibility for cybersecurity onto individuals. Australia's high level of awareness is similar to the UK, reflecting shared cultural values such as low uncertainty avoidance and high individualism. The US also shows high cybersecurity awareness, driven by similar cultural factors to the UK and Australia, including low uncertainty avoidance and high individualism. South Africa has the highest score overall, which could be symptomatic of a high-threat environment and relevant resilience testing. This suggests that individuals in South Africa may be more vigilant and aware of cybersecurity threats due to the perceived higher risk.

The HAIS-Q scores highlight the influence of cultural dimensions on cybersecurity awareness. Countries with low uncertainty avoidance and high

TABLE 10.3 HAIS-Q Scores by Country

Country	HAIS-Q Scores	Comments
India	217.04	The lowest overall score, demonstrating comparatively low cybersecurity awareness across the sample.
Singapore	240.77	Moderate level of awareness potentially linked to strict regulatory frameworks and a more pragmatic cybersecurity culture.
UK	244.75	High level of awareness that is symptomatic of low uncertainty avoidance and high individualism shifting responsibility for cybersecurity onto the individual.
Australia	242.06	High level of awareness linked to similar cultural values shared by the UK.
US	243.96	High level of awareness driven by similar factors to the UK and Australia.
South Africa	253.33	Highest score overall which could be symptomatic of a high-threat environment and relevant resilience testing.

individualism, such as the UK, Australia, and the US, tend to have higher cybersecurity awareness. This is likely because individuals in these cultures take more personal responsibility for their cybersecurity practices. In contrast, India's lower score may reflect a more relaxed attitude towards uncertainty and rule-bypassing behaviours, leading to lower overall awareness. Singapore's moderate score, despite low uncertainty avoidance, can be attributed to its strong regulatory environment and long-term orientation, which promote a more calculated approach to cybersecurity. South Africa's highest score suggests that a high-threat environment can significantly enhance cybersecurity awareness, as individuals become more attuned to potential risks and the need for protective measures.

Although such differences may relate to subtle differences in cultural values across these countries, such aspects are also likely to be influenced by wider national differences related to the context (e.g., Chew & Putti, 1995; Hofstede, 1991; Paul et al., 2006). For example, it is possible that such differences may not necessarily relate to differences in cultural values per se but instead relate more to societal conditions within a particular country. Previous research considered the role of optimism in relation to people's perceptions of the likelihood that specific life events would happen to them (Sharot & Garrett, 2016). In addition to identifying the role of factors such as age in influencing how optimistic people were about avoiding negative life events, the authors also stated that people's so-called optimism bias (considering themselves more likely to avoid negative events than other people) could change in response to perceptions of wider environmental conditions. Relatively safe environments result in over-optimism, while more threatening environments lead to a more balanced consideration. If the wider societal environment (or even the wider online environment) is perceived by respondents to be safe, they may be over-optimistic in their perceptions of online risk, and vice versa with those environments considered less safe, resulting in differences in information security behaviour. This may explain why victims of online scams often highlight increased vigilance to online threats due to their experience, potentially due to decreased optimism regarding their ability to avoid such threats in the future. One crucial point from this study was that risk-taking was a far stronger predictor for scores of ISA (information security awareness) than country of origin, indicating that individual differences in risk-taking behaviour may be a more beneficial mechanism for assessing adherence to ISA versus culture.

Organisational Culture

Organisational culture is closely aligned with the construct of geographical culture. It is a set of rules, beliefs, and ways of behaving that give an organisation its own distinctive characteristics and ethos (Brown, 1995; Willcoxon & Millett, 2000). In recent years, researchers have developed the notion of cybersecurity organisational culture to describe elements that shape an organisation's approach to cybersecurity.

The concept of organisational culture was introduced during the 1970s when researchers began studying management and organisations. Pettigrew (1979) provided the first clear overview, describing it as a set of shared beliefs, values, and assumptions that govern behaviour within an organisation (Pavlova, 2020; Pettigrew, 1979). Beliefs and values are often hard to quantify, and many within an organisation hold diverse beliefs that can be difficult to understand. Schein (2009) presented several distinct levels at which culture within an organisation can be shaped, which have been adapted to fit the area of cybersecurity (Da Veiga et al., 2020; Schlienger & Teufel, 2003).

Level 1: Artifacts

Artifacts are the most tangible manifestations of culture and can be freely observed within an organisation. They include art, technology, and visual patterns of behaviour, as well as myths, heroes, rituals, and ceremonies (Pettigrew, 1979). Although these aspects of culture are readily observable, their actual meaning is often hidden. Only by delving deeper into the organisation can we understand their significance. Artifacts, though they might seem inconsequential, can embody key aspects of the organisation's culture. For example, technology within an organisation may have culturally important meanings driven by its use and the consequences of its misuse (Coombs et al., 1992).

Level 2: Espoused Values

Espoused values are the officially advertised viewpoints of the organisation and explain the existence of artifacts. These values are displayed in mission statements and other documentation that presents the organisation's values, principles, and ethos (Schein, 2009). In simple terms, these are the goals the organisation hopes to achieve.

Level 3: Shared Tacit Assumptions

Shared tacit assumptions develop as part of the organisation's evolution and form due to successful strategies or processes (Schein, 2009). When success is achieved through specific beliefs or values, these are continually adopted and gradually become ingrained in the organisation's culture. These shared assumptions emphasise a joint learning process, which is an inherent part of the human factors approach.

Having a positive organisational culture can have direct benefits for both the people who work within the organisation and the organisation itself (Liu et al., 2021; Sutton & Tompson, 2025). However, as explored in Chapter 2 and 9 regarding CWBs, many potential negatives can emerge when organisational culture is slightly 'off', leading employees to resent or rebel against the organisation's key principles or ethos. If there are significant shortfalls in the cultural priorities for cybersecurity, the organisation may become more vulnerable to both internal and external threats (Sutton & Tompson, 2025).

In recent years, there has been a concentrated move towards discussions related to cybersecurity culture (Sutton & Tompson, 2025; Uchendu et al., 2021). Various approaches have been taken to modify or update existing frameworks from organisational and information security cultures. Uchendu et al. (2021) note that cybersecurity culture extends beyond a narrow focus on information security culture within an organisation, aiming to protect both human and organisational assets. Their systematic review highlighted that very few papers have defined cybersecurity culture, reflecting the infancy of this approach (Uchendu et al., 2021). Additionally, many papers reviewed by Uchendu et al. (2021) did not specifically reference cybersecurity culture, often using the terms information security and cybersecurity interchangeably. Despite the current state of the language, there is a pressing need to develop a more consistent and well-defined approach to cybersecurity culture. This new framework should move beyond the traditional information security paradigm, addressing the unique challenges and requirements of cybersecurity. By doing so, we can ensure a comprehensive and cohesive strategy that effectively protects both human and organisational assets.

When we explore the concept of cybersecurity culture, researchers like Van Niekerk and von Solms (2010) made a clear distinction between organisational culture and cybersecurity culture. Traditional perspectives on organisational culture often ignore specific job-related information, assuming that each employee has all the necessary knowledge to perform their roles. However, this assumption does not hold for cybersecurity, where employees may lack the specific skills required to perform their job securely (Van Niekerk & von Solms, 2010).

Furthermore, Sutton and Tompson (2025) highlight that cybersecurity culture (CSC) is a key sub-component of organisational culture. Each relevant sub-component can be accurately mapped onto Schein's three-component model (2004, 2009). They emphasise the importance of developing an effective cybersecurity culture where every member of the organisation adheres to practical cybersecurity priorities.

Defining Cybersecurity Culture

CSC is viewed as the norms and values of the organisation that focus directly on cybersecurity (Sharma & Aparicio, 2022). Da Veiga et al. (2020) presented a definition of information security culture that has also been used to describe the underlying elements of cybersecurity culture:

> Contextualized to the behaviour of humans in an organisational context to protect information processed by the organisation through compliance with the information security policy and an understanding of how to implement requirements in a cautious and attentive manner as embedded through regular communication, awareness, training, and education initiatives.
>
> *(Da Veiga et al., 2020, p. 19)*

Although Da Veiga et al. (2020) used this definition to describe information security culture, many relevant elements transfer neatly into our current discussion on cybersecurity. Indeed, other researchers have used this definition to apply to cybersecurity culture (e.g., Da Veiga et al., 2020). Underlying the notion of cybersecurity culture is a set of common elements that refer to the values, assumptions, and behaviours of employees within an organisation, which can be detected as artefactual elements as presented in Schein's original categorisation (Da Veiga et al., 2020).

Other organisations such as ENISA (European Union Agency for Network and Information Security) have also presented a comprehensive definition for CSC, this being the:

Knowledge, beliefs, perceptions, attitudes, assumptions, norms, and values of people regarding cybersecurity and how they manifest themselves in people's behaviours with information technologies. CSC encompasses familiar topics including cybersecurity awareness and information security frameworks but is broader in both scope and application, being concerned with making information security considerations an integral part of an employee's job, habits, and conduct, embedding them in their day-to-day actions.

(ENISA, 2017, p. 5)

There are crucial elements to take away from this definition, which have a key bearing on how we explore CSC within an organisation. Specifically, these aspects focus on:

Knowledge can significantly impact CSC. Employee awareness and understanding of cybersecurity influence organisational cybersecurity. Well-informed employees are more likely to respond quickly and effectively to threats and recognise potential risks from certain activities or behaviours. Fostering a culture of continued learning and vigilance can help, but a fine balance is needed to avoid cybersecurity fatigue (see Chapter 12).

Attitudes of individuals within the organisation also affect CSC. Employees who appreciate the importance of cybersecurity and see it as critical to both the organisation's success and their own job security are more likely to adhere to key policies. Poor attitudes towards cybersecurity mean individuals are less likely to engage in organisational cybersecurity policies and may ignore or reject their role within the cybersecurity culture. Those with a sense of personal responsibility (note the crossover to work locus of control (WLCS) discussed further in Chapter 11) are more proactive in reporting cybersecurity incidents and following organisational policies. Personality traits such as agreeableness and conscientiousness also play a role in aligning behaviour with organisational policies.

Norms, as discussed in Chapter 11, shape acceptable behaviours within the organisation. Expressed through the organisation's commitment to cybersecurity, observed in policies and effective leadership practices, these norms create expectations for employees to follow. In organisations where cybersecurity is a clear priority, staff will adopt these norms, creating a more effective CSC. Colleagues' influence on adherence to cybersecurity practices, through social norms, also plays a role. In an organisation where everyone is accountable for their cybersecurity behaviours, an active process of strengthening CSC can be created. However, fostering such a culture requires significant input from the organisation, and in certain cultures, accountability could be interpreted as blame, which could have consequences outside of CSC.

Some researchers have expanded the original three observable layers widely applied to the information security paradigm by adding an additional layer of knowledge, arguing that knowledge influences the other three layers of cybersecurity culture (Reegärd et al., 2019; Van Niekerk & von Solms, 2010). Reegärd et al. (2019) presented a well-structured argument for viewing cybersecurity culture, noting its similarity to safety culture. Much of the work in this area focuses on preventing 'incidents' resulting from human error and miscalculation. The authors identified common elements inherent to the literature on safety culture:

- A reference to shared values amongst groups or individuals within an organisation.
- It is concerned about formal safety issues and is supported by management of safety and relevant supervisory systems.
- An emphasis on the contribution of everyone in the organisation to the concept of safety culture.
- Examines the impact of the behaviour of individual members of the organisation within the workplace.
- Is very much couched in terms of a balance between reward systems and safety performance.
- This can be easily observed in terms of how willing an organisation is to learn from their previous mistakes.
- Is an enduring process that is stable over time and is resistant to change (Reegärd et al., 2019).

If we think about this in the context of cybersecurity culture, we can say with a fair degree of certainty that each of these elements maps well onto the construct. We assume that everyone in the organisation shares a set of beliefs and behaviours regarding cybersecurity, which are reflected in fair use policies and accepted rules for using organisational devices. Balancing reward and safety systems is another aspect of safety management that applies to cybersecurity. Organisations need to create a secure environment without making tasks onerous, stifling creativity and productivity, or causing undue stress for employees.

Additionally, one of the most critical aspects of this framework is the capacity for organisations to reflect on previous mistakes or errors and implement changes to improve their overall cybersecurity culture. In our opinion this is one of the weakest elements of cybersecurity culture. Many organisations lack the critical awareness, reflection, and expertise to identify key issues that lead to incidents. Furthermore, they often fail to synthesise these points into a reflective process, instead favouring a knee-jerk response to enhance physical and technical measures in a post hoc manner (Ashenden & Sasse, 2013; Nobles, 2018).

Sutton and Tompson (2025) detailed a process framework for exploring CSC, with the inclusion of behaviour elements that can serve to influence overall CSC (see Figure 10.1).

There are several key components to this model that we should pull apart, as each needs its own level of explanation.

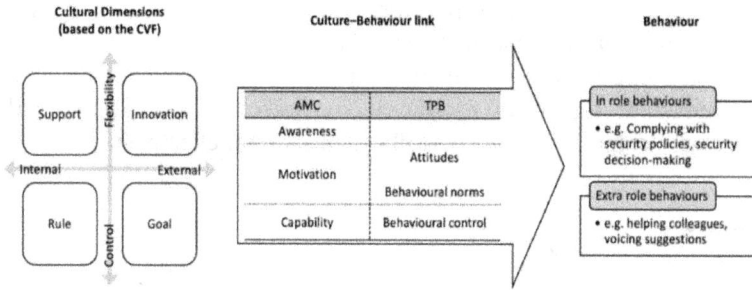

CVF = Competing Values Framework; AMC = Awareness, Motivation and Capability; TPB = Theory of Planned Behaviour.

FIGURE 10.1 The Cybersecurity Culture-Behaviour (CSCB) Framework (Sutton & Tompson, 2025)

The cultural dimensions are captured in the competing values framework (CVF) developed by Quinn and Rohrbaugh (1983, as cited in Sutton & Tompson, 2025) to understand how culture impacts organisational effectiveness. The CVF is presented using two axes: focus (internal versus external) and rigidity within the organisation (stability versus flexibility). An internal focus emphasises elements inherent to the organisation, such as employee well-being, organisational culture, and process improvement. Conversely, an external focus centres on factors outside the organisation, including market trends, key competitors, and customer experience enhancement. The other dimension, flexibility versus stability, distinguishes between a stable cultural dimension prioritizing structure, control, and efficiency, and a flexible dimension emphasizing adaptability, innovation, and openness to change. From the CVF, we can identify four distinct cultural orientations that combine these dimensions.

An internal focus with an emphasis on control aligns the organisation with a rule-oriented culture that prioritises control and efficiency, making it very process-driven. An external focus with an emphasis on control results in a goal-oriented organisation focused on competition and customer satisfaction to achieve effectiveness. An internal focus with an emphasis on flexibility creates a supportive culture emphasizing collaboration, mentorship, and team building, where human development and commitment to individuals drive overall effectiveness. An external focus with an emphasis on flexibility fosters a culture of innovation and agility, where organisations take more risks and seek new market opportunities.

Research has explored the role of organisational orientation on cybersecurity compliance behaviour. For example, Solomon and Irwin (2019) found that rule orientation had no significant impact on cybersecurity compliance within an organisation. They suggested that even though rules exist, they may not be sufficient to incentivise individuals to comply. Elements such as moral disengagement provide pathways for employees to sidestep rules and avoid engaging with cybersecurity compliance.

Understanding these cultural dimensions and their impact on organisational behaviour is crucial for developing effective strategies to enhance cybersecurity compliance and overall organisational effectiveness.

Summary

The chapter explored the intricate relationship between culture and cybersecurity, emphasizing the importance of understanding cultural dimensions to enhance cybersecurity awareness and compliance. It began by discussing the concept of culture, referencing Tylor's (1871) definition and highlighted the challenges in defining culture universally. Axelrod's (1997) perspective on culture as learned behaviour was also noted, emphasizing the role of social influence in shaping cultural norms.

The chapter also delved into national culture, using Hofstede's cultural dimensions model to explain how different cultural traits influenced cybersecurity behaviours. Key dimensions such as power distance, uncertainty avoidance, individualism versus collectivism, masculinity versus femininity, long-term versus short-term orientation, and indulgence versus restraint were discussed. The chapter highlighted how these dimensions impacted attitudes towards technology, trust in digital systems, and the prioritisation of cybersecurity. For instance, high uncertainty avoidance cultures implemented stricter cybersecurity measures, while low uncertainty avoidance cultures adopted more flexible approaches.

Organisational culture was another focal point, described as the set of rules, beliefs, and behaviours that gave an organisation its distinctive characteristics. The chapter outlined Schein's (2009) three levels of organisational culture: artifacts, espoused values, and shared tacit assumptions. It emphasised the importance of a positive organisational culture in fostering cybersecurity awareness and compliance. The concept of cybersecurity culture (CSC) was introduced as a sub-component of organisational culture, focusing specifically on cybersecurity norms and values. CSC encompasses knowledge, beliefs, perceptions, attitudes, assumptions, norms, and values regarding cybersecurity.

The chapter also addressed the interplay between trust and risk perception, noting that cultural values significantly influenced these factors. For example, collectivist cultures were more susceptible to social engineering tactics that exploited group norms and trust based on relationships. Understanding these cultural influences helped organisations tailor their cybersecurity strategies to better protect against trust-based attacks.

In summary, the chapter underscored the importance of considering cultural and contextual factors when developing cybersecurity strategies. While national and organisational cultures played significant roles, individual risk-taking tendencies were also crucial in determining cybersecurity behaviours. By integrating these cultural insights, organisations could enhance their overall security posture and resilience, creating a safer and more secure digital environment.

References

Alhasan, I. (2023). *Human factors in cybersecurity: A cross-cultural study on trust* (PhD dissertation). Purdue University.

Alowais, S., Armeen, I., Sharma, P., & Johnston, A. (2023). Cyber hygiene practices across cultures: A cross-cultural study of the US and Saudi Arabia based information systems users. *Procedia Computer Science, 219*, 744–750. doi:10.1016/j.procs.2023.01.347.

Alzubaidi, A. (2021). *Human factors in cybersecurity: A cross-cultural study on trust* (Doctoral dissertation). Queensland University of Technology.

An, D., & Kim, S. (2008). Effects of national culture on the development of consumer trust in online shopping. *Seoul Journal of Business, 14*(1), 123–151.

Arage, T. M., Belanger, F., & Tesema, T. B. (2015). Influence of national culture on employees' compliance with information systems security (ISS) policies: Towards ISS culture in Ethiopian companies. *2015 Americas Conference on Information Systems, AMCIS 2015*, 1–7. https://core.ac.uk/download/pdf/301370071.pdf.

Arage, T. M., Belanger, F., & Tesema, T. B. (2016). Investigating the moderating impact of national culture in information systems security policy violation: The case of Italy and Ethiopia. *Mediterranean Conference on Information Systems (MCIS)*. http://aisel.aisnet.org/mcis2016.

Ashenden, D., & Sasse, A. (2013). CISOs and organisational culture: Their own worst enemy? *Computers and Security, 39*(Part B), 396–405. doi:10.1016/j.cose.2013.09.004.

Axelrod, R. (1997). The dissemination of culture. *Journal of Conflict Resolution, 41*(2), 203–226. doi:10.1177/0022002797041002001.

Blais, A.-R., & Weber, E. U. (2006). A domain-specific risk-taking (DOSPERT) scale for adult populations. *Judgment and Decision Making, 1*(1), 33–47. doi:10.1037/t13084-000.

Bontempo, R. N., Bottom, W. P., & Weber, E. U. (1997). Cross-cultural differences in risk perception: A model-based approach. *Risk Analysis, 17*(4), 479–488.

Brown, A. D. (1995). *Organisational culture*. Pitman Publishing.

Chew, I. K., & Putti, J. (1995). Relationship on work-related values of Singaporean and Japanese managers in Singapore. *Human Relations, 48*(10), 1149–1170. doi:10.1177/001872679504801003.

Cockcroft, S., & Heales, J. (2005). National culture, trust and internet privacy concerns. *ACIS 2005 Proceedings – 16th Australasian Conference on Information Systems*. http://aisel.aisnet.org/acis2005/65.

Connolly, L., & Bannister, F. (2006). Factors influencing Irish consumers' trust in internet shopping. *Journal of Information Technology, 22*, 102–118.

Coombs, W. T., Holladay, S. J., & Hazleton, V. (1992). The effects of attributions of responsibility and crisis response strategies on organizational reputation. *Public Relations Review, 18*(2), 165–176.

Crespo-Pérez, G. (2021). *Factors that influence cybersecurity behavior: A cross-cultural study*. Universidad Ana G Méndez-Gurabo.

Da Veiga, A., Astakhova, L. V., Botha, A., & Herselman, M. (2020). Defining organisational information security culture – Perspectives from academia and industry.
Computers and Security, 92, 101713. doi:10.1016/j.cose.2020.101713.

Dake, K. (1991). Orienting dispositions in the perception of risk: An analysis of
contemporary worldviews and cultural biases. *Journal of Cross-Cultural Psychology*,
22(1), 61–82.

Dols, T., & Silvius, A. J. G. (2010). Exploring the influence of national cultures on
non-compliance behavior. *Communications of the IIMA*, 10(3), 10–32.
doi:10.58729/1941-6687.1140.

Doney, P. M., Cannon, J. P., & Mullen, M. R. (1998). Understanding the influence of
national culture on the development of trust. *Academy of Management Review*, 23
(3), 601–620.

Douglas, M., & Wildavsky, A. B. (1982). *Risk and culture: An essay on the selection of
technical and environmental dangers.* University of California Press.

ENISA. (2017). *Cyber security culture in organisations.* doi:10.2824/10543.

Flores, W., Antonsen, E., & Ekstedt, M. (2014). Information security knowledge
sharing in organizations: Investigating the effect of behavioral information security
governance and national culture. *Computers and Security*, 43, 90–110. doi:10.1016/
j.cose.2014.03.004.

Fukuyama, F. (1995). *Trust: The social virtues and the creation of prosperity.* Free
Press.

Hadlington, L., Binder, J., & Parsons, K. (n.d.). *Exploring the role of moral disengagement and counterproductive work behaviors in information security awareness.*
(Unpublished Manuscript.)

Hallikainen, H., & Laukkanen, T. (2018). National culture and consumer trust in e-
commerce. *International Journal of Information Management*, 38(1), 97–106.

Heales, J., Cockcroft, S., & Trieu, V. H. (2017). The influence of privacy, trust, and
national culture on internet transactions. In *Social Computing and Social Media.
Human Behavior: 9th International Conference, SCSM 2017, Held as Part of HCI
International 2017, Vancouver, BC, Canada, July 9–14, 2017, Proceedings, Part I*,
159–176. Springer International Publishing.

Hofstede, G. (1991). *Cultures and organizations: Software of the mind.* McGraw-Hill.

Hofstede, G. (2011). Dimensionalizing cultures: The Hofstede model in context.
Online Readings in Psychology and Culture, 2(1), 8.

Hofstede, G., & Minkov, M. (2010). Long-versus short-term orientation: New
perspectives. *Asia Pacific Business Review*, 16(4), 493–504.

Hsee, C. K., & Weber, E. U. (1999). Cross-national differences in risk preference and
lay predictions. *Journal of Behavioral Decision Making*, 12(2), 165–179.

Inglehart, R. (1999). Trust, well-being and democracy. *Democracy and Trust*, 88, 88–120.

Iyengar, S. S., & Lepper, M. R. (1999). Rethinking the value of choice: A cultural
perspective on intrinsic motivation. *Journal of Personality and Social Psychology*,
76, 349–366.

Johnson, B. B., & Covello, V. T. (1987). *The social and cultural construction of risk:
Essays on risk selection and perception.* Reidel Publishing.

Kanagaretnam, K., Lim, C. Y., & Lobo, G. J. (2014). Influence of national culture on
accounting conservatism and risk-taking in the banking industry. *Accounting
Review*, 89(3), 1115–1149. doi:10.2308/accr-50682.

Khosrowjerdi, M. (2020). National culture and trust in online health information.
Journal of Librarianship and Information Science, 52. doi:10.1177/
0961000619836716.

Kim, H., & Markus, H. R. (1999). Deviance or uniqueness, harmony or conformity? A cultural analysis. *Journal of Personality and Social Psychology*, 77, 785–800.

Klein, H. A., Lin, M. H., Miller, N. L., Militello, L. G., Lyons, J. B., & Finkeldey, J. G. (2019). Trust across culture and context. *Journal of Cognitive Engineering and Decision Making*, 13(1), 10–29.

Kreiser, P. M., Marino, L. D., Dickson, P., & Weaver, K. M. (2010). Cultural influences on entrepreneurial orientation: The impact of national culture on risk taking and proactiveness in SMEs. *Entrepreneurship: Theory and Practice*, 34(5), 959–983. doi:10.1111/j.1540-6520.2010.00396.x.

Kroeber, A. L., & Kluckhohn, C. (1952). *Culture: A critical review of concepts and definitions*. Peabody Museum.

Lazrus, H. (2015). Risk perception and climate adaptation in Tuvalu: A combined cultural theory and traditional knowledge approach. *Human Organization*, 74(1), 52–61. doi:10.17730/humo.74.1.q0667716284749m8.

Liu, S., Yang, X., & Mei, Q. (2021). The effect of perceived organizational support for safety and organizational commitment on employee safety behavior: A meta-analysis. *International Journal of Occupational Safety and Ergonomics*, 27(4), 1154–1165.

McEvoy, J., Gilbertz, S., Anderson, M., Ormerod, K. J., & Bergmann, N. (2017). Cultural theory of risk as a heuristic for understanding perceptions of oil and gas development in Eastern Montana, USA. *The Extractive Industries and Society*, 4 (4), 852–859. doi:10.1016/j.exis.2017.03.040.

McNeeley, S. M., & Lazrus, H. (2014). The cultural theory of risk for climate change adaptation. *Weather, Climate, and Society*, 6(4), 506–519. doi:10.1175/WCAS-D-13-00027.1.

McSweeney, B. (2002). Hofstede's model of national cultural differences and their consequences: A triumph of faith – a failure of analysis. *Human Relations*, 55(1), 89–118.

Minkov, M., & Kaasa, A. (2022). Do dimensions of culture exist objectively? A validation of the revised Minkov-Hofstede model of culture with World Values Survey items and scores for 102 countries. *Journal of International Management*, 28(4), 100971.

Moallem, A. (2018). *Cybersecurity awareness among employees: A cross-cultural study* (Doctoral dissertation). University of Twente.

Nobles, C. (2018). Botching human factors in cybersecurity in business organizations. *HOLISTICA – Journal of Business and Public Administration*, 9(3), 71–88. doi:10.2478/hjbpa-2018-0024.

Onumo, A., Cullen, A., & Ullah-Awan, I. (2017). An empirical study of cultural dimensions and cybersecurity development. In IEEE (Ed.), *2017 IEEE 5th International Conference on Future Internet of Things and Cloud (FiCloud)* (pp. 70–76). IEEE.

Paul, J., Roy, A., & Mukhopadhyay, K. (2006). The impact of cultural values on marketing ethical norms: A study in India and the United States. *Journal of International Marketing*, 14(4), 28–56. doi:10.1509/jimk.14.4.28.

Pavlova, E. (2020). Enhancing the organisational culture related to cyber security during the university digital transformation. *Information & Security: An International Journal*, 46(3), 239–249. doi:10.11610/isij.4617.

Pettigrew, A. M. (1979). On studying organizational cultures. *Administrative Science Quarterly*, 24(4), 570–581. doi:10.2307/2392363.

Quinn, R. E., & Rohrbaugh, J. (1983). A spatial model of effectiveness criteria: Towards a competing values approach to organizational analysis. *Management Science*, 29(3), 363–377. doi:10.1287/mnsc.29.3.363.

Reegärd, K., Blackett, C., & Katta, V. (2019). The concept of cybersecurity culture. *Proceedings of the 29th European Safety and Reliability Conference (ESREL)*, 4036–4043. doi:10.3850/978-981-11-2724-3_0761-cd.

Rippl, S. (2018). Cultural theory and risk perception: A proposal for a better measurement. In *The Institutional Dynamics of Culture: The New Durkheimians* (Vols. 1–2, pp. 251–269). doi:10.4324/9781315238975-13.

Sawaya, Y., Sharif, M., Christin, N., Kubota, A., Nakarai, A., & Yamada, A. (2017). *Self-confidence trumps knowledge: A cross-cultural study of security behavior*. ACM.

Schein, E. H. (2004). *Organizational culture and leadership* (3rd ed.). Jossey-Bass.

Schein, E. H. (2009). *The corporate culture survival guide* (Vol. 158). John Wiley & Sons.

Schlienger, T., & Teufel, S. (2003). *Information security culture – from analysis to change*. Information Security South Africa (ISSA).

Sharma, S., & Aparicio, E. (2022). Organizational and team culture as antecedents of protection motivation among IT employees. *Computers & Security*, 120, 102774. doi:10.1016/j.cose.2022.102774.

Sharot, T., & Garrett, N. (2016). Forming beliefs: Why valence matters. *Trends in Cognitive Sciences*, 20(1), 25–33. doi:10.1016/j.tics.2015.11.002.

Solomon, G., & Irwin, J. (2019). The influence of organisational culture and information security culture on employee compliance behaviour. *Journal of Enterprise Information Management*, 34(4), 1203–1228. doi:10.1108/JEIM-08-2019-0217.

Sutton, A., & Tompson, L. (2025). Towards a cybersecurity culture-behaviour framework: A rapid evidence review. *Computers and Security*, 148, 104110. doi:10.1016/j.cose.2024.104110.

Tansey, J., & O'Riordan, T. (1999). Cultural theory and risk: A review. *Health, Risk and Society*, 1(1), 71–90. doi:10.1080/13698579908407008.

Thampi, P. P., Jyotishi, A., & Bishu, R. (2015). Cultural characteristics of small business entrepreneurs in India: Examining the adequacy of Hofstede's framework. *International Journal of Business and Globalisation*, 15(4), 475–495. doi:10.1504/IJBG.2015.072534.

Tsohou, A., Karyda, M., & Kokolakis, S. (2015). Analyzing the role of cognitive and cultural biases in the internalization of information security policies: Recommendations for information security awareness programs. *Computers & Security*, 52, 1–24. doi:10.1016/j.cose.2015.04.006.

Tylor, E. B. (1871). *Primitive culture: Researches into the development of mythology, philosophy, religion, art, and custom*. J. Murray.

Uchendu, B., Nurse, J. R. C., Bada, M., & Furnell, S. (2021). Developing a cyber security culture: Current practices and future needs. *Computers and Security*, 109, 102387.

van Baaren, R. B., Maddux, W. W., Chartrand, T. L., de Bouter, C., & van Knippenberg, A. (2003). It takes two to mimic: Behavioral consequences of self-construals. *Journal of Personality and Social Psychology*, 84, 1093–1102.

van de Graaff, S. (2016). Understanding the nuclear controversy: An application of cultural theory. *Energy Policy*, 50, 50–59.

Van Niekerk, J. F., & von Solms, R. (2010). Information security culture: A management perspective. *Computers and Security*, 29(4), 476–486. doi:10.1016/j.cose.2009.10.005.

Weber, E. U., & Hsee, C. K. (1998). Cross-cultural differences in risk perception, but cross-cultural similarities in attitudes towards perceived risk. *Management Science*, 44(9), 1205–1217.

Willcoxon, L., & Millett, B. (2000). The management of organisational culture. *Australian Journal of Management and Organisational Behaviour*, 3(2), 91–99.

Williams, E. J., Beardmore, A., & Joinson, A. N. (2017). Individual differences in susceptibility to online influence: A theoretical review. *Computers in Human Behavior*, 72, 412–421. doi:10.1016/j.chb.2017.03.002.

Williamson, D. (2002). Forward from a critique of Hofstede's model of national culture. *Human Relations*, 55(11), 1373–1395.

Xue, W., Hine, D. W., Loi, N. M., Thorsteinsson, E. B., & Phillips, W. J. (2014). Cultural worldviews and environmental risk perceptions: A meta-analysis. *Journal of Environmental Psychology*, 40, 249–258. doi:10.1016/j.jenvp.2014.07.002.

Yoon, C. (2009). The effects of national culture values on consumer acceptance of e-commerce: Online shoppers in China. *Information & Management*, 46(5), 294–301.

Yuki, M., Maddux, W. W., Brewer, M. B., & Takemura, K. (2005). Cross-cultural differences in relationship- and group-based trust. *Personality and Social Psychology Bulletin*, 31(1), 48–62. doi:10.1177/0146167204271305.

11

COUNTERPRODUCTIVE WORK BEHAVIOUR AND CYBERSECURITY

Introduction

We all love our work, and every day we leap out of bed, singing, looking forward to the next challenge that might face us when we get there. Sound familiar? If not, do not worry, you are not alone. Statistics from the US demonstrate that just over half (51%) of employees are satisfied with their job (www.pewresearch.org/social-trends/2023/03/30/how-americans-view-their-jobs/). For most people, we get on with our work and that is it; we do not feel the need to exact revenge or engage in questionable behaviours. However, in any given organisation there will be a group of individuals who will engage in deviant behaviours, and will go to great lengths to disrupt the normal functioning of their place of work. As we have seen in Chapter 2, the incidence of malicious insider threats is commonplace and can present a damaging force to the internal security of any organisation. These activities are not only detrimental to productivity and general well-being but also have far-reaching implications for cybersecurity. In the remainder of the chapter, we will explore the aetiology of these behaviours and examine what they mean for the cybersecurity stance of the organisation.

Counterproductive Work Behaviours

Exploring the role of deviant and counterproductive work behaviours (CWB) has often been linked to employee activities that go contrary to their role or organisational standards. Researchers have defined CWB as 'scalable actions and behaviours that employees engage in that detract from organisational goals or well-being and include behaviours that bring about undesirable consequences for the organisation or its stakeholders' (Ones & Dilchert,

DOI: 10.4324/9781003509011-11

2013, p. 645). CWBs are seen as violations of workplace rules and sit outside of actions that might be mandated by their current employer or are accidental in nature (Fox et al., 2012; Hadlington et al., 2021).

Some behaviours categorised as CWBs include absenteeism, inter-employee aggression, interpersonal conflict, sabotage, and theft (Fox et al., 2001; Gruys & Sackett, 2003). The common strand tying all elements of CWB together is that they harm the organisation or reduce employee effec-tiveness (Fox et al., 2001). Individuals may engage in CWB as a type of pro-test behaviour to redress a perceived injustice or organisational dysfunction (Hadlington et al., 2021).

Additionally, researchers have noted that CWBs can be categorised according to the perceived target of the behaviour, either interpersonal tar-gets or organisational targets (Berry et al., 2007; Mercado et al., 2017; Robinson & Bennett, 1995). CWBs related to interpersonal targets (CWB-I) include behaviours such as cyberbullying, harassment, and direct physical harm, which damage the well-being of individuals within the organisation and other stakeholders, including customers (Ones & Dilchert, 2013; Robin-son & Bennett, 1995). CWBs targeting the organisation (CWB-O) include theft, sabotage, hacking, or absenteeism.

Recently, researchers have identified counterproductive work behaviours specifically associated with technology, labelled as cyber-CWB (C-CWB) (Howard & Spector, 2020). These behaviours include cyberloafing, cyber-sabotage, cyber-theft, and cyber-incivility (Howard & Spector, 2020).

Cyber-Counterproductive Work Behaviours

Modern technology has had a massive impact on the workplace, from the development of videoconferencing, to email, online storage systems, and the joys of online learning and training. However, there is an often-overlooked consequence for the presence of such technologies in the workplace, that being the introduction of new ways in which employees can engage in coun-terproductive work behaviours (Howard & Spector, 2020; Mercado et al., 2018; Ones & Dilchert, 2013). These behaviours stand as an additional clas-sification of CWB, and centre around activities that would not be possible if the internet and digital technology were not present within the workplace. These behaviours, C-CWB, have been defined as 'employee behaviours that, utilizing information communication technology, detract from legitimate organisational goals or well-being and include behaviours that bring about undesirable consequences for the organisation or its stakeholders' (Mercado, 2017, p. 5). Mercado (2017) presented a detailed list of activities that could be classified as being C-CWB, including:

- Accessing adult websites: As we will see later in this chapter, the propensity for individuals to access and view online pornographic content is something that falls into the realms of extreme or major cyberloafing. The actual statistics on how many people engage in this activity show that it is far more widespread than would first be assumed. Nearly 60% of respondents questioned in a 2018 survey admitted to watching pornography at work; a further 50% of these admitted to watching it monthly, whilst 10% admitted to viewing adult content daily (McDonald, 2018); 50% of those people suggested that the main reason for engaging in this type of behaviour was boredom. In most instances, individuals were using their own devices (77%) to watch adult content, with a smaller amount (15%) admitting to using their work devices to watch (www.sugarcookie.com/2018/OI/watch-porn-at-work). As we will explore later, the consequences for accessing such websites does not just create an issue for the wider work community and could make many in an organisation feel uncomfortable with their colleagues but can also present a direct threat to organisational cybersecurity (Blanchard & Henle, 2008).

- Cybergriping: Often labelled as e-complaining (Mills et al., 2008) it is the use of the internet and associated communication technologies to complain about unfair treatment. Often employees will use digital platforms, such as social media, to make public their perceived grievances associated with their workplace, their colleagues, their bosses, or general organisational policies. The usual modus operandi for cybergriping is to take to social media to have a good moan about unmanageable workloads, or a boss that has been seen to dispense what the employee sees as unfair judgement or admonishment. From a cybersecurity perspective, one of the key issues here is where the post contains certain information that might be related to internal processes, systems, or internal projects that the employee might be working on, leaving open the potential for social engineering attacks. Another associated danger that could result from such activities is reputational damage, where details of negative experiences and information about the organisation are being shared online (Howard & Spector, 2020; Mercado, 2017).

- Cyberharassment: This term can include a variety of other terms and concepts that are all interlinked. For example, cyberharassment is seen as a personal attack against an individual that uses any form of technology (Workman, 2010). Aligned with this is the concept of cyber-incivility, which is typically seen as any behaviour that violates workplace norms of treating everyone with respect and dignity, usually mediated by some form of computer technology (e.g., email or SMS; Lim & Teo, 2009). Alongside these we have cyberbullying, often seen as a sub-category of cyberharassment, and although it has often been typically explored within younger populations, there is ample evidence that such activities do also occur within the workplace. Cyberharassment as an attack or CWB has been typified as a way of presenting misleading or false information against a victim, with the aim being to either damage them, create some level of interference, or to lay the groundwork for some form of extortion (Workman, 2010). Cyberbullying has been defined as 'inappropriate, unwanted social exchange behaviours initiated by a perpetrator via online or wireless communication technology and devices (Piotrowski, 2012, p. 45). Grigg (2010) noted that cyberbullying can take many forms, and include fraudulent and anonymous messages, the proliferation of rumours, hacking into email accounts or other online accounts. The consequences of cyberharassment in the workplace are manifold and can include impairments in both physical and mental health (Ford, 2013; Gardner et al., 2016) as well as a decrease in the overall quality of social interactions (Kopecký & Szotkowski, 2017). There are even further impacts related to cyberbullying, where elements such as job satisfaction (Farley et al., 2015) and work engagement (Howard & Spector, 2020) could have a direct impact on the overall productivity and performance of the organisation (D'Souza et al., 2021; Jönsson et al., 2017). In this regard, such C-CWB have a clear and direct impact on the organisation and its cybersecurity posture and are not something that only impacts the individual victim.

- Cyberloafing: One of the most heavily researched of all the C-CWB listed here, cyberloafing is seen as employee use of company-based internet technology to perform non-work-based tasks during work time (Lim, 2002). Cyberloafing is seen as the voluntary use of company provided technology, email, and internet for non-work purposes whilst being at work (Blanchard & Henle, 2008; Hadlington & Parsons, 2017). We will cover cyberloafing in more detail in Chapter 12.

- Cybersabotage: This is where an employee intentionally damages or disrupts the digital systems of an organisation, including data and infrastructure. This could include deleting important or critical information, introducing malware into the system, or simply shutting down critical systems within the organisation. A lot of this type of activity fits into the typical malicious insider threat category, and the literature is littered with examples of how disgruntled employees have taken revenge on organisations after they have been fired. The actions individuals can take can be varied, and include holding passwords to critical systems ransom, deleting critical pieces of data, disabling security systems, or sabotaging customer service systems (Maasberg et al., 2020).

As we can see from this list, the presence of C-CWB in the workplace is of key importance when we are discussing cybersecurity and human factors. All the behaviours present a clear and present danger to the overall cybersecurity posture of the organisation, having serious ramifications for not only protection of data but also the infrastructure that governs that data.

In terms of cybersecurity behaviours, some previous work has touched on CWB and ICT misuse in the workplace (Hadlington et al., 2021; Weatherbee,

2010). Hadlington et al. (2021) noted that poorer engagement in aspects of information security awareness could be linked to a form of ICT misuse, and in turn could be linked to CWBs in general. In their findings, they noted that an individual with higher propensity to engage in CWBs was more likely to have lower levels of information security awareness.

Predictors for Counterproductive Work Behaviours

There has been a considerable amount of research that explores the reasons why individuals engage in CWB, and these variables included a wide range of factors, ranging from the psychological to aspects of the workplace culture and supervision. In this next section we will go over some of the key reasons for people engaging in CWB and explore their potential link with cybersecurity awareness.

Boredom

Boredom in the workplace results from low levels of arousal and general feelings of dissatisfaction that are usually linked to a workplace environment that provides limited stimulation (Pindek et al., 2018; Schaufeli & Salanova, 2014). Boredom has been defined as 'a state of relatively low arousal and dissatisfaction which is attributed to an inadequately stimulating environment' (Mikulas & Vodanovich, 1993, p. 3). Feelings of being bored at work are common, and researchers have estimated that anywhere between 15% and 87% of employees experience some form of boredom at work (van Hooff & van Hooft, 2017). Boredom can be the direct result of the environment in which the individual finds themselves, and as such is labelled as state boredom, because it makes references to the situation or 'state' the individual experiences such a feeling in. Some individuals can be predisposed to experience boredom as part of their personality characteristics, such as trait boredom (Harju et al., 2014; Kass et al., 2001). State boredom has been shown to be a direct reaction to the conditions of the job (Kass et al., 2001). Research has noted that where individuals are faced with jobs that are repetitive in nature, have a limited capacity to provide mental stimulation, or require a low level of skill, they are more likely to experience job boredom (Melamed et al., 1995). Under-stimulation or work underload has been noted to have a clear psychological impact on the individual (Pindek et al., 2018). Researchers have noted higher levels of sleep disturbance, increased anxiety, and general feelings of fatigue in those individuals who report feelings of work underload (Pindek et al., 2018; Shultz et al., 2010).

Higher levels of job boredom have been shown to be associated with higher levels of absenteeism (Kass et al., 2001; Melamed et al., 1995), higher levels of withdrawal (Spector et al., 2006), lower levels of job satisfaction (Melamed et al., 1995), and reduced work effectiveness (Drory, 1982). Game

(2007) noted that employees can engage in a wide variety of ways to cope with boredom, which can be classified as either engagement coping strategies to make the work more interesting, or disengagement coping strategies which are typically behaviours that move the individual away from the boring task. Cyberloafing for example has been typically highlighted as a disengagement strategy to relieve job boredom (Pindek et al., 2018).

There has been considerable work exploring the concept of boredom proneness as a trait, with researchers offering a variety of ways of categorising the construct (Farmer & Sundberg, 1986; Kass et al., 2001; Vodanovich et al., 2005). For example, Vodanovich et al. (2005) differentiated between boredom prone external stimulation individuals, where a person's experience of boredom is linked to their view that the external environment presents them with low levels of stimulation. In contrast, boredom prone internal stimulation individuals are those who have an inability to keep themselves occupied or lack the capacity to create a stimulating environment (Bruursema et al., 2011; Sung et al., 2021; Vodanovich et al., 2005). Additional research has noted that boredom prone external stimulation individuals exhibit maladaptive behaviours, such as experiencing higher levels of anger, displaying higher levels of hostility, and lacking honesty (Dahlen et al., 2004).

There is a clear relationship between boredom proneness and counterproductive work behaviours. For example, Bruursema et al. (2011) noted that individuals who scored higher in the boredom prone external stimulation category were more likely to score higher on CWB linked to abuse, sabotage, withdrawal, production deviance, theft, and horseplay. Of all the sub-categories for CWB, Bruursema et al. (2011) noted that the highest level of correlation was between boredom prone external stimulation and withdrawal, with the authors suggesting that this was symptomatic of workers engaging in longer work breaks or doing fewer work hours than was expected. It could also be the case that individuals engage in withdrawal behaviours to escape from stressful workplace situations that would otherwise cause the individuals psychological harm (Bruursema et al., 2011; Spector et al., 2006). In contrast, individuals who scored higher on the boredom proneness internal stimulation scale had no such correlations to the CWB examined in the Bruursema et al. (2011) study, which suggests that much of the CWB engaged in within the workplace is a result of an individual's inability to derive stimulation from their external environment.

In terms of what this means for the workplace and cybersecurity, it is obvious that workplace boredom is strongly connected to an individual's capacity to engage in CWBs. As we have noted, these CWB could include withdrawal from effective cybersecurity practices that serve to safeguard the organisation from internal and external threats, hence boredom would appear to make this situation worse. Similarly, and individual could actively engage in activities that serve to increase the likelihood of the organisation being targeted by cybercriminals, whether this be through negligence or malicious intent, to increase their level of stimulation in the workplace. Bruursema et al. (2011) noted that one of the key strategies to overcome this situation is to reduce the potential for individuals to experience workplace boredom. Although this is a positive suggestion, the actual mechanics of achieving this is a lot harder than first appears. One suggestion is to increase the integration of technology into the workplace to take over some of the more monotonous and repetitive elements of the workplace. However, as we will see in Chapter 12 in a section on technostress, integrating technology into the workplace could replace one issue with another (that of techno-insecurity).

Workplace Stress

There has been an extensive amount of research exploring the link between job stressors and counterproductive work behaviours. A workplace stressor can be anything that an individual sees as threatening to their overall psychological or physical well-being (Spector, 2002). There are a long list of psychological strains that can impact on an individual within the workplace, including (but not limited to) anxiety, feelings of frustration, depression, overall dissatisfaction with work, commitment to the job, and an intention to quit (Jex, 1998; Jex & Beehr, 1991; Spector, 2002). Workplace stressors present as events that we interpret as threats to our personal well-being and in return they result in the individual experiencing negative emotions such as anger and anxiety (Goh, 2007; Spector & Fox, 2002; Spector & Jex, 1998).

For example, it has been noted that elements of role ambiguity, role conflict, perceived workload, organisational constraints, and conflict between employees have all been linked to CWBs (Chen & Spector, 1992; Fox & Spector, 1999; Fox et al., 2001; Penney & Spector, 2005).

Goh (2007) provided a good overview of the types of job stressors people can experience which can be divided according to their origins within the workplace. The first of these categories is that of psychosocial workplace stressors which originate because of the interaction between the individual and key facets of the workplace. They include:

- **Interpersonal Conflict**

    Let's face facts, there is always someone in the office that we do not get on with, or someone that always seems to get on our nerves just a little bit. Then we have the other intra-office spats that the United Nations would have trouble trying to sort out – messy kitchen manners, the fridge raider who likes to steal other people's food, the person who always uses your special coffee cup... yes, we all know them. Interpersonal conflict can arise as one source of job stress, and the extent to which an individual gets on with people in their organisation has been shown to be a key predictor for CWB (Goh, 2007; Miles et al., 2002). Interpersonal conflict has been associated with overall measures of CWB, as well as CWB-I and CWB-O forms of CWB (Goh, 2007), with Spector et al. (2006) noting that interpersonal conflict is more likely to predict CWB-I rather than CWB-O (Goh, 2007).

• Incivility

The often rude, insensitive, or just plain disrespectful interactions we have with colleagues in the office can be seen to influence the stress we experience within the workplace (Goh, 2007; Marcus & Schuler, 2004; Miles et al., 2002). There is an associated concept that is presented as cyber-incivility (Lim & Teo, 2009) that is defined as 'communicative behaviour exhibited in computer-mediated interactions that violate workplace norms of mutual respect' (Lim & Teo, 2009, p. 419). Lim and Teo (2009) noted that cyber-incivility was negatively associated to employee satisfaction and organisational commitment, whilst being positively associated with an intention to quit their current job and increased engagement in CWB-O.

• Organisational Injustice

The perception of fair or just treatment by organisation forces has been demonstrated to be a key factor in the elicitation of job stress, where perceptions of situations that are seen as unfair (e.g., getting passed over for promotion, or receiving a lower-than-expected appraisal rating) serve to increase the experiences of negative emotion (Fox et al., 2001). Spector and colleagues have noted that CWBs act as an emotional response to stressful workplace conditions (Fox & Spector, 1999; Fox et al., 2001) and as a reaction to perceived organisational injustices, such as unfair treatment (Fox et al., 2001).

In contrast, non-social job stressors are linked to factors outside of direct workplace interactions and often beyond our immediate control. These stressors are closely related to the concept of work locus of control which we discuss later in this chapter. Individuals frequently develop strategies to manage these stressors, which can sometimes lead to CWBs. One significant non-social stressor is organisational constraints, which are perceived as obstacles or interferences in our work tasks.

From the perspective of cybersecurity awareness and behaviour, over-complicated or burdensome cybersecurity compliance requirements can be seen as such stressors. These constraints can hinder employees' ability to perform their duties effectively, leading to increased stress and potential engagement in CWB.

Peters and O'Connor (1988) listed no less than 11 individual sources of organisational constraints that can serve to impact our daily work lives, including job-related information; budgetary constraints; required support; materials and supplies; required services and help from others; task preparation; time availability; work environment; scheduling of activities; transportation; and job-related authority (Goh, 2007). In terms of cybersecurity compliance, stressors such as time availability (not being able to do your normal work, so you have little or no time to engage in additional tasks), task preparation (engaging in cybersecurity training or doing tasks that are related to cybersecurity which need additional time to prepare for that is not provided), required support (the information needed to complete the current task or training is not directly obvious, leading to frustration). Organisational constraints have been shown to have a clear link to an individual's propensity to engage in CWB, so these should be considered as part of any strategy that serves to reduce the potential for their emergence in the workplace (Goh, 2007; Spector & Jex, 1998).

Job Attitudes

In general, the research that explores counterproductive work behaviours suggests that employees are more likely to engage in such activities when they have a negative attitude towards their job (Judge et al., 2006; Liberman et al., 2011). Blau et al. (2006) noted that employees were more likely to engage in cyberloafing activities when they experienced lower levels of organisational justice. In instances where individuals feel that they have been treated unfairly at work, such as being passed over for promotion, or not receiving praise or support, they are more likely to engage in cyberloafing (Blau et al., 2006; Lim, 2002). The extent to which an individual feels involved and invested in their work is also an important determiner when it comes to predicting CWB. Intrinsic involvement, defined as the extent to which an employee feels that their work is meaningful, and they are making an important contribution to the organisation (George, 1992; Liberman et al., 2011), can serve to shape an individual's likelihood to cyberloaf. This links to the notion of boredom at work, where employees who see little worth in their contribution to the workplace are more likely to engage in counterproductive work behaviours (Liberman et al., 2011). Indeed, Liberman et al. (2011) demonstrated a clear link between intrinsic involvement and cyberloafing, where higher levels of intrinsic involvement predicted lower levels of cyberloafing. Perceived behavioural control has also been documented as being an antecedent to CWB. Behavioural control is seen as the individual's capacity to be able to engage in CWB without getting caught (Askew et al., 2014). Askew et al. (2014) noted that the level at which an individual can hide their cyberloafing activity was a clear predictor for cyberloafing, with greater perceived self-efficacy being linked to higher levels of cyberloafing.

Social Norms

The social norms of the environment in which we are choosing to engage in a certain behaviour can be an important determiner in that decision-making process. Social norms are conceptualised as unwritten rules for behaviour that is viewed as as being socially acceptable within the society or organisational group (Bicchieri & Mercier, 2014). Social norms can be seen as a set of collective rules shared by individuals that are indicative of the behaviour expected of members of that group. For example, the good old-fashioned fart; now, in the UK, even though the behaviour is typically the source of many a giggle, passing wind in public is frowned upon. There is no law that bans farting, and I am yet to find any objective evidence where someone has been sentenced or fined for letting out a fart in public, but if you are 'that' person, you face the wrath of public disapproval. A similar example could be breaking the rules of queuing, the great British pastime – to jump a well-established queue in the UK is to run the gauntlet of disapproving looks and evil stares, but there are no rules or laws that govern such activities other than those social norms that everyone (well almost everyone!) ascribes to. Social norms have been described as some of the most powerful determiners for behaviour (Cialdini et al., 1990).

Descriptive norms are related to the individual's perception of the prevalence of a behaviour, which in turn allows them the capacity to justify their engagement in such behaviour (Ajzen, 1991). Descriptive norms are associated with the perception of 'how much' a behaviour occurs within a given population (Cialdini et al., 1990). Here people ask the question 'what are most other people doing around me' when employing descriptive norms to assess what they should do in instances of uncertainty (Brauer & Chaurand, 2010). In contrast, prescriptive norms relate to the extent to which co-workers and managers approve of cyberloafing in the workplace (Askew et al., 2014; Blanchard & Henle, 2008; Karabiyik et al., 2021; Soh et al., 2018). Research has noted that approval of co-workers and supervisors for cyberloafing can lead to a direct increase in involvement in cyberloafing activities (Murodilla et al., 2020).

Moral Disengagement

Moral disengagement was originally featured in the work of Albert Bandura (1986) who argued that we have the capacity to govern our own actions, but this process is very selective in nature. This means we can decide when we ditch our internal moral standards to behave in a way that could be deemed morally questionable (Moore, 2015). By engaging these mechanisms an individual can disavow responsibility for their behaviour and avoid the respective feelings of distress that would usually accompany such actions (Moore et al., 2012). Bandura (1986) noted eight mechanisms via which moral disengagement can be achieved, these being:

- Moral justification: This is where the questionable behaviour is made more acceptable by modifying it to be seen as having a noble purpose. For example, someone may justify an aggressive act in the pursuit of protecting reputation or preventing further transgressions (Bandura et al., 1996). In the instance of cybersecurity behaviours, this might be sidestepping accepted security protocols to get work done on time.
- Euphemistic Labelling: The use of language to mask harmful actions, or even to make them sound more socially acceptable (Bandura et al., 1996). For example, the use of the term 'pacification' is often used in military contexts to cover up violent suppression, and in the same sense 'neutralising' the enemy replaces the notion of killing someone. In the context of cybersecurity, such a mechanism might be used to soften the impact of some of the key issues that come about because of end user error – for instance, labelling something as an 'incident' rather than a 'cyberattack' removes the threatening overtones of the latter term, and also reduced the perceived seriousness of the term. In a similar vein, end users who are guilty of errors or lapses in their cybersecurity behaviour can adopt a similar stance, such as using a term like 'Oversight' or 'Unintentional error' where they have accidentally opened a phishing email or clicked on a malicious link in an email resulting in a security breach.
- Advantageous Comparison: This is an effective way of deflecting the seriousness of a behaviour by making comparisons between the current morally questionable act and something that is more serious. For example, someone who is caught cheating in a sporting event might make the claim that it is not as bad as being someone that uses performance enhancing drugs. Often people who are caught drink-driving will make the statement that it is not as bad as killing someone or being a burglar, and will also be heard asking the arresting officers why they are not out arresting 'real' criminals. For cybersecurity behaviours, this mechanism is often used by individuals who have made transgressions in protocol, and they will make comparisons to what they see as being more serious lapses in concentration. Some of the ways in which they might excuse their actions might be to claim that their actions did not lead to a major data breach, even though clicking on a dubious email may have caused some serious downtime for the organisation. Other mechanics at work could be to claim that other people are worse at keeping their cybersecurity behaviours in check.
- Displacement of Responsibility: People often see their behaviour as being the result of external pressures from others around them, rather than accepting responsibility for their own morally questionable actions. If an individual can cast off their behaviours as being the result of such external pressures, they can avoid the negative consequences associated with such. Often individuals in such circumstances will claim that they

were 'just doing what they were told' by their superiors to exonerate themselves from the punishment attached to any wrongdoing. For the cybersecurity context, an individual might claim that they have not received an adequate or appropriate amount of training in cybersecurity awareness, hence why they missed the tell-tale signs of a malicious email. Other mechanisms such as claiming they missed things because of time-related pressures to meet deadlines can also be used to shift the blame away from the individual towards those who are in power.

- Diffusion of Responsibility: In any circumstance where labour or decisions are shared by a team, the capacity for an individual to pass off morally questionable decisions to the wider group is increased. Often individuals will hide behind the wider group to excuse action or inaction which results in negative consequences, but means they are not personally responsible and therefore remove themselves from direct blame. In the context of cybersecurity, there are many ways diffusion of responsibility can come into play. Assuming that someone else will do something when it comes to cybersecurity is the most critical aspect of diffusion of responsibility, where individuals will claim that someone else will report an issue, take care of critical updates, or dismiss their role in the process because it is a shared responsibility.

- Distortion of Consequences: This is generally evident when someone attempts to reduce the overall impact of their actions by claiming the effects are not as serious as they first appear. For example, a company CEO might downplay the loss of customers' personal data by stating that only a small percentage of customers were impacted, even though the breach is a serious event. In terms of cybersecurity behaviours and employees, there is abundant evidence that distortion of consequences come into play. For example, individuals will often take the stance that missing one phishing email and clicking on links contained within it is not that much of a big deal and will downplay the consequences attached to their transgression. Another favourite is the 'it will never happen to me', something we hear repeatedly when it comes to cybersecurity and cybercrime and is often used as an excuse to engage in actions such as reusing passwords or ignoring security updates.

- Dehumanisation: This is the psychological and social process through which individuals or groups are stripped of their humanity, dignity, and individuality, which in turn allows them to treat others in a less positive way. In modern business practices, individuals are often relabelled as 'clients' or 'customers' which removes some of their human vestiture by removing their names. In terms of cybersecurity behaviours, individuals might use a similar set of processes to remove themselves from the results of questionable actions by claiming that the victims of their mistakes are just faceless customers, hence they have no personal relationship or reference to them. As people create a distance between themselves and the potential victims of their lapses in concentration or morally questionable behaviours, they can reduce their own guilt.

- Attribution of Blame: The final mechanism for moral disengagement is one where the individual shifts the blame from themselves to the victim of the morally questionable behaviour. Someone who decides to engage in cyberbullying might claim that the individual on the receiving end deserved it because they were weak or needed to be taught a lesson (good old karma!). For employee cybersecurity behaviours, there are several avenues an individual could go down to use this mechanism, such as blaming the IT department for issues with updates or their inability to follow accepted rules on password creation, or blaming a co-worker in an instance where someone has forgotten their login details and sharing a password has resulted in the loss of sensitive data.

Moral disengagement has previously been explored as an antecedent to individuals carrying out counterproductive work behaviours (e.g., Barsky, 2011; Fida et al., 2015; Hystad et al., 2014; Moore et al., 2012). According to Moore et al. (2012) the workplace presents a wide range of opportunities for the individual to disengage their morality and do things that could be quite questionable. For example, Alnuaimi et al. (2010) showed that moral disengagement was associated with higher levels of social loafing, and this was more apparent where individuals were members of a larger team (Hadlington et al., 2021). In today's work environments, most organisations exhibit hierarchical structures that facilitate the capacity for individuals to displace responsibilities to individuals who they are subordinate to (Moore et al., 2012). Diffusion of responsibility also presents another ideal opportunity for an individual to make the assertion that someone else within the team is doing the thing that they should be doing, therefore they no longer need to engage in that behaviour (Hadlington et al., 2021).

In terms of links between moral disengagement and cybersecurity behaviours, there has been some limited work conducted in this area. Initial work conducted by D'Arcy et al. (2014) noted that moral disengagement was a good predictor for intentional violations of information security awareness (Hadlington et al., 2021). In further work, Hadlington et al., (2021) examined how moral disengagement shaped knowledge, attitudes, and behaviours linked to information security awareness. The results demonstrated that across the board, moral disengagement acted as a significant negative predictor for information security awareness, so as moral disengagement increased, an individual's propensity to adhere to accepted information security rules decreased. Crucially diffusion of responsibility was shown to be the main contributor to decreased engagement in information security awareness. As noted by Hadlington et al. (2021) this is potentially one of the most challenging aspects of getting individuals within larger teams and organisations to engage in active cybersecurity protection. In big organisations individuals may feel it easier to devolve their own responsibilities for cybersecurity to others in their team, often relying on others in the team to support their shortcomings (Hadlington et al., 2021). Another interesting finding was that increases in moral disengagement led to a significant decrease in knowledge regarding protective information security behaviours, suggesting people devolved their respective knowledge about cybersecurity-related behaviours with the assumption that others within the organisation would make up the deficit (Hadlington et al., 2021).

Work Locus of Control

As we introduced way back in Chapter 4, the concept of locus of control was first discussed in work by Rotter (1966) and is a way of classifying how an individual views their control over their life decisions. In a brief recap, individuals who have a more external locus of control believe that many of the decisions and events that occur within their lives sit outside of their sphere of influence and instead tend to see such things being down to fate or luck. In contrast, those individuals who have a more internally focused locus of control see events and life outcomes as a direct result of their own actions, and the work that they have conducted to get to those points (Rotter, 1966). In the original work by Rotter, it was suggested that individuals with an internal locus of control are more likely to have higher levels of job satisfaction, are less likely to report job stress, and overall see themselves as being more in control of the workplace.

More recently the concept of work locus of control has emerged from research into the way in which people approach decisions about their work life (Spector, 1988). In Spector's (1988) work, a model of job stress is presented where a perception of control increases the individual's anger and frustration (Hadlington et al., 2021; Spector, 1988; Sprung & Jex, 2012). Several studies have previously highlighted that an external locus of control was positively associated with an individual's experience of frustration within the workplace as well as the increased likelihood of them engaging in counterproductive work behaviours (Fox & Spector, 1999; Sprung & Jex, 2012). In additional work that explored work locus of control specifically, Sprung and Jex (2012) noted that where employees perceived a lack of control over decisions within their workplace, they were increasingly more likely to engage in counterproductive work behaviours.

In the context of cybersecurity, previous definitions of information security awareness have posited that the key factor is the extent to which an individual commits to the organisational policies aligned with such mechanisms (Hadlington et al., 2019; Parsons et al., 2017). It would therefore seem logical to assume that anyone who has a poor engagement with their workplace or sees their role within the organisation as having limited influence will in turn have a limited incentive to engage in effective cybersecurity practices (Hadlington et al., 2019).

In an original piece of research, Hadlington et al. (2019) set about exploring the role work locus of control has in cybersecurity awareness. Individuals who exhibited a more external locus of control scored significantly lower on a measure of cybersecurity awareness compared to those who had a more internal work locus of control. We postulated that individuals with a more internal work locus of control are more likely to see their actions related to cybersecurity as having a demonstrable benefit to themselves and also the organisation. However, those individuals who have a more external work locus of control are those who assume that irrespective of their actions when it comes to cybersecurity, the organisation will still be vulnerable to attack (Hadlington et al., 2019). There is also the possibility that individuals with a more external work locus of control have adopted an acute sense of devolved responsibility when it comes to their responsibilities for organisational cybersecurity (Hadlington et al., 2019). As we noted, externals will have a perception that they have a very limited control over the outcomes related to their daily work lives with this also including key aspects of cybersecurity. Forces outside of the influence of the individual for the externally positioned employee will serve to impact on the likelihood of the organisation being targeted by a cyberattack, so they have little incentive to engage in cybersecurity.

Strategies for Dealing with Counterproductive Work Behaviours

There has been some research that has explored the best ways to avoid the appearance of CWB in the workplace, and therefore (hopefully) limit their impact on cybersecurity. One of the most often and obvious mechanisms that organisations can employ to minimise the potential for threats from technology-related CWBs is to engage in some form of electronic monitoring (Dalal & Girab, 2016; Howard & Spector, 2020). However, this does not come without disadvantages, and there are a variety of issues that need to be explored before organisations go down this route. There are some benefits, the primary one being that in instances where transgressions against individuals have taken place (for example in the form of cyberaggression, cyberbullying, and cyber-incivility) there is a way of establishing a body of evidence to be used in conflict resolution (Howard & Spector, 2020). There is also the potential for organisations to be better able to monitor excessive or derisive cyberloafing activities that fall outside of the acceptable IT use policy and establish relevant remedial training for those individuals who have transgressed these policies (Howard & Spector, 2020). However, as with anything that appears to be an easy win, there are a set of issues that can arise from the use of such monitoring practice. For example, employees might become resentful of such policies which could in turn result in feelings of anger, frustration, and stress (Alge & Hansen, 2014; Howard & Spector, 2020). As we have seen in this chapter, one of the key antecedents to individuals engaging in CWBs is the feeling of loss of control, or that of frustration and a perception of organisational injustice which electronic monitoring could exacerbate further. Organisations could make a very minor issue even worse by enraging those individuals who are already cybersecurity compliant using monitoring policies that are ill thought out and poorly implemented (Howard & Spector, 2020).

Of course, establishing what employees should and should not be doing means that there should be a clear set of guidelines set out which established what is and what is not acceptable behaviour in the workplace, especially when it comes to the use of work-based digital technology. Ensuring that everyone understands these guidelines would appear to be a critical step in establishing a base-rate for accepted use and minimising the potential for people to claim ignorance of such rules. Of course, this can be slightly problematic as the hard-core group of individuals who will serve as the hardest to reach or the most resilient to engaging in accepting these policies are those that will likely form the greatest threat to organisational cybersecurity and will see this as an opportunity to engage in CWB.

Summary

So, we have been discussing the main aspects of counterproductive work behaviours in this chapter, but can we isolate why they are so damaging when it comes to cybersecurity within an organisation. From a global perspective individuals who engage in CWBs that are damaging to the organisation present a clear threat to organisational cybersecurity and position themselves as clear insider threats. Intentionally engaging in CWBs could lead to a variety of intended and unintended outcomes, not least the loss of important company data, compromises to organisational systems, and the potential for irreparable damage to organisational reputation (Hadlington & Parsons, 2017). As we have seen, one potential CWB, cyberloafing, has been noted as having some significant ramifications for organisational cybersecurity including the potential for employees to unwittingly download malware from unsecure websites, or using work-based technology for other unscrupulous activities. There may also be the potential for individuals to pay less attention to critically important aspects of their daily work environment whilst they are engaging in cyberloafing activities, which mean that they miss the tell-tale signs of a potential cybersecurity violation in the offing.

References

Ajzen, I. (1991). The theory of planned behaviour. *Organisational Behaviour and Human Decision Processes*, 50(2), 179–211.

Alge, B. J., & Hansen, S. D. (2014). Workplace monitoring and surveillance research since '1984': A review and agenda. In M. D. Coovert & L. F. Thompson (Eds), *The psychology of workplace technology* (pp. 209–237). Routledge.

Alnuaimi, O. A., Robert, L. P., & Maruping, L. M. (2010). Team size, dispersion, and social loafing in technology-supported teams: A perspective on the theory of moral disengagement. *Journal of Management Information Systems*, 27(1), 203–230.

Askew, K., Buckner, J. E., Taing, M. U., Ilie, A., Bauer, J. A., & Coovert, M. D. (2014). Explaining cyberloafing: The role of the theory of planned behavior. *Computers in Human Behavior*, 36, 510–519.

Bandura, A. (1986). *Social foundations of thought and action: A social cognitive theory*. Prentice Hall.

Bandura, A., Barbaranelli, C., Caprara, G. V., & Pastorelli, C. (1996). Mechanisms of moral disengagement in the exercise of moral agency. *Journal of Personality and Social Psychology*, 71(2), 364.

Barsky, A. (2011). Investigating the effects of moral disengagement and participation on unethical work behavior. *Journal of Business Ethics*, 104(1), 59–75. doi:10.1007/s10551-011-0889-7.

Berry, C. M., Ones, D. S., & Sackett, P. R. (2007). Interpersonal deviance, organizational deviance, and their common correlates: A review and meta-analysis. *Journal of Applied Psychology*, 92, 410–424.

Bicchieri, C., & Mercier, H. (2014). Norms and beliefs: How change occurs. In M. Xenitidou & B. Edmonds (Eds), *The complexity of social norms* (pp. 37–54). Springer International Publishing.

Blanchard, A. L., & Henle, C. A. (2008). Correlates of different forms of cyberloafing: The role of norms and external locus of control. *Computers in Human Behavior*, 24(3), 1067–1084. doi:10.1016/j.chb.2007.03.008.

Blau, G., Yang, Y., & Ward-Cook, K. (2006). Testing a measure of cyberloafing. *Journal of Allied Health*, 35(1), 9–17.

Brauer, M., & Chaurand, N. (2010). Descriptive norms, prescriptive norms, and social control: An intercultural comparison of people's reactions to uncivil behaviors. *European Journal of Social Psychology*, 40(3), 490–499. doi:10.1002/ejsp.640.

Bruursema, K., Kessler, S. R., & Spector, P. E. (2011). Bored employees misbehaving: The relationship between boredom and counterproductive work behaviour. *Work & Stress*, 25, 93–107.

Chen, P. Y., & Spector, P. E. (1992). Relationships of work stressors with aggression, withdrawal, theft and substance use: An exploratory study. *Journal of Occupational and Organizational Psychology*, 65, 177–184.

Cialdini, R. B., Reno, R. R., & Kallgren, C. A. (1990). A focus theory of normative conduct: Recycling the concept of norms to reduce littering in public places. *Journal of Personality and Social Psychology*, 58(6), 1015–1026. doi:10.1037/0022-3514.58.6.1015.

D'Arcy, J., Herath, T., & Shoss, M. K. (2014). Understanding employee responses to stressful information security requirements: A coping perspective. *Journal of Management Information Systems*, 31(2), 285–318. doi:10.2753/MIS0742-1222310210.

D'Souza, N., Forsyth, D., & Blackwood, K. (2021). Workplace cyber abuse: Challenges and implications for management. *Personnel Review*, 50(7/8), 1774–1793.

Dahlen, E. R., Martin, R. C., Ragan, K., & Kuhlman, M. M. (2004). Boredom proneness in anger and aggression: Effects of impulsiveness and sensation seeking. *Personality and Individual Differences*, 37, 1615–1627.

Dalal, R. S., & Girab, A. (2016). Insider threat in cyber security: What the organizational psychology literature on counterproductive work behavior can and cannot (yet) tell us. In S. J. Zaccaro, R. S. Dalal, L. E. Tetrick, & J. A. Steinke (Eds), *Psychosocial dynamics of cyber security* (pp. 122–140). Routledge.

Drory, A. (1982). Individual differences in boredom proneness and task effectiveness at work. *Personnel Psychology*, 35, 141–151.

Farley, S., Coyne, I., Sprigg, C., Axtell, C., & Subramanian, G. (2015). Exploring the impact of workplace cyberbullying on trainee doctors. *Medical Education*, 49(4), 436–443.

Farmer, R., & Sundberg, N. D. (1986). Boredom proneness: The development and correlates of a new scale. *Journal of Personality Assessment*, 50, 4–17.

Fida, R., Paciello, M., Tramontano, C., Fontaine, R. G., Barbaranelli, C., & Farnese, M. L. (2015). An integrative approach to understanding counterproductive work behavior: The roles of stressors, negative emotions, and moral disengagement. *Journal of Business Ethics*, 130(1), 131–144.

Ford, D. P. (2013). Virtual harassment: Media characteristics' role in psychological health. *Journal of Managerial Psychology*, 28(4), 408–428.

Fox, S., & Spector, P. E. (1999). A model of work frustration–aggression. *Journal of Organizational Behavior*, 20, 915–931. doi:10.1002/(SICI)1099–1379(199911)20:6% 3C915:AID-JOB918%3E3.3.CO;2-Y.

Fox, S., Spector, P. E., Goh, A., Bruursema, K., & Kessler, S. R. (2012). The deviant citizen: Measuring potential positive relations between counterproductive work behaviour and organizational citizenship behaviour. *Journal of Occupational and Organizational Psychology*, 85(1), 199–220. doi:10.1111/j.2044-8325.2011.02032.x.

Fox, S., Spector, P. E., & Miles, D. (2001). Counterproductive work behavior (CWB) in response to job stressors and organizational justice: Some mediator and moderator tests for autonomy and emotions. *Journal of Vocational Behavior*, 59(3), 291–309. doi:10.1006/jvbe.2001.1803.

Game, A. M. (2007). Workplace boredom coping: Health, safety, and HR implications. *Personnel Review*, 36, 701–721.

Gardner, D., O'Driscoll, M., Cooper-Thomas, H. D., Roche, M., Bentley, T., Catley, B., ... & Trenberth, L. (2016). Predictors of workplace bullying and cyber-bullying in New Zealand. *International Journal of Environmental Research and Public Health*, 13(5), 448.

George, J. M. (1992). The role of personality in organizational life: Issues and evidence. *Journal of Management*, 18(2), 185–213.

Goh, A. (2007). *An attributional analysis of counterproductive work behavior (CWB) in response to occupational stress.* University of South Florida.

Grigg, D. (2010). Cyber-aggression: Definition and concept of cyberbullying. *Australian Journal of Guidance and Counselling*, 20(2), 143–156. http://journals.cam bridge.org/abstract_S1037291100001084.

Gruys, M. L., & Sackett, P. R. (2003). Investigating the dimensionality of counterproductive work behavior. *International Journal of Selection and Assessment*, 11(1), 30–42. doi:10.1111/1468-2389.00224.

Hadlington, L., & Parsons, K. (2017). Can cyberloafing and internet addiction affect organisational information security? *Cyberpsychology, Behaviour, and Social Networking*, 20(9). doi:10.1089/cyber.2017.0239.

Hadlington, L., Binder, J., & Stanulewicz, N. (2021). Exploring role of moral disengagement and counterproductive work behaviours in information security awareness. *Computers in Human Behaviour*, 114, 106557. doi:10.1016/j. chb.2020.106557.

Hadlington, L., Popovac, M., Janicke, H., Yevseyeva, I., & Jones, K. (2019). Exploring the role of work identity and work locus of control in information security awareness. *Computers and Security*, 81. doi:10.1016/j.cose.2018.10.006.

Harju, L., Hakanen, J. J., & Schaufeli, W. B. (2014). Job boredom and its correlates in 87 Finnish organizations. *Journal of Occupational and Environmental Medicine*, 56 (9), 911–918. doi:10.1097/JOM.0000000000000248.

Howard, D. J., & Spector, P. E. (2020). The dark side of workplace technology. In B. J. Hoffman, M. K. Shoss, & L. A. Wegman (Eds), *The Cambridge handbook of the changing nature of work* (pp. 509–531). Cambridge University Press. doi:10.1017/9781108278034.024.

Hystad, S. W., Mearns, K. J., & Eid, J. (2014). Moral disengagement as a mechanism between perceptions of organisational injustice and deviant work behaviours. *Safety Science*, 68, 138–145. doi:10.1016/j.ssci.2014.03.012.

Jex, S. M. (1998). *Stress and job performance: Theory, research, and implications for managerial practice*. Sage Publications.

Jex, S. M., & Beehr, T. A. (1991). Emerging theoretical and methodological issues in the study of work-related stress. *Research in Personnel and Human Resources Management*, 9, 311–365.

Jönsson, S., Muhonen, T., Forssell, R. C., & Bäckström, M. (2017). Assessing exposure to bullying through digital devices in working life: Two versions of a cyber-bullying questionnaire (CBQ). *Psychology*, 8(3), 477–494. doi:10.4236/psych.2017.83030.

Judge, T. A., Scott, B. A., & Ilies, R. (2006). Hostility, job attitudes, and workplace deviance: Test of a multilevel model. *Journal of Applied Psychology*, 91, 126–128.

Karabıyık, C., Baturay, M. H., & Özdemir, M. (2021). Intention as a mediator between attitudes, subjective norms, and cyberloafing among preservice teachers of English. *Participatory Educational Research*, 8(2), 57–73. doi:10.17275/per.21.29.8.2.

Kass, S. J., Vodanovich, S. J., & Callender, A. (2001). State–trait boredom: The relationship to absenteeism, tenure and job satisfaction. *Journal of Business and Psychology*, 16, 317–327.

Kopecký, K., & Szotkowski, R. (2017). Specifics of cyberbullying of teachers in Czech schools-a national research. *Informatics in Education*, 16(1), 103–119.

Liberman, B., Seidman, G., McKenna, K., & Buffardi, L. (2011). Employee job attitudes and organizational characteristics as predictors of cyberloafing. *Computers in Human Behavior*, 27, 2192–2199.

Lim, V. K. (2002). The IT way of loafing on the job: Cyberloafing, neutralizing and organizational justice. *Journal of Organizational Behavior*, 23, 675–694.

Lim, V. K., & Teo, T. S. (2009). Mind your E-manners: Impact of cyber incivility on employees' work attitude and behavior. *Information & Management*, 46(8), 419–425.

Maasberg, M., Zhang, X., Ko, M., Miller, S. R., & Beebe, N. L. (2020). An analysis of motive and observable behavioral indicators associated with insider cyber-sabotage and other attacks. *IEEE Engineering Management Review*, 48(2), 151–165. doi:10.1109/EMR.2020.2989108.

Marcus, B., & Schuler, H. (2004). Antecedents of counterproductive behavior at work: A general perspective. *Journal of Applied Psychology*, 89(4), 647–660. doi:10.1037/0021-9010.89.4.647.

McDonald, T. (2018). *How many people watch porn at work will shock you*. https://sugarcookie.com/2018/01/watch-porn-at-work.

Melamed, S., Ben-Avi, I., Luz, J., & Green, M. S. (1995). Objective and subjective work monotony: Effects on job satisfaction, psychological distress, and absenteeism in blue-collar workers. *Journal of Applied Psychology*, 80, 29–42.

Mercado, B. K. (2017). *Cyber counterproductive work behaviors: Measurement, prediction, and means for reduction*. City University of New York.

Mercado, B. K., Dilchert, S., Giordano, C., & Ones, D. S. (2018). Counterproductive work behaviors. In D. S. Ones, N. Anderson, C. Viswesvaran, & H. K. Sinangil (Eds), *The Sage handbook of industrial, work and organizational psychology* (Vol. 1, pp. 109–210). Sage Publications.

Mercado, B. K., Giordano, C., & Giordano, C. (2017). A meta-analytic investigation of cyberloafing. *Career Development International*, 22(5), 546–564.

Mikulas, W. L., & Vodanovich, S. J. (1993). The essence of boredom. *Psychological Record*, 43, 3–12.

Miles, D. E., Borman, W. C., Spector, P. E., & Fox, S. (2002). Building an integrative model of extra role work behaviors: A comparison of counterproductive work behavior with organizational citizenship behavior. *International Journal of Selection and Assessment*, 10(1/2), 51–57.

Mills, B. J. E., Tyrell, B. J., Werner, W. B., & Woods, R. H. (2008). Cybergriping: Violating the law while e-complaining. *Hospitality Review*, 26(1), 55–73.

Moore, C. (2015). Moral disengagement. *Current Opinion in Psychology*, 6, 199–204. doi:10.1016/j.copsyc.2015.07.018.

Moore, C., Detert, J. R., Klebe Treviño, L., Baker, V. L., & Mayer, D. M. (2012). Why employees do bad things: Moral disengagement and unethical organizational behavior. *Personnel Psychology*, 65(1), 1–48. doi:10.1111/j.1744-6570.2011.01237.x.

Murodilla, S., Dadaboyev, U., & Baek, Y. (2020). Victimizing innovative employees: Joint roles of in-role behavior and task interdependence. *International Journal of Conflict Management*, 1044. doi:10.1108/IJCMA-05-2020-0090.

Ones, D. S., & Dilchert, S. (2013). Counterproductive work behaviors: Concepts, measurement, and nomological network. In K. F. Geisinger, B. A. Bracken, J. F. Carlson, J.-I. C. Hansen, N. R. Kuncel, S. P. Reise, & M. C. Rodriguez (Eds), *APA handbook of testing and assessment in psychology: Test theory and testing and assessment in industrial and organizational psychology* (Vol. 1, pp. 643–659). APA. doi:10.1037/14047-035.

Parsons, K., McCormac, A., Pattinson, M., Butavicius, M., & Jerram, C. (2017). The Human Aspects of Information Security Questionnaire (HAIS-Q): Two further validation studies. *Computers & Security*, 66, 40–51.

Penney, L. M., & Spector, P. E. (2005). Job stress, incivility, and counterproductive work behavior (CWB): The moderating role of negative affectivity. *Journal of Organizational Behavior*, 26(7), 777–796. doi:10.1002/job.336.

Peters, L. H., & O'Connor, E. J. (1988). Measuring work obstacles: Procedures, issues, and implications. In F. D. Schoorman & B. Schneider (Eds), *Facilitating work effectiveness* (pp. 105–123). Lexington Books.

Pindek, S., Krajcevska, A., & Spector, P. E. (2018). Cyberloafing as a coping mechanism: Dealing with workplace boredom. *Computers in Human Behavior*, 86, 147–152. doi:10.1016/j.chb.2018.04.040.

Piotrowski, C. (2012). From workplace bullying to cyberbullying: The enigma of e-harassment in modern organizations. *Organization Development Journal*, 30(4), 44–53.

Robinson, S. L., & Bennett, R. J. (1995). A typology of deviant workplace behaviors: A multidimensional scaling study. *Academy of Management Journal*, 38(2), 555–572. doi:10.5465/256693.

Rotter, J. B. (1966). Generalized expectancies for internal versus external control of reinforcement. *Psychological Monographs: General and Applied*, 80(1), 1–28.

Schaufeli, W. B., & Salanova, M. (2014). Burnout, boredom, and engagement in the workplace. In M. C. W. Peeters, J. De Jonge, & T. W. Taris (Eds), *An introduction to contemporary work psychology* (pp. 293–320). Wiley-Blackwell.

Shultz, K. S., Wang, M., & Olson, D. A. (2010). Role overload and underload in relation to occupational stress and health. *Stress and Health*, 26(2), 99e111. doi:10.1002/smi.1268.

Soh, P. C. H., Koay, K. Y., & Lim, V. K. (2018). Understanding cyberloafing by students through the lens of an extended theory of planned behavior. *First Monday*. https://firstmonday.org/ojs/index.php/fm/article/download/7837/7417.

Spector, P. E. (1988). Development of the Work Locus of Control Scale. *Journal of Occupational Psychology*, 61(4), 335–340.

Spector, P. E. (2002). Employee control and occupational stress. *Current Directions in Psychological Science*, 11(4), 133–136.

Spector, P. E., & Fox, S. A. (2002). An emotion-centered model of voluntary work behavior: Some parallels between counterproductive work behavior and organizational citizenship behavior. *Human Resource Management Review*, 12, 269–272.

Spector, P. E., & Jex, S. M. (1998). Development of the work locus of control scale. *Journal of Occupational Psychology*, 61(4), 335–340.

Spector, P. E., Fox, S., Penney, L. M., Bruursema, K., Goh, A., & Kessler, S. (2006). The dimensionality of counterproductivity: Are all counterproductive behaviors created equal? *Journal of Vocational Behavior*, 68(3), 446e460. doi:10.1016/j.jvb.2005.10.005.

Sprung, J. M., & Jex, S. M. (2012). Work locus of control as a moderator of the relationship between work stressors and counterproductive work behavior. *International Journal of Stress Management*, 19(4), 272–291. doi:10.1037/a0030320.

Sung, B., Lee, S., & Teow, T. (2021). Revalidating the Boredom Proneness Scales Short From (BPS-SF). *Personality and Individual Differences*, 168. doi:10.1016/j.paid.2020.110364.

van Hooff, M. L. M., & van Hooft, E. A. J. (2017). Boredom at work: Towards a dynamic spillover model of need satisfaction, work motivation, and work-related boredom. *European Journal of Work and Organizational Psychology*, 26(1), 133–148. doi:10.1080/1359432X.2016.1241769.

Vodanovich, S. J., Wallace, J. C., & Kass, S. J. (2005). *A confirmatory approach to the factor structure of the boredom proneness scale: Evidence for a two-factor short form*. http://istprojects.syr.

Weatherbee, T. G. (2010). Counterproductive use of technology at work: Information & communications technologies and cyberdeviancy. *Human Resource Management Review*, 20(1), 35–44. doi:10.1016/j.hrmr.2009.03.012.

Workman, M. (2010). A behaviorist perspective on corporate harassment online: Validation of a theoretical model of psychological motives. *Computers & Security*, 29(8), 831–839.

12

THE DARK SIDE OF TECHNOLOGY IN THE WORKPLACE

Implications for Cybersecurity

Introduction

Let's face it, technology has brought us a raft of advantages in our everyday work lives. Email, the internet, smartphones, digital storage systems, and video-conferencing (which might also be a curse, but let's not go down that particular rabbit hole) all exist thanks to advances in digital technology and aligned services. Technology supports numerous activities in the workplace, enhancing productivity and stimulating creativity and collaboration across projects. However, as with any potential benefits there are usually some residual downsides. There are numerous negatives associated with the use of digital technology in our everyday work lives and some researchers have also linked technology use to issues with cybersecurity compliance. We often forget that we are at the constant disposal of our smartphones, leaping to pick them up when we get a new notification, even in the middle of the night. Sahami Shirazi et al. (2014) made the astounding observation that, on average, smartphone users take 30 seconds from receiving a notification to interacting with it, irrespective of its origin (Hadlington, 2017). Research has noted that 79% of smartphone users have their smartphones on or near them for all but 2 hours of their working day (Hadlington, 2017; Levitas, 2013). Our smartphones often accompany us throughout our daily lives, from the moment we wake up to the moment we drift off to sleep. Many people are unable to fall asleep without their faithful sleep companion positioned next to them in bed. It is no surprise then that technology has been positioned as creating an atmosphere of stress and fatigue in some individuals, impacting their capacity to work effectively and follow basic aspects of cybersecurity.

The constant lure of technology can lead to maladaptive behaviours, with research showing that technology addictions can deteriorate cybersecurity

DOI: 10.4324/9781003509011-12

awareness. Additionally, the presence of technology brings unexpected consequences, such as interruptions and distractions from constant notifications, which take our focus away from current tasks. This is a direct result of the digital 'push economy', where numerous notifications from apps and devices vie for our limited attention (Basoglu et al., 2009; Bawden & Robinson, 2008). Some have referred to this as 'continual partial attention', describing a state where we are never fully paying attention to one thing but instead paying a small amount of attention to multiple activities and devices (Hadlington, 2017; Stone, 2009).

In this chapter, we will focus on these specific aspects of technology use in more depth and examine how each can have a detrimental effect on cybersecurity awareness and behaviours in individuals.

Technostress

Let us consider some scenarios that might be familiar to some people:

- Sarah is a project manager for a busy architectural company; she is always juggling tasks and is constantly overwhelmed by the sheer volume of notifications that she gets on her smartphone, her laptop, and even her smartwatch. Whilst in the middle of doing several tasks, she gets an email from her manager that asks her to review a document urgently. As she has so much going on, and because the deadline is so urgent, she misses the tell-tale signs of a spear-phishing attack and inadvertently enters her login credentials onto a fake website. These are later used to compromise the company's internal systems.
- Mark is a customer service representative for a large car sales company and feels like he is on the verge of a breakdown due to the long hours and the task of managing a large volume of calls on a digital system. The company Mark works for has a password policy that means passwords must be changed every few weeks, which Mark finds annoying, frustrating, and something that takes up a lot of his time preventing him from getting on with his normal work. To counteract this, Mark adopts the strategy of reusing a password that is taken from his personal non-work platforms (such as social media accounts). When one of these platforms suffers a hack, and account information is leaked online, and the reused password is used to access the company's internal systems, causing disruption and loss of reputation.

Technology's integration into our daily work lives has a clear dichotomy that Tarafdar et al. (2011) were keen to highlight. On the one hand technology allows us to access unlimited amount of information and gives us the capacity to work in a variety of diverse ways. On the other hand, as these researchers have noted, there is a dark side to the use of digital technology within the workplace. The presence of digital technology in our daily work lives can lead people to experience feelings of compulsion to stay connected to multiple streams of information, to be trapped in a continual loop of multitasking behaviours and to feel compelled to respond immediately to notifications (Tarafdar et al., 2011). These feelings can cumulate in what has been termed 'technostress' and has been typified as an individual experiencing stress because of using technology, most specifically ICT. The term technostress has been defined as 'a modern disease of adaptation caused by an inability to cope with new computer technologies in a healthy manner' (Brod, 1984, p. 16). Technostress has been linked to a variety of psychological and physiological issues. These include high blood pressure, heart disease, and musculoskeletal disorders (Pransky et al., 2002). Additionally, technostress has been linked to perceptions of work overload, information overload, loss of motivation, and job dissatisfaction (Weil & Rosen, 1997).

Technostress is seen as separate and additive to general work stress. It is experienced when an individual carries out tasks using technology in the workplace (Ahuja et al., 2007; Moore, 2000).

Tarafdar et al. (2011) presented a framework for conceptualising technostress, and highlighted five interrelated factors that can serve as predictors for an individual experiencing technostress.

- Techno-Overload: This is where an individual is faced with multiple streams of information; the constant presence of technology creates a situation where the individual feels compelled to work faster. Multiple different platforms and technologies create an environment where we are faced with a multitude of constant, simultaneous streams of real-time information creating the potential for information overload, multitasking, and interruptions. There has been some extensive work conducted exploring these aspects of technology use that we will explore later in this chapter.
- Techno-Invasion: The steady and persistent creep of technology that permeates throughout our daily lives. Techno-invasion is typically viewed as a perceived inability to escape from technology, or the feeling of constantly being connected to the internet, work, and our devices. There is an inherent feeling of being constantly tied to technology and that it intrudes on our personal time outside of work, creating feelings of stress and frustration.
- Techno-Complexity: Ever had that feeling where you just have no idea what you are doing with technology? Techno-Complexity is a situation where individuals are forced to engage with additional learning to understand and use new forms of technology or applications. Obviously, such a process can take considerable time and effort, and even then, users may feel that they do not have the full grasp of the full

functionality of the system. This in turn can lead to feelings of confusion, intimidation, and stress as a result.

- Techno-Insecurity: In situations where individual exhibit fear or feel threatened by the potential for individuals who have a better grasp of technology than themselves to take their jobs.
- Techno-Uncertainty: The constant march of change that is often accompanied with the use of technology in the workplace means that individuals do not have a sufficient time to establish a firm grounding with systems, applications, and devices. Although individuals may initially have a good understanding of technology and feel a degree of excitement and enthusiasm for using these systems, they soon become disillusioned as these systems constantly get refreshed, updated, or replaced. This creates feelings of uncertainty, which in turn can also turn to frustration and stress.

Tarafdar et al. (2011) went on to detail how technostress can impact an individual, and the wider ramifications of the phenomenon. For example, technostress has been noted to create feelings of overload, particularly where aspects such as techno-complexity mean that individuals need to expand additional time and effort learning a new system on top of their existing workload. Techno-overload can also mean that an individual is pressured to engage in processing more information and to attempt to fit more into a much more condensed amount of time. Technostress can also lead to an increase in what Tarafdar et al. (2011) termed role conflict, meaning that individuals perceive an increasing level of contradictory and conflict roles and situations. For example, the ever-present nature of technology associated with techno-invasion means that individuals suffer from a conflict between work and home life. Individuals can also experience levels of dissatisfaction with the technology they are using which can also create conditions where the individual reduces their overall commitment to the organisation they work for.

Technostress and Cybersecurity Fatigue

There has been some work exploring the role of technostress in the manifestation of a concept that has been labelled 'cybersecurity fatigue' in the literature (Nobles, 2022; Reeves et al., 2021). Cybersecurity fatigue is a situation in which an individual finds themselves overwhelmed with the pressures of maintaining an adequate level of cybersecurity awareness and experience levels of 'weariness, aversion, or manifested lack of motivation in regard to cybersecurity' (Reeves et al., 2021, p. 2). Cybersecurity fatigue is seen to emerge as a response to a continued, high-level exposure to cybersecurity initiatives, including training, messaging, and other workplace demands around the topic (Reeves et al., 2021). Researchers have noted that there is a significant positive relationship between techno-invasion and cybersecurity fatigue, suggesting that as technology is seen to transgress beyond the limits of the workplace and begins to invade our outside-of-work lives, we start to reject the continued messages about cybersecurity (Mangundu & Mayayise, 2023). This could also mean that as we engage in the use of technology outside of work, we may take for granted the risks that arise from our use of digital technology, choosing instead to neglect protective cybersecurity behaviours altogether. Techno-complexity and techno-overload were also seen to have a positive influence on cybersecurity fatigue, again suggesting that as people experience increased levels of stress due to the perceived complexity of technology, and where they feel that technology creates a situation of information overload, they are more likely to disengage from cybersecurity rules and procedures. These are interesting findings and demonstrate that the impact of technostress can and does have a direct impact on an individual's approach to cybersecurity in the workplace. As such, there are clear implications for how organisations integrate the use of technology in the workplace, and how this serves to impact the cybersecurity posture of the organisation. For example, organisations that have higher levels of individuals who experience techno-invasion, techno-complexity, and techno-overload may have to consider the implementation of mitigation strategies that serve to either reduce the impact of such on their overall cybersecurity posture, or look to make technology less invasive, complex, and reduce the potential for overload.

Other researchers have mapped the underlying concept of technostress directly on to cybersecurity requirements that individuals within the workplace must adhere to. This concept, labelled 'security-related stress' (SRS; D'Arcy et al., 2014), describes the stress that is elicited because of the demands associated with adherence to cybersecurity. The concept focuses on workplace stress because of compliance with organisational cybersecurity requirements rather than a more general form of workplace stress. There has been some previous empirical support for this, and researchers have noted that individuals develop stress-related responses to organisational policies on things such as secure email use (Puhakainen & Siponen, 2010). Herath and Rao (2009a, 2009b) also noted that there was a significant negative relationship between the severity of punishment for a violation of organisational security policies and the intention to comply with such rules. Posey et al. (2011) also noted in environments where there are dramatically changing rules and expectations from organisational cybersecurity policies these can create a potential for CWBs in the form of computer abuse. Organisational practice, such as monitoring employee computer use, can serve to create negative perceptions of the organisation and increase the occurrence of undesirable employee behaviour (Alge, 2001; Posey et al., 2011).

In the framework of SRS presented by D'Arcy et al. (2014) psychological stress is created as a function of both external and internal demands made on the individual because of cybersecurity policies. As with the framework presented by Tarafdar et al. (2011) there are five key pillars that serve to create SRS.

- SRS Overload: Situations where the security requirements presented by the organisation increase employees' perceived workload and therefore create additional pressure on the individual. In instances where someone might not have relevant administrative access to download a relevant program or file, you might have to expand considerable effort emailing the relevant support team, waiting for a reply, and then getting a resolution to the issue. In turn, this may mean the initial task that you started that needed that program or file has now increased in urgency, meaning that you must work harder and faster (D'Arcy et al., 2014). Findings from research have supported these aspects related to SRS overload, where individuals have detailed the often-cumbersome nature of cybersecurity protocols which create unnecessary demands on them, and which in turn can impact stress levels and frustration (D'Arcy et al., 2014).
- SRS Complexity: Features in an individual's work life when the requirements to comply with cybersecurity rules are seen as overwhelming or complex, meaning that individuals must spend a considerable amount of time and effort engaging in additional training to understand what is required of them. The use of technical information and jargon, or the requirement to engage in multiple different steps to ensure compliance, is a sure-fire way to create an unnecessary level of complexity for end users. This means they must devote increasing amounts of time to decipher the things that are requested of them, and complex requirements are seen to generate stress. Many employees have exhibited feelings of intimidation when it comes to the rules they are asked to follow in terms of cybersecurity, feelings that are often accompanied by misunderstanding and misinterpretation (D'Arcy et al., 2014).
- SRS Uncertainty: In situations where organisations present a continuous cycle of updates related to cybersecurity requirements that individuals need to fulfil as part of their job roles, this can serve to create feelings of uncertainty. These changes may be driven by any number of forces that sit within the organisation or are positioned outside of the organisation in terms of regulatory requirements. Often such changes require organisations to push through new training or initiatives to enhance perceived compliance with these regulations, which in turn means employees are bombarded with a raft of new things to do (D'Arcy et al., 2014).

D'Arcy et al. (2014) explored the relationship between SRS and violations of accepted cybersecurity protocols and found evidence that when individuals perceived stress because of cybersecurity requirements within the organisation, they were more likely to attempt to use moral disengagement to excuse this transgression. Later work by D'Arcy and Teh (2019) proposed that SRS had a direct influence on the emotional reactions of individuals, where the experience of SRS increased the likelihood of individuals experiencing frustration and fatigue. In addition, frustration and fatigue were seen to have a clear impact on the tendency for individuals to engage in active neutralisation strategies. Neutralisation is something that we explored back in Chapter 7; it provides individuals with the capacity to minimise or downplay the potential impact of illicit behaviours. In the study by D'Arcy and Teh (2019), the illicit behaviour they focused on was the tendency for individuals to engage in violations of accepted cybersecurity rules and procedures. The pattern of behaviour that emerges from this research is less complicated than it may first appear; people experience higher levels of SRS, which increases their experience of frustration and fatigue. In turn frustration and fatigue leads to a higher propensity for individuals to use neutralisation techniques that excuse their lack of engagement with cybersecurity rules within the organisation. Such a pattern means that individuals who experience higher levels of SRS are more likely to be at risk of engaging in compromising organisational cybersecurity behaviours. D'Arcy et al. (2014; D'Arcy & Teh, 2019) suggested engaging in strategies to reduce the perceived complexity of cybersecurity compliance could be initiated, alongside a reduction in the use of unnecessary jargon and the use of legal/technical terminology. D'Arcy and Teh (2019) also suggested that steps should be taken to ensure that employees reduce their potential to engage in neutralisation behaviours through more effective training programmes. However, there is no indication of how successful such processes could be and adding another layer of training to cybersecurity compliance would seem to be counterproductive when the very basis of the stressful situation is an overabundance of cybersecurity training information.

Mitigating Technostress and Cybersecurity Fatigue

Addressing technostress is crucial for reducing cybersecurity fatigue, as highlighted by Mangundu and Mayayise (2023). They found that techno-complexity, techno-invasion, and techno-insecurity significantly predict cybersecurity fatigue. This underscores the importance of helping individuals understand technology better and reducing its complexity in the workplace. Mangundu and Mayayise (2023) noted that effective cybersecurity awareness training served to moderate the relationship between technostress creators and cybersecurity fatigue, suggesting this as one essential strategy that could be deployed to tackle technostress. This use of effective training programmes that enhance employees' technological skills and knowledge has also garnered attention from other researchers. For example, Berger et al. (2023) presented no less than 24 individual preventative measures that were synthesised from the existing literature in the area. These techniques included fostering a cooperative workplace culture, developing group norms for the use of ICT, applying human-focused ICT design, and training technostress coping mechanisms. By ensuring that employees feel confident and competent in using new technologies, organisations can reduce feelings of techno-uncertainty and techno-complexity. Training should be tailored to different skill levels and include practical, hands-on sessions that allow employees to familiarise themselves with new systems in a supportive environment (Berger et al., 2023).

Another important approach is to simplify technology use within the organisation. This can be achieved by selecting user-friendly software and systems, minimizing unnecessary features, and providing clear, concise instructions and support materials. Regularly reviewing and streamlining technological processes can help reduce the cognitive load on employees, making technology less intimidating and more manageable. In their opinion piece on the topic, Brivio et al. (2018) expressed the virtues of adopting an approach labelled as Positive Technology (Brivio et al., 2018; Calvo & Peters, 2012; Riva et al., 2012). Positive technology essentially focuses on the use of technology that leads to an improvement in the quality of our personal experiences (Riva et al., 2012). This could include a variety of different initiatives, including the promotion of well-being using digital tools, using e-learning platforms to enhance individual training and development opportunities, or integrating aspects of gamification into daily tasks and activities (Brivio et al., 2018). However, it is important to note that many of the suggested interventions for overcoming technostress in the workplace have limited empirical evidence to support their overall effectiveness, with some researchers noting that there is a real gap in the literature on preventative measures (Rohwer et al., 2022).

Multitasking

As we have seen in the previous section on technostress, one of the elements embodied in the concept of techno-overload is linked to the constant state of connectivity we experience due to the ubiquitous nature of technology. One of the key aspects associated with techno-overload is the potential for constant interruptions, distractions, and the need to engage in extreme levels of multitasking, which can lead to stress and anxiety.

The concept of multitasking, defined as the execution of two or more tasks simultaneously by an individual (Lui & Wong, 2012; Yuan & Zhong, 2024), has become a key skill that many employers emphasise in their job specifications. Multitasking has become a hallmark of modern productivity, often celebrated as a way to accomplish more in less time. However, research demonstrates that humans are incapable of true multitasking (Carrier et al., 2015; Rosen, 2008). Unlike computers, which can execute multiple operations simultaneously due to hardwired logic, humans engage in rapid task-switching – alternating attention between tasks rather than performing them concurrently. Herbert Simon (1971) famously noted that 'a wealth of information creates a poverty of attention' (p. 40), emphasizing the challenge of managing focus in the modern era. Similarly, Rosen (2008) critiques the hijacking of the term multitasking, redefining it as the human attempt to manage multiple tasks simultaneously, often with the aid of technology. However, these attempts frequently fail, as evidenced by consistent research showing increased errors and reduced efficiency when individuals try to multitask.

Researchers have noted that multitasking can lead to feelings of cognitive overload, decreased productivity, and poorer quality of work (Carrier et al., 2015; Steege et al., 2015). Yuan and Zhong (2024) noted that multitasking had a significant negative impact on task performance, with lower accuracy and increased reaction times to complete set tasks. This inefficiency in our capacity to multitask stems from the finite nature of human attention. As we have noted previously, attention operates as a limited resource, and when we attempt to divide it between tasks, we reduce the cognitive resources available for each. While practice and repetition may improve certain aspects of multitasking, individual differences significantly influence performance. Some individuals appear less susceptible to cognitive overload due to greater working memory capacity or superior task prioritisation skills. However, even these individuals cannot match the efficiency of single-task focus. William James (1890) likened multitasking to a child-like inability to maintain focused attention. His observation resonates strongly today, where digital devices and social media frequently lure attention away from critical tasks. While the term suggests simultaneous engagement, what truly occurs is a sequence of cognitive shifts – a process riddled with inefficiencies and limitations.

Dzubak (2007) argued that multitasking is more accurately described as task switching. This involves shifting attention from one task to another in rapid succession, selecting information, processing it, and encoding it into memory. Delbridge (2001) reinforces this view, describing multitasking as the pursuit of multiple goals within the same period through frequent attention shifts. These shifts, while necessary, often come at a cost.

Multitasking and Cybersecurity

Multitasking can significantly influence cybersecurity awareness and behaviours due to its impact on cognitive resources and attention. When individuals engage in multitasking, they often experience cognitive overload, which can impair their ability to process information effectively and make sound decisions. This cognitive strain can lead to increased susceptibility to risky cybersecurity behaviours. Technology can in turn often serve to amplify the allure of multitasking. Devices and applications designed to capture attention create a constant battle for focus. The integration of technology into daily routines has transformed multitasking into a cultural norm, despite its inefficiencies. The over-reliance on technology for simultaneous task management frequently leads to cognitive fatigue, reduced productivity, and compromised accuracy. Another consequence of the modern digital age is the phenomenon of media multitasking (MMT) which has been previously demonstrated to have a detrimental effect on an individual's propensity to engage in risky online activities (Hadlington & Murphy, 2018). MMT has been defined as the simultaneous use of two or more types of media, or a consistent pattern of switching between media types (Hadlington & Murphy, 2018; Minear et al., 2013; Ophir et al., 2009). Ever had the television on, whilst also surfing the internet, watching a YouTube video, and listening to the radio (of course this is something the authors never ever do, and we have never been reprimanded for such behaviours!) – this is a clear example of MMT in the wild. It is more common than we would first assume, and research has noted that in the age group between 13 and 65 years old, individuals on average engaged in at least one hour of MMT during their daily life (Voorveld & Van der Groot, 2013).

The consequences of MMT are far-reaching. Individuals who report higher levels of MMT also display higher levels of attentional failures, poorer planning capabilities, organisation, and task monitoring (Hadlington & Murphy, 2018; Magen, 2017; Ralph et al., 2014). The impact on cybersecurity activities is similarly extensive. Higher levels of MMT are associated with cognitive limitations, making individuals more prone to distraction and less likely to identify risks in their immediate environment (Hadlington & Murphy, 2018).

Research has shown that individuals who score higher on measures of MMT also score significantly higher on measures of online risky behaviours. This suggests that those who engage in multiple forms of digital technology may be more likely to take risks online. This relationship may be due to the distractibility of individuals who engage in MMT, as they may lack the impulse control to regulate their online behaviours, increasing their risk of cyberattacks (Hadlington & Murphy, 2018). Additionally, the sheer volume of information consumed by high-level MMT users means they may miss important cues that highlight potential risks, leaving them open to further risks (Hadlington & Murphy, 2018).

This work demonstrates that multitasking with digital technology can have a detrimental effect on an individual's cybersecurity posture. Addressing this behaviour is complex and requires careful consideration. Organisations need to map the incidence of MMT within their population, which is no small feat. Isolating individuals who engage in higher levels of MMT and providing them with targeted interventions (such as placing them in an environment with limited digital media) is both ethically unviable and impractical.

Understanding the limitations of multitasking is critical for both individuals and organisations. Productivity can be improved by minimizing distractions and fostering environments that encourage single-task focus. Techniques such as time blocking, mindfulness, and deliberate task prioritisation can help mitigate the detrimental effects of task-switching. While multitasking is often heralded as a skill, its benefits are illusory. Acknowledging its cognitive costs allows for more effective task management and a better appreciation of focused attention as a cornerstone of productivity and learning.

Interruptions

As we have seen from the evidence above, multitasking presents a wide variety of challenges and means that our attention is often divided across any number of different and distinct activities. There is another facet that is linked to the construct of techno-overload, this being the role of interruptions and task switching. Interruptions, though often dismissed as minor, can significantly disrupt focus and hinder task completion, especially in digital environments where they are frequent and unpredictable. In turn, interruptions can also have a deterrent effect on cybersecurity, particularly where individuals are interrupted by notifications or other tasks that mean their attention is taken away from concurrent and important tasks. Interruptions can be viewed as discrete, externally generated events that disrupt the flow of our focus on a primary task (Coraggio, 1990; Hadlington, 2017). In terms of the difference between a distraction and an interruption, both can occur whilst we are engaged in another primary task. However, the key difference is the way in which they are detected by our senses. Distractions are detected by senses that sit outside of those currently being used for the primary task, so there is limited interference with the content of the task, and we can make the choice to ignore that stimulus or not. In contrast, an interruption will usually take up the same senses as those being used in the task we are currently engaged in, meaning they are a lot harder to ignore (Hadlington, 2017; Speier et al., 2003).

In digital contexts, these may include system notifications, pop-ups, or unrelated adverts. Unlike voluntary shifts in attention where we make the decision to change task or shift attention, interruptions are unplanned and intrusive, making them particularly disruptive to performance. They can lead to error-prone behaviours, diminished memory retention, and frustration, particularly when the interruption is irrelevant to the task.

Not all interruptions have the same impact. For example, relevant interruptions – those offering new information pertinent to the task – are less disruptive and can even facilitate task completion (Czerwinski et al., 2000). For example, receiving additional details about a project may allow us to streamline our current activities and move forward with the current task in hand. However, to do this we must devote additional time to assess the relevance of the interruption to our current task, meaning we have to divert attention from the primary task, reducing efficiency. Irrelevant interruptions cause frustration and impair performance by introducing unnecessary cognitive demands. The degree of disruption also depends on the complexity of the primary task and the timing of the interruption (Czerwinski et al., 2000; Hadlington, 2017; Kalyanaraman et al., 2005; Roda, 2011).

Interruptions and Cybersecurity

There has been some exploration of how interruptions impact cybersecurity. For example, researchers have noted that in instances where individuals were interrupted by a security task that prevented them from accomplishing their primary tasks, the interruption was shown to detrimentally impact cybersecurity behaviour. In instances where participants were time pressured to complete a primary task, they would often ignore additional notifications that occurred (Chowdhury et al., 2019; Kirlappos & Sasse, 2012; Vance et al., 2018, 2022). Acar et al., (2016) also noted that in instances where individuals were under significant time pressures they ignored security protocols to avoid an interruption. Other researchers noted that interruptions to a task that required participants to handle and input sensitive information created a series of extraneous costs in terms of time taken to recheck work, or errors that emerged because of not checking their work once they resumed the task (Williams et al., 2020). As the authors of this research noted, where checks were not made when they resumed their primary task this could result in sensitive information being sent out to an unintended party or being logged incorrectly, both of which impair organisation cybersecurity (Williams et al., 2020).

Interruptions are an inevitable part of modern, technology-driven workflows, but their impact is neither uniform nor negligible. Understanding how interruptions interact with task complexity, timing, and content can guide strategies to mitigate their effects. For users engaged in demanding cognitive tasks, reducing unnecessary interruptions, and designing user-centred notification systems can enhance focus, efficiency, and task satisfaction. Future research should explore how to optimise notification systems further and tailor them to individual task demands and user capacities. To reduce cognitive interference, designers must balance the need for timely notifications with minimizing distractions. Notifications should align with task goals and avoid interrupting high-load activities.

Internet Addiction

One of the concepts that is often discussed in modern research exploring the impact of digital technology on everyday life is the concept of technology addictions. Often when we think about addictions the immediate reaction is to think about substances like drugs, and the consequences of such addictions have long been explored in research. However, there is an emergent strand of work spurred on by the rise of cyberpsychology that focuses directly on the rise of behavioural addictions, including those linked to technology. These addictions often mirror substance dependencies in their psychological patterns, including salience, mood modification, tolerance, and withdrawal symptoms (Griffiths, 1996).

Internet addiction is seen as another form of behavioural dependency, often acting as a conduit for other addictions like gaming or gambling (Griffiths, 2010). It has been linked to poor academic performance, fatigue from late-night usage, and sleep disturbances, which further impair cognition (Kubey et al., 2001). Additionally, individuals with traits like impulsivity or ADHD symptoms appear more susceptible to excessive internet use (Yen et al., 2007). Internet addiction correlates with higher instances of cognitive failures. These failures stem from impaired working memory and reduced attentional control, making individuals more prone to distractions and errors in daily life (Unsworth et al., 2012). While causation remains speculative, the association underscores the cognitive strain imposed by excessive digital engagement. In terms of the workplace, internet addiction could be seen to be an umbrella concept that covers a wide range of deviant CWB in the workplace (Griffiths, 2010).

In terms of the impact internet addiction can have on cybersecurity, researchers have noted some connections between the two concepts. For example, Hadlington and Parsons (2017) identified a relationship between internet addiction acting as a significant negative predictor for scores on the HAIS-Q. Additional work was conducted by Hadlington (2017) exploring the role internet addiction played in predicting the potential for individuals to engage in risky cybersecurity behaviours. In these results internet addiction acted as a significant positive predictor for an individual's self-reported engagement in risky cybersecurity behaviours (e.g., sharing passwords with friends, using the same password for multiple accounts, using free to access public Wi-Fi). These results were later replicated in a further study by Aivazpour and Srinivasan Rao (2018), demonstrating that such a relationship is robust and is found even in diverse cultures outside of the UK. In additional work, Cudo and Ablian (2023) reviewed a collection of papers which focused on problematic internet use and the respective negative consequences associated with such behaviour, and they noted an overall negative impact on cybersecurity awareness, in turn being associated with an increased risk from cyber threats.

Tackling the issue of internet addiction and its respective impact on cybersecurity awareness is somewhat complicated. First, the label of internet addiction has often been used to describe a plethora of other behavioural addictions that are fuelled by access to the internet. For example, someone who is addicted to online gambling is not inherently addicted to the internet per se but may display excessive consumption of the internet to satisfy their primary addiction (Griffiths, 2010). Finding a way to explore these issues within a workplace environment highlights some further issues as well.

First, investigating the prevalence of particular technology-based addictions among employees, such as excessive smartphone use, social media dependency, or compulsive internet browsing, and how these may influence their adherence to cybersecurity awareness, involves navigating sensitive and ethically complex territory. Such inquiries risk infringing on employee privacy, particularly if they require monitoring personal behaviours or collecting self-reported data on potentially stigmatised habits. Without clear ethical guidelines, informed consent, and robust data protection measures, this type of research could easily overstep boundaries and erode trust within the organisation. As highlighted throughout this book, initiating any action that an employee perceives as a violation of organisational justice, whether related to fairness in decision-making, resource distribution, or interpersonal treatment, could trigger a range of adverse responses. These may include CWBs such as reduced productivity, rule-breaking, or sabotage, and in more severe cases, the emergence of malicious insider threats. When employees feel that they have been treated unfairly or excluded from transparent processes, their sense of loyalty and trust in the organisation can erode, increasing the likelihood of retaliatory or disengaged behaviour. Second, if you have a fuller understanding of the issues, what methods do you initiate to prevent the behaviour occurring going forward. Punitive action would seem to be one route, but there again we are faced with the same issues highlighted previously where individuals could become more withdrawn, seeking to engage in some form of retribution against what they see as unnecessary restrictions. Monitoring could go down the same route as that as cyberloafing, with individuals seeing the benefits they obtain from engaging in the behaviour as outweighing the potential sanctions that could be levelled against them.

Our take on this would be to initiate an approach that serves to understand the underlying causes for the observed behaviours rather than tackling the outcome of such behaviours. Whilst this might appear to be a very counterintuitive approach, it would mean that employees get relevant support to help them tackle any problematic issues they might be experiencing which are leading them to spend more time online. Giving an individual more support can remove the potential for them to go down a CWB route and may be the most appropriate intervention if organisations want to avoid the potential for later issues that might come from malicious insider threats.

The Social Media Paradox and the Fear of Missing Out

Social media addiction represents a growing sub-category of technology dependence. Platforms like Facebook exploit the human need for connection, creating cycles of compulsive checking and overuse. A case study by Karaiskos et al. (2010) illustrated this phenomenon with a case report that followed a young woman who displayed compulsive Facebook use that in turn lead to job loss, sleep disturbances, and social withdrawal. This individual had been spending in excess of five hours per day checking her Facebook account and had lost her job waitressing at a local cafe because she often left to visit the nearest internet cafe. This case study presents just one example of how excessive and problematic levels of social media use can impact an individual's work life. There is another layer that typifies the contribution of social media use to aspects of cybersecurity and this links to the amount of information people share online, often without a thought about how that information could be used and who might be able to access it. Gharibi and Shaabi (2012) noted that information released via social media can serve to increase an individual's vulnerability to cybersecurity threats. The potential for cybercriminals to scan social media and utilise information they obtain to formulate further attacks has also been well documented in the research literature (e.g., Khan et al., 2021; Loiacono, 2015; Mouton et al., 2016; Robinson, 2017). Interestingly Khan et al. (2021) noted that those individuals reporting higher levels of cyber protective behaviours demonstrated an increase in the amount of information they disclosed on social media, potentially highlighting a perceived overconfidence in their capacity to protect themselves online (see Chapter 6).

Social media platforms also contribute to phenomena like fear of missing out (FOMO; Hadlington et al., 2020; Przybylski et al., 2013), where users feel compelled to stay continuously connected. Such compulsions divert cognitive resources away from other tasks, impacting memory, decision making, and overall well-being. Fear of missing out has been typically described as an individual's compulsion to stay connected and online for fear of missing social experiences (Przybylski et al., 2013; Riordan et al., 2015). Researchers have noted that individuals who score higher on measures of FOMO are less risk adverse than those who have lower levels (Buglass et al., 2017; Riordan et al., 2015). This has been demonstrated in a variety of studies that have shown that FOMO can lead to an increased tendency to disclosure more information online, therefore increasing vulnerability (Buglass et al., 2017; Dredge et al., 2014; Trepte & Reinecke, 2013). In additional work conducted by Hadlington et al. (2020) it was noted that FOMO predicted employee information security awareness above other factors such as age, gender, and personality traits, which was an interesting finding. We suggested that individuals who exhibited higher levels of FOMO may already be engaged in higher levels of risky behaviour that spread over into their online activities (Hadlington et al., 2020). The drive for individuals to stay online and stay connected may also mean that they are more likely to take risks with their online safety and security, therefore they are less likely to adhere to accepted cybersecurity protocols (Hadlington et al., 2020).

Cyberloafing

We touched upon the concept of cyberloafing earlier on in Chapter 11 as one potential CWB, and here we extend that exploration to investigate how it can impact cybersecurity in the workplace. Researchers have investigated employees' use of their own devices as a form of distraction at work, referring to 'technologically mediated non-work behaviours' to describe cyberloafing and 'personal Internet use in the workplace' (Huma et al., 2017, p. 98). There are a variety of estimates as to how much time individuals spend engaged in cyberloafing at work, with some estimating that employees can spend up to two hours each day engaged in non-work-based activities (Zakrzewski, 2016). Others have noted that around about 62% of employees questioned wasted around about 60 minutes of their workday engaged in personal mobile phone use. Earlier research suggested that cyberloafing was typically widespread within the workplace, with around about 44% of employees questioned citing personal internet use as one of the top distractors at work (Malachowski, 2005). Other researchers have noted that 90% of employees had received, checked, and replied to personal emails during work hours, sometime using work-based equipment to do so (Blanchard & Henle, 2008; Hadlington & Parsons, 2017).

Cyberloafing has been described in terms of the perceived seriousness of the activities that the individual engages in within the workplace. There are two distinct categories that have been defined as:

- Minor Cyberloafing: These are seen as low-level misdemeanours and are often overlooked by organisations and accepted as frequent practice. Such behaviours are less problematic compared to more serious cyberloafing activities and include sending and receiving personal emails whilst at work, surfing mainstream news websites or banking websites, and shopping online (Blanchard & Henle, 2008; Venkatraman et al., 2018).
- Major Cyberloafing: These are the behaviours that stretch the boundaries of what is acceptable to do in the workplace and can also include some activities that could be seen as potentially illegal. Such behaviours can include visiting adult websites, maintaining and posting to personal websites or blogs, spending time interacting in chatrooms, online gambling, and downloading music/films (Blanchard & Henle, 2008; Venkatraman et al., 2018).

Cyberloafing – Surely It Does Not Impact Cybersecurity

Sending emails at work for non-work purposes, having a quick browse on the internet for news stories, or looking at a potential short getaway – what is the harm? Researchers have noted that there are wider risks associated with minor cyberloafing activities outside those of a general impact on productivity and output (Askew et al., 2014; Henle & Blanchard, 2008). Even though minor cyberloafing is often viewed as being more socially acceptable within an organisation there is a risk that browsing non-work-related websites can introduce unnecessarily higher levels of cybersecurity risks (Vernon-Bido et al., 2018), but there are certain caveats that need to be mentioned here. Defining what websites and activities are non-work related is hard to determine especially when the world of employment is so wide and varied. For an academic researcher, browsing a news website or looking for material in less well documented areas is par for the course, but could also been seen as cyberloafing in the formally defined sense of the term. Inherently the risk for organisations comes when individuals stretch the boundaries of their activities to include elements that could include the illegal, or those that transgress the fair usage policy of their host organisation. Blanchard and Henle (2008) noted that cyberloafing activities could place an organisation at risk if the activities being engaged in were illegal in nature or created workplace norms where sending and viewing offensive material is acceptable. Other issues could include malware being inadvertently downloaded onto organisational systems due to individuals visiting unsecure websites, in turn raising the potential cyber-risk (Hadlington & Parsons, 2017). In work conducted by Hadlington and Parsons (2017) they explored the potential relationship between cyberloafing and cybersecurity awareness. The results demonstrated that major cyberloafing acted as a significant negative predictor for scores on a measure of cybersecurity awareness. Those individuals who admitted to engaging in more frequent major cyberloafing activities scored significantly lower on a measure of cybersecurity awareness compared to those individuals not frequently engaging in these activities. There was also a significant negative correlation between minor cyberloafing and cybersecurity awareness, so as minor cyberloafing increased, cybersecurity awareness decreased (Hadlington & Parsons, 2017). So even in instances where individuals are engaged in what are seen as subjectively acceptable cyberloafing activities in the workplace, these are still seen to have a significant impact on cybersecurity awareness. Such a trend is worrying, particularly as many see minor cyberloafing activities as more widely acceptable, which in turn raises questions about how cyberloafing should be viewed in the workplace (Hadlington & Parsons, 2017). Other researchers have noted similar trends, showing that cyberloafing can have a strong negative influence on intention to comply with accepted cybersecurity protocols (Chiu et al., 2024).

Mitigation Strategies for Cyberloafing

As we have seen in the context of cyberloafing, the behaviours that people engage in during their work hours will in part be influenced by how acceptable they think their behaviours are when compared to their colleagues and managers. In research by Askew et al. (2014) they noted that descriptive norms, attitudes towards cyberloafing, and the capacity to hide cyberloafing activities all acted as significant predictors for cyberloafing activities. People often have the motive and intention to engage in cyberloafing, but they resist the temptation to do so when they believe that people around them will disprove of this activity, and where the risk of them getting caught doing so is increased. If organisations want to avoid more strict measures when it comes to curbing cyberloafing activity in the workplace, Askew et al., (2014) suggested that removing the capacity for people to hide this type of activity could be one possible strategy. In shared office environments, this could be as simple as orientating desks and screens so that the material being accessed on computers is visible by everyone else in the office. Askew et al. (2014) noted that having this level of transparency in the workplace should lead to a reduction in excessive levels of cyberloafing, particular the more serious forms noted above, but would still allow employees some freedom in being able to engage in online activities that alleviate stress. Of course, this suggestion comes with its own set of provisos, including the need to ensure that sensitive data is protected from the view of others who should not have access to it. The other consideration is the descriptive norms of the work environment – if no one else thinks that cyberloafing is a problem, they may turn a blind eye to this type of activity in the first place.

If organisations wish to go down the technical intervention approach, there are some potential issues that have been highlighted in previous research. For example, Khansa et al. (2017) examined the impact of technological interventions on cyberloafing and found that while these interventions were effective at controlling cyberloafing, they are associated with perceptions of unfairness among employees, which can negatively impact employee loyalty. Employees often perceived monitoring-based interventions as being an invasion of their privacy, which in turn led to a decrease in loyalty to the company (Khansa et al., 2017). Remember that perceptions of organisational injustice can act as a significant motivator for CWBs and could be a potential antecedent to malicious insider threat, so a word of caution should be exercised. Khansa et al. (2017) also noted that perceptions of fairness related to the use of technology-based interventions aimed at curbing cyberloafing behaviours did not have a significant effect. This suggests that while transparency measures as suggested by Askew et al. (2014) could reduce cyberloafing, they must be implemented in a way that does not compromise employee perceptions of fairness and privacy.

Borrowing from neutralisation theory and general deterrence theory, Cheng et al. (2013) explored the influence of neutralisation techniques, severity of punishment, and likelihood of detection on personal internet use at work. They found that neutralisation techniques and perceived benefits of cyberloafing had a strong positive effect on personal internet use, while perceived detection certainty had a negative effect. The severity of potential sanctions did not significantly deter cyberloafing. This aligns with the findings of Askew et al. (2014) that increasing the visibility of online activities thereby increasing detection certainty could be a feasible way of reducing cyberloafing. However, it also underscores the importance of addressing the justifications employees use to rationalise their behaviour and the perceived benefits they gain from cyberloafing, and further suggested that admonishing such behaviours has a limited impact.

We would suggest organisations review their current policies as well as making a clear assessment of the current impact from cyberloafing on cybersecurity. It would be wrong to suggest organisations engage in wide-ranging changes and initiatives to tackle a behaviour that is currently having a limited impact on their cybersecurity posture. Initiating what could be seen as draconian measures to tackle what is actually a fairly minor issue could serve to create more issues: we probably want to avoid 'using a sledgehammer to crack a nut', as the saying goes.

Summary

Technology has significantly transformed our work lives, bringing numerous advantages such as enhanced productivity, creativity, and collaboration. However, it also introduces several challenges, including technostress, cybersecurity fatigue, and the negative impacts of multitasking and interruptions. Technostress, a modern phenomenon, arises from the demands of using technology in the workplace and is linked to various psychological and physiological issues, including high blood pressure, heart disease, and job dissatisfaction. Factors contributing to technostress include techno-overload, techno-invasion, techno-complexity, techno-insecurity, and techno-uncertainty.

Cybersecurity fatigue occurs when individuals become overwhelmed by the constant demands of maintaining cybersecurity awareness, leading to weariness, aversion, and a lack of motivation regarding cybersecurity practices. High levels of technostress, particularly techno-invasion and techno-complexity, exacerbate cybersecurity fatigue, causing individuals to disengage from cybersecurity protocols. Multitasking, often celebrated as a hallmark of modern productivity, is shown by research to be inefficient. Humans engage in rapid task-switching rather than true multitasking, leading to increased errors and reduced efficiency. The constant connectivity facilitated by technology results in frequent interruptions and distractions, further diminishing productivity and cybersecurity awareness.

Technology addictions, such as internet and social media addiction, mirror substance dependencies and have significant implications for workplace efficiency and cybersecurity. These addictions lead to cognitive failures, poor decision making, and increased vulnerability to cybersecurity threats. The fear of missing out exacerbates these issues by compelling individuals to stay continuously connected, often at the expense of their cybersecurity practices. Cyberloafing, or the use of technology for personal activities during work hours, poses additional cybersecurity risks. While minor cyberloafing activities are often overlooked, they can introduce vulnerabilities and reduce overall cybersecurity awareness. Major cyberloafing activities, such as visiting adult websites or engaging in online gambling, significantly increase cybersecurity risks.

Addressing technostress is crucial for reducing cybersecurity fatigue. Effective cybersecurity awareness training can moderate the relationship between technostress creators and cybersecurity fatigue. Simplifying technology use within the organisation, fostering a cooperative workplace culture, and developing group norms for the use of ICT can help reduce technostress. Additionally, understanding the limitations of multitasking and minimizing distractions can improve productivity and cybersecurity awareness. Organisations need to balance technology use with effective cybersecurity practices to maintain a productive and secure work environment.

References

Acar, Y., Backes, M., Fahl, S., Kim, D., Mazurek, M., & Stransky, C. (2016). You get where you're looking for – The impact of information sources on code security. In IEEE (Ed.), *IEEE Symposium on Security and Privacy* (pp. 289–305). IEEE.

Ahuja, M. K., Chudoba, K. M., Kacmar, C. J., McKnight, D. H., & George, J. F. (2007). IT road warriors: Balancing work-family conflict, job autonomy, and work overload to mitigate turnover intentions. *MIS Quarterly*, 1–17. https://misq.umn. edu/it-road-warriors-balancing-work-family-conflict-job-autonomy-and-work-overl oad-to-mitigate-turnover-intentions.html.

Aivazpour, Z., & Srinivasan Rao, V. (2018). Impulsivity and risky cybersecurity behaviors: A replication. *Americas Conference on Information Systems 2018: Digital Disruption, AMCIS 2018.* www.researchgate.net/profile/Zahra-Aivazpour/p ublication/334726198_Impulsivity_and_Risky_Cybersecurity_Behaviors_A_Replica tion/links/60fb55722bf3553b29096e73/Impulsivity-and-Risky-Cybersecurity-Behavi ors-A-Replication.pdf.

Alge, B. J. (2001). Effects of computer surveillance on perceptions of privacy and procedural justice. *Journal of Applied Psychology*, 86(4), 797.

Askew, K., Buckner, J. E., Taing, M. U., Ilie, A., Bauer, J. A., & Coovert, M. D. (2014). Explaining cyberloafing: The role of the theory of planned behavior. *Computers in Human Behavior*, 36, 510–519.

Basoglu, K. A., Fuller, M. A., & Sweeney, J. T. (2009). Investigating the effects of computer mediated interruptions: An analysis of task characteristics and interruption frequency on financial performance. *International Journal of Accounting Information Systems*, 10(4), 177–189. doi:10.1016/j.accinf.2009.10.003.

Bawden, D., & Robinson, L. (2008). The dark side of information: Overload, anxiety and other paradoxes and pathologies. *Journal of Information Science*, 35(2), 180–191. doi:10.1177/0165551508095781.

Berger, M., Schäfer, R., Schmidt, M., Regal, C., & Gimpel, H. (2023). How to prevent technostress at the digital workplace: A Delphi study. *Journal of Business Economics*. doi:10.1007/s11573-023-01159-3.

Blanchard, A. L., & Henle, C. A. (2008). Correlates of different forms of cyberloafing: The role of norms and external locus of control. *Computers in Human Behavior*, 24(3), 1067–1084. doi:10.1016/j.chb.2007.03.008.

Brivio, E., Gaudioso, F., Vergine, I., Mirizzi, C. R., Reina, C., Stellari, A., & Galimberti, C. (2018). Preventing technostress through positive technology. *Frontiers in Psychology*, 9, 2569.

Brod, C. (1984). *Technostress: The human cost of the computer revolution.* Addison-Wesley.

Buglass, S. L., Binder, J. F., Betts, L. R., & Underwood, J. D. M. (2017). Motivators of online vulnerability: The impact of social network site use and FOMO. *Computers in Human Behavior*, 66, 248–255. doi:10.1016/j.chb.2016.09.055.

Calvo, R. A., & Peters, D. (2012). Positive computing: technology for a wiser world. *Interactions*, 19(4), 28–31.

Carrier, L. M., Rosen, L. D., Cheever, N. A., & Lim, A. F. (2015). Causes, effects, and practicalities of everyday multitasking. *Developmental Review*, 35, 64–78. doi:10.1016/j.dr.2014.12.005.

Cheng, L., Li, Y., Li, W., Holm, E., & Zhai, Q. (2013). Understanding the violation of IS security policy in organisations: An integrated model based on social control and deterrence theory. *Computers & Security*, 39, 447–459.

Chiu, C. M., Cheng, H. L., Hsu, J. S. C., Tan, C. M., & Huang, C. H. (2024). Employees' intention to comply with information security policies: The impacts of loafing and commitment. *International Journal of Human–Computer Interaction*, 1–17. doi:10.1080/10447318.2024.2422757.

Chowdhury, N. H., Adam, M. T. P., & Skinner, G. (2019). The impact of time pressure on cybersecurity behaviour: A systematic literature review. *Behaviour and Information Technology*, 38(12), 1290–1308. doi:10.1080/0144929X.2019.1583769.

Coraggio, L. (1990). *Deleterious effects of intermittent interruptions on the task performance of knowledge workers: A laboratory investigation* (Unpublished doctoral dissertation). University of Arizona, Tucson.

Cudo, A. V., & Ablian, J. D. (2023). Assessing the knowledge on internet addiction and cybersecurity: A literature review. *American Journal of Humanities and Social Sciences Research (AJHSSR)*, 7(2), 81–89.

Czerwinski, M., Cutrell, E., & Horvitz, E. (2000). Instant messaging and interruption: Influence of task type on performance. *OZCHI 2000 conference proceedings*, 356–361. https://citeseerx.ist.psu.edu/document?repid=rep1&type=pdf&doi=639e5 34bae7bafe80cb7fb0efcd5fac91ed22c78.

D'Arcy, J., Herath, T., & Shoss, M. K. (2014). Understanding employee responses to stressful information security requirements: A coping perspective. *Journal of Management Information Systems*, 31(2), 285–318. doi:10.2753/MIS0742-1222310210.

D'Arcy, J., & Teh, P. L. (2019). Predicting employee information security policy compliance on a daily basis: The interplay of security-related stress, emotions, and neutralization. *Information and Management*, 56(7). doi:10.1016/j.im.2019.02.006.

Delbridge, K. A. (2001). *Individual differences in multi-tasking ability: Exploring a nomological network* (Unpublished doctoral dissertation). Michigan State University, East Lansing, MI.

Dredge, R., Gleeson, J., De, X., & Garcia, P. (2014). Presentation on Facebook and risk of cyberbullying victimisation. *Computers in Human Behavior*, 40, 16–22. doi:10.1016/j.chb.2014.07.035.

Dzubak, C. M. (2007). Multitasking: The good, the bad and the unknown. *Association for the Tutoring Profession*, 53(9), 1689–1699. doi:10.1017/CBO9781107415324.004.

Gharibi, W., & Shaabi, M. (2012). Cyber threats in social networking websites. *International Journal of Distributed and Parallel Systems*, 3(1), 119–126. doi:10.5121/ijdps.2012.3109.

Griffiths, M. (1996). Behavioural addiction: An issue for everybody? *Journal of Workplace Learning*, 8(3), 19–25. doi:10.1108/13665629610116872.

Griffiths, M. (2010). Internet abuse and internet addiction in the workplace. *Journal of Workplace Learning*, 22(7), 463–472. doi:10.1108/BIJ-10-2012-0068.

Hadlington, L. (2017). Human factors in cybersecurity; examining the link between internet addiction, impulsivity, attitudes towards cybersecurity, and risky cybersecurity behaviours. *Heliyon*, 3(7), e00346. doi:10.1016/j.heliyon.2017.e00346.

Hadlington, L., & Murphy, K. (2018). Is media multitasking good for cybersecurity? Exploring the relationship between media multitasking and everyday cognitive failures on self-reported risky cybersecurity behaviours. *CyberPsychology, Behaviour & Social Networking*, 21. doi:10.1089/cyber.2017.0524.

Hadlington, L., & Parsons, K. (2017). Can cyberloafing and internet addiction affect organisational information security? *Cyberpsychology, Behaviour, and Social Networking*, 20(9). doi:10.1089/cyber.2017.0239.

Hadlington, L., Binder, J., & Stanulewicz, N. (2020). Exploring role of moral disengagement and counterproductive work behaviours in information security awareness. *Computers in Human Behaviour*, 114, 106557. doi:10.1016/j.chb.2020.106557.

Herath, T., & Rao, H. R. (2009a). Encouraging information security behaviours in organisations: Role of penalties, pressures and perceived effectiveness. *Decision Support Systems*, 47(2), 154–165.

Herath, T., & Rao, H. R. (2009b). Protection motivation and deterrence: A framework for security policy compliance in organisations. *European Journal of Information Systems*, 18(2), 106–125.

Huma, Z. E., Hussain, S., Thurasamy, R., & Malik, M. I. (2017). Determinants of cyberloafing: A comparative study of a public and private sector organization. *Internet Research*, 27(1), 97–117.

James, W. (1890). *The principles of psychology* (Vols. 1 & 2). Henry Holt and Company. doi:10.1037/10538-000.

Kalyanaraman, S., Ivory, J., & Maschmeyer, L. (2005). Interruptions and online information processing: The role of interruption type, interruption content, and interruption frequency. *Proceedings of the 2005 Annual Meeting of International Communication Association*, 1–32.

Karaiskos, D., Tzavellas, E., Balta, G., & Paparrigopoulos, T. (2010). Social network addiction: A new clinical disorder? *European Psychiatry*, 25(1), 855–856. doi:10.1016/S0924-9338(10)70846-70844.

Khan, B., Alghathbar, K., Nabi, S. I., & Khan, M. K. (2021). Effectiveness of information security awareness training programs: A systematic review. *Computers & Security*, 95, 101–115.

Khansa, L., Kuem, J., Siponen, M., & Kim, S. S. (2017). To cyberloaf or not to cyberloaf: The impact of the announcement of formal organizational controls. *Journal of Management Information Systems*, 34(1), 141–176.

Kirlappos, I., & Sasse, M. A. (2012). Security education against phishing: A modest proposal for a major rethink. *IEEE Security & Privacy*, 10(2), 24–32.

Kubey, R. W., Lavin, M. J., & Barrows, J. R. (2001). Internet use and collegiate academic performance decrements: Early findings. *Journal of Communication*, 51(2), 366–382.

Levitas, D. (2013). Always connected: How smartphones and social keep us engaged. In *IDC Research Report, Sponsored by Facebook*. https://stareintothelightsmypret ties.jore.cc/files/IDCFacebook-AlwaysConnected.pdf.

Loiacono, E. T. (2015). Self-disclosure behavior on social networking web sites. *International Journal of Electronic Commerce*, 19, 66–94.

Lui, K. F. H., & Wong, A. C.-N. (2012). Does media multitasking always hurt? A positive correlation between multitasking and multisensory integration. *Psychonomic Bulletin & Review*, 19(4), 647–653. doi:10.3758/s13423-012-0245-7.

Magen, H. (2017). The relations between executive functions, media multitasking and polychronicity. *Computers in Human Behavior*, 67, 1–9. doi:10.1016/j.chb.2016.10.011.

Malachowski, D. (2005). Wasted time at work costing companies billions. *Asian Enterprise*, 14–16.

Mangundu, J., & Mayayise, T. (2023). The impact of technostress creators on academics' cybersecurity fatigue in South Africa. *Issues in Information Systems*, 24(4), 294–310.

Minear, M., Brasher, F., McCurdy, M., Lewis, J., & Younggren, A. (2013). Working memory, fluid intelligence, and impulsiveness in heavy media multitaskers. *Psychonomic Bulletin & Review*, 20, 1274–1281. doi:10.3758/s13423-013-0456-6.

Moore, J. (2000). One road to turnover: An examination of work exhaustion in technology professionals. *MIS Quarterly*, 24(1), 141–168.

Mouton, F., Leenen, L., & Venter, H. S. (2016). Social engineering attack examples, templates and scenarios. *Computers and Security*, 59, 186–209.

Nobles, C. (2022). Stress, burnout, and security fatigue in cybersecurity: A human factors problem. *HOLISTICA – Journal of Business and Public Administration*, 13 (1), 49–72. doi:10.2478/hjbpa-2022-0003.

Ophir, E., Nass, C., & Wagner, A. D. (2009). Cognitive control in media multitaskers. *Proceedings of the National Academy of Sciences of the United States of America*, 106(37), 15583–15587. doi:10.1073/pnas.0903620106.

Posey, C., Bennett, B., Roberts, T., & Lowry, P. B. (2011). When computer monitoring backfires: Invasion of privacy and organizational injustice as precursors to computer abuse. *Journal of Information System Security*, 7(1), 24–47.

Pransky, G., Robertson, M. M., & Moon, S. D. (2002). Stress and work related upper extremity disorders: Implications for prevention and management. *American Journal of Industrial Medicine*, 41, 443–455.

Przybylski, A. K., Murayama, K., Dehaan, C. R., & Gladwell, V. (2013). Motivational, emotional, and behavioral correlates of fear of missing out. *Computers in Human Behavior*, 29(4), 1841–1848. doi:10.1016/j.chb.2013.02.014.

Puhakainen, P., & Siponen, M. (2010). Improving employees' compliance through information systems security training: an action research study. *MIS Quarterly*, 34 (4), 757–778.

Ralph, B. C. W., Thomson, D. R., Cheyne, J. A., & Smilek, D. (2014). Media multitasking and failures of attention in everyday life. *Psychological Research*, 78(5), 733–748. doi:10.1007/s00426-013-0523-7.

Reeves, A., Delfabbro, P., & Calic, D. (2021). Encouraging employee engagement with cybersecurity: How to tackle cyber fatigue. *SAGE Open*, 11(1). doi:10.1177/ 21582440211000049.

Riordan, B. C., Flett, J. A. M., Hunter, J. A., Scarf, D., & Conner, T. S. (2015). Fear of missing out (FOMO): The relationship between FOMO, alcohol use, and alcohol-related consequences in college students. *Annals of Neuroscience and Psychology*, 2(9), 7. doi:10.7243/2055-3447-2-9.

Riva, G., Baños, R. M., Botella, C., Wiederhold, B. K., & Gaggioli, A. (2012). Positive technology: Using interactive technologies to promote positive functioning. *Cyberpsychology, Behavior, and Social Networking*, 15(2), 69–77.

Robinson, S. C. (2017). Self-disclosure and managing privacy: Implications for interpersonal and online communication for consumers and marketers. *Journal of Internet Commerce*, 16(4), 385–404.

Roda, C. (2011). *Human attention in digital environments.* Cambridge University Press.

Rohwer, E., Flöther, J. C., Harth, V., & Mache, S. (2022). Overcoming the 'dark side' of technology – A scoping review on preventing and coping with work-related technostress. *International Journal of Environmental Research and Public Health*, 19 (6). doi:10.3390/ijerph19063625.

Rosen, C. (2008). The myth of multitasking. *The New Atlantis*. www.thenewatlantis.com/publications/the-myth-of-multitasking.

Sahami Shirazi, A., Henze, N., Dingler, T., Pielot, M., Weber, D., & Schmidt, A. (2014). Large-scale assessment of mobile notifications. *Proceedings of the SIGCHI conference on Human factors in computing systems*, 3055–3064. www.nhenze.net/uploads/Large-Scale-Assessment-of-Mobile-Notifications.pdf.

Simon, H. A. (1971). Designing organizations for an information-rich world. In M. Greenberger (Ed.), *Computers, communications, and the public interest* (pp. 37–72). The Johns Hopkins Press.

Speier, C., Vessey, I., & Valacich, J. S. (2003). The effects of interruptions, task complexity, and information presentation on computer-supported decision-making performance. *Decision Sciences*, 34(4), 771–797. doi:10.1111/j.1540-5414.2003.02292.x.

Steege, L. M., Drake, D. A., Olivas, M., & Mazza, G. (2015). Evaluation of physically and mentally fatiguing tasks and sources of fatigue as reported by registered nurses. *Journal of Nursing Management*, 23(2), 179–189.

Stone, L. (2009). *Continuous Partial Attention.* www.lindastone.net/qa/continuous-partial-attention.

Tarafdar, M., Tu, Q., Ragu-Nathan, T. S., & Ragu-Nathan, B. S. (2011). Crossing to the dark side: Examining creators, outcomes, and inhibitors of technostress. *Communications of the ACM*, 54(9), 113–120. doi:10.1145/1995376.1995403.

Trepte, S., & Reinecke, L. (2013). The reciprocal effects of social network site use and the disposition for self-disclosure: A longitudinal study. *Computers in Human Behavior*, 29(3), 1102–1112. doi:10.1016/j.chb.2012.10.002.

Unsworth, K. L., Dmitrieva, A., & Adriasola, E. (2012). Changing behaviour: Increasing the effectiveness of workplace interventions to reduce injury. *Safety Science*, 50(4), 623–629.

Vance, A., Eargle, D., Eggett, D., Straub, D., & Ouimet, K. (2022). Do security fear appeals work when they interrupt tasks? A multi-method examination of password strength. *MIS Quarterly*, 45(3), 1721–1738. doi:10.25300/misq/2022/15511.

Vance, A., Jenkins, J. L., Anderson, B. B., Bjornn, D. K., & Kirwan, C. B. (2018). Tuning out security warnings: A longitudinal examination of habituation through fMRI, eye tracking, and field experiments. *MIS Quarterly: Management Information Systems*, 42(2), 355–380. doi:10.25300/MISQ/2018/14124.

Venkatraman, S., Cheung, C. M. K., Lee, Z. W. Y., Davis, F. D., & Venkatesh, V. (2018). The "darth" side of technology use: An inductively derived typology of cyberdeviance. *Journal of Management Information Systems*, 35(4), 1060–1091. doi:10.1080/07421222.2018.1523531.

Vernon-Bido, D., Grigoryan, G., Kavak, H., & Padilla, J. (2018). Assessing the impact of cyberloafing on cyber risk. *Simulation Series*, 50(2), 116–124. doi:10.22360/springsim.2018.anss.020.

Voorveld, H. A., & Van der Groot, M. (2013). Age differences in media multitasking: A diary study. *Journal of Broadcasting & Electronic Media*, 57(3), 392–408. doi:10.1080/08838151.2013.816709.

Weil, M. M., & Rosen, L. D. (1997). *Technostress: Coping with technology @work @home @play*. John Wiley & Sons.

Williams, C., Hodgetts, H. M., Morey, C., Macken, B., Jones, D. M., Zhang, Q., & Morgan, P. L. (2020). Human error in information security: Exploring the role of interruptions and multitasking in action slips. *Communications in Computer and Information Science*, 1226, 622–629. doi:10.1007/978-3-030-50732-9_80.

Yen, J. Y., Ko, C. H., Yen, C. F., Wu, H. Y., & Yang, M. J. (2007). The comorbid psychiatric symptoms of internet addiction: Attention deficit and hyperactivity disorder (ADHD), depression, social phobia, and hostility. *Journal of Adolescent Health*, 41, 93–98.

Yuan, X., & Zhong, L. (2024). Effects of multitasking and task interruptions on task performance and cognitive load: Considering the moderating role of individual resilience. *Current Psychology*, 43(28), 23892–23902.

Zakrzewski, C. (2016). The key to getting workers to stop wasting time online. *Wall Street Journal*. www.wsj.com/articles/the-key-to-getting-workers-to-stop-wasting-time-online-1457921545.

13

THE PSYCHOLOGY OF CYBERCRIME

Introduction

Much of this book is devoted to the psychology of the individual that shapes their responses to cybersecurity incidents, and the ways in which they cope with decisions that they are uncertain about. On the opposing side are the tactics that are often employed by attackers to take advantage of some innate processes that are in part linked to cognitive processes, and in part linked to the pull of social norms. If you think about it, humans represent a system that has not been patched correctly, meaning that cybercriminals can take advantage of these processes to execute their scams and exploits. There are a wide range of psychological tactics that are employed in cybersecurity scams, with many falling into the categories of influence and persuasion. We must remember that for most scams, the individuals responsible for creating and deploying them are not playing about – there are some serious actors at large in the cybercrime sphere that have considerable time and resources to devote to honing their craft. So, when we talk about the use of psychological tactics, these are being used at a high level and are becoming increasingly sophisticated as they evolve. Many scammers will rely on borrowing key tactics from existing frauds that have worked in the past or will adapt these tactics to be used in a new way, with the same underlying processes being used.

By understanding the psychological tactics that are employed in the realm of cybercrime we can ensure that end users are better prepared to deal with them and are more able to spot the tell-tale signs of a scam quickly and easily. Remember that to be forewarned is to be forearmed and this is never truer than when we are discussing the psychological tactics in cybercrimes.

DOI: 10.4324/9781003509011-13

The Psychological Foundations of Cybercrime

Cialdini (2007) discussed the concept of fixed action patterns (FAPs) in the context of behaviours we can observe in the animal world. FAPs are automatic or reflexive behaviours that are triggered because of an organism being subjected to a particular stimulus. The key to FAPs is that the same behaviour will be elicited in the same way for the same stimulus, repeatedly. One example that Cialdini presents is a behaviour that is peculiar to Greylag geese. When this species of goose sees an egg outside of its nest, it will instinctively use its beak to roll the egg back into the nest. However, if the egg is removed whilst the goose is mid-action, the goose will continue to engage in the retrieval process as though the egg is still there. The trigger to the FAP in this instance is the appearance of a round object that is near the nest. Another example is from the male stickleback who will fight other male sticklebacks during the mating season. Male sticklebacks are distinguished by their red underside – the FAP in this instance is that the male stickleback can and will attack anything that is red in colour mistaking the relevant object for an enemy stickleback.

Cognitive Biases and Heuristics in Cybercrime

Obviously, humans are slightly more complex in terms of their behaviours, but they can still be seen to engage in behaviours that can be triggered in predictable ways. For example, have you ever been in a position where an alarm sounds and no one else responds in the way you would normally expect? When we hear a fire alarm we would start to move towards the nearest fire exit, but in an instance where we see the rest of the people in the same environment ignoring the alarm we tend to follow their behaviour and assume that the situation is not that serious. We have heuristics to thank for this, as this is a clear example of the bystander effect which tends to mean that we are less likely to act in a helpful or facilitating manner in a critical situation when there are others around us (Fischer et al., 2011). The bystander effect is evident in situations where an individual perceives a situation to be less dangerous, so the likelihood of this process kicking in during a cybersecurity attack is high (Widdowson & Goodliff, 2015).

The key to exploring processes that are like FAPs in humans is to start to focus in on the cognitive biases and heuristics that we explored in Chapter 5. These mechanisms are an excellent way to get people to do something in an automatic way. Heuristics can be useful in day-to-day decisions because we, as humans, are cognitive misers (Fiske & Taylor, 1991), and we just do not have the capacity to analyse every single person or situation that we encounter. However, whilst heuristics may have their benefits this also means that in set situations, we can almost form an expectation about how a person will behave (Attrill-Smith & Wesson, 2020) – and if played out correctly, lead a person to make a poor decision leading to severe errors and outcomes (Jansson & von Solms, 2010).

There are a variety of classic studies from social psychology that demonstrate how easy it is to get someone to do something you want without them thinking about it. For example, Langer et al. (1978) set up an experiment as follows: a confederate of the researchers (someone who is in on the experiment) would approach a participant who was about to use a photocopier. The confederate would request to 'cut in' the line and ask to make some photocopies before them. In the experiment the confederate would use one of three reasons for wanting to cut in:

1. May I use the photocopy machine.
2. May I use the photocopy machine because I am in a rush.
3. May I use the photocopy machine because I have to make copies.

Which one of these arguments resulted in the highest level of compliance to allow the confederate to cut in front of the person about to use the photocopier? Well, the first statement resulted in the lowest level of compliance, but the latter two arguments resulted in almost identical levels of compliance (94% and 93% respectively). The researchers suggested that this was a clear example of mindless conformity, where individuals fall foul of the 'because' heuristic. Individuals ignore the actual reason presented after the word 'because' due to an assumption that anything that follows the word would be a valid reason for wanting to push in front of the participant doing the photocopies. These findings have been replicated in several later pieces of research (e.g., Key et al., 2009). These researchers noted that overall, individuals who complied with the request took less time to respond to the request in comparison to those individuals who refused to allow the request (Key et al., 2009). They also noted that those individuals who scored higher on a measure of self-monitoring, or the capacity to observe and control their behaviour or presentation to comply with perceived social norms (Key et al., 2009; Snyder, 1974), were more likely to give way to requests, to present a more agreeable and likeable nature and avoid confrontation that could damage their social standing (Key et al., 2009; Snyder & Gangestad, 1986).

There are some clear examples of how cognitive biases can creep into elements of cybercrime, and we have already noted that elements of confirmation, optimism, and anchoring biases can make individuals more susceptible to cybercrime.

Influence and Persuasion

Attackers will leverage any advantage they can get over an individual in order to get what they want. They will leverage psychological manipulation to reveal sensitive information, and there are various strategies that can be implemented to do this – when we think about more specific social engineering techniques, these essentially rely on the deceptive use of social influence and emotional techniques to divulge confidential information (Naidoo, 2020). Cialdini's (2007) six principles of persuasion have been fundamental in understanding how individuals can be influenced in cybercrime. As discussed earlier, attackers will manipulate and exploit the heuristics and cognitive shortcuts that individuals go through when making decisions – and the following tactics draw upon these to encourage victims to make a quick decision without stopping and evaluating the information they are faced with. These six principles of influence are:

Authority

The role of authority in the context of influence and persuasion has been well documented in a variety of different contexts (e.g., Burger, 2009; Bushman, 1984; Miller et al., 1995; Slater et al., 2006) The influence of authority has its roots in source credibility theory (Algarni, 2014; Serman & Sims, 2022), whereby source credibility is based on an individual being more persuaded and compliant when the source presents as being credible. That is, individuals are more likely to be influenced and persuaded by people they perceive as authoritative figures or credible experts. There are two types of authority – one which is based on expertise, and the other relying on hierarchical position within an organisation or society (Uebelacker & Quiel, 2014). The perception of authority also works with symbols related to authority too, for example apparel in the form of uniforms (Bushman, 1984). In Bushman's (1984) experiment the dress of a confederate was manipulated so they were either a homeless person, a business executive, or a firefighter. Compliance rates differed significantly between these conditions, where the homeless person obtained 45% compliance, the business executive 50%, and the firefighter 82%. Participants were also seen to give fewer hostile reasons for not complying with the request when the perceived authority of the individual increased, and the time to respond to the request was also faster in the authority conditions. This is a crucial point to note, as authority is often leveraged in conjunction with other mechanics (such as scarcity and urgency) to get individuals to respond quickly, therefore engaging heuristic-driven processes rather than the more systematic processes that could pinpoint a threat.

When it comes to cyberattacks and cybercrime the role of authority is usually obvious, and the reasons why people comply with the demands of the people instructing them are clear. For example, let us take the common CEO fraud spear-phishing attack. This type of exploit usually targets an employee within an organisation by sending an email that looks like it has come from their boss or someone in authority within their organisation. A request will be made of the employee, usually asking them to do a job for them because they do not have current access to the system they need because they are in a meeting or are travelling and do not have a stable connection. The request will usually involve the transfer of money to a bank account that is owned by the cybercriminal or will request some sensitive information from the individual. The manipulation will also include some element of urgency as well to engage heuristic processing. The use of CEO-based spear-phishing attacks has been well documented, and it was reported that the Austrian aerospace component manufacturer Fischer Advanced Composite Components, who supply parts for both Airbus and Boeing, lost approximately $55.8 million in such an attack (www.infosecurity-magazine.com/news/aircraft-maker-lo ses-50-million-in).

The Role of Obedience in Authority

For those of you who do not have a background in psychology this next study may not be familiar to you, but for most psychologists this is perhaps one of the most disturbing and well-known examples of how far authority can be pushed. In Milgram's (1963) study, the procedure went as follows: at the beginning of the study the participant was introduced to another participant, who was a confederate of the researcher. They drew straws to determine which person was going to be the 'learner' or the 'teacher' – however, the roles were pre-determined, and the confederate was always going to be the learner. There was also another confederate in the room who was dressed in a grey lab coat who played the role of the 'experimenter'. The learner was taken to one room where the teacher was told they were being placed into an electric chair. The experimenter and the teacher were in another room where there was an electric shock generator which the participant was led to believe was connected to the electric chair in the other room. Communication between the two rooms was conducted via a two-way speaker that connected the two rooms. The learner was asked to learn a list of word pairs, and then they were asked to recall the partner word when they were presented with the trigger word. The teacher was told they had to administer an electric shock every time the learner made a mistake, and these were increased in strength for each incorrect word recalled. The shock strength was marked from 15 volts (slight shock) up to 450 volts (marked with three X's to indicate a potentially lethal electric shock). The learner got the answers to the probes wrong, and the experimenter would prompt the teacher to deliver the electric shock using a variety of prods (e.g., 'it is absolutely essential that you continue'). There were some surprising results that served to shape our understanding of how authority can influence obedience. Over 65% of participants continued to deliver the highest level of electric shock to the learner, which could have been a potentially fatal shock. All the participants continued to deliver shocks up to the 300 volts level which could also have had some serious health effects. Obviously, the learner never actually received any of the shocks delivered, but where the teacher delivered the potentially fatal shocks, they would go quiet and not respond via the two-way radio.

So, what does Milgram's (1963) study show us when we are talking about obedience? The experiment was a clear demonstration that obedience operates in concert with authority, where authority provides the framework or justification for obeying an order or request that the individual may feel uncomfortable completing. Indeed, Milgram documented some of the intense stress that was experienced by many of the individuals who carried out the instructions of the experimenter. Milgram (1963) recounted an observation of an individual who, after being engaged in the experiment for 20 minutes, was reduced to the point of nervous collapse, but continued to follow the instructions from the experimenter. This demonstrated that even though an individual might exhibit incompatibility between their emotions and the behaviour they are carrying out, the drive to perform in situations of social pressure serves to override this (Miller et al., 1995). Obedience is the behaviour that is induced by authority being directed towards an individual, and is one of the key reasons why individuals fall foul of so many diverse types of authority-based scams.

Social Proof

According to the principle of social proof, we make a judgement about the type of behaviours that are acceptable or appropriate based on an observation of the behaviours of other similar people around us (Cialdini, 1993; Cialdini et al., 1999). We have explored some examples of social proof in the context of cyberloafing (see Chapters 11 and 12) where individuals will make a judgement about how acceptable their use of work-based technology is for personal reasons based on what other people around them are doing. If we view the behaviour to be acceptable, and colleagues are seen to be engaged in similar types of behaviour, then we will deem the behaviour okay to do.

Social proof can be initiated in a wide variety of ways and is often captured in several distinct ways, most of which can be captured in specific heuristics processes. For example, let us take the bandwagon effect (Schmitt-Beck, 2015). The heuristic is initiated when people engage in a particular behaviour or trend because everyone else in their reference groups (e.g., friends, colleagues, other online shoppers) is doing the same thing. The power of the bandwagon effect should be familiar to anyone who has viewed viral videos, or engaged in any TikTok related challenge, and the feeling to get involved because 'everyone else is doing it' is immense. The bandwagon effect also comes into play when individuals engage in buying specific brands of smartphones, usually because of the influence of their peers around them, or a particular app.

The power of the bandwagon effect means that it can also serve as a powerful influencing tactic that can be used in a wide variety of scams.

Investment frauds are a popular way of engaging the bandwagon effect where the cybercriminal will create the illusion of a successful opportunity to invest in something with the provision of testimonials or reviews from a wide range of people. Individuals are usually encouraged to invest because they see others making a profit, but usually there is no quick money to be made, and people lose their money. Other associated frauds that employ the use of the bandwagon effect are commonly seen on social media, where scammers will use the metrics available to them in terms of fake shares, fake comments, or fake likes to create an air of legitimacy to their current exploit. One common method to initiate this process is to create a fake give away where the scammer will use the tag line of 'Look at the thousands of winners who have already received their prizes', and this is usually supported by fake likes or fake comments from the 'winners'. The fraud relies on the individuals who fall foul of it to send a small amount of money for shipping to get their prize, and of course the prize never appears.

Conformity and Social Proof

The power of social proof is heavily reliant on another psychological construct that has been researched extensively in the field of social psychology, and that is conformity. Conformity is seen as an individual's tendency to change their behaviours to fit in with the norms or behaviours of the group, and it is the process that underlies why social proof is so powerful.

The research on conformity originated with the now famous piece of research conducted by Asch (1955, 1956, 1958) that showed individuals will sometimes alter their responses to match those of the majority, even though they believe that the group has made the wrong decision (Mori & Arai, 2010). The experiment collects a group of people together where everyone must make a judgement about matching a line with the length of three reference lines. The group is comprised of confederates of the researcher who have been instructed to respond incorrectly to the presented stimulus, and to present a unanimous group decision (Mori & Arai, 2010). In his research Asch noted that around 30% of the participants overrode their belief that they had made the right decision and instead conformed to the majority (Mori & Arai, 2010). The findings from Asch's original research have been replicated numerous times since (Franzen & Mader, 2023) showing that conformity is a robust and persistent psychological phenomenon. People will change their attitudes or behaviours to align with the group's expectations as they are influenced by the norms of that group environment – whether this be in a social or professional context.

Behaviours that are shared or performed by a group are viewed as appropriate and 'correct' behaviours, as they are representative of consensus within a group of individuals (Masland & Lease, 2013). In previous literature, it was indicated that conformity is normally driven by the desire to fit in, avoid conflict, or adhere to group expectations (Cialdini & Goldstein, 2004), and there are different factors that can affect conformity such as the group size, group cohesion and group unanimity – for example a small group can lead to a big conformity effect in comparison to when a group is larger (Zheng et al., 2021). It has also been found that individuals will exhibit more conformity behaviours when faced with high-ambiguity contexts (in comparison to low-ambiguity contexts), or when there was conflict between an individual's own opinion and the group's views (Chen et al., 2021).

In the process of conformity, there are two types of influence which attackers leverage to manipulate their victim's behaviour. The first is *normative* influence, which relies on our human need for social acceptance and desire to fit in, and occurs when an individual conforms to a group's behaviour or expectations, even if it does not align with their beliefs, or if they do not fully understand what is being asked of them. When it comes to cybercrime, attackers will create a situation where their victim feels pressure to comply with their request to avoid social judgment or rejection. This can be implicit in nature, that is, an individual acts or engages in a behaviour based on social norms. An example of this may be that a cybercriminal gains access to a company group email and pretends to be another employee of the company promoting a new 'productivity tool' which helps employees manage their tasks more effectively – and subtly implies that other people in the company have tried it or are already using it. In this case, the target may feel pressured to download the 'tool', because they are under the impression that it is becoming popular in the company, and do not want to feel left out of using it.

Normative influence can also be explicit in nature, whereby the pressure to conform is much more directly communicated, using language which plainly states what other people are doing, or suggests potential social consequences if a person is non-compliant in engaging with a particular action or behaviour. For example, the attacker may pose as someone from the HR department from a company and send a phishing email to employees about a 'mandatory security update' they need to do. In this email, they might also state that most of the employees in the company have already completed the update, and that failure to do so will lead to restricted access to the companies' facilities. In this case, the target may feel pressured to click the 'update' link to avoid social judgement or negative consequences (e.g., restricted access).

The second type of influence that attackers will leverage is *informational* influence, which is when an individual will conform in a situation where they believe that others possess more accurate information – especially when the situation is ambiguous or unfamiliar. This is known as social proof (and as we have seen, is one of the principles of persuasion) – though you may also know it more colloquially as 'herd mentality'. Cybercriminals will exploit this by emphasising uncertainty in their attack, for example by creating a sense of urgency to complete an action within a certain time limit. They may also exploit gaps in technical knowledge by using jargon which the victim may not understand, situating the attacker as an 'expert' and holding accurate information.

Liking/Similarity

It is human nature to be more receptive to people we know and like, and because of this, we tend to comply more with requests from such people, as doing so helps to maintain and strengthen social bonds. Cialdini (2007) showed that individuals who are rated as being more likeable are also seen to be more influential, with factors such as physical attractiveness or similarity being key determiners of likeableness (Guadagno et al., 2013). Work by Parsons et al. (2019) noted that liking was one of the most successful techniques in predicting an individual's likelihood to respond to a phishing email, behind the techniques of consistency and reciprocity.

In other work Guadagno et al. (2013) explored the role of the key pillars of influence on participants' willingness to volunteer time to a fictional event. They noted that in an online situation where the individuals were not engaged in more salient forms of interaction (e.g., verbal or face-to-face) the influence of likability was diminished and did not have a significant impact on participants' compliance. However other researchers have noted that individuals demonstrate an increased change in attitudes and a change in behavioural intentions when they are communicating with someone online that they like (Guadagno & Cialdini, 2002, 2007; Holzwarth et al., 2006; Muscanell et al., 2014).

The mechanics of liking come into play in a wide variety of online scams. Firstly, we have the 'Stranded Traveller' scam, which is usually initiated by email, and targets an individual in a spear-phishing attack. The victim will be approached via email by someone who purports to be their friend, stating they are currently stranded in a foreign country after some misfortune has befallen them (usually they have had their wallet stolen). The scammer will then proceed to ask the victim to send them money via transfer so that they can get tickets home. The scam is set up in a way that means the victim sends cash over to the scammer who is not of course a friend. The mechanism of liking is obvious here and relies on the existing friendship between the proposed target and the stranded traveller (Leamy & Hawkins, 2012; Muscanell et al., 2014). There are a variety of other scams that employ the element of liking to initiate the process of influence, such as the 'friend request' scam that is common to social media platforms such as Facebook. Usually, an individual will be approached with a friend request from someone who is an old friend. Once the request is accepted, the scammer will initiate a conversation with the victim that will usually discuss the benefits of engaging in a particular investment scheme that they themselves have also taken part in, encouraging the victim to part with their own money. Obviously, the investment scheme is completely fictitious, or perhaps another pyramid investment scheme where no one gets anything in return (Muscanell et al., 2014).

Commitment and Consistency

You want to be someone that people can depend on, and you also want to be seen as someone that is consistent in their treatment of others – this is the fundamental driver of the commitment and consistency process (Cialdini & Goldstein, 2004; Cialdini & Trost, 1998). If we are inconsistent in our behaviours this can be a red flag to others around us and will result in being socially excluded (Muscanell et al., 2014). Commitment can also bind individuals to behaviours in the future (think New Year's Resolutions) which in turn provides the mechanism for consistency to be demonstrated (Isenberg & Brauer, 2022). The concept of commitment and consistency is based in older research from the field of social psychology, particularly that of Festinger (1957) who noted that people tend to try to rationalise their inconsistency, or they engage in a process that means they must change their attitudes or beliefs. Obviously not having to go through this process is more favourable hence why people like to remain consistent with their beliefs and their behaviours (Festinger, 1957; Isenberg & Brauer, 2022).

The use of the commitment and consistency mechanic in scams is usually initiated by the foot-in-the-door technique (Burger, 1999; Dillard, 1991; Freedman & Fraser, 1966). The process usually follows a set pattern where the scammer will target an individual with a small, insignificant request. If the victim agrees to this initial request, the scammer will then follow up with a larger, more significant request. This technique is often used in online romance fraud, where an individual will be asked to give the scammer a small gift or small amount of money, and once they have engaged in that process the scammer will follow up with requests that increase in value (Anesa, 2020). Commitment and consistency are also used in social media posts that offer free vouchers for well-known supermarkets. The process asks people to share, like, or comment on posts on social media. However, the fraud progresses beyond this and engages individuals in increased time and money as well as the potential to hand over your personal details in the process (www.which.co.uk/news/article/beware-of-social-media-posts-offering -free-asda-and-tesco-vouchers-ae81E6P2rpPu). When individuals comment on the posts that are offering the prizes, they are then contacted by an external company not affiliated with the supermarkets in question. They are then engaged in a survey conducted via phone with the premise of verifying their account details – often the phone call takes a considerable amount of time and is to a premium phone number, therefore racking up additional costs.

The foot-in-the-door process can also be leveraged in the context of organisational fraud, particularly where individuals are initially approached for some personal information. In situations where individuals are presented with repeated requests for information, the amount of information they divulge increases exponentially (Fleming et al., 2023). Obviously, this can have a clear and significant impact on confidential information in the workplace, not only in terms of customer information, but also personal sensitive information that could be used to compromise work-based accounts.

Scarcity

The idea of not being able to have something or losing something that we could have had forms a powerful driver in the decisions that we make (Bullée et al., 2015). The concept has been well demonstrated in the field of health, where pamphlets that detail the potential losses of not engaging in a screening campaign have a more significant impact on patient sign-up compared to those that detail a potential gain (Bullée et al., 2015; Meyerowitz & Chaiken, 1987). We tend to perceive something as having more value when we think it's rare or of limited availability (i.e., scarce) and because of this, we will respond by wanting to have that item or 'thing' (e.g., the latest iPhone release, or Taylor Swift concert tickets!) as soon as it's available. With this principle, time constraints are normally used to persuade a buyer to buy a product before time runs out, and the product either sells out, or the price increases – for example, a scammer may send out emails stating, 'limited time offer!' or 'only a few spots left!'. This tactic also taps into a fear of missing out (FOMO) by driving individuals to act before they miss a 'scarce' opportunity. Due to the time-sensitive nature of this technique, victims are also less likely to step back and scrutinise the legitimacy of the offer.

In a review of the typical mechanisms that are used in phishing emails, Akbar (2014) noted that scarcity was used in just over 40% of the emails analysed, although there was no objective measurement of how successful such appeals were in getting people to comply with demand in the email. Morrow (2024) also noted that the use of the scarcity tactic featured highly in a corpus of 2300 emails that targeted higher education institutions, with Wright et al., (2014) noting that scarcity acted as one of the most effective influence techniques used in phishing emails.

Reciprocation

The process of reciprocation is well demonstrated in a study that was conducted by Regan (1971). The experiment is set up as follows:

Participants are invited to take part in judging entries in an art competition. Two individuals are asked to rate art, one being the participant and the other a confederate of the researcher; they both sit outside of a room waiting to go in to judge the art. There are two conditions – in one condition the confederate wanders off for a brief period, and when they return, they bring with them two drinks, one for the participant and one for the confederate. In the other condition the confederate does not perform any additional favours for the participant. After the judging session, the confederate delivers the coup de grace, which is a request for a small favour – would the participant mind buying some raffle tickets. In the condition where the confederate has done the participant the favour the participant purchases twice as many raffle tickets in comparison to the no favour condition; reciprocation can be quite a powerful driver in terms of influence!

A classic example of the principle of reciprocity is the door-in-the-face technique (Cialdini et al., 1975) which follows the premise that individuals are more likely to comply with a request if it comes after they have been presented with a much larger request previously. The initial request that is presented to individuals is impossible to fulfil but allows the individual making the request the freedom to follow up with a smaller request that is usually accepted (Cialdini et al., 1975). This technique differs from the normal mechanisms of influence as many of the others described here are based on a perception of attractiveness for the proposal, whereas the door-in-the-face technique relies on a contrast between the unattractiveness of the original request and the follow-up request (Mauny et al., 2023).

Social Engineering

> Only amateurs attack machines; professionals target people.
>
> *(Schneier, 2000)*

Social engineering is a catch-all term that is used to reference the use of psychological manipulation to get people to perform actions or behaviours without them being fully aware that they are being manipulated. The key tactics involved are those that we have discussed in the preceding part of this chapter, and these form the essential weapons that equip many scammers to do their daily work. In comparison to more 'traditional' hacking that is seen to employ more technical methods of infiltrating a system, social engineering leverages psychological manipulation to reveal sensitive information (whether this be personal or organisational information), to perform actions which allow the attacker to gain access to systems. Many individuals refer to social engineering as 'hacking the human' to reflect the similarity to the process of using backdoors or flaws in software to access a physical system, and the tactics employed by social engineers seek to leverage the same flaws in human psychology.

Social engineering has a wide range of implications for those who have the onerous task of protecting information systems from security breaches, and adds another layer of susceptibility to organisational cybersecurity (Salahdine & Kaabouch, 2019). The previous focus for much of the development of cybersecurity has been extensively based around the provision of technical measures designed to protect systems. However, as you may be aware because you are reading this book, these technical measures become inert when we engage in the process of social engineering.

When it comes to social engineering, researchers have noted that most attacks will follow a common pattern of four phases (Gallegos-Segovia et al., 2017; Salahdine & Kaabouch, 2019):

1. Collect information about the target: The attacker attempts to research and gather as much information about the target either via websites, physical interactions, or public documents. However, one of the most easily accessible places an attacker can gather information about an individual is social networking sites such as Instagram or Facebook. Self-disclosure on social media has been demonstrated to have a clear impact on cybersecurity and privacy risks, with the key reason behind this being that it makes more information available to the social engineer (Calic et al., 2018).
2. Building trust: The attacker will try to find a way to 'hook' the target (e.g., by starting a conversation), and begin building a trust relationship with the victim. Trust has been demonstrated to be a key facilitator in the process of self-disclosure (Calic et al., 2018) and researchers have noted that participants who reported a greater potential to trust were also more likely to share personally sensitive information, such as family names and places of birth (Tait & Jeske, 2015).
3. Exploitation and play: Once trust has been built, the attacker exploits this by manipulating the victim to perform actions or give information requests, to set up the execution of the attack.
4. Ending/exit: In the final phase, the attacker executes their attack and exits with no traces.

There are several different variations for the way in which social engineering will take place, but usually they will follow the set pattern detailed above. Sometimes the elements of influence will be implemented it a more ad hoc way, where some elements of the framework will be utilised in a less structured way, usually as part of a more general phishing email attack.

Marking Your Target

Picking a target to exploit as part of a social engineering attack can also be something of a meticulously crafted art. Steinmetz (2022) interviewed social engineers and explored the way in which they extract information to create a profile of the perfect target. The work suggested that social engineers employ the use of heuristic principles and traits to allow them to identify the best target. These shortcuts included looking at age and gender, where younger individuals are more likely to comply with authority, and are more likely to have a larger online footprint due to a preference to engage in social media. It was also noted that they were more likely to go after men, but use a female to engage in the demands, as they noted this yielded more compliance.

In terms of traits, those questioned by Steinmetz (2022) noted that those who were unconcerned with their potential to be targeted by social engineering tactics presented an ideal mark. Typically, these are people who are passive, complacent, and display a general apathy to their online security as well as having an unwillingness to engage in more meaningful and critical analysis of situations (Steinmetz, 2022). They also noted that a distracted target makes a good target, and this is borne out by the research we have explored earlier in terms of the limitations of the human information processing system. Those people who are outgoing also present an opportunity to engage them in social engineering attacks. Friendly people are more likely to exhibit qualities that align well to social proof, reciprocity, and liking, making them easier to engage and to establish a rapport with, meaning that trust can be established easily between them and the social engineer (Steinmetz, 2022). Social engineers avoid the unhelpful, the rude, the grumpy, or the jaded – none of these are traits that facilitate trust or allow the capacity for the key mechanics of influence to be engaged easily.

Mitigation Strategies

So, as we noted at the start of this chapter, there is an extremely easy way of mitigating the threat from social engineering, and that is to be aware of the tactics that are employed as part of an attack. For example, Sagarin and Mitnick (2012) noted that teaching individuals about the potential techniques that could be used as part of a social engineering attack can and does decrease their likelihood of being vulnerable to these types of attacks. Steinmetz (2022) undertook a unique piece of research which presented the results of interviews conducted with social engineers, and they discussed the methods they use to engage their perfect target. One of the key traits they looked for in their exploration of potential targets was being uninformed about the potential risks of social engineering, either through a lack of training or through ignorance. The most common target in this instance was the new hire, who typically does not know the correct internal processes and procedures and is less likely to know who to approach if something does go wrong. They are also keener to impress authority, which means this element of influence can also be leveraged to get them to comply with demands (Steinmetz, 2022).

Muscanell et al. (2014) noted that for each of the core pillars of influence detailed above there are relevant tactics that can be employed by individuals to overcome the threat posed. For example, for liking, they suggest the best defence against this is to attempt to separate the request that is being made from the individual who is making that request. They suggest that a good prompt to ask yourself in these situations is to reflect on the 'Would I say yes to this request if someone else was making it?' This makes a lot of sense, but the actual application of this process may prove trickier that it first appears, especially as the mechanics of social engineering and influence can and do act in concert, meaning that other aspects such as scarcity could serve to undermine a more protracted consideration. Implementing a series of questions that can be employed by individuals as part of the checks they do when responding to emails could be feasible, but the mechanisms suggested by Muscanell et al. (2014) offer no objective data on how successful this self-reflective style of questioning is when it comes to countering the threat posed by social engineering tactics. As mentioned above, the key facet of preventing people from falling foul of these types of attacks is to give them the relevant information in a palatable format that shows them the potential dangers that can come from social engineering attacks. We would suggest moving towards an integrated process that incorporates aspects of cybersecurity judgement (see Chapter 14) where individuals are afforded the freedom to explore the potential results of their decisions in the context of attacks that employ the use of social engineering mechanics and scaffold learning around the errors of judgement or faulty decision-making processes.

Summary

The psychology of individuals plays a crucial role in shaping their responses to cybersecurity incidents. Attackers often exploit cognitive processes and social norms to execute their scams, taking advantage of the fact that humans, like unpatched systems, can be manipulated through predictable behaviours. Psychological tactics used in cybercrime often fall into the categories of influence and persuasion, with scammers continuously refining their methods to exploit these human vulnerabilities.

One foundational concept is the fixed action patterns, which are automatic behaviours triggered by specific stimuli. While humans are more complex, they still exhibit predictable behaviours influenced by cognitive biases and heuristics. For instance, the bystander effect can lead individuals to downplay the seriousness of a cybersecurity threat if others around them do not react. Heuristics, while useful for everyday decisions, can lead to poor choices in cybersecurity contexts, making individuals susceptible to scams.

Influence and persuasion tactics are central to many cybercrimes. Cialdini's principles of persuasion – authority, social proof, liking, commitment and consistency, scarcity, and reciprocation – are frequently leveraged by attackers. Authority figures, whether real or impersonated, can compel individuals to comply with requests, as seen in CEO fraud spear-phishing attacks. Social proof and conformity drive individuals to follow the behaviours of others, making them more likely to fall for scams that appear popular or endorsed by peers.

Liking and similarity are exploited in scams where attackers pose as friends or trusted contacts, leveraging existing relationships to gain compliance. Commitment and consistency are used in techniques like the foot-in-the-door method, where small initial requests lead to larger ones. Scarcity creates a sense of urgency, compelling individuals to act quickly without scrutinizing the legitimacy of the offer. Reciprocation, where individuals feel obliged to return favours, can also be manipulated to extract information or compliance.

Social engineering, a form of psychological manipulation, is a key tactic in cybercrime. It involves building trust with the target and then exploiting that trust to achieve the attacker's goals. Social engineers meticulously profile their targets, looking for traits such as passivity, distraction, and a lack of awareness about social engineering risks. They avoid targets who are unhelpful or sceptical, focusing instead on those who are more likely to comply.

Mitigating the threat of social engineering involves educating individuals about these tactics and encouraging critical thinking. Awareness and training can significantly reduce vulnerability to these attacks. By understanding the psychological foundations of cybercrime, individuals can better recognise and resist manipulation, enhancing their overall cybersecurity posture.

References

Akbar, N. (2014). *Analysing persuasion principles in phishing emails* (Master's thesis). University of Twente.

Algarni, A. A. M. G. (2014). Social engineering in social networking sites: How good becomes evil. In AIS (Ed.), *Proceedings of the 18th Pacific Asia Conference on Information Systems (PACIS)* (pp. 1–10). Association for Information Systems (AIS).

Anesa, P. (2020). Lovextortion: Persuasion strategies in romance cybercrime. *Discourse, Context & Media*, 35, 100398. doi:10.1016/j.dcm.2020.100398.

Asch, S. E. (1955). Opinions and social pressure. *Scientific American*, 193(5), 31–35. doi:10.1038/scientificamerican1155-31.

Asch, S. E. (1956). Studies of independence and conformity: I. A minority of one against a unanimous majority. *Psychological Monographs: General and Applied*, 70 (9), 1–70. doi:10.1037/h0093718.

Asch, S. E. (1958). Effects of group pressure upon modification and distortion of judgments. In E. E. Maccoby, T. M. Newcomb, & E. L. Hartley (Eds.), *Readings in social psychology* (3rd ed.). Holt, Reinhart & Winston.

Attrill-Smith, A., & Wesson, C. (2020). The psychology of cybercrime. In T. J. Holt & A. M. Bossler (Eds.), *The Palgrave handbook of international cybercrime and cyberdeviance* (pp. 653–678). Springer.

Bullée, J.-W. H., Montoya, L., Pieters, W., Junger, M., & Hartel, P. H. (2015). The persuasion and security awareness experiment: Reducing the success of social engineering attacks. *Journal of Experimental Criminology*, 11(1), 97–115. doi:10.1007/s11292-014-9222-7.

Burger, J. M. (1999). The foot-in-the-door compliance procedure: A multiple-process analysis and review. *Personality and Social Psychology Review: An Official Journal of the Society for Personality and Social Psychology*, 3(4), 303–325. doi:10.1207/s15327957pspr0304_2.

Burger, J. M. (2009). Replicating Milgram: Would people still obey today? *American Psychologist*, 64(1), 1–11. doi:10.1037/a0010932.

Bushman, B. J. (1984). Perceived symbols of authority and their influence on compliance. *Journal of Applied Social Psychology*, 14(6), 501–508. doi:10.1111/j.1559-1816.1984.tb02255.x.

Calic, D., Brushe, M., Parsons, K., & Brittain, C. (2018). Self-disclosing on Facebook can be risky: Examining the role of trust and social capital. *HAISA*, 225–235.

Chen, X., Liu, J., Luo, Y., & Feng, C. (2021). Brain systems underlying fundamental motivations of human social conformity. *Neuroscience Bulletin*, 37(10), 1361–1372. doi:10.1007/s12264-022-00960-4.

Cialdini, R. B. (1993). *Influence: Science and practice* (3rd ed.). HarperCollins College Publishers.

Cialdini, R. B. (2007). *Influence: The psychology of persuasion* (Rev. ed.). Collins.

Cialdini, R. B., & Goldstein, N. J. (2004). Social influence: Compliance and conformity. *Annual Review of Psychology*, 55, 591–621. doi:10.1146/annurev.psych.55.090902.142015.

Cialdini, R. B., & Trost, M. R. (1998). Social influence: Social norms, conformity and compliance. In D. T. Gilbert, S. T. Fiske, & G. Lindzey (Eds), *The handbook of social psychology* (Vols. 1–2, 4th ed., pp. 151–192). McGraw-Hill.

Cialdini, R. B., Vincent, J. E., Lewis, S. K., Catalan, J., Wheeler, D., & Darby, B. L. (1975). Reciprocal concessions procedure for inducing compliance: The door-in-the-face technique. *Journal of Personality and Social Psychology*, 31(2), 206–215. doi:10.1037/h0076284.

Cialdini, R. B., Wosinska, W., Barrett, D. W., Butner, J., & Gornik-Durose, M. (1999). Compliance with a request in two cultures: The differential influence of social proof and commitment/consistency on collectivists and individualists. *Personality and Social Psychology Bulletin*, 25(10), 1242–1253. doi:10.1177/0146167299258006.

Dillard, J. P. (1991). The current status of research on sequential-request compliance techniques. *Personality and Social Psychology Bulletin*, 17(3), 283–288. doi:10.1177/0146167291173008.

Festinger, L. (1957). *A theory of cognitive dissonance*. Row, Peterson.

Fischer, P., Krueger, J. I., Greitemeyer, T., Vogrincic, C., Kastenmüller, A., Frey, D., ... Kainbacher, M. (2011). The bystander-effect: A meta-analytic review on bystander intervention in dangerous and non-dangerous emergencies. *Psychological Bulletin*, 137(4), 517–537. doi:10.1037/a0023304.

Fiske, S. T., & Taylor, S. E. (1991). *Social cognition* (2nd ed.). McGraw-Hill.

Fleming, P., Edwards, S. G., Bayliss, A. P., & Seger, C. R. (2023). Tell me more, tell me more: Repeated personal data requests increase disclosure. *Journal of Cybersecurity*, 9(1), tyad005. doi:10.1093/cybsec/tyad005.

Franzen, A., & Mader, S. (2023). The power of social influence: A replication and extension of the Asch experiment. *PloS One*, 18(11), e0294325. doi:10.1371/journal.pone.0294325.

Freedman, J. L., & Fraser, S. C. (1966). Compliance without pressure: The foot-in-the-door technique. *Journal of Personality and Social Psychology*, 4(2), 195–202. doi:10.1037/h0023552.

Gallegos-Segovia, P. L., Bravo-Torres, J. F., Larios-Rosillo, V. M., Vintimilla-Tapia, P. E., Yuquilima-Albarado, I. F., & Jara-Saltos, J. D. (2017). Social engineering as an attack vector for ransomware. *2017 CHILEAN Conference on Electrical, Electronics Engineering, Information and Communication Technologies (CHILECON)*, 1–6. doi:10.1109/CHILECON.2017.8229528.

Guadagno, R. E., & Cialdini, R. B. (2002). Online persuasion: An examination of gender differences in computer-mediated interpersonal influence. *Group Dynamics: Theory, Research, and Practice*, 6(1), 38–51. doi:10.1037/1089-2699.6.1.38.

Guadagno, R. E., & Cialdini, R. B. (2007). Persuade him by email, but see her in person: Online persuasion revisited. *Computers in Human Behavior*, 23(2), 999–1015. doi:10.1016/j.chb.2005.08.006.

Guadagno, R. E., Muscanell, N. L., Rice, L. M., & Roberts, N. (2013). Social influence online: The impact of social validation and likability on compliance. *Psychology of Popular Media Culture*, 2(1), 51–60. doi:10.1037/a0030592.

Holzwarth, M., Janiszewski, C., & Neumann, M. M. (2006). The influence of avatars on online consumer shopping behavior. *Journal of Marketing*, 70(4), 19–36. doi:10.1509/jmkg.70.4.19.

Isenberg, N., & Brauer, M. (2022). *Commitment and consistency*. Routledge. doi:10.4324/9780367198459-REPRW126-1.

Jansson, K., & von Solms, R. (2010). Social engineering: Towards a holistic solution. *SAISMC*. www.semanticscholar.org/paper/Social-Engineering%3A-Towards-A-Holistic-Solution-Jansson-Solms/4089c6a6fb3403c5e32d007f316935ebafe73f9a.

Key, M. S., Edlund, J. E., Sagarin, B. J., & Bizer, G. Y. (2009). Individual differences in susceptibility to mindlessness. *Personality and Individual Differences*, 46(3), 261–264. doi:10.1016/j.paid.2008.10.001.

Langer, E. J., Blank, A., & Chanowitz, B. (1978). The mindlessness of ostensibly thoughtful action: The role of 'placebic' information in interpersonal interaction. *Journal of Personality and Social Psychology*, 36(6), 635–642.

Leamy, E., & Hawkins, S. (2012, July 13). 'Stranded traveler' scam hacks victims' emails, asks their contacts for money. *ABC News*. http://abcnews.go.com/Technology/stranded-traveler-scam-hacks-victims-emails-asks-contacts/story?id=16774896

Masland, L. C., & Lease, A. M. (2013). Effects of achievement motivation, social identity, and peer group norms on academic conformity. *Social Psychology of Education: An International Journal*, 16(4), 661–681. doi:10.1007/s11218-013-9236-4.

Mauny, N., Mange, J., Mortier, A., Somat, A., & Sénémeaud, C. (2023). When a refusal turns into donation: The moderating effect of the initial position toward blood donation in the door-in-the-face effectiveness. *The Journal of Social Psychology*, 163(2), 212–229. doi:10.1080/00224545.2022.2043815.

Meyerowitz, B. E., & Chaiken, S. (1987). The effect of message framing on breast self-examination attitudes, intentions, and behavior. *Journal of Personality and Social Psychology*, 52(3), 500–510. doi:10.1037/0022-3514.52.3.500.

Milgram, S. (1963). Behavioral study of obedience. *The Journal of Abnormal and Social Psychology*, 67(4), 371–378. doi:10.1037/h0040525.

Miller, A. G., Collins, B. E., & Brief, D. E. (1995). Perspectives on obedience to authority: The legacy of the Milgram experiments. *Journal of Social Issues*, 51(3), 1–19. doi:10.1111/j.1540-4560.1995.tb01331.x.

Mori, K., & Arai, M. (2010). No need to fake it: Reproduction of the Asch experiment without confederates. *International Journal of Psychology*, 45(5), 390–397. doi:10.1080/00207591003774485.

Morrow, E. (2024). Scamming higher ed: An analysis of phishing content and trends. *Computers in Human Behavior*, 158, 108274.

Muscanell, N. L., Guadagno, R. E., & Murphy, S. (2014). Weapons of influence misused: A social influence analysis of why people fall prey to internet scams. *Social and Personality Psychology Compass*, 8(7), 388–396. doi:10.1111/spc3.12115.

Naidoo, R. (2020). A multi-level influence model of COVID-19 themed cybercrime. *European Journal of Information Systems*, 29(3), 306–321. doi:10.

Parsons, K., Butavicius, M., Delfabbro, P., & Lillie, M. (2019). Predicting susceptibility to social influence in phishing emails. *International Journal of Human-Computer Studies*, 128, 17–26. doi:10.1016/j.ijhcs.2019.02.007.

Regan, D. T. (1971). Effects of a favor and liking on compliance. *Journal of Experimental Social Psychology*, 7(6), 627–639. doi:10.1016/0022-1031(71)90025–90024.

Sagarin, B. J., & Mitnick, K. D. (2012). The path of least resistance. In D. T. Kenrick, N. J. Goldstein, & S. L. Braver (Eds.), *Six degrees of social influence: Science, application, and the psychology of Robert Cialdini*. Oxford University Press. doi:10.1093/acprof:osobl/9780199743056.003.0003.

Salahdine, F., & Kaabouch, N. (2019). Social engineering attacks: A survey. *Future Internet*, 11(4), Article4. doi:10.3390/fi11040089.

Schmitt-Beck, R. (2015). Bandwagon effect. In G. Mazzoleni (Ed.), *The international encyclopaedia of political communication*. John Wiley & Sons. doi:10.1002/9781118541555.wbiepc015.

Schneier, B. (2000). Semantic attacks: The third wave of network attacks. *Cryptogram Newsletter*. www.schneier.com.

Serman, Z. E., & Sims, J. (2022). Source credibility theory: SME hospitality sector blog posting during the Covid-19 pandemic. *Information Systems Frontiers: A Journal of Research and Innovation*, 1–18. doi:10.1007/s10796-022-10349-3.

Slater, M., Antley, A., Davison, A., Swapp, D., Guger, C., Barker, C., … Sanchez-Vives, M. V. (2006). A virtual reprise of the Stanley Milgram obedience experiments. *PloS One*, 1(1), e39. doi:10.1371/journal.pone.0000039.

Snyder, M. (1974). Self-monitoring of expressive behavior. *Journal of Personality and Social Psychology*, 30(4), 526–537. doi:10.1037/h0037039.

Snyder, M., & Gangestad, S. (1986). On the nature of self-monitoring: Matters of assessment, matters of validity. *Journal of Personality and Social Psychology*, 51(1), 125–139. doi:10.1037/0022-3514.51.1.125.

Steinmetz, K. F. (2022). The identification of a model victim for social engineering: A qualitative analysis. In D. Rebovich & J. M. Byrne (Eds), *The new technology of financial crime* (pp. 213–237). Routledge.

Tait, S. E., & Jeske, D. (2015). Hello stranger! Trust and self-disclosure effects on online information sharing. *International Journal of Cyber Behavior, Psychology and Learning (IJCBPL)*, 5(1), 42–55.

Uebelacker, S., & Quiel, S. (2014). The social engineering personality framework. *2014 Workshop on Socio-Technical Aspects in Security and Trust*, 24–30. doi:10.1109/STAST.2014.12.

Widdowson, A. J., & Goodliff, P. B. (2015). CHEAT: An approach to incorporating human factors in cyber security assessments. *IET Conference Proceedings*, 5. www.researchgate.net/profile/Amanda-Widdowson-2/publication/311606003_CHEAT_an_approach_to_incorporating_human_factors_in_cyber_security_assessments/links/5fae4921a6fdcc9389b20120/CHEAT-an-approach-to-incorporating-human-factors-in-cyber-security-assessments.pdf.

Wright, R. T., Jensen, M. L., Thatcher, J. B., Dinger, M., & Marett, K. (2014). Research note – Influence techniques in phishing attacks: An examination of vulnerability and resistance. *Information Systems Research*, 25(2), 385–400. doi:10.1287/isre.2014.0522.

Zheng, J., Hu, L., Li, L., Shen, Q., & Wang, L. (2021). Confidence modulates the conformity behavior of the investors and neural responses of social influence in crowdfunding. *Frontiers in Human Neuroscience*, 15, 766908. doi:10.3389/fnhum.2021.766908.

14

THE FINAL FRONTIER

Introduction

Well, the title for this chapter is a little dramatic and rightly so. In this chapter we attempt to bring together all the bits we have discussed in the rest of the book and try to form some clear suggestions about how to tackle the individuating factors that makes the human factors approach so interesting, but also at the same time so complicated. At the very start of this book, we set out to examine how the human factors paradigm could be applied to the field of information security awareness, and in the intersecting chapters we have explored a wide variety of factors, both individual and situational, that can serve to influence adherence to cybersecurity policies and rules. Now we understand that many people who have read this book will be searching for answers to a lot of questions, and most of these will surround one central, pivotal objective – how do I get my employees to engage in cybersecurity awareness? Well, if we had the answer to that question, we would be setting up our own consultancy business and earning millions selling the best cybersecurity products the market had ever seen. However, the answer is never as straightforward as one might think, and there is no magic silver bullet that will deal with employee disengagement from cybersecurity policies. Training forms just one part of the process and is often erroneously seen as the key mechanism that will serve to prevent all the woes of organisations' CISOs. However, as we have seen from the research, training is only one part of the equation when it comes to cybersecurity. You cannot train people to be better humans, you cannot train out biases and heuristics, and you cannot improve the cognitive processes that underlie a lot of the decision-making and attentional processes that govern our day-to-day engagement with cybersecurity. You can bring an awareness to individuals about these things,

DOI: 10.4324/9781003509011-14

which can in turn help them to understand the issues they may bring to cybersecurity. So, in this chapter we will try to bring the book to a (sort of) conclusion by trying to impart some of the things that we have learned from experience and some of the elements we can bring in from research. When we say a sort of conclusion, the movements that shape cybersecurity mean that some elements we talk about may become outdated or may be superseded by other theories, but hopefully the things that we talk about will give professionals, practitioners, and those interested in the field of human factors a good basis to move forward.

Training

There are numerous different forms of training that have been designed and implemented to raise the awareness of employees when it comes to cybersecurity. Some are better designed that others; some are just generic tick boxes in an extensive list of compliance factors that organisations must complete (e.g., regulatory rules, ethical standards, risk mitigation strategies). The breadth of training types that come into play when we look at cybersecurity is immense, and to cover each in sufficient depth and detail would take up most of this book. Instead, we will summarise the key types that have been well documented in the research literature and explore their relative merits alongside some of the detracting elements that accompany each. One of the key things that has been noted from the research reviewing the design of interventions is the sheer number of products that lack any significant basis in theory (Prummer et al., 2024). As we have seen in the context of our journey through the chapters in this book, the human factors approach to cybersecurity is not straightforward and stands outside of a common-sense approach to training, something that Prummer et al. (2024) are also keen to point out. We feel that this is one of the most frustrating elements of current training provision, particularly where multiple organisations sell products that claim to have a clear underlying basis in established theory, but once you delve a little deeper, such theoretical underpinnings are limited or non-existent.

Prummer et al. (2024) presented a review of current cybersecurity training methods and highlighted that the most frequently mentioned training methods were game-based training, presentation-based training, simulation-based training, information-based training, video-based training, text-based training, and discussion-based training. Game-based training was seen as the most frequently employed and often the most effective in improving cybersecurity awareness and behaviours. Game-based training and simulation methods often yielded more consistent ratings when it came to the retention of information and were also seen as being more engaging. Simulated phishing attacks where participants are presented with immediate feedback are also seen as being particularly effective when it comes to reducing risky behaviours in these circumstances, and these fit into the feedback processes detailed in the previous chapter when looking at TPB and PMT. Other training mechanics employed involved presentation methods such as lectures and seminars. The provision to using these types of methods is that they must be well structured and clearly presented and have a clear link back to theoretical underpinnings (Prummer et al., 2024). If these conditions are met, improvements in both knowledge and awareness can be observed. Prummer et al. (2024) noted that in the studies they reviewed, using this form of training method resulted in significant changes in phishing detection skills. Both text and video-based training are often the mainstays of organisation cybersecurity training and can be seen integrated in online courses and e-learning packages. Prummer et al. (2024) noted that such training methods are less effective in comparison to more interactive methods when it comes to engaging individuals and often result in limited retention of information. They are also view less favourably when compared to other approaches such as game-based methods.

One of the key findings to be drawn out of the review by Prummer et al. (2024) was that there were a wide variety of limitations associated with the training methods employed in cybersecurity awareness. Primarily most of studies focused on small populations that were not comparable to larger scale organisations, and many used undergraduate students as participants. Whilst using students is a usual and accepted practice for a great deal of research, in this context where we are assessing the capacity of workers to engage in learning material it may not be the most productive or ecologically valid approach. Primarily, students are already used to learning and engaging in a wide variety of different presentation methods, so they may already be primed to have certain preferences for different forms of presentation methods. Learning is also their primary goal when they engage in their studies and they have no main job role to fulfil, unlike employees who often have primary job roles to carry out in addition to cybersecurity training and awareness. The other aspect of the work that has been done exploring training provision in cybersecurity is that many of the studies examined training effectiveness over a brief period, usually within the space of a few months, rather than longer term effectiveness. By gaining a better understanding of the effectiveness of different methods, employers can base their decisions to implement certain training methods on a more cost-benefit basis.

Gamification

Gamification is a concept that has been widely explored in several different settings and involves engaging an individual's predisposition to engage in games and gaming. As such, the approach serves to use similar methods and mechanisms to those employed in more traditional video games to get people to engage in real-world activities (Kappen & Nacke, 2013; Larson, 2020; Ong,

2013). The concept of gamification stretches into the realm of 'serious games', or those that are designed for purposes that stretch beyond pure entertainment (Azadegan et al., 2012). Deterding et al. (2011) defined gamification as 'the use of video game elements in non-gaming systems to improve user experience and user engagement' (p. 11). The use of gaming mechanics or features for use in aspects of employee training and engagement has become extremely popular (Deterding et al., 2011). Mechanics such as 'levelling up', where people progress onto further, more advanced stages of a system after they have completed certain activities or quizzes, or beaten end-of-level bosses (this usually involves completing some form of multiple-choice test or quiz) have often been implemented. The extent to which gamification provides positive effects on training and learning depends on a vast number of different underlying variables, including the context in which it is being used and the users who are being targeted by its use (Hamari et al., 2014). Researchers have noted that gamification-based learning sessions lead to higher levels of behavioural and emotional engagement, above those of traditional lecture-based learning or multiple quiz type sessions (Thomas & Baral, 2022). Thomas and Baral (2022) suggested that this process was mediated by the involvement of the process of 'flow', commonly thought of as 'being in the zone' when doing a task such as learning (Thomas & Baral, 2022). They suggested that gamification environments lead to better engagement because they lead to the psychological state of flow which is typically viewed as a sensation of being completely absorbed in a task or situation (Csikszentmihalyi, 1975). Flow has been widely explored in the video game environment and has been linked to the positive experiences an individual has when playing such games (Hoffman & Novak, 1996; Nah et al., 2014; Quinn, 2005).

Gamification Mechanics

Gamification borrows elements from video gaming to enhance an individual's experience of a real-world activity and increases their motivation to engage in specific activities or tasks. There are a wide range of specific mechanisms that can be used to accomplish this, including the use of points-based systems, leaderboards, achievements and badges, levels and levelling up, and rewards (Hamari et al., 2014). Indeed Marczewski (2018) noted no less than 52 individual mechanics and elements that have been employed in a variety of gamification contexts. The most common elements that are used are points, badges, and leaderboards (Koivisto & Hamari, 2019). Points refer to numerical tokens that are awarded to people for completing tasks or performing well, and the leaderboard uses these points to represent an individual's ranking within the gaming world alongside other individuals within the same environment (Ferro, 2021). Badges are visual representations that display an achievement that has been obtained within the gaming environment, such as completing a particular task or objective (Ferro, 2021).

Gamification and Cybersecurity

There have been numerous attempts to leverage the power of gamification in cybersecurity awareness (e.g., Brady & M'manga, 2022; Carreiro et al., 2024; Diakoumakos et al., 2025; Filipczuk et al., 2019; Malone et al., 2021; Scholefield & Shepherd, 2019). It has been noted that gamification can serve to significantly boost employee engagement and motivation to engage in certain aspects of cybersecurity, but such schemes need to be personalised and targeted (Shahzadi et al., 2025). DeCarlo (2017) presented findings which focused on the use of gamification-based training strategies for knowledge retention and the frequency of internal compromises in a health-care setting. This research compared results across three different conditions, these being a gamification-style learning environment, a traditional learning environment (audio recording with slide deck) and no specific learning environment. Participants were tested on both pre- and post-training knowledge, and the results demonstrated that those in the gamified group scored significantly higher than those in the other two test conditions. The results further noted that the gamification groups also experienced the lowest number of security incidents over the two-month period after the training had taken place. This is useful information to have, as it shows that this form of training has longevity in terms of its impact on employee engagement with cybersecurity rules and behaviours. Other researchers have noted that employing the use of gamification strategies in cybersecurity awareness can be effective in making the topic more interesting, particularly to those who do not have any in-depth technical knowledge (Gwenhure & Rahayu, 2024). However, in their review of the research that has been conducted in the area, Gwenhure and Rahayu (2024) noted that most of the findings showed that gamification strategies results in mostly short-term engagement in cybersecurity awareness, and there was no substantive evidence that longer term engagement resulted from the training. Gwenhure and Rahayu (2024) noted that in most of the cases they had studied, the observed positive influence of the gamification strategies employed usually lasted just a few months. Obviously for many organisations this will have some cost-benefit implications attached to it and should be a key consideration for implementing these strategies over the lifetime of an organisation's cybersecurity programme.

Barriers to Implementation of Gamification

It has been noted that companies often seek to engage in the use of gamification because of the perceived popularity of the term and attempt to introduce elements of games and associated terminology in the workplace but then lack the capacity to support the framework which in turn fails to make the gamification approach less appealing (Landers, 2014, 2019; Larson, 2020). Poor design elements mean that companies often fail to engage the needs and wants of employees when it comes to the relevance of the engaging elements or the rewards that are being offered to participants (Larson, 2020). There can also be a perceived lack of continuity between the needs of the business and the goals of the gamification process, as well as the perceived goals for the employees for engaging in the gamification process, which overall results in a very inefficient use of time and resources (Callan et al., 2015). It is important to understand that gamification is not a one-size-fits-all approach and there are a lot of issues we need to explore when trying to initiative such frameworks. For example, as noted by Larson (2020), organisations are multifaceted and diverse – they are multicultural and multigenerational, and each person brings with them a diverse range of psychological and emotional needs when it comes to motivation to engage in elements such as gamification. For example, males are seen to have preferences for games that are competitive and aggressive in nature, whereas females are more likely to engage in games that support more social elements and relationship forming (Larson, 2020). Younger workers are more orientated towards reward-based and task-driven games, whereas older workers are more motivated by social facets of games but are also less likely to engage in gamification overall (Larson, 2020). Finally cultural differences also serve to influence engagement in gamification because they attach different meanings to achievements, as well as differing in terms of their motivation to engage in gamification (Larson, 2020).

Behavioural Nudges

What is a behavioural nudge? This concept was introduced by Thaler and Sunstein (2008, p. 6) who defined a nudge as 'any aspect of the choice architecture that alters people's behaviour in a predictable way without forbidding any options or significantly changing their economic incentives'. Choice architecture is just another way of saying the situation or context in which an individual decides, and a nudge is a mechanism that allows us to push an individual in the preferred direction without engaging in any form of coercion or pressuring them away from another choice (Damgaard & Nielsen, 2017; Damgaard, 2020).

There are a wide variety of forms of behavioural nudges, and each can interact with the individual on several distinct levels while tapping into the underlying psychology of influence. We have highlighted the main ones here and make some links to the cybersecurity awareness field to show how they might be used.

- **Defaults**: This nudge automatically sets the desired or most beneficial option as the default one, but still allows the individual the opportunity to opt out of that choice. These default nudges are seen to influence behaviour because they require less energy and effort from the end user and because people tend to go with the default option (Lemken, 2024; Von Bergen & Miles, 2015).

- **Commitment Devices**: Are you the type of person who lacks follow-through when it comes to doing something? Do you like to procrastinate patholo- gically when it comes to looming deadlines? The use of commitment devices could serve to help you! Commitment devices are a tool or strategy that encourages someone to stick to their future goals by creating some form of psychological incentive to follow through (Damgaard & Nielsen, 2017). As these are part of the behavioural nudges process, they are self-imposed mechanisms that an individual agrees to themselves (e.g., if you are losing weight, you make a target of losing X amount by a certain date). Commit- ment devices can in turn take a variety of forms, such as pre-commitment contracts where an individual will make a statement about some action they will take in the future (Bryan et al., 2010; Derksen et al., 2021; Rogers et al., 2014). This could be an individual signing up to a pledge that they will follow best practice when it comes to trying to detect and report suspicious emails in work over the next six months.

Goal-tracking is another useful commitment device and is often used in health-related behaviours where individuals will track their progress on their way to their goal with the use of manageable sub-goals (e.g., training for a marathon, you track your progress from 0 km to full distance). Time-limited constraints linked to behaviours can also be implemented as commitment devices, such as the tried and tested 'your password will expire in X number of days, please change it now'. The usual mechanism used here is that non- compliance will result in the individual being locked out of the system until they change their password, hence they are nudged towards that behaviour. The good thing about commitment is that although they require individuals to buy into the process, this process can yield results in terms of engagement. Commitment devices also offer specific and clear goals against which an individual behaviour can be measured without ambiguity creeping into the process (you either fulfilled the commitment or you did not, easy as that). They are also incredibly hard from a psychological perspective to reverse, and backing out of a commitment device often involves some tangible impact on the individual, usually in terms of damage to self-esteem or per- ceived self-efficacy. Commitment devices are particularly useful for cyberse- curity awareness because much of what we ask individuals to do in this context is outside of their normal work life pattern, so they might forget or be complacent – by adding in a commitment to do something they will find it harder to overlook that behaviour, therefore encouraging it to become part of their normal work life activities.

- **Providing Accessible Information**: Providing individuals with information in a more accessible and understandable way is another mechanism for introducing nudges. One of the key criticisms that have been levied at cybersecurity protocols often employed by organisations is that the information presented to end users is overly complex and technical (e.g., Grobler et al., 2021; Nurse et al., 2011), so simplifying the information people get would seem like an effective way of encouraging positive behaviours. This can take several forms, including:

a   Reminders: Presenting people with informative reminders that alert them to a risk or to act when their attention might be directed elsewhere. Many email clients have explicit warning reminders that are pasted somewhere into the body of emails that come from external email addresses to remind individuals that such information could contain malicious links or may not be subject to the same security requirements as internally generated emails.

b   Easy-to-access information: Providing information that is easy to act upon and does not require an enormous amount of effort to decipher and engage with is also another way of overcoming barriers to engagement (Damgaard & Nielsen, 2017). This could be exemplified in terms of the creation of secure passwords, where clear, simple, step-by-step instructions give an individual actionable information that they can use.

- **Framing**: How information is presented to people can also have a significant impact on their intention to act on that information. Framing is the mechanism used to convey a complex problem or request in a way that is both simple and yet still convinces the individual to comply with the request (de Bruijn, 2017; de Bruijn & Janssen, 2017). Generally framing can be either positive where following the advice or behaviour in question will result in some form of potential gain, or it can be negative in nature, where failure to follow the advice will result in a loss (de Bruijn & Janssen, 2017). For example, stating that 'Using a two-factor authentication tool can effectively increase your account security by up to 80%' is a clear example of a positively framed message where users are encouraged to adopt 2FA to obtain a positive outcome. However, if we change this to 'If you fail to use two-factor authentication you could increase your exposure to potential hackers by up to 80%', we have changed the outcome to a negative one, meaning people will change optimism to fear of loss. De Bruijn and Janssen (2017) cautioned the use of negative framing for cybersecurity awareness initiatives, claiming that constantly presenting a dystopian perspective on cybersecurity can result in a heady mixture of denial, apathy, and fatalism (de Bruijn & Janssen, 2017; O'Neill & Nicholson-Cole, 2009). If you think about it, this is an obvious pattern of behaviour, because if you feel like cybersecurity issues are everywhere and they are always serious and you are going to get caught out eventually, what is the point of following all the rules? This is where our external locus of control might kick in, and we resign ourselves to luck or fate taking over cybersecurity awareness and behaviour. Positively framed messages can also have drawbacks and can lead individuals to develop overconfidence or underestimate the potential risks. For example, if we look at our example related to 2FA above and we focus on the 80% of secured accounts, we tend to ignore the fact that there are another 20% of accounts that are not secure.

- **Social Nudges**: These are mechanisms that are largely based on social norms that govern society and actually have a great deal in common with the aspects of social engineering we explored in Chapter 13. Essentially social nudges use accepted social norms to engage individuals in positive and proactive behaviours because they want to adhere to the norms of the group to which they belong (Damgaard & Nielsen, 2017). Research by Venema et al. (2020) has noted that social nudges can be effective in guiding an individual towards a decision in situations where they have no clear preferences or are uncertain about their decisions. The authors suggested that in some instances certain behaviours in certain populations may be more susceptible to social nudges versus others and this might be true for cybersecurity behaviours, as most individuals will not have any direct preference for these types of behaviours since they fall outside of their everyday work life activities, and may also be surrounded by a high degree of uncertainty (Venema et al., 2020).

- **Incentives**: Providing the right incentives to individuals as a reward or punishment for engaging / not engaging in the behaviour that is desired has also been used in a variety of different contexts. Incentives come under the category of extrinsic motivation or an externally generated source of making someone engage in the desired behaviour. Incentives can come in a wide range of different guises and can be both financial and non-financial in nature. As we will see in the section on gamification, the use of virtual badges and rewards of this nature can serve to influence behaviour especially in group settings (Acquisti et al., 2017). Other forms of non-financial incentives could include the use of grades or feedback which have no inherent value for the individual other than to indicate a level of performance and nudge the individual towards improvement (the desired behaviour) (Damgaard & Nielsen, 2017). Other researchers have explored the use of financial incentives when it comes to cybersecurity compliance (Goel et al., 2021). In their research, Goel et al. (2021) compared vigilance for detecting phishing emails and likelihood of clicking links within suspicious looking emails across three groups – a control group that had no financial incentive for compliance, a positive frame group where participants could gain up to $5 for compliance, and a negative frame group where participants were awarded $5 for compliance, but would lose a portion of this if they failed to detect a phishing email. Overall, the financial incentives served to increase individuals' vigilance towards detecting phishing emails, as well as decreasing the likelihood of an individual clicking on a link. The negative, loss framed incentive was seen to have the strongest impact on vigilance and compliance (Goel et al., 2021).

On the Effectiveness of Nudges

As we have touched upon, there are some issues with using behavioural nudges and even though some may appear to be a cost effective and simple solution to all that ails cybersecurity, they are not as straightforward as they might seem. For instance, there has been a wide range of variation in results for studies that have used nudge interventions (Ioannou et al., 2021). Nudge interventions are also seen to be less effective where individuals have strong prior preferences towards a particular choice of action (Venema et al., 2020). In an extensive review of the literature exploring the use of nudge interventions in a variety of contexts, Hummel and Maedche (2019) demonstrated that almost one third of the results reported were statistically insignificant, with the authors suggesting that this value may even be lower since other non-significant results did not reach publication. However, overall default nudges are those that are the most effective when compared to any other form of nudge type (Beshears & Kosowsky, 2020; Hummel & Maedche, 2019; Johnson et al., 2012; Lemken, 2024).

Specific uses of nudges in the context of cybersecurity have so far been limited, but there have been some attempts to apply them to both the privacy and cybersecurity domains (Acquisti et al., 2017; Hartwig & Reuter, 2021; Ioannou et al., 2021; Zimmermann & Renaud, 2021). Hartwig and Reuter (2021) assessed general attitudes towards nudges and noted that most participants viewed them in a positive way when it comes to their use in cybersecurity contexts. They noted that 64% of participants found nudges helpful, with a further 38% noting that they thought priming in cybersecurity was a necessary mechanism.

Social and Peer-Led Learning

In workplaces where resources are limited and there might be a lack of specialised experts who can engage in teaching the key elements of cybersecurity awareness, the use of peer-led learning strategies might offer an alternative approach. These approaches are appealing because they can remove the perception of an 'us versus them' attitude when it comes to employees' view of cybersecurity and the inherent battles they might have with the IT department. It can also engender feelings of collaboration and collegiality and increase a perception of overall control in the context of employee cybersecurity. Peer-based learning has been seen to increase motivation, engagement, and overall confidence in an individual's capacity and knowledge (Loh & Ang, 2020; Qureshi et al., 2023; Tran, 2019).

Peer-based instruction has been used widely to create aspects of active engagement in student populations (Ahmed & Roussev, 2018; Deshpande et al., 2019; Schneider & Asprion, 2023; Straub, 2019). The nature of peer-based instruction differs from situation to situation, but there are some general elements that we can isolate as being common across most of these strategies:

1. Students are presented with some form of problem-based learning activity that requires some form of individual preparation or analysis.
2. There is an objective measure of the problem-based learning activity in which learners will respond to some form of multiple-choice test in order assess initial knowledge retention.
3. Sessions are led by students/peers who usually act in a facilitative role, encouraging individuals to engage in the material and to act to impart some of the essential aspects of information needed to complete the task.
4. Discussion-based activities form a large part of peer-led learning activities, and it is through these discussion-based activities that individuals are encouraged to further engage in the subject matter and given an opportunity to learn more about the topic through other individuals' experiences.

Straub (2019) reported the results of a study that was conducted at North Dakota State University examining student experiences of cybersecurity peer learning activities. These activities typically involved a learning leader demonstrating a key skill or delivering some element of knowledge whilst the learners follow along, utilising the same tools to achieve the same goal or practice the same skill. The success of these activities relies in part on the enthusiasm of the peer learning leaders and individuals within the sessions see that the material is accessible to them because one of their peers is presenting that material (Straub, 2019). Peer learning groups were developed to have one or more leaders that were students, and the groups were open to choose the time they met. They could also have additional breakout meetings or working meetings, and topics were self-selected, taken from a list of relevant cybersecurity-related topics. Straub (2019) noted that such activities resulted in a wide range of benefits, with respondents claiming improvements in their technical skills, their overall comfort with the technical elements of the course and their excitement about the topic area. Comparable results have been found in the context of cybersecurity education, particularly in studies focusing on younger learners. However, these have been largely limited to primary school settings, as noted by Videnovik et al. (2024). This suggests that while early interventions can be effective, further research is needed to determine whether similar approaches yield comparable outcomes in secondary or adult education contexts.

It is important to acknowledge that much of the existing research in this area has been conducted in educational settings that differ significantly from organisational or business environments. These studies often take place in contexts where learning is the primary focus, such as schools or training programmes, and where participants are embedded in environments designed to support instruction and knowledge acquisition. As a result, the findings may not fully translate to workplace settings, where competing priorities, time constraints, and varying levels of motivation can influence the effectiveness of cybersecurity education initiatives.

As we have noted consistently throughout this book, cybersecurity is often one of the elements that is overlooked and forgotten within the workplace (Alsharnouby et al., 2015). However, we believe that peer-led learning offers a real opportunity for organisations to engage their employees in some key aspects of cybersecurity awareness – still, there are some provisions we would like to stress. Peer-led learning needs to be carefully thought out, and as with anything will only be as successful as the planning and preparation that goes into it. As with training and awareness campaigns, creating peer-led learning initiatives that lack theoretical basis or a clear objective will result in poor outcomes alongside wasted time and money. At the heart of peer-led learning is a need to tap into the enthusiasm of the learning leads, so making sure that individuals who are suited to the role is an important part of the process. Similarly, making sure peer-led sessions are well planned and coordinated whilst still retaining the essential element of learning is also a crucial part of the process and something that needs to be carefully crafted. In our experience peer-led sessions that lack a clear aim or objective can often descend into a series of chaotic discussions; the role of the peer facilitator is another critical element here. We have used peer-led sessions for a variety of cybersecurity-related activities, including an exploration of student perceptions around barriers to engagement in cybersecurity awareness and behaviours, with some excellent results. Often the discussion parts of these sessions yield the most fruitful learning experiences, with individuals sharing their experiences about various aspects of their cybersecurity journey, which in turn can be turned into a teaching opportunity. With the use of careful and thoughtful facilitation, a deeper understanding of the current issues that surround engagement in cybersecurity can be extracted, and we have found that the people involved in our sessions learn a great deal about elements of protective behaviours that they would not have engaged in through more traditional learning routes. In an organisational setting thought needs to be given to how these experiences can be integrated into the overall cybersecurity culture, as well as having an understanding of who will be taking part and how the experiences are advertised to individuals within the organisation.

Cybersecurity Awareness Campaigns

When we talk about cybersecurity awareness campaigns, we must stress that this is not just about training, but training can form a part of an awareness campaign. Awareness campaigns are widely regarded as an effective means of directing individual attention toward specific aspects of cybersecurity. They serve not only to inform but also to empower individuals by providing them with the knowledge and tools necessary to respond to threats in a manner that aligns with their own capacity and understanding (Bada et al., 2014). These campaigns often aim to shift attitudes and behaviours by making cybersecurity more personally relevant and actionable, thereby fostering a more security-conscious culture within organisations. It is important to acknowledge that despite the launch of hundreds, if not thousands, of cybersecurity awareness campaigns over recent decades, the incidence of cyberattacks and the prevalence of cybersecurity-related fraud remain persistently high. Researchers, including Bada et al. (2014), suggest that a key reason for this disconnect lies in the mismatch between the information provided in these campaigns and the actionable intelligence that individuals can realistically apply. In many cases, the content of awareness initiatives may be too generic, overly technical, or insufficiently tailored to the specific contexts and capabilities of their target audiences, thereby limiting their practical impact on behaviour. Government-led cybersecurity campaigns are not cheap. For example, the UK Government's 'Cyberaware' campaign was reported to have cost £12 million and was widely seen as a complete flop (www.buzzfeed.com/jimwaterson/governments-cybercrime-website-tha t-costs-ps630-per-visitor). According to one report, the website received less than 5,000 visitors in one one-month period, and was estimated to have cost, on average, £6.37 for each person who visited the website. The metrics used to demonstrate the effectiveness of the initiative were also based on faulty statistics that used a sub-sample of 2,000 participants and only examined claimed behavioural change, not actual behaviour change (https://ques tions-statements.parliament.uk/written-questions/detail/2016-04-20/3484).

Most of the time awareness campaigns that are designed to influence behaviours are centred around an assumption that making people aware of a risk will in turn lead them to act in a way that counters that risk (van Steen et al., 2020). However, there is an inherent problem with presenting information onto the public in a passive way – they do not always pay attention. Early theories that explored the way in which the public absorbs information from awareness campaigns noted that some individuals will be more interested in that information than others, and it is the others who are the hardest group to reach (Hyman & Sheatsley, 1947). Nothing has changed in the intervening years to say that the public interact with government messages and information campaigns any differently, and we must remember that again psychology comes into play when we present information to people that tries to engage them in behavioural change. Health-related behaviours, such as exercise, smoking cessation, eating a low-fat diet, and eating five vegetables a day, have all been the focus of many information awareness campaigns, yet unhealthy behaviours persist and the resilience to change is still maintained in some pockets of the population.

Doing something that goes contrary to your current practice or behaviour is hard and many of our current habits have been engrained over the course of years. If we learn that something that we have been doing for the past ten years is bad for us, but is something we enjoy, we could stop that behaviour immediately and by doing so reduce the 'dissonance' or difference between the behaviour we are doing and the potential negative effects that could occur. However, this would be far too easy, so instead we engage in a process of changing the way we think about the negative impact of the unhealthy thing that we are doing, choosing instead to search for the positives associated with that behaviour. This process is at the heart of something that is called cognitive dissonance (Festinger, 1957), where individuals who are faced with two or more aspects of knowledge that are associated with each other, but are incompatible, are put into a state of discomfort (or dissonance). They then engage in a process to reduce the discomfort by putting effort into justifying continuing the behaviour in question (Festinger, 1957; Harmon-Jones & Harmon-Jones, 2012; Harmon-Jones & Mills, 2019). The neutralisation techniques that individuals engage in that we reviewed in Chapter 7 are a good example of how individuals will counter inconsistencies between their current cognitions and the processes that they are being asked to engage in, and some researchers have noted that cognitive dissonance can actually be used to counteract these processes (Siponen et al., 2020). These researchers showed that training that was based around the use of cognitive dissonance (engaging the difference between current behaviour and desired behaviour to increase discomfort) was more effective at increasing likelihood to change behaviour (Siponen et al., 2020). The important thing to note here is that this is not passive transference of information as we might usually expect with information awareness campaigns – it requires individuals to engage in an effortful process to change their behaviours.

Bada et al. (2014) noted that there are several factors that serve to create the ideal conditions for cybersecurity awareness campaigns to work. Key to this is the use of effective and engaging communication processes that allow individuals the capacity to learn, and to learn in a way that is productive and aligned with the risks they may face (Bada et al., 2014). Bada et al. (2014) were keen to note that often, awareness campaigns require individuals to exert a great deal of effort in terms of their engagement, but there are no real objective measures for the benefits of such campaigns. They further noted that the alignment between the assumptions made about the individuals engaging in the awareness campaigns and their motivations to take part are misjudged, meaning that outcomes are also often unmet (Bada et al., 2014).

We have noted that these issues can often creep into a lot of awareness campaigns organisations engage in, particularly in the context of cybersecurity awareness. Often organisations will start with a very top-down process when it comes to presenting the types of behaviours employees should be engaging in when it comes to effective cybersecurity, making an extremely broad assumption that these are the behaviours or skills individuals are deficient in. However, as we have noted, this can serve to annoy or irritate employees who already have good knowledge in certain areas of cybersecurity awareness but lack better understanding in other areas. We suggest organisations wishing to engage in such processes adopt a bottom-up approach to cybersecurity awareness campaigns and conduct focus groups and interviews with employees to gauge a better understanding of the type of issues and barriers they are facing when it comes to cybersecurity awareness. This approach means employees feel more empowered and crucially feel listened to, which in turn can enhance their adherence to rules and policies they feel that they have shaped (Bada et al., 2014).

Cybersecurity Judgement and Decision Making

Something that has been discussed in some parts of the literature on cybersecurity awareness is the concept of cybersecurity judgement (Roghanizad & Neufeld, 2015; Rosoff et al., 2013; Yan & Gozu, 2012; Yan et al., 2018). The concept brings together three key research areas including attitudes and awareness to cybersecurity, underlying skills and knowledge, and the actual behaviour individuals engage in (Yan et al., 2018). The overall concept aligns with decision-making processes that we explored in Chapter 4 and the discussion of cognitive biases in Chapter 6, and refers to the ability of individuals to make clear evaluations, assessments and then to make appropriate decisions about responses to cybersecurity-related risks. Yan et al. (2018) explored the cybersecurity judgement in a group of undergraduate students and noted that rather than taking end users as a homogenous group where cybersecurity judgement was the same across all individuals, there were three distinct group, aligned to low, medium, and high cybersecurity judgement. In terms of how this translated into risk, they proposed that 23% fell into the riskiest category, and there were 73% that were in the medium risk category, with only 4% belonging to the safe group (Yan et al., 2018). The authors noted that these groups differed significantly in their capacity to make judgements on cybersecurity-based scenarios, but also that performance on these scenarios differed according to the difficulty of the scenario. The most challenging scenario was one that involved an aspect of failed attention, where a manager fails to report a potential cybersecurity breach. However, the authors noted that students were good at detailing how they would deal with pop-ups, which demonstrated that there is a clear heterogeneity in terms of the judgements individuals are making. It could be that individuals are better able to formulate responses to situations as they have had more experience of them, hence they are less reliant on heuristic judgements, but the proviso the authors make here is that they must have the right level of information to make these judgements (Yan et al., 2018). So, from this perspective cybersecurity judgement is about empowering individuals in a way that gives them a sufficient level of knowledge and awareness to make critical decisions around cybersecurity, but also acknowledges that there are clear differences in existing knowledge and experience already in the population. As an area of research, cybersecurity judgement is one that is still in its infancy, and it warrants a lot more attention in terms of a focus on how such a concept features in organisational cybersecurity culture, and is something that we are currently focusing our efforts on.

Summary

In this chapter we aimed to synthesise the various aspects of human factors in cybersecurity discussed throughout the book, offering practical suggestions for improving employee engagement in cybersecurity awareness. The chapter acknowledges the complexity of human factors and the absence of a one-size-fits-all solution. We present training as a crucial component, but it is emphasised that training alone cannot address all issues related to cybersecurity. The chapter critiques the lack of theoretical underpinnings in many training programmes and underscores the importance of well-structured, theory-based training methods.

We review different training methods, noting that game-based and simulation-based training are often the most effective in improving cybersecurity awareness and behaviours. These methods are engaging and provide immediate feedback, which helps in retaining information. Presentation-based training, if well-structured, can also be effective, while text and video-based training are less engaging and less effective in retaining information.

Gamification is explored as a promising approach to enhance cybersecurity training. By incorporating game elements like points, badges, and leaderboards, gamification can increase engagement and motivation. However, the effectiveness of gamification depends on various factors, including the context and the target audience. The chapter highlights the importance of designing gamified training programmes that are personalised and targeted to the specific needs of the users. We also discuss the barriers to implementing gamification, such as poor design, lack of continuity between business needs and gamification goals, and the diverse preferences of a multicultural and multigenerational workforce. It emphasises that gamification is not a one-size-fits-all solution and must be carefully tailored to the specific context and audience.

Behavioural nudges are presented as another strategy to improve cybersecurity awareness. Nudges like defaults, commitment devices, goal-tracking, and providing accessible information can influence behaviour without coercion. The chapter discusses the effectiveness of different types of nudges and their application in cybersecurity contexts.

Peer-led learning is suggested as a cost-effective alternative to traditional training methods, especially in resource-limited settings. Peer-led sessions can increase motivation, engagement, and confidence, but they require careful planning and enthusiastic facilitators to be effective.

We conclude this chapter by discussing the importance of cybersecurity awareness campaigns and the need for effective communication strategies. It critiques the top-down approach often used in these campaigns and advocates for a bottom-up approach that involves employees in the process. The chapter also introduces the concept of cybersecurity judgment, which combines attitudes, skills, and behaviours to make informed decisions about cybersecurity risks.

Overall, the chapter provides a comprehensive overview of various strategies to improve cybersecurity awareness, emphasizing the need for a multifaceted approach that combines training, gamification, behavioural nudges, peer-led learning, and effective communication.

References

Acquisti, A., Adjerid, I., Balebako, R., Brandimarte, L., Cranor, F., Komanduri, S., ... Wilson, S. (2017). Nudges for privacy and security: Understanding and assisting users' choices online. *ACM Computing Surveys*, 50(3). doi:10.1145/3054926.

Ahmed, I., & Roussev, V. (2018). Peer instruction teaching methodology for cybersecurity education. *IEEE Security & Privacy*, 16(4), 1–10.

Alsharnouby, M., Alaca, F., & Chiasson, S. (2015). Why phishing still works: User strategies for combating phishing attacks. *International Journal of Human Computer Studies*, 82, 69–82. doi:10.1016/j.ijhcs.2015.05.005.

Azadegan, A., Riedel, J. C., & Baalsrud Hauge, J. (2012). Serious games adoption in corporate training. In *Serious Games Development and Applications: Third International Conference, SGDA 2012, Bremen, Germany, September 26–29, 2012. Proceedings 3* (pp. 74–85). Springer Berlin Heidelberg.

Bada, M., Sasse, A., & Nurse, J. (2014). Cyber security awareness campaigns: Why they fail to change behavior. *Proceedings of the International Conference on Cyber Security for Sustainable Society*, 38. doi:10.48550/arXiv.1901.02672.

Beshears, J., & Kosowsky, H. (2020). Nudging: Progress to date and future directions. *Creating Habit Formation for Behaviors*, 161(Suppl), 3–19.

Brady, C., & M'manga, A. (2022). Gamification of cyber security training: EnsureSecure. In IEEE (Ed.), *2022 IEEE International Conference on e-Business Engineering (ICEBE)* (pp. 1–10). IEEE. doi:10.1109/ICEBE55470.2022.00010.

Bryan, G., Karlan, D., & Nelson, S. (2010). Commitment devices. *Annual Review of Economics*, 2, 671–698. doi:10.1146/annurev.economics.102308.124324.

Callan, R. C., Bauer, K. N., & Landers, N. (2015). How to avoid the dark side of gamification: Ten business scenarios and their unintended consequences. In T. Reiners & L. Wood (Eds.), *Gamification in education and business* (pp. 553–568). Springer.

Carreiro, A., Silva, C., & Antunes, M. (2024). The use of gamification on cybersecurity awareness of healthcare professionals. *Procedia Computer Science*, 239, 526–533.

Csikszentmihalyi, M. (1975). *Beyond boredom and anxiety*. Jossey-Bass Publishers.

Damgaard, M. T. (2020). A decade of nudging: What have we learned? *Economics Working Papers*. https://pure.au.dk/portal/files/191597643/wp20_07.pdf.

Damgaard, M. T., & Nielsen, H. S. (2017). The use of nudges and other behavioural approaches in education. *EENEE Analytical Reports*, 29. https://eric.ed.gov/?id=ED574102.

De Bruijn, H. (2017). *The art of framing: How politicians convince us that they are right*. Etopia BV.

De Bruijn, H., & Janssen, M. (2017). Building cybersecurity awareness: The need for evidence-based framing strategies. *Government Information Quarterly*, 34(1), 1–7. doi:10.1016/j.giq.2017.02.007.

DeCarlo, S. M. (2017). *Measuring the application of knowledge gained from the gamification of cybersecurity training in healthcare*. Robert Morris University.

Derksen, J. T., Kerwin, N. O., Reysoso, N. O., & Sterck, O. (2021). Appointments: A more effective commitment device for health behaviors. *SSRN Electronic Journal*. doi:10.2139/ssrn.3939283.

Deshpande, P., Lee, C. B., & Ahmed, I. (2019). Evaluation of peer instruction for cybersecurity education. In ACM (Ed.), *Proceedings of the 50th ACM Technical Symposium on Computer Science Education* (pp. 1–10). ACM.

Deterding, S., Sicart, M., Nacke, L., O'Hara, K., & Dixon, D. (2011). Gamification: Using game design elements in non-gaming contexts. In ACM (Ed.), *Proceedings of the 2011 Annual Conference on Human Factors in Computing Systems* (pp. 2425–2428). ACM.

Diakoumakos, J., Chaskos, E., Kolokotronis, N., & Lepouras, G. (2025). Cyber-security gamification in federation of cyber ranges: design, implementation, and evaluation. *International Journal of Information Security*, 24. doi:10.1007/s10207-024-00974-1.

Ferro, L. S. (2021). The Game Element and Mechanic (GEM) framework: A structural approach for implementing game elements and mechanics into game experiences. *Entertainment Computing*, 36, 100375. doi:10.1016/j.entcom.2020.100375.

Festinger, L. (1957). *A theory of cognitive dissonance*. Row, Peterson.

Filipczuk, D., Mason, C., & Snow, S. (2019). Using a game to explore notions of responsibility for cyber security in organisations. *Conference on Human Factors in Computing Systems – Proceedings*, 1–6. doi:10.1145/3290607.3312846.

Goel, S., Williams, K. J., Huang, J., & Warkentin, M. (2021). Can financial incentives help with the struggle for security policy compliance? *Information and Management*, 58(4), 1–25.

Grobler, M., Gaire, R., & Nepal, S. (2021). User, usage and usability: Redefining human centric cyber security. *Frontiers in Big Data*, 4. doi:10.3389/fdata.2021.583723.

Gwenhure, A. K., & Rahayu, F. S. (2024). Gamification of cybersecurity awareness for non-IT professionals: A systematic literature review. *International Journal of Serious Games*, 11(1), 83–99. doi:10.17083/ijsg.v11i1.719.

Hamari, J., Koivisto, J., & Sarsa, H. (2014). Does gamification work? A literature review of empirical studies on gamification. *Proceedings of the Annual Hawaii International Conference on System Sciences*, 3025–3034. doi:10.1109/HICSS.2014.377.

Harmon-Jones, E., & Harmon-Jones, C. (2012). Cognitive dissonance theory. In J. Y. Shah & W. L. Gardner (Eds.), *Handbook of motivation science* (pp. 71–83). Guilford Press.

Harmon-Jones, E., & Mills, J. (2019). An introduction to cognitive dissonance theory and an overview of current perspectives on the theory. In E. Harmon-Jones (Ed.), *Cognitive dissonance: Reexamining a pivotal theory in psychology* (2nd ed., pp. 3–24). American Psychological Association. doi:10.1037/0000135-001.

Hartwig, S., & Reuter, C. (2021). Nudge or restraint: How do people assess nudging in cybersecurity – A representative study in Germany. *ACM International Conference Proceeding Series*, 141–150. doi:10.1145/3481357.3481514.

Hoffman, D. L., & Novak, T. P. (1996). Marketing in hypermedia computer-mediated environments: Conceptual foundations. *Journal of Marketing*, 60, 50–68.

Hummel, D., & Maedche, A. (2019). How effective is nudging? A quantitative review on the effect sizes and limits of empirical nudging studies. *Journal of Behavioral and Experimental Economics*, 80, 47–58. doi:10.1016/j.socec.2019.03.005.

Hyman, H. H., & Sheatsley, P. B. (1947). American Association for Public Opinion Research: Some reasons why information campaigns fail. *The Public Opinion Quarterly*, 11(3), 412–423.

Ioannou, A., Tussyadiah, I., Miller, G., Li, S., & Weick, M. (2021). Privacy nudges for disclosure of personal information: A systematic literature review and meta-analysis. *PLoS ONE*, 16. doi:10.1371/journal.pone.0256822.

Johnson, E. J., Shu, S. B., Dellaert, B. G. C., Fox, C. R., Goldstein, D. G., Häubl, G., … Weber, E. U. (2012). Beyond nudges: Tools of a choice architecture. *Marketing Letters*, 23(2), 487–504. doi:10.1007/s11002-012-9186-1.

Kappen, D. L., & Nacke, L. (2013). The kaleidoscope of effective gamification: Deconstructing gamification in business applications. In *Proceedings of the First International Conference on Gameful Design, Research, and Applications*, 119–122. doi:10.1145/2583008.2583029.

Koivisto, J., & Hamari, J. (2019). The rise of motivational information systems: A review of gamification research. *International Journal of Information Management*, 45, 191–210. doi:10.1016/j.ijinfomgt.2018.10.013.

Landers, R. N. (2014). Developing a theory of gamified learning: Linking serious games and gamification of learning. *Simulation and Gaming*, 45(6), 752–768.

Landers, R. N. (2019). Gamification misunderstood: How badly executed and rhetorical gamification obscures its transformative potential. *Journal of Management Inquiry*, 28(2), 137–140.

Larson, K. (2020). Serious games and gamification in the corporate training environment: A literature review. *TechTrends*, 64(2), 319–328.

Lemken, D. (2024). Options to design more ethical and still successful default nudges: A review and recommendations. *Behavioural Public Policy*, 8, 349–381. doi:10.1017/bpp.2021.33.

Loh, R. C.-Y., & Ang, C.-S. (2020). Unravelling cooperative learning in higher education. *Research in Social Sciences and Technology*, 5(2), 22–39.

Malone, M., Wang, Y., James, K., Anderegg, M., Werner, J., & Monrose, F. (2021). To gamify or not? On leaderboard effects, student engagement and learning outcomes in a cybersecurity intervention. *SIGCSE 2021 – Proceedings of the 52nd ACM Technical Symposium on Computer Science Education*, 1135–1141. doi:10.1145/3408877.3432544.

Marczewski, A. (2018). *52 gamification mechanics and elements.* Gamified UK – #Gamification Expert. www.gamified.uk/user-types/gamification-mechanics-elements.

Nah, F. F. H., Zeng, Q., Telaprolu, V. R., Ayyappa, A. P., & Eschenbrenner, B. (2014). Gamification of education: A review of literature. In F. H. H. Nah (Ed.), *Proceedings of 1st International Conference on Human-Computer Interaction in Business* (pp. 401–409). LNCS Springer.

Nurse, J. R. C., Creese, S., Goldsmith, M., & Lamberts, K. (2011). Trustworthy and effective communication of cybersecurity risks: A review. *Proceedings – 2011 1st Workshop on Socio-Technical Aspects in Security and Trust, STAST 2011*, 60–68. doi:10.1109/STAST.2011.6059257.

O'Neill, S., & Nicholson-Cole, S. (2009). 'Fear won't do it' promoting positive engagement with climate change through visual and iconic representations. *Science Communication*, 30(3), 355–379.

Ong, M. J. K. (2013). *Gamification and its effect on employee engagement and performance in a perceptual diagnosis task* (Unpublished Master's Thesis). University of Canterbury.

Prummer, J., van Steen, T., & van den Berg, B. (2024). A systematic review of current cybersecurity training methods. *Computers and Security*, 136, 103585. doi:10.1016/j.cose.2023.103585.

Quinn, R. W. (2005). Flow in knowledge work: High performance experience in the design of national security technology. *Administrative Science Quarterly*, 50, 610–641. doi:10.2189/asqu.50.4.610.

Qureshi, M. A., Khaskheli, A., Qureshi, J. A., Raza, S. A., & Yousufi, S. Q. (2023). Factors affecting students' learning performance through collaborative learning and engagement. *Interactive Learning Environments*, 31(4), 2371–2391.

Rogers, R. W., Milkman, K. L., & Volpp, K. G. (2014). Commitment devices: Using initiatives to change behavior. *JAMA*, 311(20), 2065–2066. doi:10.1001/jama.2014.3485.

Roghanizad, M. M., & Neufeld, D. J. (2015). Intuition, risk, and the formation of online trust. *Computers in Human Behavior*, 50, 489–498. doi:10.1016/j.chb.2015.04.025.

Rosoff, H., Cui, J., & John, R. S. (2013). Heuristics and biases in cyber security dilemmas. *Environment Systems and Decisions*, 33, 517–529.

Schneider, B., & Asprion, P. (2023). Peer instruction as teaching method in cybersecurity and data privacy. *International Journal of Management, Knowledge and Learning*, 12, 1–7.

Scholefield, S., & Shepherd, L. A. (2019). Gamification techniques for raising cyber security awareness. *Lecture Notes in Computer Science (Including Subseries Lecture Notes in Artificial Intelligence and Lecture Notes in Bioinformatics)*, 11594 LNCS, 191–203. doi:10.1007/978-3-030-22351-9_13.

Shahzadi, A., Ishaq, K., Nawaz, N. A., & Rosdi, F. (2025). Unveiling personalized and gamification-based cybersecurity risks within financial institutions. *PeerJ Computer Science*, 2598, 1–36. doi:10.7717/peerj-cs.2598.

Siponen, M., Puhakainen, P., & Vance, A. (2020). Can individuals' neutralization techniques be overcome? A field experiment on password policy. *Computers & Security*, 88, Article101617.

Straub, J. (2019). Assessment of the educational benefits produced by peer learning activities in cybersecurity. In *2019 ASEE Annual Conference & Exposition, Tampa, Florida*. doi:10.18260/1-2–32131.

Thaler, R., & Sunstein, C. R. (2008). *Nudge: Improving decisions about health, wealth, and happiness*. Penguin.

Thomas, N. J., & Baral, R. (2022). Gamification for synchronous and asynchronous learning. In P. Kumar & J. Eisenberg (Eds.), *Synchronous and asynchronous approaches to teaching: Higher education lessons in post-pandemic times* (pp. 203–222). Palgrave Macmillan.

Tran, V. D. (2019). Does cooperative learning increase students' motivation in learning? *International Journal of Higher Education*, 8(5), 12–20.

van Steen, T., Norris, E., Atha, K., & Joinson, A. (2020). What (if any) behaviour change techniques do government-led cybersecurity awareness campaigns use? *Journal of Cybersecurity*, 6(1), 1–8. doi:10.1093/CYBSEC/TYAA019.

Venema, T. A., Kroese, F. M., Benjamins, J. S., & de Ridder, D. T. (2020). When in doubt, follow the crowd? Responsiveness to social proof nudges in the absence of clear preferences. *Frontiers in Psychology*, 11, 1385.

Videnovik, M., Trajkovik, V., Vold, T., Kiønig, V., Madevska Bogdanova, A., & Filiposka, S. (2024). Using peer-learning and game-based instruction for achieving long-lasting knowledge of cybersecurity in primary schools. *IEEE Access*, 11679–11688. doi:10.1109/ACCESS.2024.3479921.

Von Bergen, C. W., & Miles, M. P. (2015). Social negative option marketing. *Journal of Social Marketing*, 5(2), 125–138.

Yan, Z., & Gozu, H. Y. (2012). Online decision-making in receiving spam emails among college students. *International Journal of Cyber Behavior, Psychology and Learning*, 2(1), 1–12. doi:10.4018/ijcbpl.2012010101.

Yan, Z., Robertson, T. W., Yan, R., Park, S. Y., Bordoff, S., & Chen, Q. (2018). Finding the weakest links in the weakest link: How well do undergraduate students make cybersecurity judgment? *Computers in Human Behavior*, 84, 375–382. doi:10.1016/j.chb.2018.03.015.

Zimmermann, V., & Renaud, K. (2021). The nudge puzzle: Matching nudge interventions to cybersecurity decisions. *ACM Transactions on Compute–Human Interaction (TOCHI)*, 28(1), 1–45.

INDEX

For Product Safety Concerns and Information please contact our EU
representative GPSR@taylorandfrancis.com
Taylor & Francis Verlag GmbH, Kaufingerstraße 24, 80331 München, Germany

www.ingramcontent.com/pod-product-compliance
Lightning Source LLC
Chambersburg PA
CBHW052120230326
41598CB00080B/3908